ANSELM OF HAVELBERG

STUDIES IN THE HISTORY
OF
CHRISTIAN THOUGHT

EDITED BY

HEIKO A. OBERMAN, Tucson, Arizona

IN COOPERATION WITH
HENRY CHADWICK, Cambridge
JAROSLAV PELIKAN, New Haven, Connecticut
BRIAN TIERNEY, Ithaca, New York
ARJO VANDERJAGT, Groningen

VOLUME LXXIX

JAY T. LEES

ANSELM OF HAVELBERG

ANSELM OF HAVELBERG

DEEDS INTO WORDS IN THE TWELFTH CENTURY

BY

JAY T. LEES

BRILL
LEIDEN · NEW YORK · KÖLN
1998

This book is printed on acid-free paper.

Library of Congress Cataloging-in-Publication Data

Lees, Jay T. (Jay Terry), 1948–
     Anselm of Havelberg : deeds into words in the twelfth century / by
Jay T. Lees.
     p.   cm. — (Studies in the history of Christian thought, ISSN
0081–8607 ; v. 79)
     Includes bibliographical references and index.
     ISBN 9004109064 (cloth : alk. paper)
     1. Anselm, bishop of Havelberg, d. 1158.   2. Catholic Church–
–Germany—Bishops—Biography.   I. Title.   II. Series.
BX4705.A62L44   1997
282'.092—dc21
[B]   97–40019
                                                                   CIP

Die Deutsche Bibliothek - CIP-Einheitsaufnahme

Lees, Jay T.:
Anselm of Havelberg: deeds into words in the twelfth century / by
Jay T. Lees. – Leiden ; New York ; Köln : Brill, 1997
(Studies in the history of Christian thought ; Vol. 79)
ISBN 90–04–10906–4

ISSN   0081-8607
ISBN   90 04 10906 4

PRINTED IN THE NETHERLANDS

Dedicated to
Charles T. Davis
and in memory of
Peter Classen

CONTENTS

ACKNOWLEDGMENTS

I am indebted to many people who have helped me in many ways. First and foremost, I would like to express my deep appreciation for the guidance of Charles Till Davis of Tulane University who took me under his wing and taught me to look at the sources of the past with new eyes; and for that of the late Peter Classen of the University of Heidelberg, strolling with whom in the orchards overlooking the Neckar Valley while talking about Anselm remains unforgettable.

I am grateful to the Fulbright Commission for a grant allowing me to do research in Germany and study at the University of Heidelberg. Among those who have aided me in the United States, I would like to thank John van Engen of the University of Notre Dame and Giles Constable of the Institute for Advanced Study along with several anonymous readers for reading early drafts of the manuscript and giving me much advice and support. Thanks are also due to Charles H. Carter, Caecilia Davis-Weyer, George Fick, Becky Lees, Britta-Paule Lees, Brynn Lees, Patricia Lees, Sal McLemore, Noemie Merrick, James Myers, Jr., William Pulsipher, Jr., Carol Neel, George Schmitt, Stephen D. Uhl, and John Waldmer. My colleagues at the University of Northern Iowa have given conversation and support, especially those who have taken a particular interest in my project: Gregory Bruess, Judith Dohlman, Vickie Hanson, John Johnson, David McKibbin, Timothy O'Connor, Aaron Podolefsky, Roy Sandstrom, Donald Shepardson, David Walker, Charlotte Wells, Donald Whitnah, and Harold Wohl.

In Germany, many people have helped to make my visits pleasant and fruitful. Among my friends at the University of Heidelberg, I would like to thank Jürgen Miethke for setting me on the right track, Walter Berschin for reading and critiquing an early draft, as well as Reinhard Düchting, and Hermann Jakobs. Of my other friends in and near Heidelberg, many have lent me assistance: in particular Friederike and Günther Roegler have become my German parents, truly making their home my own, and virtually making my trips to Germany possible. Thanks also to Ilsa and Fritz Bopp, Johannes Fried, Waldtraud and Hans Kuhn, Susanne and Peter Roegler, and Fritz Schmidt. Finally in Heidelberg, I will be forever grateful to Mechthild Classen who has been a mainstay of kind encouragement.

I have been fortunate in receiving assistance in other parts of Germany, as well. In Freiberg, I am grateful to Katerina and Achim Aurnhammer; in Berlin to Gertrud Roegler and Monica Preisler, in Potsdam to Liselott Enders; in Friedland to Andreas Werner, former pastor of the Cathedral of Havelberg, and his wife Anna Maria. The people in and around Havelberg have overwhelmed me with their kindness. My heartfelt thanks to Ellen and Klaus Kubat for opening their home to me, to Hanns-Joachim Fincke, the unofficial town historian, who has so often shared his boundless knowledge of Havelberg's past with me, to Torsten Buchholz of the Prignitz Museum and Elke and Albrecht Seeger for the serious discussions we had about Anselm. Also thanks to Andreas König of the Havelberger Volksstimme, Bürgermeister Bernt Poloski, Erwin and Ingrid Pusch, Antje Reichel of the Prignitz Museum, Fred and Barbara Sobik, and Herbert Sterz of the Heimatverein Havelberg.

I would also like to express my appreciation to Professor Heiko A. Oberman of the University of Arizona for selecting this book for Brill's series Studies in the History of Christian Thought. It has been a pleasure to work with him and my editors at Brill, including Elisabeth Venekamp, Julian Deahl, Gera van Bedaf, Theo Joppe, and Tanja de Hoog.

My thanks also to the editors of the *Analecta Praemonstratensia*, *Benedictina*, and *Viator* for publishing some of what follows in different form.

Finally, my wife Julie Lowell has been my most loyal editor and made many suggestions regarding the book. The strengths of what follows are due to the help of these people and many more; the weaknesses remain my own.

J.T.L.
July, 1997
Cedar Falls, Iowa

ABBREVIATIONS

Antik.	Anselm of Havelberg, *Antikeimenon*, PL 188
Ber. 1	Berlin manuscript: Staatsbibliothek der Stiftung Preussischer Kulturbesitz, theol. fol. 80, saec. XV
Mun.	Munich manuscript: Bayerische Staatsbibliothek, lat. 6488 (anno 1437) aus Freising
Wolf. 1	Wolfenbüttel manuscript: Herzog-August-Bibliothek, 2135 (August. 11.14), saec. XVI
AP	*Analecta Praemonstratensia*
CCSL	Corpus Christianorum. Series Latina
CCCM	Corpus Christianorum. Continuatio mediaevalis
DA	*Deutsches Archiv für Erforschung des Mittelalters*
Epist. apol.	Anselm of Havelberg, *Epistola apologetica*, PL 188
Ber. 2	Berlin manuscript: Staatsbibliothek der Stiftung Preussischer Kulturbesitz, Theol. fol. 80, saec. XV, fols 252v-261r.
Wolf. 2	Wolfenbüttel manuscript: Helmstedt 494, saec. XII, fols. 9r-10v (frag.)
GQPS, GQPS NR	Geschichtsquellen der Provinz Sachsen und des Freistaates Anhalt, Neue Reihe
HJ	*Historisches Jahrbuch*
HZ	*Historische Zeitschrift*
JGMOD	*Jahrbuch für die Geschichte Mittel- und Ostdeutschlands*

MGH   Monumenta Germaniae Historia
  Const.   Constitutiones et acta publica imperatorum et
                 regum
  DD   Diplomata regum et imperatorum Germaniae
  Epis. sel.   Epistola selectae
  Lib.   Libelli de Lite
  Sch   Schriften
  SS   Scriptores (in Folio)
  SS r. G.,   Scriptores rerum Germanicarum in usum scho-
    SS r. G. NS larum separatim editi, Nova Series

PL   Migne, Patrologia Latina

RHE   Revue d'histoire ecclésiastique

UB   Urkundenbuch

UF, UF 2   Urkunden Friedrichs I. MGH DD 10.1, 10.2

UK   Urkunden Konrads III. und seines Sohnes Heinrich
                 MGH DD 9

UL, ULR   Urkunden Lothars III. und der Kaiserin Richenza
                 MGH DD 8

Vita Norberti A Vita Norberti archiepiscopi Magdeburgensis, MGH SS
                 12

Vita Norberti B Vita Norberti archiepiscopi Magdeburgensis, Acta
                 Sanctorum, Juni 1

Wibald   Wibald of Stablo, Epistolae. Ed. Philip Jaffé.
                 Bibliotheca rerum Germanicarum 1. Monu-
                 menta Corbeiensia. Berlin, 1864

ZKG   Zeitschrift für Kirchengeschichte

INTRODUCTION

In the Middle Ages, biblical exegesis fashioned tools from the words of Scripture to pry open the windows of heaven and obtain a view beyond the mundane and into the realm of the Spirit. Shaping and reshaping Holy Writ through different methods of interpretation, the exegete ran the risk of forgetting that the base metal of his tools, that which had given rise to the words in the first place, was to be found in deeds performed in this world by the faithful. The Scriptures presented the holy servants of God doing His will. Christ Himself, the Word, had become flesh and dwelt in the world, and His life had been captured in the words of Scripture. The task of the exegete, however, was to find a spiritual significance in these words that went beyond the historical action. Thus the twelfth-century canon Hugh of St. Victor (1096-1141) could refer to the ark as something built by a man named Noah and then move on to shape a grand allegory. Noah using his axe to build a boat was replaced by Christ using his preachers to build the church, or wisdom using meditation to fill the heart, or grace using the virtues to create love.[1]

Through allegory, Hugh sought escape from the transient historical deed to the immutable God because, he says, he and his brethren had been sighing over the restlessness and instability of the world.[2] And certainly, the history of their own time gave them reason to sigh. Since the middle of the eleventh century, restless men had fought over the reform of the church. The dramatic events of the period known as the Investiture Controversy or the Gregorian Reform fired imagination and indignation. On whichever side one might stand in the battle between old and new, there could be no doubt that the deeds of the contestants had an effect. Allegory was not needed to

---

[1] *De arca Noe morali* 1, 2, PL 176:621-25. On medieval exegesis P. C. Spicq, *Esquisse d'une histoire de l'exégèse latine au Moyen Âge* (Paris, 1944); Beryl Smalley, *The Study of Bible in the Middle Ages* (Notre Dame, Indiana, 1964); Henri de Lubac, *Exégèse médiévale: Les quatre sens de l'écriture*, 2 vols., vol. 2 in 3 pts. (Aubier, 1959-64); G. R. Evans, *The Language and Logic of the Bible: The Earlier Middle Ages* (Cambridge, 1984). Rupert of Deutz, another contemporary of Anselm, found the spiritual meaning to be at the center of Scripture, the literal to enclose it like the husk surrounding the grain. Evans, pp. 14-15.

[2] *De arca Noe morali*, prologue, PL 176:617.

give those contemporary deeds the power to build or to destroy, to
attack or to defend, to inspire or to dismay.

This monograph deals with the deeds and the words of Anselm of
Havelberg. In the middle of the twelfth century, Bishop Anselm
wrote of people like Hugh and his brothers who were horrified by the
many changes around them and dreamed of a stable world, free from
buffeting events where they could find a secure place to rest their
weary heads. Such a world, cautioned Anselm, is not to be found, not
in the past, not in the present, and not until Christ returns. Anselm's
message was, however, not one of despair for he argued that this
world could be changed for the better by active efforts to address its
ills. A man of high intellectual ability, on several occasions Anselm
put pen to parchment to investigate how words used to describe past
deeds communicate the importance of this active involvement. The
active efforts of which Anselm wrote very much concerned the clerical segment of medieval society. One of the successes of the papacy
in the late eleventh and early twelfth centuries in trying to create a
centralized ecclesiastical hierarchy was an increased distinction between the clergy and the laity. The former came to claim a position
of sanctity akin to that of the monk. This claim entailed a
reexamination and redefinition of clerical service and what it meant
to live a life active in the world as opposed to withdrawn from it in
cloistered seclusion. Anselm of Havelberg is a valuable source for this
reevaluation.

Anselm is at least mentioned in most studies of medieval ideas of
history, Latin-Byzantine relations in the Middle Ages, the flourishing
of new religious orders in the early twelfth century, and medieval
theories of papal primacy, among others. While there have been
many narrowly focused studies of different aspects of Anselm's writings or brief surveys of his career, there is no book-length study of his
life and literary production.[3] In recent years, scholars have in general

---

[3] The fullest studies of Anselm remain the non-judgmental biography by Eugen
Dombrowski, Anselm von Havelberg, Inaugural-Dissertation (Königsberg, 1880),
which ignores his writings entirely, and Kurt Fina's "Anselm von Havelberg: Untersuchungen zur Kirchen- und Geistesgeschichte des 12. Jahrhunderts," *AP* 32 (1956),
69-101, 193-227; 33 (1957), 5-39, 268-301; 34 (1958), 13-41. Fina's excellent work
neglects the biographical dimension and deals for the most part with Anselm's
Epistola apologetica. On some of the problems of evaluating Anselm's life and writings,
see Jay T. Lees, "Charity and Enmity in the Writings of Anselm of Havelberg,"
Viator: Medieval and Renaissance Studies 25 (1994), 53-62.

assumed that Anselm's career had been accurately assessed in the early part of this century. In 1933, Gottfried Wentz published an itinerary for Anselm.[4] Kurt Fina, author of the fullest treatment of Anselm, referred to this itinerary as "almost complete" and thus discouraged research into Anselm's biography in further detail.[5] This is unfortunate, for in spite of some few historians who have called for a more nuanced interpretation of Anselm's career,[6] the voices of his critics remain the loudest.[7] Their criticism has rested on a single event in Anselm's career. After having been exiled from the court of King Conrad III, he wrote that he was resigned to spend the rest of his life in Havelberg. Then, at the accession of Frederick Barbarossa, he promptly returned to court. In this return historians have inferred gross hypocrisy which has then been read into the bishop's entire career: By returning to court Anselm showed himself to be enamored of life near the king—perhaps even to be a sycophant. When at times he appears to have supported the pope against the king, this has been taken as evidence of a man who could, with considerable dexterity, change sides if it were to his personal advantage. And, finally, in leaving Havelberg, Anselm demonstrated his disdain of humble diocesan duties. Thus, whether one speaks of Anselm as a royal adviser or

---

[4] Gottfried Wentz, *Das Bistum Havelberg*, Germania sacra 1.2 (Berlin, 1933), pp. 37-40.

[5] Fina, "Anselm von Havelberg," *AP* 32, p. 79.

[6] Most importantly Wilhelm Berges, "Anselm von Havelberg in der Geistesgeschichte des 12. Jahrhunderts," *Jahrbuch für die Geschichte Mittel- und Ostdeutschlands* 5 (1956), 39-57: "Die Tatsachen sind...nuancenreicher und interessanter als Vokabeln und Schemata aus dem Schulbuch" (p. 41). See also Hans-Dietrich Kahl, *Slawen und Deutsche in der Brandenburgischen Geschichte des Zwölften Jahrhunderts: Die letzten Jahrzehnte des Landes Stodor* 1 (Cologne, 1964), pp. 229-33.

[7] The uncomplimentary appraisal of Anselm by Wilhelm Bernhardi in *Lothar von Supplinburg*, Jahrbücher der Deutschen Geschichte (Leipzig, 1879) and *Konrad III.*, Jahrbücher der Deutschen Geschichte (Leipzig, 1883) (here esp. pp. 775-76, 849) has held the field. See Hans Lauerer, *Die theologischen Anschauungen des Bischofs Anselm von Havelberg (+1158) auf Grund der kritischgesichteten Schriften dargestellt* (Erlangen, 1911); Wentz, *Das Bistum Havelberg*, 35; more recently, Dietrich Claude, *Geschichte des Erzbistums Magdeburg bis in das 12. Jahrhundert*, 2 vols. Mitteldeutsche Forschungen 67/1-2 (Cologne, 1972, 1975), 2.49. Other works dealing with Anselm's career include: Franz Winter, *Die Prämonstratenser des zwölften Jahrhunderts und ihre Bedeutung für das nordöstliche Deutschland. Ein Beitrag zur Geschichte der Christianisierung des Wendenlandes* (1865, reprint Aslen, 1965); Henry Simonsfeld, *Jahrbücher des Deutschen Reichs unter Friedrich I (1152-1158)* 1, Jahrbücher der Deutschen Geschichte (Leipzig, 1908); Johannes Dräseke, "Bischof Anselm von Havelberg und seine Gesandtschaftsreisen nach Byzanz," *ZKG* 21 (1901), 160-85. See also p. 5 n. 9 and p. 11 n. 1 below.

as a bishop, he appears to fall short, the sense being that he manipulated his episcopal charge to enjoy a life spent in high political circles.

If this image of the bishop of Havelberg has not been quite so forcefully maintained in recent years, it is not the result of further biographical investigation into his career either as a royal adviser or as a bishop. It is rather because attention has been focused on Anselm's writings. Anselm's scholarly side has been emphasized in part by historians interested in his history of the faithful, *De una forma credendi*, which forms the opening section of a larger work titled the *Antikeimenon* or *Book of Antitheses*. Those concerned with medieval ideas of history and how the past might be divided up into periods have been impressed by Anselm who, in this relatively short work, managed to make use of an astonishing number of schemes of periodization. The questions here have revolved around how Anselm's schemes resemble and differ from those of other twelfth-century exegetes such as Hugh of St. Victor, Rupert of Deutz, and Joachim of Fiore.[8]

---

[8] Suggesting Joachim was influenced by Anselm, Herbert Grundmann, *Studien über Joachim von Floris*, Beiträge zur Kulturgeschichte des Mittelalters und der Renaissance 32 (Leipzig, 1927), pp. 92-95. Critical of Grundmann, George La Piana, "Joachim of Flora: A Critical Survey," *Speculum* 7 (1932), 267. Circumspect but still claiming Joachim could have read Anselm: Grundmann, *Neue Forschungen über Joachim von Fiore*, Münstersche Forschungen 1 (Marburg, 1950), p. 79 n. 1. See also Morton Bloomfield, "Joachim of Flora: A Critical Survey of His Canon, Teachings, Sources, Biography, and Influences," *Traditio* 13 (1957), 278-81; Marjorie Reeves "History and Prophecy in Medieval Thought," *Medievalia et Humanistica: Studies in Medieval and Renaissance Culture*. New Series 5 (1974), 54-55; idem, *Joachim of Fiore and the Prophetic Future* (New York, 1976), p. 2; idem, "The Originality and Influence of Joachim of Fiore," *Traditio* 36 (1980), 85-286; Delno C. West and Sandra Zimdars-Swartz, *Joachim of Fiore: A Study in Spiritual Perception and History* (Bloomington, 1983), pp. 37-38; Bernard McGinn, *The Calabrian Abbot: Joachim of Fiore in the History of Western Thought* (New York, 1985), p. 68.

Many studies treat Anselm's ideas in the context of twelfth-century views of history, among them: Johannes Spörl, *Grundformen hochmittelalterlicher Geschichtsanschauungen: Studien zum Weltbild der Geschichtsschreiber des 12. Jahrhunderts* (Munich, 1935); Wilhelm Kamlah, *Apokalypse und Geschichtstheologie. Die Mittelalterliche Auslegung der Apokalypse vor Joachim von Fiore* (1935, reprint: Vaduz, 1965); M. van Lee, "Les idées d'Anselme de Havelberg sur le developpement des dogmes," *AP* 14 (1938), 5-35; Joseph de Ghellinck, *Le mouvement théologique du XIIe siècle*, 2nd ed. (Bruges, 1948); M.-D. Chenu, *La theologie au douzième siècle*, Etudes de philosophie médiévale 45 (Paris, 1957); Lawrence F. Barmann, "Reform Ideology in the *Dialogi* of Anselm of Havelberg," *Church History* 30 (1961), 379-95; Amos Funkenstein, *Heilsplan und natürliche Entwicklung: Formen der Gegenwartsbestimmung im Geschichtsdenken des hohen Mittelalter* (Munich, 1965); R. W. Southern, "Aspects of the European Tradition of Historical Writings. 2. Hugh of St. Victor and the Idea of Historical Development," *Trans-*

The image of Anselm that has emerged through the study of his written works is of a man of intelligence who appears as a champion of Christian unity, understanding, and compromise. Here the bishop's reputation rests primarily on the remaining and longer section of the *Antikeimenon* in which he claims to recount in dialogue format two debates he had held with a Greek archbishop in Constantinople concerning issues dividing the church into East and West. These debates appear to contrast dramatically with other meetings of Latins and Greeks where the aggressive and dogmatic stance of both sides only etched the divisions deeper. In Anselm's account, the bishop of Havelberg and the Greek archbishop distinguish themselves by honestly trying to find solutions to divisive issues.[9]

These views of Anselm contradict each other: On the one hand, Anselm is seen as a man who acted in his own best interest and for personal advancement; on the other, he is seen as a man who unselfishly served the ideal of a united Christendom. This monograph seeks to resolve this contradiction first of all by looking at the bishop of Havelberg's life within the context of the court society in which he moved and the models of behavior that it provided those who, like

---

actions of the Royal Historical Society 5th ser. 21 (1971), 159-79; Walter Edyvean, *Anselm of Havelberg and the Theology of History* (Rome, 1972); Horst Dieter Rauh, *Das Bild des Antichrist im Mittelalter: Von Tyconius zum deutschen Symbolismus*, 2nd ed., Beiträge zur Geschichte der Philosophie und Theologie des Mittelalters, NS 9 (Münster, 1973), pp. 268-302; Peter Classen, "*Res Gestae*, Universal History, Apocalypse: Visions of Past and Future," in Robert L. Benson and Giles Constable, eds., *Renaissance and Renewal in the Twelfth Century* (Cambridge, Mass., 1982), pp. 387-417; Walter Berschin, "Anselm von Havelberg und die Anfänge einer Geschichtstheologie des hohen Mittelalters," *Literaturwissenschaftliches Jahrbuch im Auftrage der Görres-Gesellschaft*, NF 29 (1988), 225-32.

[9] On the debates: Georg Schreiber, "Anselm von Havelberg und die Ostkirche: Begegnung mit der byzantinischen Welt. Morgenländisches und abendländisches Zönobium," *ZKG* 60 (1941), 354-411; Johannes Beumer, "Ein Religionsgespräch aus dem zwölften Jahrhundert," *Zeitschrift für katholische Theologie* 78 (1951), 465-82; Martin Fitzthum, "Anselm von Havelberg als Verteidiger der Einheit mit der Ostkirche," *AP* 36 (1961), 137-41; Gillian Evans, "Anselm of Canterbury and Anselm of Havelberg: The Controversy with the Greeks," *AP* 53 (1977), 158-75; Theodore N. Russell, "Anselm of Havelberg and the Union of the Churches," *Kleronomia* 10 (1978), 85-120; Hermann-Josef Sieben, *Die Konzilsidee des lateinischen Mittelalters (847-1378)*, Konziliengeschichte: Reihe B, Untersuchungen (Paderborn, 1984), pp. 219-51; Karl F. Morrison, "Anselm of Havelberg: Play and the Dilemma of Historical Progress," in *Religion, Culture and Society in the Early Middle Ages: Studies in Honor of Richard E. Sullivan*, ed. Thomas F. X. Noble and John J. Contreni, Studies in Medieval Culture 23 (Kalamazoo, 1987), pp. 219-56; Evans, "Unity and diversity: Anselm of Havelberg as Ecumenist," *AP* 67 (1991), 42-52.

Anselm, aspired to clerical and advisory positions at royal and ecclesiastical courts. Anselm sought to model his active life on the pattern set by the educational system for court bishops and on the life of his mentor, Norbert of Xanten, the archbishop of Magdeburg. While Anselm achieved some success by taking on the roles of diplomat, bishop, and adviser to kings and popes, there was always an element of frustration in this performed life. The harmony the peace-making Norbert was so capable of fashioning often slipped through Anselm's fingers. In times of crisis, Norbert had the charisma to function not only as performer but as playwright, determining the direction of the action and moving his fellow performers toward his goal. Anselm's life appears more at the mercy of Fortune's wheel. The results were not always pleasant for Anselm, but the life of withdrawal from the political stage had little appeal, a fact expressed in his writings.

Lacking a fundamental understanding of Anselm's career, scholars have placed his written works within a variety of contexts which, while certainly not without value, have made it difficult to draw them together as a single mind's coherent reflections on its world. His *Epistola apologetica* has been placed in the context of the polemic literature produced in the disputes between monks and canons, old orders and new. This has obscured how similar the biblical exegesis in this work, with its emphasis on literal meaning, is to that found in the first book of the *Antikeimenon*. That first book, *De una forma credendi*, has been placed in the context of medieval ideas of history, periodization, and the Antichrist. Since it is difficult to place the second part of the *Antikeimenon* and its debates with the Greek archbishop into these contexts, the assumption has been that the debates and *De una forma credendi* have little to do with each other, and the essential integrity of the *Antikeimenon* has been missed. Moreover, the debates have too often been taken to represent Anselm's attempt to describe accurately an event from his own life. This they most certainly are not, and their literary nature needs evaluation.

This book seeks to reconstruct Anselm's life in Part One and to give a detailed reading of his written works in Part Two with the intent of demonstrating that those written works cannot be properly understood apart from his life nor apart from each other. I will argue that the *Epistola apologetica* is an early attempt by Anselm to conceptualize his active life by comparing the actions of biblical figures with the deeds of men active in the clerical hierarchy. In his later *De una forma credendi*, he takes his concern for action a step further by formulating a progressive idea of history in which actions have a cause and effect relation to other actions. Finally, in the debates, Anselm takes an event from his own life and dramatically reshapes it through words to present a model of action and to illustrate the potential such action has for promoting a united Christendom. Here he also creates something of an apologia for his own life by using words to turn a less than successful deed into a triumph. In so doing, he gives us a written description of the model he aspired to, a model inspired by the teachers of his youth who themselves wrote little.

A technical note on Anselm's writings. There is no critical edition of Anselm's works. Some years ago, Johann Braun began work on producing one for the Monumenta Germaniae Historica; but for now, one must fall back on the edition found in J. P. Migne, *Patrologia Latina*, volume 188,[10] an edition which poses many problems. Braun has written at length both about the Migne edition and about the thirteen manuscripts he has found for the *Antikeimenon*, as well as mentioning seven for the *Epistola*. While I refer the reader to his thorough discussion,[11] let me mention that four manuscripts of the *Antikeimenon* are in Prague. That the work of a follower of St. Norbert should be found there is not surprising, for Norbert's own body was removed to this Premonstratensian center in 1627. However, all four manuscripts were made in the fifteenth century, indicating some real interest in Anselm during this period, a subject worthy of further research. None of the manuscripts of the *Antikeimenon* date from before the fifteenth century. I have looked at two of the manuscripts of the *Antikeimenon* and a third on microfilm, as well as two manuscripts—one complete, one fragment—of the *Epistola* in order to use them as a control on Migne. These are listed in the bibliography. My selection of manuscripts is based on Braun's stemma which breaks the manuscripts for the *Antikeimenon* into three groups.[12] I have used one manuscript from each group. In those places where I feel the manuscripts have allowed a better reading than Migne, I have

---

[10] In Migne, the edition of the *Epistola apologetica* is from E. Amort, *Vetus disciplina canonicorum regularium et saecularium* (Venice, 1747), 1117-40; that of the *Antikeimenon* is from St. Baluze, E. Martène, F. J. de la Barre, *Spicilegium sive collectio veterum aliquot scriptorum*, new edition, 1 (Paris 1723), 160-207 which itself is a reworking of J.L. D'Achery, *Spicilegium sive collectio veterum aliquot scriptorum* 13 (Paris, 1677), pp. 88-252. See Braun's article, n. 11 below.

[11] "Studien zur Überlieferung der Werke Anselms von Havelberg I: Die Überlieferung des Anticimenon," *DA* 28 (1972), 133-209.

[12] Braun, "Überlieferung," p. 166.

given in the notes the corresponding column number for the Migne edition, cited the manuscripts and folio numbers on which those changes are based, and given my revised Latin text in full.

Scholars have generally referred to Anselm's *Antikeimenon* as the *Dialogi*;[13] but *Antikeimenon* is Anselm's chosen title, and I have therefore used it in what follows. The title generally given to the first book of the *Antikeimenon* is *De unitate fidei et multiformitate vivendi ab Abel justo usque ad novissimum electum*, often shortened to *De unitate fidei*. For reasons which will be made clear, when referring to this book as distinct from the two books of debates, I have used the title *De una forma credendi*, though the notes will give the reference *Antik.* 1.

Finally, for Latin quotations, I have given the spelling and punctuation of the editions used.

---

[13] Migne gives the title of the work as *Dialogi*. Braun says that the manuscript tradition stands on the side of Antikeimenon, "Überlieferung," pp. 135-36. The three mss. I have used all have the title *Antikeimenon* in the incipit to the prologue (Ber. 1; Mun.) or book one (Wolf. 1). See also Berschin, "Anselm von Havelberg," p. 227.

PART ONE

ANSELM OF HAVELBERG

CHAPTER ONE

EARLY LIFE AND FRIENDSHIPS WITH
WIBALD OF STABLO AND ARNOLD OF WIED
1095-1129

Anselm of Havelberg's life (ca. 1095-1158) spans the first half of the twelfth century from the time of the Investiture Controversy through the beginning of the reign of Frederick Barbarossa.[1] By the time of Anselm's birth, church reformers had sought to address the problems of a clergy lax in its morals and decentralized in its administration. The result was to draw the papacy into a bitter struggle with the German ruler over the control of ecclesiastical offices. In 1122, the Concordat of Worms marked at least a truce between the pope and the emperor. All of Anselm's politically active life falls in the period when the viability of that uneasy truce was put to the test.[2]

Anselm was a product of this age of ecclesiastical reform, himself caught up in the forces the reformers had tried to harness to forward their goals. At the end of the eleventh century, the papacy capitalized on a spirituality both militant and lay by promoting the First Crusade, and saw considerable success in the capture of Jerusalem. By the middle of the twelfth century, a second crusade not only to the Holy Land but across the Elbe River and into the territory of the

---

[1] There are many brief summaries of Anselm's life. The most useful are Johann W. Braun, "Anselm von Havelberg," *Die deutsche Literatur des Mittelalters, Verfasserlexikon*, 2nd ed., 1 (New York, 1978), pp. 384-91; and the beginning of the article by Barmann, "Reform Ideology," pp. 379-95. Others include A. Versteylen, "Anselme d'Havelberg," *Dictionnaire de spiritualité: ascétique et mystique: doctrine et histoire* 1 (Paris, 1937), pp. 697-98; J. R. Sommerfeldt, "Anselm of Havelberg," *New Catholic Encyclopedia* 1 (New York, 1967), pp. 583-84; Karl Bosl, "Anselm von Havelberg," *Biographisches Wörterbuch zur deutschen Geschichte* (Munich, 1973), pp. 113-14; Johann W. Braun, "A[nselm] von Havelberg," *Lexikon des Mittelalters* 1 (Munich, 1980), pp. 678-79; Walter Berschin, "Anselm von Havelberg," pp. 225-32. Still of value, Adolph Friedrich Riedel, "Nachrichten über den Bischof Anselm von Havelberg, Gesandten der deutschen Kaiser Lothar und Friedrich I. am kaiserlichen Hofe zu Constantinopel, nachmaligen Erzbischof und Exarchen von Ravenna," *Leopold von Ledeburs Allgemeines Archiv für die Geschichtskunde des preussischen Staates* 8 (1832): 97-136, 225-67.
[2] On the post-Concordat of Worms period see Peter Classen, "Das Wormser Konkordat in der deutschen Verfassungsgeschichte," *Vorträge und Forschungen* 17: *Investiturstreit und Reichsverfassung*, ed. Josef Fleckenstein (Sigmaringen, 1973), 411-60.

pagan Wends was preached by Bernard of Clairvaux. For a considerable part of his life, Anselm was the bishop of Havelberg, a town on
the pagan side of the Elbe. Thus, he had a vested interest in this
crusade against the Wends. The Second Crusade, however, accomplished little and left Bernard with the sinking feeling that the Antichrist was on the way.

Like Bernard, Anselm was a participant in that other spiritual
force of this half century, the new religious orders. The Norbertine or
Praemonstratensian Order of canons regular, to which Anselm be-
longed, and the Cistercians, among whom Bernard was numbered,
were just two of many new forms of religious life springing up
throughout Europe. But as with the crusades, what seemed such a
marvelous tool to renew spiritual commitment and enthusiasm became mired in problems. The old orders criticized the new for being
upstart innovators; the new pointed fingers at the old as decrepit and
decadent. Anselm was in the trenches of this battle between old and
new, a battle which by its very nature could reveal an uncharitable
side of men otherwise dedicated to a spiritual life. This side, too,
would be shown by Anselm of Havelberg.

Anselm's life was by no means free of the problem of the secular
authority's role in the church. The wounds of the Investiture Controversy were deep. Though the Concordat provided a chance for those
wounds to heal, it also left many on both the royal and papal sides of
the conflict with a bitter sense that defeat had been masked with the
appearance of compromise. A reformer and negotiator of the
Concordat, Archbishop Adalbert of Mainz, was soon moaning that
"the church of God must undergo the same slavery as before, or an
even more oppressive one,"[3] and the German ruler Lothar III held
tight to a strong tradition of ecclesiastical domination by demanding
"that the investiture of bishops, which the Roman church had taken
away from his predecessor, ... should be restored to himself."[4] The
possibility of a renewal of the papal-imperial conflict was therefore a
very real one. German prelates such as Anselm found themselves in
a difficult situation. On the one hand, they were unwilling to disasso-
ciate their offices from the power and wealth bestowed on them by
the ruler and desired strong secular leadership to maintain peace; on

---

[3] P. Jaffé, *Bibliotheca rerum Germanicarum* 5:519; cited and translated by Robert L.
Benson, *The Bishop-Elect: A Study in Medieval Ecclesiastical Office* (Princeton, 1968), p.
305.
[4] Ernald, *Vita Bernhardi* 2.1.5, *PL* 185:271f. Quoted by Benson, *Bishop-Elect*, p. 253.

the other, their loyalty was demanded by an aggressive papacy which saw them as part of a centralized ecclesiastical bureaucracy. Pulled in both directions, they lived with the memory of how contentious rulers and popes could rend this delicate interweaving of church and state. Anselm served on both sides of the papal-imperial equation and was rewarded toward the end of his life by being made archbishop of Ravenna. His political activities are most often interpreted as an indication of weakness of character, as if the lure of an easy life at court had tempted him away from his diocesan duties as bishop of Havelberg. However, life at court was never easy for those who tried to maintain the equilibrium between the pope and the ruler; and among such admirable men, it will be argued, was Anselm.

Anselm became bishop of Havelberg in 1129.[5] If canon law was followed, he was at least thirty years old at the time of his ordination[6] and was thus born no later than 1099. His place of birth is unknown. Various arguments have been put forward for the area of Lorraine-Burgundy. Franz Winter suggested that the name Anselm is prevalent in that region,[7] and Georg Schreiber pointed to Anselm's mention of Burgundy twice in the first book of the *Antikeimenon* as evidence[8] for what has become the generally accepted hypothesis.[9] However, Winter changed his mind when he came upon specific evidence that indicated Saxony as more likely. In a document dated April 17, 1187—that is, some twenty-nine years after Anselm's death in 1158—the provost of the cathedral chapter of Halberstadt, also named Anselm, gives money for an annual donation to the poor along with the burning of two candles on the anniversary of his own death and that of "his relative the lord Anselm, reverend archbishop

---

[5] Riedel, "Nachrichten," pp. 103-8; Winter, *Die Prämonstratenser*, pp. 299-300; Dombrowski, *Anselm*, pp. 4-5. The ordination is determined from the foundation charter of the Norbertine chapter of Jerichow of 1144 (pp. 64-68 below) which is dated to the fifteenth year of Anselm's episcopacy. Edited by Winter, *Die Prämonstratenser*, p. 352.

[6] Burchard of Worms, *Decretum* 2.9, PL 140:627A; Ivo of Chartres, *Decretum* 6.29, PL 161:451D.

[7] *Die Prämonstratenser*, p. 56.

[8] "Anselm von Havelberg und die Ostkirche," p. 354.

[9] So for example U. Berlière, "Anselme d'Havelberg," *Dictionnaire de théologie Catholique* 1.2 (Paris, 1909), p. 1360; Martin Grabmann, "Anselm," *Neue Deutsche Biographie* 1 (Berlin, 1953), p. 309; A. Bayol, "Anselme," *Dictionnaire d'histoire et de géographie ecclésiastiques* 3 (Paris, 1924), p. 458; Barmann, "Reform Ideology," p. 379; François Petit, *La spiritualité des Prémontrés aux XIIe et XIIIe siècles*, Études de théologie et d'histoire de la spiritualité 10 (Paris, 1947), p. 56; Karl Bosl, "Anselm von Havelberg," p. 113.

of Ravenna."[10] Here is evidence for at least one more Anselm east of
Burgundy, and a relative of Anselm of Havelberg's at that. It has
been suggested that almost all of the canons of Halberstadt came
from the town or the surrounding area,[11] and thus the chapter provost probably came from the vicinity of Halberstadt and Anselm of
Havelberg, as well. One can at least say that the contention that
Anselm was of Saxon origin has the virtue of basing itself on more
concrete historical evidence than the arguments for Lorraine or Burgundy.[12]

The single piece of evidence for Anselm's early life strongly suggests that as a young man, he received his education in Liège,[13] and
there, sometime after 1115, met Wibald, the future abbot of Stablo
and Corvey, and Arnold of Wied, the future chancellor of Conrad III
and archbishop of Cologne.[14] In a letter written in 1149, Wibald
refers to Arnold and Anselm as friends "whom since our youth we
have embraced in the greatest love and venerated in diligent devotion with ever growing affection."[15] Wibald, who was born in 1098,

---

[10] Edited by Winter in "Zur Geschichte des Bischofs Anselm von Havelberg,"
ZKG 5 (1882), 141-43. Kurt Fina cautiously concedes Winter's argument "einige
Wahrscheinlichkeit," *AP* 32 (1956), 79-80; Berges agrees with Winter, "Anselm von
Havelberg in der Geistesgeschichte," p. 43 n. 12.

[11] Walter Schlesinger, *Kirchengeschichte Sachsens im Mittelalter* 2 vols. (Cologne, 1962),
1:278; 2:534-37; Winter, "Zur Geschichte des Bischofs Anselm von Havelberg,"
p. 140.

[12] Berges, "Anselm von Havelberg," p. 43 n. 12.

[13] On Germans who moved west to study in this period such as Hugh of
St. Victor and Gerhoch of Reichersberg see Joachim Ehlers, "Deutsche Scholaren in
Frankreich während des 12. Jahrhunderts, *Schulen und Studium im sozialen Wandel des
hohen und späten Mittelalters*, ed. Johannes Fried, *Vorträge und Forschungen* 30 (Sigmaringen, 1986), pp. 97-120; Jerome Taylor, *The Origin and Early Life of Hugh of St. Victor*,
Texts and Studies in the History of Medieval Education 5 (Notre Dame, 1975),
pp. 67-69; Peter Classen, *Gerhoch von Reichersberg: Eine Biographie* (Wiesbaden, 1960),
p. 15.

[14] Heinz Wolter, *Arnold von Wied, Kanzler Konrads III. und Erzbischof von Köln*, Veröffentlichungen des Kölnischen Geschichtsvereins e.V. 32 (Cologne, 1973), pp. 5-6;
Friedrich Hausmann, *Reichskanzlei und Hofkapelle unter Heinrich V. und Konrad III.*, MGH
Sch 14 (Stuttgart, 1956), p. 181; Franz-Josef Jakobi, *Wibald von Stablo und Corvey
(1098-1158): Benediktinischer Abt in der frühen Stauferzeit*, Veröffentlichungen der Historischen Kommission für Westfalen 10, Abhandlungen zur Corveyer Geschichtsschreibung 5 (Münster, 1979), p. 41.

[15] Wibald of Stablo, *Epistolae*, ed. Philip Jaffé, *Monumenta Corbiensia, Bibliotheca rerum
Germanicarum* 1 (Berlin, 1864), 150, p. 241. On the problems of determining the
meaning of *iuventus* in the Middle Ages, Adolf Hofmeister, "Puer, Iuvenis, Senex.
Zum Verständnis der mittelalterlichen Altersbezeichnungen," in *Papstum und Kaisertum: Forschungen zur politischen Geschichte und Geisteskultur des Mittelalters. Paul Kehr zum*

spent some years at the monastery school of Stablo, and then in 1115 went to study in Liège.[16] In 1117, he left to become a monk at Waulsort and by early 1118 had returned to Stablo where he was made abbot in 1130.[17] Given that neither Arnold nor Anselm chose the monastic life, the period 1115 to 1117 is the most likely time for them to have met Wibald. Moreover, all three demonstrate an acquaintance with Rupert of Deutz, the famous biblical exegete who resided in Liège at that time. In 1118, Wibald left Stablo to return to Liège to see Rupert.[18] Arnold was also influenced by Rupert and clearly admired him. At the height of his career as archbishop of Cologne, he had the lower chapel of his famous church of Schwarzrheindorf painted with scenes from the Book of Ezekiel as interpreted by Rupert in his commentary on Ezekiel.[19] Finally, Anselm wrote that he "saw and knew" Rupert, though his opinion of him was rather lower than that of his friends.

Since the tenth century, Liège had acquired considerable fame as a veritable Athens of the West. However, in the late eleventh and early twelfth centuries, the schools of Liège remained conservative in regards to the growing enthusiasm for dialectic and rhetoric being promoted in northern France.[20] As has been mentioned, Wibald fell

---

65. *Geburtstag dargebracht*, ed. Albert Brackmann (Munich, 1926), p. 316; Wilfried Marcel Grauwen, "Norberts reis naar Laon, Kamerijk en Nijvel en de inbezitneming van Prémontré, 1120," *AP* 69 (1993), 41-50.

[16] Wibald, 395, p. 526.

[17] Jakobi, *Wibald von Stablo*, pp. 40-45; Hausmann, *Reichskanzlei*, pp. 180-82.

[18] Wibald, 1, p. 77; Jakobi, *Wibald von Stablo*, pp. 40-41; John van Engen, *Rupert of Deutz* (Berkeley, 1983), p. 219; Herbert Silvestre, "Notes sur la controverse de Rupert de Saint-Laurent avec Anselme de Laon et Guillaume de Champeaux," in *Saint-Laurent de Liège: Église, Abbaye et Hopital militaire: Mille ans d'histoire* (Liège, 1968), pp. 71-73.

[19] Wolter, *Arnold von Wied*, p. 6; Wilhelm Neuss, *Das Buch Ezechiel in Theologie und Kunst bis zum Ende des XII Jahrhunderts*, Beiträge zur Geschichte des alten Mönchtums und des Benediktinerordens (Münster, 1912), pp. 285ff; Johannes Kunisch, *Konrad III., Arnold von Wied und der Kapellenbau von Schwarzrheindorf* (Düsseldorf, 1966), pp. 93-95. Anne Derbes points to the possible influence of Rupert's *In XII Prophetas minores*, "The Frescoes of Schwarzrheindorf, Arnold of Wied and the Second Crusade," in Michael Gervers, *The Second Crusade and the Cistercians* (New York: 1992), pp. 142-43.

[20] On the declining importance of Liège as a center of education at the beginning of the twelfth century, see Christine Renardy, "Les écoles Liégeoises du IXe au XIIe siècle: Grandes lignes de leur évolution," *Revue belge de Philologie et d'Histoire* 57 (1979), 309-28; Renardy, *Le monde des maîtres universitaires du diocèse de Liège 1140-1350: Recherches sur sa composition et ses activités*, Bibliothèque de la Faculté de Philosophie et Lettres de l'Université de Liège 227 (Paris, 1979), pp. 16-18; Jean-Louis Kupper, *Liège et l'église impériale, XIe-XIIe siècles*, Bibliothèque de la Faculté de Philosophie et

under the spell of Rupert of Deutz. While Rupert reinvigorated
Scriptural exegesis with imaginative and innovative interpretations,
these remained firmly grounded on traditional monastic contemplation; and he battled fiercely with those giving their allegiance to the
new dialectic's emphasis on demonstrating rather than contemplating truth.[21] Wibald followed the monastic path set out by Rupert, but
Anselm did not. Here we must jump ahead in Anselm's life by several
decades to a tract he wrote in which he demonstrated nothing but
contempt for Rupert.

In Anselm's *Epistola apologetica*, he wrote that he knew Rupert, read
some of his works, and found him to be a fat man of limited intelligence whose writings were of no particular consequence.[22] Anselm
penned the *Epistola* to defend the notion that a canon held the highest
position on the hierarchy of spiritual lives. Here he entered a battle
that had been going on since the eleventh century over what the
monastic and the clerical lives entailed and which was the superior. It
was a battle that became more heated as the new religious orders of
monks and canons, each with its own contending claims of sanctity,
grew in number.[23] It was also a battle engaged in by Rupert of Deutz
and fought with particular intensity in Liège at the very time Anselm
would have been a student there. A real lightening rod went up for
drawing the bolts of champions of monks and canons alike when a
clergyman or a monk decided to switch professions. As will be seen,
the *Epistola apologetica* addressed just such and incident; and Liège lost

---

Lettres de l'Université de Liège 28 (Paris, 1981), pp. 361-65, 380-83; Charles De-
reine, "Clercs et moines au diocèse de Liège du Xe au XIIe siècles," *Annales de la
Société archéologique de Namur* 45 (1949-1950), 183-203. See also van Engen, *Rupert of
Deutz*, 14-26.

[21] Van Engen, *Rupert of Deutz*, pp. 72-94

[22] *Epist. apol.*, 1120B; see also pp. 139 below.

[23] The literature on this issue is extensive. See Dereine, *Les chanoines réguliers au
diocèse de Liège avant saint Norbert* (Bruxelles, 1952; cf. Kupper, *Liège et l'église imperiale*,
pp. 369-70 with ns. 113, 116); J. Leclercq, "La crise du monachisme aux XIe et XIIe
siècles," *Bullettino dell'Istituto Storico Italiano per il Medio Evo* 70 (1958), 19-41; M.-D.
Chenu, "Moines, clercs, laics au carrefour de la vie évangélique (XIIe siècle)," *La
théologie au douzième siècle*, Etudes de philosophie médiévale 45 (Paris, 1957), pp. 225-
51; Lester K. Little *Religious Poverty and the Profit Economy in Medieval Europe* (Ithaca,
1978), pp. 59-112; Caroline Walker Bynum, *Docere verbo et exemplo: An Aspect of Twelfth-
Century Spirituality*, Harvard Theological Studies 31 (Missoula, 1979); Henrietta
Leyser, *Hermits and the New Monasticism: A Study of Religious Communities in Western Europe
1000-1150* (London: 1984); Giles Constable, "Renewal and Reform in Religious
Life: Concepts and Realities," in *Renaissance and Renewal in the Twelfth Century*, ed.
Robert L. Benson and Giles Constable (Cambridge, Mass., 1982), pp. 37-67.

many of its canons and some of its best teachers to monasteries.[24] Was the direction of such a move up or down on the scale of perfection?

In this debate, Rupert argued that a monk could not move down to what for him was the less spiritual life of the secular canon but that a cleric could become a monk because this was a move to a higher form of spiritual life. He also addressed the position of those calling themselves canons regular, that is clergy who took vows of obedience to a rule. These either lived in houses virtually indistinguishable from monasteries or continued to serve as active clergy, a flexibility that made their profession a particularly difficult one to define. Rupert, however, had no doubts as to where they should be placed on the spiritual hierarchy. He defended a secular cleric's right to join a house of canons regular[25] and a regular's right to become a monk.[26] The movement toward higher sanctity thus was from secular clergy to canon regular to monk. The context of Anselm's derogatory remarks about Rupert indicate that it is these writings to which he referred.

It should also be noted that after Rupert left Liège, he continued his defense of the monastic life in a debate conducted in all likelihood with Norbert of Xanten who founded an order of canons regular and would become Anselm's mentor.[27] This debate revolved around Rupert's contention that ordained monks had the rights to preach and to the care of souls, the traditional rights of the clergy. This contention further complicated the distinctions between secular clergy, canons regular, and monks; and Rupert's expansive definition of the monastic life was one Anselm did not refer to in the *Epistola*. For him, the monk was contemplative and bound to the monastery. Service in the clerical hierarchy was the prerogative of secular and regular clergy. Anselm, in fact, defined the regular's life in much the same way as Rupert had defined the monk's, only with a different

---

[24] Renardy, "Les Écoles Liégeoises," pp. 320-21; Dereine, *Clercs et moines*, pp. 199-200; Dereine, *Les Chanoines réguliers*, pp. 42, 50-51.

[25] The tract defending this position has been lost, but see van Engen, *Rupert of Deutz*, pp. 308-9.

[26] *Super quaedam capitula regulae Benedicti* 4:.13, PL 170:536-37; van Engen, *Rupert of Deutz*, pp. 309-10.

[27] On the possibility that Rupert's adversary was someone other than Norbert see van Engen, *Rupert of Deutz*, pp. 311-12. Rupert recounted his debate in his *Altercatio monachi et clerici quod liceat monacho praedicare*, PL 170:537-42.

emphasis. Whereas Rupert found room for some activity within the basically contemplative life of the monk, Anselm encouraged contemplation in the basically active life of the canon regular. Anselm's choice of career and his *Epistola* with its antipathetic description of Rupert indicate that he was early on touched with a desire to commit himself to clerical service.

The extent to which Anselm's scorn may have been directed not only at Rupert's defense of monasticism but at his criticism of dialectic as well is difficult to determine, though there can be no doubt that Anselm was influenced by the new learning. He demonstrates a knowledge of the tools of dialectic and takes delight in pointing out the false logic of an opponent's syllogisms. However, in his later writings, Anselm recognized full well the limitations of the new learning.[28] Nothing is known about what contact Anselm had with the teachers of dialectic,[29] but Liège was known for another kind of education that profoundly influenced him.

Using the *vitae* of German bishops, C. Stephen Jaeger has presented us with a general model for the ideal career of what he terms a "courtier bishop" in the central Middle Ages: A man of nobility is sent to school by his parents, taken into the service of a bishop, made head of the school, then provost. Through one means or another, he comes to the attention of the king; and when the bishop/patron dies, he is promoted to his place.[30] The vital point Jaeger makes is that this career was best launched by the education of a cathedral school such as Anselm would have found in Liège. In contrast to the monastic school, the cathedral school was designed specifically to meet "the needs of administration at secular and ecclesiastical courts" so that "cathedral school education becomes identical with preparation for service at court."[31] Liège had considerable renown for this sort of education.[32] Though the sources leave a decade of silence concerning Anselm's life after Liège, the bare facts for the few years after this

---

[28] See *Epist. apol.* 1122CD; *Antik.* 2.5, 1171D. For Rupert's use of periodization as a comparison to Anselm's, see pp. 179-83 below.

[29] On the suggestion that Anselm studied in Laon, see p. 30 n. 33 below.

[30] C. Stephen Jaeger, *The Origins of Courtliness: Civilizing Trends and the Formation of Courtly Ideals, 939-1210* (Philadelphia, 1985), pp. 28-29.

[31] C. Stephen Jaeger, "Cathedral Schools and Humanist Learning, 950-1150," *Deutsche Vierteljahrsschrift für Literaturwissenschaft und Geistesgeschichte* 61 (1987), 569-616, here citing pp. 571, 575. Also Jaeger, *The Origins of Courtliness*, pp. 19-53, 213-19.

[32] Renardy, "Les Écoles Liégeoises," pp. 312-13.

hiatus strongly indicate that he was pursuing a niche in the administrative, clerical hierarchy: He found a patron in an archbishop, was elevated by that archbishop to the office of bishop and introduced to the ruler who then used him in diplomatic missions.

Professor Jaeger makes another point which gives us a grasp on the formative nature of Anselm's education. Jaeger has demonstrated that the teachers in cathedral schools taught basically by becoming living examples to their students of "eloquence, gravity and dignity." The teacher's "personal presence was a text from which the students learned." What the student studied, then, was a living model of action appropriate to service in an ecclesiastic or royal court.[33] As will be shown, in the written works of Anselm's later life his overwhelming concern would be to present models of action worthy of imitation. In fact, in the final part of the *Antikeimenon*, he would present himself as the model with his student-like brothers as the audience observing not only what he says but how he says it.

While Anselm's movements until his emergence as a disciple of Archbishop Norbert of Magdeburg in 1129 remain impenetrable, his friendships with Wibald of Stablo and Arnold of Wied are another indication that his education was for administrative service, for this would be the career path of both of his friends. These friendships proved lasting. The trust and openness shared by Wibald and Anselm is clearly demonstrated in the letters they exchanged later in life.[34] In these few letters the two joke with and confide in each other. Here is Anselm, lonely in Havelberg, chastising his friend for not writing. The tone is light, but the bishop's real desire to hear from his friend comes through:

> A certain wise man said, "To be with friends requires little excuse." But you have long since had neither little nor great excuse, nor have you sent me so much as a single letter even though you, not I, have plenty of messengers. What is going on? Where are you? Where have you vanished to? What has happened to us? Why have you dismissed me? O Weser [i.e. Wibald living on the Weser River], go ahead and flow

---

[33] Jaeger, "Cathedral Schools and Humanist Learning," pp. 585-91, here citing pp. 588-89.

[34] Wibald, 158, p. 263; 221, pp. 339-41 (Anselm to Wibald); Wibald, 159, pp. 263-65; 211, p. 330 (Wibald to Anselm). Anselm may have been the senior of the two for Wibald begins his letters on a note of deference: "Reverendo patri suo A(nselmo)," and "Reverendo patri suo et domino Anselmo." Anselm writes to Wibald as an equal: "Carissimo fratri et speciali amico W[ibaldo]" and "W[ibaldo] venerabili abbati, carissimo sibi."

> backwards; the Havel still flows properly. In spite of your absence, you
> are always in my thoughts whether you wish it or not.[35]

Wibald responds apologetically, playing gently on Anselm's river
metaphor ("Far be that Lethean forgetfulness from me, dearest father"), and assuring Anselm, "Believe me, bishop, if I had the whole
world but did not have you and friends like you who are very few, I
would be poor."[36] The abbot of both Stablo and Corvey, Wibald
faced staggering problems in setting the affairs of his abbeys in order.
Nevertheless, he describes his relation with his two "wives" in terms
which try to wring a smile from a friend:

> If indeed, beloved father, my first wife [Stablo] was half blind, infertile,
> and emaciated to boot, truly this second one [Corvey] with whom I am
> joined in matrimony is certainly fatter, but no less blind and sterile, and
> more contentious, as well.[37]

While we have none of the correspondence between Anselm and
Arnold,[38] there is still good evidence that these three men worked
well together. In 1146, Conrad III chose Wibald and Anselm to go to
Dijon to meet with pope Eugenius III, and soon after the two men
went together on the crusade against the Wends. In 1155, Frederick
Barbarossa called on Anselm and Arnold to lead a delegation to Pope
Hadrian IV, and shortly after this the two played a role in avoiding
a confrontation when pope and ruler met at Sutri.[39]

The friendship of these three students, then, carried on into their
professional lives at court. The general way in which they viewed
their world was at least similar enough that there is no indication of
any great disagreement among them. They worked together and
relied on each other for advice, assistance, and support. When they
had problems, they went to each other not just seeking a sympathetic
ear but with the expectation of obtaining the sort of help that would
resolve the problem. They all had difficulties or disagreements with
the rulers they served, particularly with Conrad III, and it was at
precisely these times that they conferred with each other or at least
expressed the desire to speak in private rather than risk putting their

---

[35] Wibald, 158, p. 263.

[36] Wibald, 159, p. 264.

[37] Wibald, 159, p. 264; Jakobi, *Wibald von Stablo*, p. 243 (who, however, misses the humor in the passage); Hausmann, *Reichskanzlei*, pp. 201-4.

[38] For evidence that there was correspondence, Wibald, 211, p. 330; 221, p. 339.

[39] For Wibald and Arnold's mutual service to Conrad III, Jakobi, *Wibald von Stablo*, pp. 151-54, 158-63; Wolter, *Arnold von Wied*, pp. 40-47, 80-84.

thoughts in writing. In 1146, a surprised and horrified Wibald was pressured by Conrad to become abbot of Corvey. Wary of accepting such a task on top of his onerous responsibility to Stablo, Wibald sought out both Anselm and Arnold for advice and asked them to try to dissuade the king.[40] Three years later when Anselm felt that Conrad had unjustly banished him from court, he first asked Arnold for help and then wrote Wibald: "If we only had a few days when we could sit with our chancellor [Arnold] between us, so that together we could share those thoughts which now each must keep to himself."[41]

In Arnold and Wibald, Anselm found friends not only of a high intellectual caliber but men who, through personal ambition and circumstance, were caught up in the same world of high politics as he. While Arnold had a vested interest in the episcopacy of Cologne[42] and Wibald had the heavy responsibility for two imperial abbeys, they both also served in the royal chancery. Men of great diplomatic ability, they frequently found themselves enmeshed in disputes between their ruler and the pope. However much personal ambition one may attach to them, neither saw himself as the servant of a *Reichspolitik* against the pope or as an absolute defender of papal interests in the empire. If their concerns were in many ways with their local ecclesiastical or monastic interests, their association with the German ruler meant that they were there when popes and rulers began to collide. In such cases and in sharp contrast to advisers like Rainald of Dassel who followed after, Wibald and Arnold did not encourage confrontation but worked on the side of compromise. In this they served an ideal of the peaceful unity of Christendom rather than the interests of a particular ruler. It may be said that this commitment not only cemented their friendship with Anselm, whose view of his role as royal adviser was the same, but in so far as all three had the ear of the ruler, it made them a powerful force for compromise.

---

[40] See p. 73 below.

[41] Wibald, 221, p. 339. Arnold expressed the same concern about committing too much to writing, Wibald, 223, p. 342.

[42] Wolter, *Arnold von Wied*, p. 42.

CHAPTER TWO

ANSELM AND NORBERT OF XANTEN
1129-1134

Sometime before 1129, Anselm met and became one of the followers of Norbert of Xanten, the archbishop of Magdeburg. It was Norbert who gave Anselm his first documented ecclesiastical position by choosing him as bishop of Havelberg, Norbert who introduced him into the court of Lothar III, and Norbert at whose side Anselm remained as the archbishop moved between service to his archdiocese, his ruler, and his pope. In the words of Norbert's modern biographer Wilfried Marcel Grauwen, Anselm was the archbishop's "most faithful follower;"[1] and almost to the time of Norbert's death in 1134, the documentary evidence leaves Anselm very much in his mentor's shadow.

What it meant to be a follower of Norbert of Xanten was, however, not easy to define in the twelfth century, and Anselm's own life and writings can be seen as a struggle to reach some clear sense of what his own dedication to Norbert meant. By the time Anselm can be found at his side, Norbert was already in his mid to late forties and had moved from his home near Xanten in Lorraine to the eastern border of the empire. His earlier life reflects the spiritual fervor which both stimulated and fed on eleventh- and early twelfth-century attempts to reform monastic and ecclesiastical institutions. Norbert was among those who found, through personal experience, a dull edge to the spiritual life provided by traditional monastic communities and the clerical hierarchy. Many turned their backs on both to begin a personal quest for a satisfying spiritual way of life: men like Robert of Arbrissel, archpriest of Rennes, who took refuge in the forest of

---

[1] *Norbertus Aartsbisshop van Maagdenburg (1126-1134)*, Verhandelingen van de Koninklijke Academie voor Wetenschappen, Letteren en Schone Kunsten van België: Klasse der Letteren, Jaargang XL nr. 86 (Brussels: Paleis de Academiën, 1978), pp. 225-26. The best work on Norbert is Grauwen; good, brief accounts are found in Dietrich Claude, *Geschichte des Erzbistums Magdeburg* 2:1-38 and Wolfgang Petke, *Kanzlei, Kapelle und Königliche Kurie unter Lothar III. (1125-1137)*, Forschungen zur Kaiser- und Papstgeschichte des Mittelalters: Beihefte zu J. F. Böhmer, Regesta Imperii 5 (Cologne, 1985), pp. 303-22. See also the articles in Kaspar Elm, ed., *Norbert von Xanten Adliger-Ordensstifter-Kirchenfürst* (Cologne, 1984).

Craon in disgust at the unreformed clergy; Robert's companion Bernard of Tiron, prior at St. Savin, who felt his own abbot to be guilty of simony and then, as abbot himself of St. Cyprian near Poitiers, could not reform his own monks; and Vitalis of Mortain, who renounced his life as chaplain of Count Robert of Mortain as too worldly and spent seventeen years as a hermit at Dompierre.[2]

Norbert tried to dedicate himself both to the active life of engagement with the world and to the contemplative life of withdrawal. For an understanding of Anselm, whose *Epistola apologetica* was written to defend this mixed life combining the *vita contemplativa* with the *vita activa*, it is important to recognize the inherent contradiction in the two ways of life his mentor pursued. The eremitical life of withdrawal was directed inward to meditate on the word of God, while that of clerical service was directed outward toward bringing that word to others. This is to say that Norbert was involved in the same controversy over the issues of the relative importance of service and withdrawal and the extent to which both could be pursued by one man that Anselm probably saw hotly debated in Liège.

In 1115, Norbert left the court of Emperor Henry V and began to experiment with various forms of religious life. He moved with remarkable speed between the monastery of Siegburg, the foundation for canons regular at Klosterrath, the hut of the hermit Liudolf, and the open road of the wandering preacher. A good indication of the difficulties of separating the active and contemplative lives into canonical and eremitical/monastic camps is the fact that Norbert would have found the canons of Klosterrath turning away from taking on pastoral duties while the monks of Siegburg wanted to care for

---

[2] Ernst Werner, *Pauperes Christi: Studien zu sozial-religiösen Bewegungen im Zeitalter des Reformpapstums* (Leipzig, 1956); *L'eremitismo in Occidente nei secoli XI et XII*, Pubblicazioni dell' Università Cattolica del Sacro Cuore, Miscellanea del Centro di studi medioevali 4 (Milan, 1965); R. I. Moore, *The Origins of European Dissent*, 2nd edition (Oxford, 1985), pp. 23-114; Malcolm D. Lambert, *Medieval Heresy: Popular Movements from Bogomil to Hus* (New York, 1976), pp. 43-47; Rolf Zerfass, *Der Streit um die Laienpredigt: Eine pastoralgeschichtliche Untersuchung zum Verständnis des Predigtamtes und zu seiner Entwicklung im 12. und 13. Jahrhundert*, Untersuchungen zur praktischen Theologie 2 (Freiburg, 1974), pp. 134-45; Leyser, *Hermits and the New Monasticism*; Derek Baker, "Reform as protest: the evidence of western eremitical movements," in *The Church in a Changing Society: Conflict—Reconciliation or Adjustment?*, Proceedings of the CIHEC Conference in Uppsala August 17-21, 1977, Publications of the Swedish Society of Church History, New Series 30 (Uppsala, 1978), pp. 55-62. Though Baker does not mention Norbert, he shows how rapidly these wandering preachers moved their foundations into mainstream ecclesiastical organizations. In this too, Norbert held true to their pattern.

the souls of the needy and considered this *cura animarum* to be their right; and the hermit Liudolf stirred up resentment by actively criticizing the world he had supposedly abandoned.[3] At Norbert's ordination to the priesthood, he took a more straightforward approach to combining action and contemplation by insisting on wearing monastic garb and shortly thereafter beginning to preach.[4] Hauled before a church council in Fritzlar, he was challenged on his right to do either.[5] Eventually, he established his own religious foundation at Prémontré near Laon. In 1121, he chose the Augustinian Rule for his followers, a rule for clergymen which was adaptable to emphasizing either the active or the contemplative life.[6]

Where Norbert placed his own emphasis was a serious problem for his followers. At no time does he appear to have envisaged an order of active clergymen with its center in Prémontré,[7] nor did he see his

---

[3] *Vita Norberti* A 3, pp. 672-73; *Vita Norberti* B 4.19, p. 826. On Siegberg: Stefan Weinfurter, "Norbert von Xanten als Reformkanoniker und Stifter des Prämonstratenserordens," in Elm, *Norbert von Xanten*, pp. 165-66; J. Semmler, *Die Klosterreform von Siegburg. Ihre Ausbreitung und ihr Reformprogramm im 11. und 12. Jahrhundert*, Rheinisches Archiv 53 (Bonn, 1959), pp. 47, 256-81; Erich Wisplinghoff, *Die Benediktinerabtei Siegburg, Das Erzbistum Köln 2, Die Bistumer der Kirchenprovinz Köln*, Germania Sacra NF 9 (New York: 1975), pp. 24-27. On Klosterrath: Helmut Deutz, "Norbert von Xanten bei Propst Richer im Regularkanonikerstift Klosterrath," *AP* 68 (1992), 5-16; Weinfurter, "Norbert von Xanten als Reformkanoniker," p. 166; C. Dereine, *Les Chanoines réguliers au diocèse de Liège avant Saint Norbert*, Memoires de l'Academie royale de Belgique, Classe des Lettres et des Science morales et politiques, Mémoires 47 (Brussels, 1952), pp. 69-70; Friedrich Wilhelm Oediger, *Das Bistum Köln von den Anfängen bis zum Ende des 12. Jahrhunderts*, 2nd ed., *Geschichte des Erzbistums Köln* 1 (Cologne, 1972), pp. 130, 394-95, 402-3; Oediger, *Vom Leben am Niederrhein: Aufsätze aus dem Bereich des alten Erzbistums Köln* (Düsseldorf, 1973), pp. 107-8. On Liudolf: Charles Dereine, "La réforme canoniale en Rhénanie (1070-1150)," *Memorial d'un voyage d'études de la Société Nationale des Antiquaires de France en Rhénanie* (Paris, 1953), pp. 237, 240 n. 50.

[4] *Vita Norberti* A 2, pp. 671-73; *Vita Norberti* B 2.9-10, p. 823; 4.19, p. 826.

[5] *Vita Norberti* A 4, p. 673; *Vita Norberti* B 4.19, p. 826.

[6] *Vita Norberti* A 12, p. 683; *Vita Norberti* B 9.51, p. 836; Grauwen, *Norbertus Aartsbisshop*, pp. 32-44; François Petit, "L'ordre de Prémontré de Saint-Norbert à Anselme de Havelberg," *La vita comune del clero nei secoli XI e XII*, Atti del settimana di studio: Mendola, settembre 1959 1, Relazioni e questionario (Milan, 1962), pp. 459-60, 474; F. W. Klebel, "Norbert von Magdeburg und Gerhoch von Reichersberg," *AP* 38 (1962), 330-31; Felton, "Norbert von Xanten: Vom Wanderprediger zum Kirchenfürsten," in Elm, *Norbert von Xanten*, pp. 93-95; Weinfurter, "Norbert von Xanten —Ordensstifter und 'Eigenkirchenherr,'" *Archiv für Kulturgeschichte* 59 (1977), 70; and esp. Deutz, "Norbert von Xanten bei Propst Richer," pp. 11-16.

[7] Petit, "L'ordre de Prémontré," p. 470; Pl. Lefèvre, "Prémontré, ses origines, sa première Liturgie, les relations de son Code législatif avec Citeaux, et les Chanoines du Saint-Sépulcre de Jérusalem," *AP* 25 (1949), 99.

community as a place that would grow by virtue of its own renown with himself as its resident leader. Instead, he spent his time going forth to preach and sending those who wanted to emulate his austerities back to settle down at Prémontré.[8] On the other hand, he appeared to expect different behavior from his brethren, whom he instructed on love, work, eating, clothing, silence, obedience and duty, but not on the virtues of precisely what he himself was doing, preaching.[9]

Though historians have sometimes suggested that an active engagement with the world through preaching was not particularly important to Norbert,[10] the sources for his life show a reformer trying to make contemplation compatible with his preaching rather than a contemplative trying to reconcile himself to the need for action. Twice he sought papal permission to preach;[11] time and again he left Prémontré to proclaim the Gospel;[12] and in 1124, he combated the anticlerical heresy of Tanchelin in Antwerp.[13] It was said that he chose the Augustinian Rule because "he now wished to live according to the apostolic life which he had assumed with his preaching;"[14] and the Council of Fritzlar's first charge against him was that he had usurped the office of a preacher.[15] When Norbert went to Pope Honorius II in Rome in 1126, he may have chosen to travel in the winter because the climate north of the Alps did not lend itself to preaching out of doors.[16] Certainly, the trip was purchased at the cost of leaving his followers at Prémontré. Spending time with them appears to have come fairly far down on his list of priorities.

Most profoundly, however, Norbert's love of the active life is found in his acceptance of (and possible promotion of his own candi-

---

[8] *Vita Norberti* A 9-12, pp. 679-82; *Vita Norberti* B 7-8, pp. 832-35; 10-14, pp. 847-48.

[9] *Vita Norberti* A 12, pp. 683-84; *Vita Norberti* B 9.54, pp. 836-37.

[10] Petit, "L'Ordre de Prémontré," p. 463; Felton, "Norbert von Xanten: Vom Wanderprediger zum Kirchenfürsten," pp. 71-93.

[11] To Pope Gelasius II, *Vita Norberti* A 5, p. 674; *Vita Norberti* B 4.22-23, p. 827; to Pope Calixtus II, *Vita Norberti* A 9, p. 678.

[12] *Vita Norberti* A 9-13, pp. 679-85; *Vita Norberti* B 7-8, pp. 832-38; 10-14, pp. 847-48.

[13] *Vita Norberti* A 16, pp. 690-91; *Vita Norberti* B 13, pp. 843-44; Lambert, *Medieval Heresy*, pp. 55-57; Moore, *Origins of European Dissent*, pp. 63-66.

[14] *Vita Norberti* A 12, p. 683; *Vita Norberti* B 9.51, p. 836.

[15] *Vita Norberti* A 3, p. 673; *Vita Norberti* B 4.21-22, p. 826.

[16] Grauwen, *Norbertus Aartsbisshop*, pp. 69, 89.

dacy for) the position of archbishop of Magdeburg in 1126.[17] This was the Norbert who promoted Anselm to the office of bishop of Havelberg; and while Norbert's followers living a contemplative life in Prémontré may have felt abandoned and hurt by his decision, Anselm wrote about his mentor's earlier life by emphasizing the *vita activa* and, most remarkably, without even mentioning Prémontré:

> In the time of Pope Gelasius, there arose in this order [of St. Augustine] and in imitation of the apostolic life a certain devout priest, Norbert by name, who, on account of his piety, and because of the many dissolute acts and divisions which then were occurring in the western church, accepted from the Roman Pope Gelasius the privilege and authority to preach.

Clearly, preaching was not an end in itself for Anselm; it was the answer to the *enormitates et schismata* in the church. Norbert, Anselm went on, "wandered through diverse provinces, and by his preaching gathered a by no means small following of pious souls, created numerous foundations and by word and example guided them to the perfection of the apostolic life."[18] Norbert, in his deeds and words, was Anselm's guide to the apostolic life. With no reference to the contemplative pattern of life practiced at Prémontré, Anselm praised the fruits of Norbert's activity: his many religious foundations and their wide geographical dispersement.[19]

In Anselm's description of Norbert teaching by word and deed we find a phrase which Caroline Walker Bynum has used as a key to canonical spirituality: to instruct *verbo et exemplo*. Noting how often this phrase appears in the writings of the regulars, Professor Bynum says the canons "felt a commitment to educate others that was no longer attached to the role of the preacher or leader, a commitment that gave a new importance to example as well as speech."[20] While Bynum applies this point to the canonical life as a whole, it must be said that Anselm holds up Norbert the active preacher and charismatic leader as the example to be followed. In Anselm's case, it may

---

[17] On the complicated question of Norbert's own ambitions for the position, Felton, "Norbert von Xanten: Vom Wanderprediger zum Kirchenfürsten," pp. 115-29; Grauwen, *Norbertus Aartsbisschop*, pp. 60ff; Petke, *Kanzlei*, pp. 305-7.

[18] *Antik.* 1.10, 1155A; Grauwen, *Norbertus Aartsbisschop*, p. 9.

[19] *Antik.* 1.10, 1155AC.

[20] Caroline Walker Bynum, "The Spirituality of Regular Canons in the Twelfth Century," in *Jesus as Mother: Studies in the Spirituality of the High Middle Ages* (Berkeley, 1982), pp. 22-58, here citing p. 57; also Bynum, *Docere verbo et exemplo*.

be suggested that teaching by word and example has as much or more to do with his education as with a general notion of canonical spirituality. In Norbert we find something very close to the model of the cathedral schoolteacher discussed in the last chapter: a charismatic man who writes little but whose own life is the text for his students.[21]

The question of what Norbert expected of his new bishop of Havelberg runs into the problem of an almost complete dearth of sources that mention Anselm. We can, however, ask questions of Norbert which may help to reveal the role he envisaged for Anselm: Why was Norbert chosen to become archbishop? What was expected of him? What was the current situation in his archdiocese and particularly in Havelberg?

Havelberg was one of the five suffragan episcopal sees (along with Brandenburg, Meissen, Merseburg, and Naumburg) which made up the archdiocese of Magdeburg. The history of. Magdeburg was deeply rooted in both the need for security against the Slavic peoples including the Wends east of the Elbe River and the desire to expand into their territory.[22] Under the Carolingians, Magdeburg was part of the archdiocese of Halberstadt and an outpost to guard against Slavic attacks; Meissen and Merseburg to the south served the same purpose for Henry I. In the tenth century, Otto I pushed his armies across the Elbe. As he conquered, he built fortresses to hold the newly won land, among them Brandenburg and Havelberg, the latter at the junction of the Havel and Elbe Rivers. Otto reasoned that the sword was not an adequate tool to make the conquered people part of his empire, so he sent preachers along with his armies to begin the conversion of the Wends. Between 946 and 948, episcopal sees were founded across the Elbe at Brandenburg and Havelberg[23] (the bishops being ordained by the archbishop of Mainz), and the decision was made on the eve of the Battle of the Lech to found yet another

---

[21] See p. 18 above and Jaeger's works cited in the notes.

[22] For a general introduction to Havelberg and the Wendenland before Anselm became bishop, see Charles Higounet, *Die deutsche Ostsiedlung im Mittelalter*, trans. Manfred Vasold (Berlin, 1986), pp. 49-63; Albert Hauck, *Kirchengeschichte Deutschlands* 3 (Berlin, 1954), pp. 69-149; Berent Schwineköper, "Norbert von Xanten als Erzbischof von Magdeburg," in Elm, *Norbert von Xanten*, pp. 195-97.

[23] Brandenburg was founded in 948, but there is considerable disagreement about whether Havelberg was founded in the same year or in 946. For the two views see the articles by Lieselott Enders and Clemens Bergstedt in the forth-coming Jahrbuch für Berlin-Brandenburgische Kirchengeschichte (1997).

see at Merseburg. Otto then created a new archbishopric in Magdeburg from which the missionary work in the Wendenland could be directed.[24]

However, in his belief that conversion was the answer to securing the Wendenland, Otto was badly mistaken. The Wends' hatred of the Germans and their religion went to the marrow. In 983, they revolted, and the bishoprics of Brandenburg and Havelberg, beyond the safety of the Elbe border, were hit hardest. The church in Havelberg was looted, the bishop of Brandenburg ran for his life, and the Wends dug up and desecrated his predecessor's corpse.[25] Almost a century and a half later Magdeburg had far from recovered. The line of Christianity was still drawn at the Elbe, and most of the lands east of the river, including Havelberg and Brandenburg, were still in the hands of the Wends. There continued to be bishops of Havelberg after the disaster of 983. The last of eight, Gumbert by name, died in 1125, the year before Norbert became archbishop of Magdeburg. All of these bishops lived outside of their charge as bishops in exile or *episcopi in partibus infidelium*.[26]

In the same year as Gumbert's death, Lothar of Supplinburg succeeded to the royal throne of Germany. As duke of Saxony, Lothar had shown considerable interest in advancing across the Elbe, and he may have seen Norbert as a man of action who could restore Magdeburg's reputation for missionary work among the Slavs.[27] At

---

[24] For eastern missionary work in Otto's conception of *imperator*, Erich Weise, *Die Amtsgewalt von Papst und Kaiser und die Ostmission besonders in der 1. Hälfte des 13. Jahrhunderts*, Marburger Ostforschungen 31 (Marburg/Lahn, 1971), pp. 36-40; Eduard Otto Schulze, *Die Kolonisierung und Germanisierung der Gebiete zwischen Saale und Elbe* (1896; repr. Wiesbaden: 1969), p. 57.

[25] Thietmar of Merseburg, *Chronicon* 3.17, ed. Robert Holtzmann, MGH SS rer. Germ. NS 97 (Berlin, 1935), pp. 119-20. The church building in Havelberg was not destroyed as has often been assumed by historians. See p. 48 n. 2 below.

[26] For the bishops of Havelberg before Anselm, see Torsten Buchholz, "Die Havelberger Bischöfe von Dudo bis Gumpert und ihre Zeit (946/48-1125), *Havelberger Regionalgeschichtliche Beiträge* 4 (1995), 4-23; Wentz, *Bistum Havelberg*, pp. 29-32.

[27] On Lothar's policy toward the territories to the east of Saxony, Karl Jordan, *Die Bistumsgrundungen Heinrichs des Löwen. Untersuchungen zur Geschichte des Ostdeutschen Kolonization*, MGH Sch 3 (Leipzig, 1939), pp. 74-76; Adolf Hofmeister, "Kaiser Lothar und die grosse Kolonizationsbewegungen des 12. Jahrhunderts," *Zeitschrift der Gesellschaft für schleswig-holsteinische Geschichte* 43 (1913), 353-60; Heinz Stoob, "Gedanken zur Ostseepolitik Lothars III.," in *Festschrift Friedrich Hausmann*, ed. Herwig Ebner (Graz, 1977), pp. 531-51; Horst Fuhrmann, *Germany in the High Middle Ages: c. 1050-1200*, trans. Timothy, Reuter (Oxford, 1986), pp. 122-25; Karl Jordan, *Investiturstreit und frühe Stauferzeit (1056-1197)*, Gebhardt Handbuch der Deutschen Geschichte 4 (Stuttgart, 1970), pp. 95-98; Bernhardi, *Lothar*, pp. 16-20.

any rate, when the cathedral canons divided into rival factions over the election of a new archbishop, Lothar consented to support Norbert as a compromise candidate.[28] That Norbert accepted this appointment and may even have advanced his own candidacy while he was in Rome must not be passed over lightly. Though at his investiture, the pastoral staff had to be forced into the hand of a tearful Norbert,[29] clutch it he did; and in so doing, he turned his back on Prémontré. The distance that staff placed between him and his foundation both in terms of geography and way of life was an unbridgeable gulf.[30] Magdeburg lay far to the east on the borders of the empire. Two of its five dioceses were out of its archbishop's control, held by hostile and heathen Wends. The path to a very active life both in terms of missionary work and colonization lay open to Norbert.

Abandoned by Norbert, Prémontré went its own way, finding leadership in one of Norbert's early followers, the contemplative Hugh of Fosses, and inspiration in the monastic way of life championed by the Cistercians.[31] The order which grew up around Norbert in Magdeburg moved in a quite different direction, becoming the new archbishop's tool to control his episcopal charge and expand his influence into pagan territory. In short, it reflected much more closely the way of life Norbert had himself chosen to emphasize, the *vita activa*.

The split in Norbert's order ran deep,[32] a fact reflected by Norbert's faithful follower, Anselm of Havelberg. When Anselm's name first appears in the documentary evidence, Norbert had already been archbishop of Magdeburg for three full years, and Anselm emerges not as one of the early disciples who listened to Norbert and then went into seclusion, but rather as the bishop of Havelberg, suffragan servant to the archbishop. So far as his writings

---

[28] Grauwen, *Norbertus Aartsbisschop*, pp. 134-38.

[29] *Vita Norberti* A 18, p. 694; Grauwen, *Norbertus Aartsbisschop*, pp. 142ff.

[30] See Weinfurter, "Norbert von Xanten—Ordensstifter," pp. 71-72 on the sometimes bitter portrayal of Norbert by the brothers he left behind.

[31] Petit, *La spiritualité des Prémontrés*, pp. 44-49; J. C. Dickinson, *The Origin of the Austin Canons and Their Introduction into England* (London, 1950), p. 74.

[32] H. M. Colvin speaks of the two different directions the order took in terms of a "schism." *The White Canons in England* (Oxford, 1951), pp. 6-10. Also Dickinson, *Origin of the Austin Canons*, pp. 72-77; Petit, *La spiritualité des Prémontrés*, pp. 51-53, 167; Kaspar Elm, "Norbert von Xanten: Bedeutung-Persönlichkeit-Nachleben," in Elm, *Norbert von Xanten*, pp. 271-72; Weinfurter, "Norbert von Xanten als Reformkanoniker," pp. 172-75.

show, Anselm never looked west to Prémontré; he never mentions
the foundation, never calls himself a Premonstratensian. How or
where Anselm became one of Norbert's disciples is not known,
though the likelihood is that he met Norbert after the latter became
archbishop.[33] The first secure date for Anselm's life is 1129 when
Norbert chose him as the new bishop of Havelberg.[34]

As bishop of Havelberg, Anselm emerges as someone marked to
play a role in this eastward missionary effort; but this was mitigated
by the fact that Norbert was pulled in different directions: His own
position in Magdeburg was threatened, and he was called into service
at his king's court.[35] In these circumstances it was difficult for him to
preserve even Magdeburg's jurisdictional claim to the Havelland.
When, in 1128, Bishop Otto of Bamberg, a man who had already
preached among the Slavs, proposed to return to the Havelland,
Norbert refused to grant him permission. Otto was neither a member
of Norbert's order nor a suffragan bishop, and was moreover patron-
ized by the duke of Poland.[36] None of this boded well for tying a
successfully Christianized Havelland to Magdeburg. As a first step
toward clarifying Magdeburg's claims across the Elbe, Norbert chose

---

[33] We know nothing about Anselm's relationship with Norbert before 1129. Beginning with Franz Winter (*Die Prämonstratenser*, p. 56), historians have pointed to
Hermann of Laon's story of Norbert's conversion of seven students of Raoul of Laon
(*De miraculis S. Mariae Laudunensis* 3.4, ed. R. Wilmans, MGH SS 12 (Hanover, 1856),
p. 656), and suggested or presented as proven fact that Anselm was among them or
studied at Laon. However, Norbert's *vitae*, which tend to give the names of his
traveling companions, do not mention Anselm; thus, were Anselm among the seven
students, he would have been sent to Prémontré to take up a monastic way of life.
While a scenario could be constructed to accommodate this, it would accord little
with what we know of the adult Anselm and his devotion to the active life. In his
detailed analysis of the story, Grauwen does not mention Anselm, "Norberts reis
naar Laon," pp. 41-50. Fina suggests Anselm's Saxon background as a reason the
Saxon King Lothar would support his candidacy, "Anselm," *AP* 33 (1956), 80.

[34] See p. 13 n. 5 above.

[35] Schwineköper, "Norbert von Xanten als Erzbischof," pp. 194-95.

[36] On Norbert and Otto: Grauwen, *Norbertus Aartsbisschop*, pp. 214-40; Claude,
Geschichte des Erzbistums Magdeburg 2:19-21; Eberhard Demm, *Reformmönchtum und
Slawenmission im 12. Jahrhundert: Wertsoziologisch-geistesgeschichtliche Untersuchungen zu den
Viten Bischof Ottos von Bamberg*, Historische Studien 419 (Lübeck, 1970), p. 59; Wilhelm
Berges, "Reform und Ostmission im 12. Jahrhundert," in *Heidenmission und Kreuz-
zugsgedanke in der deutschen Ostpolitik des Mittelalters*, ed. Helmut Beumann, Wege der
Forschung 7 (Darmstadt, 1973), pp. 326-31; Heinz Stoob, "Gedanken zur Ost-
seepolitik Lothars III.," pp. 542-43. Also Klaus Guth, "The Pomeranian Missionary
Journeys of Otto I of Bamberg and the Crusade Movement of the Eleventh and
Twelfth Centuries," in *The Second Crusade and the Cistercians*, pp. 13-23.

Anselm to fill the vacant seat of bishop of Havelberg. While there was no attempt to get him to Havelberg, by assuming this office, Anselm became Norbert's appointee to tie down, at least in legal terms, the archbishop of Magdeburg's claims to these lands.[37]

Not only did Norbert need loyal men to assist him with a policy of expansion, he needed them in Magdeburg itself. Hopes that the new archbishop would find local support soon proved illusory. In Magdeburg, his popularity quickly waned as he tightened the purse strings of his church in an effort to regain control over the better part of its revenues which his predecessors had given away. In order to have men around him on whom he could rely, he replaced the secular clergy of the Church of Our Lady near the bishop's palace with his own followers.[38] The dramatic results were two attempts on the archbishop's life and a general uprising of the populace.[39] In this hostile environment, it is reasonable to assume that Norbert chose a man of proven loyalty to serve as bishop of Havelberg. The fact that in his writings Anselm never refers to Prémontré is, therefore, an indication of the schism in the order into what might be called western Praemonstratensians and eastern Norbertines rather than that Anselm was not one of Norbert's canons. He frequently does call himself a "poor man of Christ" (*pauper Christi*),[40] a term which, while often used in the twelfth century to refer to wandering preachers, was also used by Norbert's followers.[41] In a document from 1146 in which

---

[37] Grauwen, *Norbertus Aartsbisshop*, pp. 439-40; Heinz Stoob, "Gedanken zur Ostseepolitik Lothars III.," p. 545.

[38] *Vita Norberti* A 18, p. 694; *Regesta archiepiscopatus Magdeburgensis* 1, ed. George Adalbert von Mülverstedt (Magdeburg, 1876), 1010, pp. 388-89; Grauwen, *Norbertus Aartsbisshop*, pp. 165-72, 263ff; Schwineköper, "Norbert von Xanten als Erzbischof," pp. 198-99; Bernhardi, *Lothar*, pp. 153-54.

[39] *Vita Norberti* A 18-19, pp. 694-99; *Vita Norberti* B 16, pp. 851-52; Grauwen, *Norbertus Aartsbisshop*, pp. 293ff.; Bernhardi, *Lothar*, pp. 222-25; Gottfried Wentz and Berent Schwineköper, *Das Erzbistum Magdeburg* 1.1, *Das Domstift St. Moritz in Magdeburg*, Germania sacra (New York, 1972), pp. 179-80, 220.

[40] Anselm's *epistolae* to Wibald of Stablo, Wibald, 158, p. 263, 221, p. 339; to Peter the Venerable, *Recueil des chartes de l'Abbay de Cluny* 5, ed. Auguste Bernard and Alexandre Bruel (Paris, 1894), 4176, p. 526; and the *Epistola apologetica* to Egbert of Huysburg, PL 188:1119. See Werner, *Pauperes Christi*, p. 19. In the *Epistola apologetica* in which Anselm defends the canons regular, he uses the term to imply that he is something more than a cleric: "Sum clericus et pauper Christi" (*Epist. apol.*, 1129D).

[41] On the term *pauper Christi*, Werner, *Pauperes Christi*, who would apply the term to wandering preachers; cf. Lambert, *Medieval Heresy*, pp. 349-52. Members of Norbert's order in Prémontré are referred to as *pauperes Christi* in the *Vita Norberti* A 12, p. 684 and the *Fundatio monasterii Gratiae Dei*, MGH SS 20:686. Lambert, using these and other examples, shows that the title *pauper Christi* tended to refer to settled canons

Anselm gives the Norbertine cloister of Jerichow rights over several
villages which had been under the jurisdiction of Havelberg, he says
that these gifts were given to support the poor men of Christ (*ad
predictorum pauperum Christi sustentationem*) in clear reference to members
of Norbert's order, and says further that the grants are made in
memory of "our father Norbert."[42] Norbert's own need for trusted
advisers and Anselm's habitual reference to himself as a *pauper Christi*
are persuasive evidence that Anselm's close relationship to Norbert
included membership in the eastern part of his mentor's order.[43]

From 1129 to 1134, Anselm's itinerary can be followed fairly
closely, but only because, exiled bishop that he was, he stayed close
to Norbert. As has been mentioned, Norbert faced constant problems
with the clergy and townspeople of Magdeburg, culminating in a
general uprising in 1129. The first mention of Anselm in the historical record places him at Norbert's side when the archbishop and his
followers were forced to take refuge in the tower of an unfinished
church while an angry mob fired arrows and shouted, "Thiet-ut!
Thiet-ut!" ("Come out! Come out!"). Norbert, splattered with the
blood of a loyal servant, barely escaped martyrdom.[44]

Norbert, in fact, behaved toward Magdeburg in a way similar to
his behavior toward Prémontré by spending little time there.
Whether it was because he felt in need of the German king's assistance to mount a concerted effort to Christianize the Wends or because he thought his ruler required advice in dealing with the Ger-

---

(the Cistercians also used the term), rather than to the wandering preachers themselves. Members of the Norbertine foundation dedicated to Mary in Leitzkau (diocese of Brandenburg) changed the term by calling themselves *pauperes beatae Mariae*.
Kahl, *Slawen und Deutsche* 1:126-27.

[42] *Hamburgisches UB* 1, ed. Johann Martin Lappenberg (Hamburg, 1907), 180, p.
170.

[43] Petke, *Kanzlei*, pp. 324-26; Braun, *Lexicon*, p. 678; Fina, "Anselm," *AP* 33 (1956),
80-83; Lauerer, *Anschauungen*, pp. 12-15.

[44] On the uprising: *Vita Norberti* A 19, pp. 697-98; *Vita Norberti* B 17, pp. 853-
54; *Annalista Saxo*, ed. Georg Waitz, MGH SS 6 (Hanover, 1844), p. 766; *Annales
Magdeburgenses*, ed. George Heinrich Pertz, MGH SS 16 (Hanover, 1859), p. 183;
Chronicon Montis Sereni, ed Ernst Ehrenfeuchter, MGH SS 23 (Hanover, 1874), p. 143;
Magdeburger Schöppenchronik 2, ed. Karl Janicke, Die Chroniken der Deutschen Städte
7 (1869; repr. Gottingen, 1962), p. 112; *Gesta archiepiscoporum Magdeburgensium*, ed.
Wilhelm Schum, MGH SS 14 (Hanover, 1883), p. 413. Secondary accounts: Dombrowski, *Anselm*, pp. 7-8; Grauwen, *Norbertus Aartsbisschop*, pp. 302-28; Claude, *Geschichte des Erzbistums Magdeburg* 2:10-14; Schwineköper, "Norbert von Xanten als
Erzbischof," pp. 199-200; Bernhardi, *Lothar*, pp. 225-27; Riedel, "Nachrichten," pp.
108-9.

man nobility and the papacy, the archbishop demonstrated an ever growing inclination to spend his time at the court of Lothar III. Even in the years before the uprising in Magdeburg, Norbert fought on Lothar's side in his ruler's successful struggle against Conrad of Hohenstaufen, who had been raised up as an anti-king.[45] These circumstances had a dramatic effect on the bishop of Havelberg's life and reversed the career track that normally went from royal adviser to bishop.[46] For while Anselm held the title *episcopus*, it was impossible for him to exercise any diocesan functions. Thus he remained with his archbishop, a man who had ingratiated himself with the German ruler and was devoting his energies to the politics of empire. While Anselm's own episcopal duties were so far out of reach and even out of mind that he was sometimes mistakenly identified as the bishop of Brandenburg,[47] he became a student of politics and diplomacy of a high order.

In the last years of Norbert's life, the sources leave Anselm in this role of the observing student without giving him a voice to comment on what he saw and heard. We can trace his movements, always near Norbert, but little else. Still, it is worth considering what Anselm witnessed because his major writings are, at heart, works about imitating a model life. The model he had before him in the flesh until 1134, and to which the sources for his later life demonstrate that he held firmly, was that of Norbert. What Anselm's writings indicate most impressed him was the archbishop's ability to place himself between contending parties and to mediate peace between them.

In general, the problem Norbert confronted as royal adviser was that of his ruler's relationship with the papacy. That problem had two sides. On the one hand, the papacy itself had fallen prey to schism. On the other, Lothar saw in this weakened papacy his chance to push aside the Concordat of Worms and its compromise settlement of the control of ecclesiastical offices. Anselm witnessed in Norbert a man devoted first and foremost to Christian unity, which in this case meant both ending the schism and maintaining the balance between ruler and pope established by the Concordat.

When, in February 1130, the college of cardinals split and elected two popes, Innocent II and Anacletus II, Norbert rapidly became

---

[45] Grauwen, *Norbertus Aartsbisshop*, pp. 178-79, 210-13; Bernhardi, *Lothar*, pp. 122-39; Petke, *Kanzlei*, pp. 308-9.

[46] See pp. 18-19 above.

[47] See p. 35 n. 55, p. 40 n. 2 below.

involved in helping the king determine the rightful candidate.[48] On
advice from friends in Italy, Norbert recommended Innocent, and
Lothar agreed.[49] Innocent, who had found his position in Italy unten-
able, came north seeking support. On March 22, 1131, he met the
German ruler in Liège. Norbert was also there with Anselm among
"a huge multitude of bishops, abbots and clerics of different orders."[50] When the pope rode into the city on a white horse, the crowd
watched as Lothar humbly played the part of Innocent's *strator* or
groom. On foot, the ruler rushed to Innocent. Fending off the crowd
with one hand, he grasped the horse's bridle with the other and then
helped the pope dismount. It was a magnificent display of royal
humility.[51]

But however humble and obedient Lothar may have appeared to
the cheering throng gathered at Liège, soon he was demanding the

---

[48] On the schism of 1130 as a conflict between an anti-imperial, hard-line
Gregorian faction (Anacletus') and a moderate faction willing to work with imperial
authorities (Innocent's): Franz-Josef Schmale, *Studium zum Schisma des Jahres 1130*,
Forschungen zur kirchlichen Rechtsgeschichte und zum Kirchenrecht 3 (Cologne,
1961); Stanley Chodorow, *Christian Political Theory and Church Politics in the Mid-Twelfth
Century: The Ecclesiology of Gratian's Decretum* (Berkeley, 1972), pp. 37-46 (with a good
summary of the literature). On the contrary interpretation of the schism as the result
of factions within the college of cardinals: W. Maleczek, "Das Kardinalskollegium
unter Innozenz II. und Anaklet II," *Archivum historiae Pontificiae* 19 (1981), 27-78;
Timothy Reuter, "Zur Anerkennung Papst Innocenz II.: Eine neue Quelle," *DA NF*
39 (1983), 395-416; Petke, *Kanzlei*, 311; Mary Stroll, *The Jewish Pope: Ideology and
Politics in the Papal Schism of 1130* (Leiden, 1987) and *Symbols as Power: The Papacy
Following the Investiture Contest* (Leiden, 1991).

[49] Schmale, "Die Bemühungen Innocenz II. um seine Anerkennung in
Deutschland," *ZKG* 65 (1953/54), 265-66; Petke, *Kanzlei*, pp. 311-14. On Norbert's
choice of Innocent, Stroll, *Jewish Pope*, pp. 153-54 with n. 23. Calling for caution in
giving Norbert credit for Lothar's choice, Petke, *Kanzlei*, p. 314; cf. Grauwen, *Norbertus Aartsbisschop*, pp. 425-28. Anselm's movements during this time: Probably with
Norbert at the Synod of Würzburg, Oct. 1130 (Innocent recognized by the German
episcopacy), *Annales Erphesfurdenses*, ed. G. H. Pertz, MGH SS (Hanover, 1844),
6:537-38, *Annalista Saxo*, MGH SS 6:767, cf. Grauwen, *Norbertus Aartsbisschop*, pp. 414-
15; provincial ecclesiastical diet at Goslar, February 1131, *UL* 31, pp. 47-48, on the
date: Dombrowski, *Anselm*, p. 9.

[50] *Annales Magdeburgenses*, MGH SS 16:183; *UL* 33, pp. 51-55; and *UL* 34, pp. 55-
57 (Norbert as witness "cum [omnibus] suis [conprovincialibus]").

[51] *Ex vita Ludovici VI. Francorum Regis auctore Sugerio* 31, ed. A. Molinier, MGH SS 26
(Hanover, 1882), p. 58; Robert Holtzmann, *Der Kaiser als Marschall des Papstes: Eine
Untersuchung zur Geschichte der Bezeihungen zwischen Kaiser und Papst im Mittelalter*,
Schriften der Strassburger Wissenschaftlichen Gesellschaft in Heidelberg, Neue
Folge 8 (Berlin, 1928), pp. 8-9; idem, "Zum Strator- und Marschalldienst," *HZ* 145
(1932), 301-50; Eduard Eichmann, *Die Kaiserkrönung im Abendland: Ein Beitrag zur
Geistesgeschichte des Mittelalters mit besonderer Berücksichtigung des kirchlichen Rechts, der Liturgie
und der Kirchenpolitik* 2 (Würzburg, 1942), pp. 291-92.

full right of pre-Concordat rulers to invest bishops and abbots in exchange for lending Innocent military assistance against Anacletus.[52] Important to Anselm's perception of Norbert is the fact that twice on Lothar's Italian campaign, the archbishop mediated between the ruler and Innocent on the question of investiture. Anselm saw Norbert skillfully walk a fine line between the two and play a significant role in holding the alliance together.

Before Lothar reached Rome, representatives of Anacletus met the king in Valentano and tried to convince him to call a tribunal to give the electors of both popes a hearing. Norbert himself was sent to Innocent to explain these dealings. There, "it was argued against Norbert that the highest pontifex ought not be subjected to the judgment of man or stand in court," says one of Norbert's *vitae*, suggesting that Norbert himself thought the idea of a tribunal a good one.[53] Norbert acted the able diplomat and suggested that Innocent raise the stakes by agreeing to come personally to the hearing on pain of accepting life imprisonment for his failure to do so, but on the condition that Anacletus would agree to the same conditions. It was an astute move, for it asked Anacletus to step into the lion's den of enemies backed by a German army, something he was unwilling to do.[54] While Norbert's tactic successfully destroyed the possibility of a tribunal, he had nevertheless touched on a sore point with the Roman Curia, namely that by indicating his willingness to submit to a tribunal, Innocent was conceding the legality of a pope being tried in a lay court. Innocent's supporters produced a version of events which made it appear that he and his curia had completely rejected the notion of a trial.[55] Norbert saw the situation somewhat differently

---

[52] Johannes Bauermann, "Die Frage der Bischofswahlen auf dem Würzburger Reichstag von 1133," in *Kritische Beiträge zur Geschichte des Mittelalters: Festschrift für Robert Holtzmann*, ed. Emil Ebering (Berlin, 1933), pp. 103-34.

[53] *Vita Norberti* A 21, p. 701.

[54] Grauwen, *Norbertus Aartsbisschop*, pp. 526-33; Hauck, *Kirchengeschichte Deutschlands* 3 (Berlin, 1954), pp. 152-54; Bernhardi, *Lothar*, pp. 466-68. Stroll, *Jewish Pope*, pp. 71-72, sees Norbert as being opposed to a tribunal from the beginning, but cf. Grauwen, p. 527; also F. X. Seppelt, *Geschichte der Päpste* 3 (Munich, 1956), p. 177.

[55] *Encyclica de Anacleto antipapa damnato*, ed. Ludwig Weiland, MGH Const. 1 (Hanover, 1893), pp. 166-67. Criticized by Bernhardi as not the work of the curia (*Lothar*, pp. 847-50), others have (without completely answering Bernhardi) considered the document authentic and suggested Norbert's own hand behind it. See Grauwen, *Norbertus Aartsbisschop*, pp. 535-37 and n. 11 with bibliography; editorial notes to *UL* 48, pp. 79-81. The *Encyclica* is the evidence for Anselm's participation on this expedition, though it identifies him as the bishop of Brandenburg.

from the curia. Whereas the curia was concerned with a principle of papal immunity, he focused on what could be done to avoid a trial while maintaining the alliance between Lothar and Innocent. Some years later, Anselm would take the same perhaps simplistic view of a similar situation.

After Lothar was crowned emperor in the Lateran in June 1133, Norbert faced yet another possible breakdown in the alliance when the ruler renewed his demand that the pope give him the full right of investing bishops—give him, that is, "the freedom of the churches [*libertas ecclesiarum*]."[56] Innocent and his followers were in a difficult position: Lothar had his army, and Anacletus still held a good part of Rome. No one dared speak against the ruler's suggestion; and when Innocent appeared willing to give way, it was Norbert who addressed his pope:

> What are you doing, father? To whom will you turn over the sheep placed in your charge to be torn apart? Would you now turn the free church you received into a slave? The chair of Peter requires the deeds of Peter. Yes, I have promised in the name of Christ obedience to the blessed Peter and to you; but if you do that which is demanded of you, behold, I speak against you in front of the church."[57]

Again Norbert acted sagely, taking his stand with St. Peter rather than expressly choosing between his ruler and his pope. By addressing his remarks to Innocent rather than to Lothar, he appeared to criticize the pope; indeed, he threatened to disobey him, while he was actually defending the papal position on investiture. In this way, Norbert turned the confrontation between Lothar and Innocent into a confrontation between himself and the pope in which the latter could both lose the confrontation and win on the issue of investiture. What went neatly unexpressed, but what must have been clear to Norbert's papal and imperial audience, is that had Norbert's gambit failed and the pope given in to Lothar's demands, the archbishop could only have followed through on his threat by withdrawing his support from Lothar. Norbert had put his loyal service in the place of the issue of investiture. A more diplomatic avoidance of a papal-imperial confrontation while still defending the principle of the *libertas*

---

[56] *Vita Norberti* A 21, p. 702.
[57] *Vita Norberti* A 21, p. 702.

ecclesiarum could scarcely have been found.[58] This is not to say that Lothar won nothing. After hard if brief negotiations, Innocent granted Lothar a charter which, however ambiguously, forbid a German bishop-elect from administering the *regalia* before his investiture. It has been suggested that Norbert was behind these negotiations on the side of the emperor.[59]

Lothar returned to Germany, leaving the schism not a step closer to resolution. There, Norbert was once again involved in a question about investiture, this time at the Diet of Würzburg in September, 1133. Anselm was very likely in attendance, as well.[60] The issue concerned the election and ordination of an archbishop by Archbishop Conrad I of Salzburg. This had been done while Lothar was in Italy, and it was in direct opposition to the emperor's right, recently confirmed by Innocent, to invest a bishop with the *regalia* of his office before the ordination. While the particulars of the case need not concern us here, the situation was the reverse of the papal-imperial meeting of a few months earlier. There, a principle of ecclesiastical authority was threatened by the emperor; now, in Germany, the emperor's authority had received cavalier treatment at the hands of an archbishop whom the ruler sternly rebuked.[61]

What was Norbert's position in this dispute? Conrad of Salzburg hotly argued that a layman, no matter whether he be king or duke, had no business enmeshing himself in ecclesiastical elections. He wrote a letter to Norbert[62] which clearly shows that the archbishop of Magdeburg took the side of the emperor by claiming that "the consent of the leading laymen [*honorati*] is necessary in elections of bishops."[63] While Conrad was horrified by this, in Norbert's position

---

[58] The only report of these events is *Vita Norberti* A 21, p. 702. It has been criticized frequently, but see Grauwen, *Norbertus Aartsbisshop*, pp. 575-87; also Benson, *The Bishop-Elect*, p. 256 n. 17; Petke, *Kanzlei*, p. 317.

[59] Benson, *The Bishop-Elect*, pp. 256-63.

[60] While there is no direct evidence for Anselm's presence in Würzburg, he was with Norbert in Mainz in the middle of October (see n. 65 below). The probability is that Anselm remained with Norbert and traveled with Lothar's court.

[61] Benson, *The Bishop Elect*, p. 273, n. 38, and for the whole dispute, pp. 263-83; see also Classen, "Wormser Konkordat," pp. 431-33.

[62] Benson describes it as "an open letter, designed for publication" though addressed to Norbert. *The Bishop Elect*, p. 264. The fragmentary remains of the letter are edited by Bauermann, "Die Frage der Bischofswahlen," pp. 132-34. Also Benson, pp. 273-74 n. 38.

[63] Bauermann, "Die Frage der Bischofswahlen," p. 132; Benson, *The Bishop Elect*, p. 266.

there is a clear sense of maintaining an equilibrium between ecclesiastical and secular leaders. The fulcrum of that equilibrium was the
control of church offices. If it moved one way or the other, as Conrad
and Lothar had each proposed, the delicate balance which brought
peace to both parties would be lost. Between Rome and Würzburg,
Norbert had not switched sides but rather fulfilled his self-imposed
role of peacemaker. The position of Conrad at Würzburg was no less
extreme, though in the opposite direction, than that of Lothar at
Rome. It was these extremities that Norbert fought to avoid.[64]

Norbert's health had been poor even before the trip to Italy,[65] and
early in March of 1134, he was taken seriously ill. After a warm
reception by the people of Magdeburg, he spent the weeks of Lent in
bed. Barely able to perform Mass on Easter Sunday, he died on June
6. Among the bishops who presided at Norbert's funeral were
Anselm and Bishop Godebold of Meissen. The two had been companions of the archbishop when, but five years earlier, they had faced
the arrows of an angry mob in the city that was now providing the
resting place for Norbert's body.[66]

In Norbert of Magdeburg, Anselm found a model. It was not that
of the early Norbert of Xanten gathering followers for a life of contemplation while personally wandering from place to place. Rather,
it was Norbert the church official and diplomat who recognized the

---

[64] Grauwen, *Norbertus Aartsbisshop*, pp. 613-14; Petke, *Kanzlei*, pp. 320-21.

[65] *Vita Norberti* A 21, p. 701; Grauwen, *Norbertus Aartsbisshop*, pp. 625-29. Anselm
and Norbert's movements after the Diet of Würzburg: Synod held at Mainz, Oct.
21, 1133, *Mainzer UB* 1; *Die Urkunden bis zum Tode Erzbischof Adalberts I. (1137)*, ed.
Manfred Stimmins (Darmstadt, 1932), 588, pp. 505-7, *Urkundenbuch des Hochstifts
Halberstadt und seiner Bischöfe* 1, ed. Gustav Schmidt, Publicationen aus den K.
preussischen Staatsarchiven 17 (1883; repr. Osnabrück, 1965), 170, pp. 141-42, 173,
pp. 144-45; Mainz, Oct 23, *UL* 54, pp. 85-87 (place mistakenly given as Bamberg by
the editors); Basel, Nov. 8, 1133 with Lothar, *UL* 55, pp. 87-88 (misdated Nov. 3 by
the editors); at the royal court in Cologne, Jan. 1, 1134, *UL* 56, pp. 88-89 and
perhaps *UL* 58, pp. 91-92, though place and date are problematic. On this last
Bernhardi, *Lothar*, pp. 526-27 n. 8; Dombrowski, *Anselm*, p. 16; dated to mid April
1134 in Halberstadt by Otto von Heinemann, *Codex diplomaticus Anhaltinus* 1, (Essau,
1867), 214, p. 166, and as such accepted by Wentz, *Bistum Havelberg*, p. 37 (surely
wrong: in April Norbert was bedridden in Magdeburg); dated Jan. 6 to 25 by the
editors of Lothar's charters; to Lothar's stay in Cologne Dec. 25 to Jan. 1 by Petke,
Kanzlei, p. 175 (probably right, Anselm was working for Lothar without Norbert in at
least part of January, see p. 40 below). Also Grauwen, *Norbertus Aartsbisshop*, pp. 554-
57, 617.

[66] *Vita Norberti* A 23, p. 703; *Gesta archiepiscoporum Magdeburgensium*, MGH SS
14:414; *Annalista Saxo*, MGH SS 6:769. The third bishop was Ludolf of Brandenburg.
See Grauwen, *Norbertus Aartsbisshop*, pp. 633-37.

fragility of a united Christendom and used perspicacity and deft diplomatic skill to keep it from crumbling. In Norbert, Anselm found a
man who played a real role in guarding the integrity of the church.
Norbert had been projected into that role precisely because he had,
in his early years, turned aside suggestions that he adopt the eremitical or monastic life of withdrawal. The life he embraced was the
active one. He became the guardian of a balance between secular
and ecclesiastical leaders, each trying to pull the weight of prerogative and power over to its own side. Norbert sensed how far the
fulcrum could move one way or the other before the balance would
be lost. That he supported a papal prerogative at the Lateran and a
royal one in Würzburg is, thus, not surprising. His devotion was to
the middle ground, and from this came his effectiveness as a mediator.

   Norbert's life from 1130 to 1134 formed a kind of rehearsal for
Anselm of Havelberg's active life. Anselm soon found himself in the
service of his ruler, and like his mentor, had to balance his devotion
to his diocese with his commitment to steering his ruler and his pope
away from divisive conflicts. The events of Valentano, Rome, and
Würzburg would replay themselves with Anselm in Norbert's role.
Anselm would not be nearly as successful as Norbert, but that he
emulated the archbishop of Magdeburg will be seen in Anselm's
literary efforts to define his mentor's spirituality.

CHAPTER THREE

IMPERIAL SERVICE AND
THE DEBATES WITH THE GREEKS
1134-1136

Anselm's relationship to Norbert of Magdeburg had helped consider-
ably to advance his career. In title, at least, he was a bishop, and he
had been given the opportunity to attend the imperial court. Continued success for Anselm meant establishing close enough ties at court
so that he could move from serving Norbert to serving Lothar on the
former's death. Evidence that Anselm had been moving in that direction is the fact that shortly before Norbert's death, he was called into
service at the imperial court. In January 1134, Lothar was in Goslar
attending to business that had been set aside during his Italian campaign. One matter concerned the abbeys of Clues and Braunshausen
in the diocese of Hildesheim. These had fallen into a state of disre-
pair and were on the verge of dissolution. As early as 1131, Lothar
had determined to turn them over to the care of Liutgard II, abbess
of the imperial abbey of Gandersheim, and at Goslar he issued a
charter to that effect.[1] Bishop Bernard I of Hildesheim was an interested party to this transaction, and Lothar's choice of Anselm to head
a delegation to the bishop was not an arbitrary one.[2] Bernard was an
old friend of Norbert, and Anselm had met the bishop at Goslar and
again at Liège in 1131.[3] The business concerning Clues and Brauns-

---

[1] *UL* 59, pp. 92-94, dated Jan. 25, 1134; Hans Goetting, *Das Bistum Hildesheim* 1,
Das reichsunmittelbare Kanonissenstift Gandersheim, Die Bistümer der kirchenprovinz
Mainz, Germania Sacra, Neue Folge 7 (New York, 1973), p. 304; idem, *Das Bistum
Hildesheim* 2, *Das Benediktiner(innen)kloster Brunshausen. Das Beneditinerinnenkloster St. Marien
vor Gandersheim. Das Benediktinerkloster Clus. Das Franziskanerkloster Gandersheim*, Germania
Sacra, Neue Folge 8 (New York, 1974), pp. 26-27, 199-201.
[2] Lothar's choice of Anselm: *UB des Hochstifts Hildesheim und seiner Bischöfe* 1, ed. K.
Janicke (1896, reprint: Osnabrück, 1965), 208, pp. 190-91. Anselm is described as *de
Brandenburhc episcopo*.
[3] Goslar, Feb. 5, *UL* 31, p. 48,; and Liège, Mar. 29, 1131, *UL* 33, p. 54. Norbert's
relations with Bernard: Grauwen, *Norbertus Aartsbisshop*, pp. 429-30, 471, 479-80, 482;
Hans Goetting, *Das Bistum Hildesheim* 3, *Die Hildesheimer Bischöfe von 815 bis 1221
(1227)*, Germania Sacra, Neue Folge 20 (New York, 1984), pp. 344-45.

hausen was not particularly difficult,[4] but Anselm had caught his ruler's attention as someone who could be placed in a modest position of authority representing the interests of the emperor.

Anselm was back in Magdeburg for Norbert's funeral in June and may have briefly met Lothar once again at the end of the month when the emperor came to Magdeburg to approve the election of Conrad, the new archbishop.[5] Still unable to get to Havelberg, Anselm probably remained close to Conrad for more than a year,[6] in one instance assisting in the dedication of a monastery.[7] Then, in August 1135, he was back at the emperor's court in Nienburg.[8] From there he accompanied Lothar to Merseburg.

---

[4] For an effort to show considerable animosity between Lothar and Bernard (which could indicate something more to Lothar's selection of Anselm), see Wolfgang Heinemann, *Das Bistum Hildesheim im Kräftesspiel der Reichs- und Territorialpolitik vornehmlich des 12. Jahrhunderts*, Quellen und Darstellungen zur Geschichte Niedersachsens 72 (Hildesheim, 1968), pp. 143-52; Marie-Luise Crone, *Untersuchungen zur Reichskirchenpolitik Lothars III. (1125-1137) zwischen reichskirchlicher Tradition und Reformkurie* (Frankfurt, 1982), pp. 197-200. However, for a forceful rejection of this thesis, see Wolfgang Petke, *Die Grafen von Wöltingerode-Wohldenberg. Adelsherrschaft, Königtum und Landesherrschaft am Nordwestharz im 12. und 13 Jahrhundert*, Veröffentlichungen des Instituts für historische Landesforschungen der Universität Göttingen 4 (Göttingen, 1971), p. 279 n. 139; Goetting, "Die Riechenberger Fälschungen und das zweite Königssiegel Lothars III.," *Mitteilungen des Instituts für österreichische Geschichtsforschung* 78 (1970), pp. 143-44; idem, *Bistum Hildesheim* 2:201-2 n. 5; summary of arguments against Heinemann: Goetting, *Bistum Hildesheim* 3:348-51, 367.

[5] Bernhardi, *Lothar*, p. 551.

[6] Anselm with Conrad in Halle, March 4, 1135, *UB des Erzstifts Magdeburg* 1, *(937-1192)*, ed. Friedrich Israël and Walter Möllenberg, GQPS NR 18 (Magdeburg, 1937), 237, pp. 296-98; also 236, pp. 293-296, dated Jan. 6, 1135 in Halle (as such in Wentz's itinerary, *Havelberg*, p. 37; also Dombrowski, *Anselm*, p. 12), however, see *Regesten der Markgrafen von Brandenburg aus Askanischem Hause*, ed. Hermannn Krabbo and Georg Winter (Berlin, 1955), 36, p. 10, concluding the date should be March 8. Anselm is also a witness to *UB des Erzstifts Magdeburg* 238, pp. 299-300, dated 1135, no location. These are the only three charters issued by Conrad before 1136 which give lists of witnesses.

[7] The monastery of Ammensleben which had been a foundation of secular canons. Norbert had supported the change from canons to monks at a synod in 1129 with Anselm present. See Grauwen, *Norbertus Aartsbisshop*, pp. 342-51. In 1140, Archbishop Conrad confirmed the change, mentioning the 1129 synod and that he had dedicated the monastery "cum domino Anselmo Hauelbergensi episcopo." *UB des Erzstifts Magdeburg* 247, pp. 309-12.

[8] *UL* 74, pp. 113-16, dated August 1, 1135. Anselm's name among the witnesses to *UL* 72, pp. 111-12, dated April 9 in Halberstadt, is an interpolation. Petke, *Kanzlei*, 39c, p. 453; Emil von Ottenthal, "Die Urkundenfälschungen von Hillersleben," *Papstum und Kaisertum: Forschungen zur politischen Geschichte und Geisteskultur des Mittelalters. Paul Kehr zum 65. Geburtstag dargebracht* (Munich, 1926), p. 341.

It was at Merseburg that the events began which, due to his own account of them, have first and foremost been associated with Anselm of Havelberg, namely his diplomatic journey to Constantinople and his debates there with the Greek Archbishop Nicetas of Nicomedia. We need not rely on Anselm's account of those debates given in the *Antikeimenon* to determine why he went to Constantinople; indeed, we cannot. This is one of the issues, in this work about the unity of the faithful, that he fails to explain.

From other sources we learn how Lothar's court had become the center of considerable diplomatic activity. Representatives of various powers tried to win the ruler's support for another campaign in Italy, this time directed primarily against Pope Anacletus' ally, Roger II of Sicily. Pope Innocent II, still trying to end the schism in his own favor, sent legates and Bernard of Clairvaux; and as Wilhelm Bernhardi has commented, "[It was] not for the sake of peace."[9] There were others who also wanted to see a German army back in Italy. The Venetians had suffered serious losses due to Roger's attacks on their shipping, and the Byzantine emperor, John II Comnenus, was concerned about Norman incursions into Africa. At Merseburg, Lothar received delegations from both the Venetians and the eastern emperor. Bearing a wealth of gifts, they offered to provide the king with men, ships, and money.[10] Suitably flattered, he responded by sending his own delegation to the Greeks. Among its members and quite probably its leader, was Anselm.[11] His close friendship with Norbert had brought him into Lothar's court where he had now won a place serving the ruler he would call "the Great"[12] and taking on

---

[9] Bernhardi, *Lothar*, p. 564.

[10] *S. Petri Erphesfurtensis Auctarium et Continuatio Chronici Ekkehardi, Monumenta Erphesfurtensia saec. XII, XIII, XIV*, ed. Oswald Holder-Egger (Hanover, 1899), MGH SS r. G., p. 42, giving the Greek and Venetian complaints against the Normans; Willy Cohn, *Die Geschichte der Normannisch-sicilischen Flotte unter der Regierung von Rogers I. und Rogers II. (1060-1154)* (Breslau, 1910), pp. 27-32; Erich Caspar, *Roger II. und die Gründung der normannisch-sicilischen Monarchie* (Innsbruck, 1904), pp. 167-71; Dräseke, "Bischof Anselm von Havelberg," pp. 163-64; Francesco Giunta, *Bizantini e bizantinismo nella Sicilia normanna* 2nd ed. (Palermo, 1950), p. 42; Bernhardi, *Lothar*, pp. 575-76; Ferdinand Chalandon, *Histoire de la domination normande en Italie et en Sicile* 2 (Paris, 1907), pp. 55-56.

[11] *Annalista Saxo*, MGH SS 6:769 ("Quibus decenter remuneratis, cum suis legatis Anselmo Havelbergensi episcopo et ceteris eos in propria remisit"); *Annales Magdeburgensis*, MGH SS 16:185; *Translatio Godehardi episcopi Hildesheimensis*, ed. Philipp Jaffé, MGH SS 12:649, naming one member of the delegation ("scilicet Eilbertum praepositum Goslariensem fratrem nostrum"), but not mentioning Anselm.

[12] *Antik*. prol., 1140B; 1.10, 1156D; Petke, *Kanzlei*, p. 328.

duties which had nothing to do with his episcopal charge in Havel-berg.

The delegation made its way by land to Venice and then went by ship to Constantinople.[13] What was Anselm commissioned to do there? In the *Antikeimenon*, he speaks of himself not only as a *legatus* but as an *apocrisiarius*.[14] Since the latter term was used by the pope to designate officials sent by him to the Byzantine court,[15] Anselm's mission has often been seen as a religious one with papal backing.[16] The term *apocrisiarius*, however, is ambiguous. It does not appear in any of the accounts of the delegation except Anselm's.[17] Even if the term had been used in 1136, it would not necessarily have had a religious connotation. Otto of Freising speaks of the *apocrisiarii* whom Emperor John II Comnenus sent to Conrad III a few years later to renew the alliance between the emperors, as do both Conrad and John in their exchange of letters.[18] Moreover, Anselm refers to him-self specifically as the *apocrisiarius* of Lothar with no reference to the pope. The *Translatio Godehardi episcopi Hildesheimensis*, the best source for the delegation, says that "Lothar...sent his legates" who "repaired the ancient pact of the emperors which at that time had been pain-fully neglected,"[19] showing the mission to have been a matter strictly between the two emperors and not involving the pope at all. The delegation was not sent to heal the religious schism but to mend and strengthen that *antiquum foedus imperatorum* by formally accepting what

---

[13] *Translatio Godehardi episcopi Hildesheimensis*, MGH SS 12:649; Bernhardi, *Lothar*, p. 577 n. 36. It is quite possible that Anselm also negotiated with the Venetians; see p. 50 below.

[14] *Apocrisiarius: Antik.* 1.10, 1156CD; *legatus: Antik.* prol., 1140B.

[15] Dräseke, "Bischof Anselm von Havelberg," p. 164. Cardinal Humbert of Silva Candida used the term for his delegation to Constantinople in 1054, Cornelius Will, ed., *Acta et scripta quae de controversiis ecclesiae graecae et latinae saeculo undecimo composita extant* (Leipzig-Marburg, 1861), p. 153. For the earlier use of the term, Jeffrey Richards, *Consul of God: The Life and Times of Gregory the Great* (Boston, 1980), pp. 73-76; Jaeger, *Origins of Courtliness*, p. 21.

[16] Lauerer, *Anschauungen*, pp. 54-55; Schreiber, "Anselm von Havelberg und die Ostkirche," pp. 358-59; Beumer, "Ein Religionsgespräch," p. 465; Martin Fitzthum, "Anselm von Havelberg als Verteidiger der Einheit mit der Ostkirche," *AP* 36 (1961), 138-39; Dombrowski, *Anselm*, p. 14.

[17] The term *Apocrisiarius* is used in reference to Anselm by Theodore of Engel-husen (1362/5-1434) in his *Chronicon continens re Ecclesiae et Reipublicae ab o.c. usque ad a.d. 1421*, ed. G. W. Leibniz, Scriptores rerum Brusvicensium 2 (1710), p. 1098; however, Theodore's account of Anselm's activities shows the *Antikeimenon* itself to have been his source.

[18] Otto of Freising, *Gesta Friderici I. imperatoris*, 3rd ed., ed. Georg Waitz and Ber-nard von Simson (Hanover, 1912), MGH SS r. G. 1.24-25, p. 37, 39-41, p. 43.

[19] *Translatio Godehardi episcopi Hildesheimensis*, MGH SS 12:649.

had been offered at Merseburg. All that can be said of Anselm's success in furthering this alliance is that although the Byzantines did not send the proffered aid for the coming campaign in Italy, a delegation from John did arrive to offer his apologies.[20]

Of any attempts to confirm a military alliance between the Germans and the Greeks, Anselm says not a word in the *Antikeimenon*. This work, the only extant account of what transpired during the delegation's stay in Constantinople, was written by Anselm some fourteen years later to address religious issues divisive to a united Christendom, not to reminisce on earlier political events. The give and take of the written debates is risky evidence for a reconstruction of what actually happened on the delegation of 1136.[21] We find here a paradox: The evidence for what has been seen as the central event of Anselm's life may, in fact, have little to do with that event. While a detailed study of Anselm's account will be presented later, here we can ask what, in general terms, he says happened and how accurately the Anselm who actually debated Nicetas is portrayed in the *Antikeimenon*.

One can glean from his account that when Anselm arrived in Constantinople he was drawn into theological discussions with Greek religious leaders. With the permission of the emperor and the patriarch of the city, it was arranged that he hold public debates with Archbishop Nicetas of Nicomedia. On April 10 ("if I remember correctly"), near the church of Hagia Eirene, the first debate was held.[22] Scribes and officials charged with maintaining order were present. Latins too had come. Because the debaters did not speak a common language, Anselm had at his side three men learned in Greek to act as translators: James of Venice, Burgundio of Pisa and, as official translator, Moses of Bergamo.[23] A second debate was held a week

---

[20] Peter the Deacon, *Chronica Monasterii Casinensis* 4.115-16, ed. Hartmut Hoffmann, MGH SS 34 (Hanover, 1980), pp. 590-91.

[21] On the historicity of the debates see the decisive work by Sieben, *Die Konzilsidee*, pp. 153-87, esp. pp. 157-163; also Morrison, "Anselm of Havelberg," p. 238. See also p. 5 n. 9 above, p. 33 above.

[22] *Antik.* 2.1, 1163AB.

[23] On these men, Peter Classen, *Burgundio von Pisa: Richter, Gesandter, Übersetzer* (Heidelberg, 1974); L. Minio-Paluello, "Jacobus Veneticus Grecus Canonist and Translator of Aristotle," *Traditio* 8 (1952), 265-304; Giovanni Cremaschi, *Mosè del Brolo e la cultura a Bergamo nei secoli XI-XII*, Collezione Storica Bergamasca 3 (Bergamo, 1945); Walter Berschin, *Griechisch-Lateinisches Mittelalter: Von Hieronymus zu Nikolaus von Kues* (Bern, 1980), pp. 261-63; Charles Homer Haskins, *Studies in the History of Mediaeval Science* (Cambridge, Mass., 1924), pp. 144-46, 149-50, 197-209, 227-30; Russell, "Anselm of Havelberg and the Union of the Churches," p. 96.

later. Because the first encounter had aroused interest, the meeting place was moved to the church of Hagia Sophia to accommodate a larger crowd.[24]

The debates as related in the *Antikeimenon* cover a fairly standard litany of contentious issues dividing the two churches: the tortuous problem of the *Filioque* concerning whether the Spirit proceeds from the Father or from the Father "and the Son"; differences in sacramental rites, and the Greek rejection of the Roman pope's claim to primacy in the church.[25] That these were the issues actually debated in 1136 would not be surprising. What has surprised many modern readers and gained their admiration is the charitable and tactful way in which Anselm engages his opponent. Less than a century earlier in 1054, religious discussions between East and West had exploded rudely when Archbishop Leo of Ochrida called Latins who used unleavened bread in the Eucharist "neither good Jews nor good Christians but similar to a leopard whose hair is neither black nor wholly white."[26] The Roman Cardinal Humbert responded, flinging the famous excommunication of Leo and the patriarch of Constantinople onto the alter in the Hagia Sophia and stalking away shaking the dust from his feet. The patriarch, Michael Cerularius, fired off a counter excommunication, calling Humbert and his party wolves and the *Filioque* an "artifice of the devil."[27] That East and West often sought better relations after 1054 was due more to threats from nearby Norman and Muslim states than to a spirit of mutual good will, and Anselm's own diplomatic delegation was itself primarily concerned with a military alliance. Yet, the Anselm of the *Antikeimenon*, written so many years after the actual events, stands out as a man interested in finding a basis for spiritual reconciliation with the Greeks. "It seems to me that I have come upon a truly catholic Westerner," says Nicetas of Anselm in the *Antikeimenon*,

---

[24] *Antik.* 3.1, 1209CD.

[25] Particulars of the exchange as Anselm relates them are discussed in Part Two. Good summaries are available: Russell, "Anselm of Havelberg and the Union of the Churches," pp. 85-120 and Beumer, "Ein Religionsgesprach," pp. 465-82, with the caveat that both of these authors are too willing to accept the historical accuracy of Anselm's account.

[26] *Epistola missa ad quemdam episcopum Romanum*, Migne, Patrologia Graeco-Latina 120:841A, partially translated by Deno John Geanakoplos, *Byzantium: Church, Society, and Civilization Seen through Contemporary Eyes* (Chicago,1984), p. 207.

[27] Will, *Acta et scripta*, pp. 155-68, trans. Geanakoplos, *Byzantium*, pp. 209-12.

If only Latins like this one would come to us in these times! But now if
any come, they walk about puffed up with their grandeur, and they
never speak of such catholic and humble things but rather of those
which are insolent and intolerable to us.[28]

While this paean is almost certainly Anselm's invention,[29] the man it
describes is the kind of person he aspired to be. With the advantages
of having time to weight the arguments in his favor and no actual
adversary to respond to them, Anselm is at pains to portray his
debates as moving toward acceptable resolutions not because of the
force of his arguments but because of his sensitivity to the opposition.[30] As Anselm reports it, he set the tenor for the discussions by
telling the assembled Greeks that he did not come seeking a quarrel,
"Rather I come to inquire and learn about the faith, yours and mine,
and most of all because you desire it."[31] Here, in his scripted dialogue, is the role which Anselm assigns himself, that of a man of
definite convictions and yet willing to take the middle ground and
begin with the assumption that the faith is a unified whole, "yours
and mine." Is this the role he tried to assume during the actual events
of 1136?

In sending this delegation to Greece, Lothar III was seizing an
opportunity to gain military support for his coming Italian campaign
and to keep the door open for further cooperation between the em-
pires. On his side, John II Comnenus had created this opportunity in
the first place. Anselm's job, first and foremost, was to keep it alive.
Seen in this context, a public debate over passionately held religious
differences presented some danger, for it would have been in no one's
interest to allow a religious squabble to jeopardize the alliance. That
the Greeks encouraged a debate is an indication that, at the very
least, they did not see an enemy in Anselm. In agreeing to the debate,
Anselm must have realized that tact was of the essence.

---

[28] *Antik.* 2.24, 1204B. Criticism of western visitors could also come from western
residents of Constantinople. Anselm's translator Moses of Bergamo wrote to his
brother in the West telling of a visit from a westerner: "Venit enim Ioannes porcus,
sus, asinus, stipes plumbeus; venit obprobrium hominum et abiectio plebis; venit
ignominias et iniurias illaturus quorum gloriabatur esse propinquus." Cremaschi,
Mosè del Brolo, p. 143.

[29] See pp. 251-52 below.

[30] Peter Classen, "Der Häresie-Begriff bei Gerhoch von Reichersberg und seinem
Umkreis," in *The Concept of Heresy in the Middle Ages (11th-13th C.)*, ed. W. Lourdaux
and D. Verhelst, Medievalia Lovaniensia, series 1, studia 4, Proceedings of the
International Conference Louvain May 13-16, 1973 (Louvain, 1976), pp. 40-41.

[31] *Antik.* 2.1, 1163C.

The *Antikeimenon* mentions Norbert of Magdeburg only briefly and in Anselm's opening book rather than in the debates themselves. Yet Anselm's mentor colors all of its pages. In effect, the role in which Anselm cast himself in the debates is modeled after Norbert of Xanten, the understanding mediator and peacemaker. In Valentano, Rome, and Würzburg, Norbert had dealt astutely and judiciously with very sensitive situations, carefully steering contending parties away from uncompromising positions. Anselm, who had been on the wings while observing Norbert, found himself at the center of the diplomatic stage in Constantinople; and Lothar III certainly did not want a Humbert to play the leading role. With Norbert gone, the ruler chose Anselm, whose own description of himself in the *Antikeimenon* shows that the mediating role of Norbert was the one to which he readily aspired.

This is, however, not to say that the success Anselm claims in moving Nicetas toward accepting the Latin point of view on dogma and ritual reflects the outcome of the actual debates or the spirit in which they were conducted. Even in Anselm's account, his Latin translators stand like seconds in a duel. The crowd that gathered at the Hagia Eirene certainly came to see the local champion win; and the happy conclusions to each debate in which Anselm describes Nicetas as coming close to embracing Latin positions would surely have disappointed or horrified a Greek audience. That the second debate drew a larger crowd speaks more for sparks in the first or, perhaps, a Greek victory than for happy understanding tending to favor the Latin side. The debates were a game, a game which Anselm probably tried to win, a game which, so long as bitterness was avoided and the military alliance not jeopardized, did not matter much one way or the other. That bitterness was avoided is the most that can be said of them, but given earlier contacts between Greeks and Latins, that is praise, indeed.

CHAPTER FOUR

FROM IMPERIAL SERVICE
TO THE HAVELLAND
1136-1144

During the final years of Lothar's reign, Anselm remained a part of the royal court and showed himself a loyal supporter of imperial policies even when, in one instance, they ran contrary to those of the papacy. Lothar's death, however, and the accession of the Hohenstaufen Conrad III to the German throne would lose Anselm his standing at court and give him a new perspective on the affairs of church and state as he finally took up his diocesan duties in the Havelland.

By June 1136 Anselm had returned from Constantinople. He met the German ruler in Goslar where Lothar had come to plan his expedition against Roger of Sicily. The records which tell of Anselm's return mention events in Havelberg, as well: In an uprising, the pagan sons of Widukind, the chief of the Wends and a Christian, had taken control of the town. These sources also say that the church in Havelberg was destroyed.[1] By church, they may mean the community of Christians, for the building survived.[2] But whether the building or the community is meant, the fact that the revolt was directed against the

---

[1] Anselm at Goslar: *UL* 85, pp. 133-34; capture of Havelberg mentioning "ecclesia destructa": *Annales Magdeburgenses*, MGH SS 16:186; *Annalista Saxo*, MGH SS 6:770.

[2] On this point see Alfred Schirge, *Dom zu Havelberg* (Berlin, 1970; Georg Staemmler, "Havelberg," in *Repertorio delle Cattedrali Gotiche*, ed. Ernesto Brivio (Milan, 1986), pp. 781-90; and Hanns-Joachim Fincke, "Wie alt ist der Havelberger Dom?" *Havelberger Regionalgeschichtliche Beiträge* 4 (1995), 55-83. These three works disagree with the oft repeated assumption that the tenth century Ottonian church was destroyed in the uprising of 983. No other church of the twelfth century has a floor plan similar to Havelberg's. Fincke traces that floor plan back to the Ottonian churches of St. Maximin in Trier and St. Willibrord in Echternach, and he concludes that the plan of the cathedral does not lend itself to the Roman liturgy but rather to that of the Greeks or to a western liturgy highly influenced by the eastern church. This he traces to the Benedictines of Gorze who built their monastery churches (like St. Maximin) in such a way that liturgies other than the Roman (perhaps the eastern-influenced Gallican) could be conducted.

ecclesia is some indication that Christianity had made its mark on the Wends of Havelberg in the absence of Anselm. Bishop Otto of Bamberg, who visited Havelberg in 1128, had apparently steered Widukind toward Christianity in spite of Norbert's refusal to sanction his missionary efforts there.[3] In 1136, Albert the Bear, the margrave of the North March, led an expedition against the Slavs, forcing Lothar to delay his Italian expedition. Whether this had anything to do with the uprising in Havelberg is not known,[4] and there is little evidence to support the argument that Albert actually conquered the Havelland and captured Havelberg. The expedition was probably more akin to a raid than a conquest, and it certainly had no bearing on getting Anselm into his diocese.[5] It was the court of Lothar III to

---

[3] Ebo, *Vita Ottonis Episcopi Babenbergensis*, ed. R. Köpke (Hanover, 1856), MGH SS 12:861, portraying the Wends as willing to listen to Otto but wanting nothing to do with Norbert. Demm, *Reformmönchtum und Slawenmission*, p. 59; Kahl, *Slawen und Deutsche* 1:90-91; 2:651 n. 98; Crone, *Untersuchungen zur Reichskirchenpolitik Lothars III.*, pp. 230-32. Also, p. 30 above.

[4] The *Annales Patherbrunnenses* says only that Albert moved against Slavs who had themselves invaded parts of Saxony. *Annales Patherbrunnenses. Eine Quellenschrift des 12. Jahrhunderts, aus Bruchstücken wiederhergestellt*, ed. Paul Scheffer-Boichorst (Innsbruck, 1870), p. 163. See Petke, *Kanzlei*, p. 359 with n. 77; Fritz Curschmann, *Die Diozese Brandenburg: Untersuchungen zur historischen Geographie und Verfassungsgeschichte eines ostdeutschen Kolonialbistums* (Leipzig, 1906), pp. 90-91; Gottfried Wentz, "Havelberg, Jerichow und Broda: Probleme der märkischen Kirchengeschichte und Beiträge zu ihrer Lösung," in *Festschrift A. Brackmann*, ed. L. Santifaller (Weimar, 1931), pp. 327-31; cf. Wolfgang Brüske, *Untersuchungen zur Geschichte des Lutizenbundes: Deutsch-wendische Beziehungen des 10.-12. Jahrhunderts*, Mitteldeutsche Forschung 3 (Münster, 1955), p. 106.

[5] In his "Bemerkungen zu der sogenannten Stiftungsurkunde des Bistums Havelberg von 946 Mai 9," *Jahrbuch für die Geschichte Mittel- und Ostdeutschlands* 5 (1956), 27-29, Walter Schlesinger suggests that after Widukind's death, Albert the Bear took Havelberg and built a church; Widukind's sons then revolted against Albert and destroyed the church; and finally, Albert retook Havelberg in 1136/37 and Havelberg "ist seither dauernd in deutscher Hand geblieben" (p. 27). There is, however, no evidence of Albert's presence in Havelberg before the Wenden Crusade of 1148. Schlesinger's statement that Albert "dem Italienzuge fernbleibt" in order to accomplish this (p. 28 n. 102) does not account for the fact that he only delayed the Italian expedition; he did, in fact, join it (see Otto von Heinemann, *Albrecht der Bär: Eine quellenmässige Darstellung seines Lebens* (Darmstadt, 1864), pp. 104, 110-12). One may suggest that the conquest of the Wends would have made it difficult for Albert to leave his newly won but still hostile lands to go to Italy. Schlesinger explains the fact that Anselm did not take up residence in Havelberg by calling it "nichts als ein vorgeschobener Aussenposten, ungeeignet als Bischofssitz" (p. 29). Since Anselm himself described Havelberg as a threatened outpost when he did take up residence in 1149 (see p. 90 below), Schlesinger has not really clarified why he did not go there earlier if it was in German hands. Given that Anselm went to considerable lengths to establish a bishop's residence in Jerichow in 1144 (see pp. 62-67 below) and that, as with Albert, there is no evidence for his presence in Havelberg until 1148, it is more

which the bishop was committed; and when Lothar's expedition began in late August, the bishop of Havelberg went with it.[6]

By the campaign of 1136, Lothar was convinced that in Anselm he had found a man on whom he could rely both for advice and to handle administrative duties. Before the year was out, the ruler had chosen Anselm and Bishop Bruno of Strasbourg to assist Queen Richenza in governing northern Italy while he took his army against Roger. The town of Reggio was chosen for her residence; and even before Lothar left, Anselm and Bruno were at Richenza's side listening to the complaints of a local bishop.[7] Early in October, Anselm was in Corregio Verde, apparently without Bruno, to witness the renewal of agreements made with the Venetians a year earlier at Merseburg.[8] It is possible that Anselm had worked out some of those agreements when he went through Venice on his way to Constantinople and that the contacts he had with the Venetians were good, for Lothar had called him from his duties in Reggio to attend the negotiations.[9]

With Lothar's success against Roger II, who was forced to take refuge in Sicily, Pope Innocent and the German ruler fell to quarreling with each other. One dispute between the pope and the ruler in which Anselm played a part concerned Rainald, the abbot of Monte Cassino. This issue is worth some scrutiny, both because it bears a marked similarity to the earlier conflicts resolved by Norbert, and because Anselm, who would later write about papal power in the *Antikeimenon*, took a position which completely ignored the claims of the papacy.

Rainald had supported Roger of Sicily and been confirmed as abbot by Pope Anacletus. With Roger's defeat and the capture of Monte Cassino, he submitted to Lothar who recognized him as abbot, a political move meant to keep Monte Cassino free of papal control.[10] Innocent grasped this motive and insisted on replacing Rainald with someone of proven loyalty to himself. Against this move,

likely that Albert's expedition was a raid and that the Christianized Widukind held Havelberg until the revolt of his sons, in whose Slavic hands it remained until the Wenden Crusade.

[6] Anselm in Würzburg August 16, 1136 for the assembly of the army: *UL* 92, pp. 143-44; Bernhardi, *Lothar*, pp. 600-1; Dombrowski, *Anselm*, pp. 18-19.

[7] *ULR* 1, pp. 227-28, dated September, 1136.

[8] *UL* 97, pp. 151-56, dated October 3, 1136.

[9] Anselm back in Reggio in early Dec. 1136: *ULR* 2-3, pp. 228-31.

[10] Stroll, *Jewish Pope*, pp. 55-64; Bernhardi, *Lothar*, pp. 678-701.

Lothar claimed that the monks were his chaplains and Monte Cassino a possession of the empire which, as part of the imperial dignity, he would never relinquish.[11] Lothar was again showing that while he might fight for the papacy, he would also take every opportunity to advance what he felt were his prerogatives. Rainald briefly submitted to Innocent, but a few weeks later, he showed his true colors by renewing his contacts with Roger.[12] The stage was now set for yet another confrontation over the control of church offices, only this time without the tactful Norbert.

In September the emperor and the pope made their way to San Germano, near Monte Cassino. Bernard of Clairvaux was in Innocent's entourage, and it was probably at this time that Anselm heard the emaciated abbot preach to the papal curia and, as he would later proudly relate, was himself chosen by Innocent to preach before the assembled prelates on the eighth of the month.[13] He related this years later in the *Antikeimenon* in order to buttress the idea that he supported the papacy and interpreted Innocent's decision to have him preach as a sign of papal approval. In this context, the upshot is interesting. Little more than a week later, Lothar went to Monte Cassino and put Rainald on trial without the approval or cooperation of Innocent.[14] Even granting Innocent's desire to replace Rainald, for Lothar to take this action with the pope almost looking over his shoulder could only highlight the fact that the ruler was flatly claiming the right to make and break church office holders. A negative reaction from Innocent, no matter what the decision of Lothar's tribunal, was only to be expected. Yet Anselm appears to have missed this completely. On the sixteenth of September, the trial proceeded with Anselm in attendance. Peter the Deacon describes the meeting, saying that it was

---

[11] *Chronica monasterii Casinensis* 4.108, MGH SS 34:572; Wibald, 8-9, pp. 82-83; *UL* 121e-f, pp. 206-7.

[12] *Chronica monasterii Casinensis* 4.115 and 1.18, MGH SS 34:589, 592.

[13] *Epist. apol.*, 1128BC, giving month and day but not year. Anselm says he preached "in Romana ecclesia" which most likely means "in the Roman Curia" rather than "in Rome." Some historians, including myself, have though that Anselm remained in Italy after Lothar's departure or made a brief trip to Germany only to return to attend Innocent's Lateran Council of 1139 in Rome: Dombrowski, *Anselm*, pp. 21-22; Lees, "Anselm of Havelberg's 'Banishment' to Havelberg," *AP* 58 (1986), 7-8; Bernhardi, *Konrad*, p. 155. n. 12; Wentz *Havelberg*, pp. 35, 38. There is no direct evidence that Anselm remained in Italy after Lothar's campaign or returned in 1138-1139. The September date and the presence of Bernard are far more compatible with the year 1137. See Petke, *Kanzlei*, p. 331.

[14] *Chronica monasterii Casinensis* 4.119-20, MGH SS 34:593-95.

argued that Rainald's election was invalid because he had been ordained by Peter Leoni (Anacletus), and that this was done while
Rainald was only a subdeacon and thus could neither perform mass
nor forgive sins. Anselm spoke up in agreement:

> While there are many things which these brothers have said about
> [Rainald's] election for which he ought to be deposed, nevertheless this
> one thing seems sufficient for his removal, namely that, by the Lord's
> testimony, a foundation which is built on sand cannot stand. Where-
> fore, if it please those who have convened to discuss this matter, we may
> put aside the other reasons and fasten on this alone.[15]

This incident gives but a brief glance at Anselm, and it comes from
the pen of Peter the Deacon, a man with no great reputation for
honesty. Still, Peter's account here is straightforward enough, and he
speaks as an eyewitness.

The story is instructive. One might say that Norbert had earlier
taken the same pragmatic, if naive, view by bringing the papacy's
immunity from legal prosecution into question in order to defeat
Anacletus.[16] However, it is difficult to believe that Norbert would
have approached Rainald's case as simplistically as did Anselm. As
we have seen, in dealing with the issue of the control of church
offices, Norbert was very cautious. The issue for him in this case
would certainly have been one of prerogative rather than the fate of
Rainald. Anselm was, in fact, ignoring the very fulcrum of power
which Norbert had worked so hard to keep in balance by seeing only
the problem of a recalcitrant and disloyal abbot who should be removed from office. The more important issue of who had the right to
remove him seems to have escaped Anselm. Acting as Lothar's counselor and looking out for the good of the empire, he had, perhaps
unconsciously, overlooked the larger issue at stake in Rainald's trial
and been at best neglectful of the pope, and this in spite of having
recently preached before the curia. This is a point to which we will
return in dealing with Anselm's assessment of papal power in the
Antikeimenon.

Innocent was furious and threatened to remove from office—
whether it be that of archbishop, bishop or abbot—all those who had
assisted Lothar in Rainald's case.[17] A confrontation was avoided
through Lothar's willingness to concede to Innocent the right to re-

---

[15] *Chronica monasterii Casinensis* 4.120, MGH SS 34:595.
[16] See pp. 35-36 above.
[17] *Chronica monasterii Casinensis* 4.121, MGH SS 34:595.

move Rainald and the choice of Wibald of Stablo, Lothar's counselor and Anselm's friend, as his replacement.[18]

Innocent and Lothar accompanied each other as far as Farfa and then separated. The pope went on to Rome while Lothar recrossed the Alps. On December 4, 1137, the ruler Anselm had served faithfully died in Tyrol. Lothar had not solved the thorny problem of the papal schism, but less than two months later it ended with the death of Anacletus in Rome.

Lothar's death presented a dilemma for Anselm. If he were to continue to serve at the royal court, it was necessary for him to win the confidence of the king's successor. Lothar left no heir, and the fast-moving family of the Hohenstaufen quickly won the crown for the former anti-king Conrad, who became King Conrad III in early March of 1138. Anselm's friend Wibald successfully moved from serving the Saxon Lothar to becoming a trusted adviser of the Hohenstaufen Conrad; but Anselm hesitated, a hesitation which, one may suggest, was to cost him dearly in his dealings with Conrad. While he had been a frequent witness to the charters of Lothar, for over a year he witnessed none for Conrad. In all probability, the problem for Anselm involved divided loyalties. Lothar's wife, Queen Richenza, resisted Conrad and the Hohenstaufen by forcefully supporting the royal candidacy of her brother-in-law, the Welf Duke Henry the Proud. Furthermore, Anselm's own metropolitan, Archbishop Conrad of Magdeburg (a relative of Lothar), also took the part of Henry along with most of the Saxon nobility.[19] Anselm's motive for staying away from the royal court may have been a sense of loyalty to Richenza, whom he had served on Lothar's second Italian campaign, or to Archbishop Conrad. However, it is more likely that he waited for the smoke to clear in the Welf-Hohenstaufen dispute before taking sides. In any event, he ended up playing his hand poorly by demonstrating loyalty neither to Richenza nor to Archbishop Conrad while at the same time failing to win the confidence of King Conrad.

---

[18] *Chronica monasterii Casinensis* 4.122-24, MGH SS 34:596-600. Wibald remained in Monte Cassino only until November 2 when Roger II moved on the monastery. Hartmut Hoffmann, "Die älteren Abtslisten von Montecassino," *Quellen und Forschungen aus italienischen Archiven und Bibliotheken* 47 (1967), 334-35. Anselm as witness to privileges granted Monte Cassino: *UL* 119-20, pp. 190-202, in Aquino, September 22.

[19] Claude, *Geschichte des Erzbistums Magdeburg* 2:43-45, 50.

Initially, Anselm returned to Magdeburg.[20] It was probably at this time that he wrote a tract concerning the apostolic life of the canon regular.[21] The incident which moved him to write concerned Peter, the provost of Hamersleben, southwest of Magdeburg, who had decided to leave his canonical duties and become a monk at Huysberg, in the diocese of Halberstadt. This event stirred up an old controversy over whether a canon could, without permission, leave his canonical order for the monastic cell and whether such a change of profession should be seen as moving up or down on the scale of perfection. Egbert, the abbot of Huysburg (1134-1155), took up his pen in defense of Peter's decision and wrote a tract championing the monastic life as superior to the clerical.[22] Anselm countered with his Letter in Defense of the Order of Canons Regular, the *Epistola apologetica*. At the beginning of this work he pictures himself sitting alone one day "as was my custom" and reading the *Epistolarium* of St. Jerome. There may be a glimpse here of a man at loose ends, as was Anselm in 1138, in his reaction to the arrival of Egbert's tract: "I snatched it up, avid for something new, and immediately began to read...." Quickly, however, he moves to the attack as he begins a biting criticism of monasticism:

> ...and [I] discovered a work which was not for leisure reading but was rather onerous, and right off I wondered greatly about the prudence of such a man as the one who had begun, put together and finished this work. And behold! The title of the work appeared unexpectedly and showed you to be its author.[23]

In spite of referring to Egbert as his "most dear brother," Anselm continues in this sarcastic vein, asking Egbert, "By what temerity do you presume to offer muddy water to simple boys by writing about God? ...I fear for you."[24]

An uncompromising side of Anselm's character comes clear. After flinging insults such as these, he turns to a serious defense of the active clerical life, asserting in no uncertain terms that the life of the canon regular is superior to that of the monk. The diplomatic An-

---

[20] Dombrowski, *Anselm*, pp. 20-21.

[21] For the date of the *Epistola apologetica* see Lees, "Charity and Enmity," 54-58.

[22] Egbert's tract is lost. See p. 136 n. 23 below.

[23] *Epist. apol.*, 1119AB. Anselm's "recentium litterarum avidus" is, perhaps, a hint that he was not in Rome when he received this tract. See p. 51 n. 13 above.

[24] *Epist. apol.*, 1120C.

selm one finds portrayed in the later *Antikeimenon*, as a man looking for compromise with the Greek Nicetas and sensitive to the position of his opponent, is hardly to be found in the *Epistola*. Egbert had hit a raw nerve. On one level, Anselm's own chosen way of life was being attacked; but Anselm had chosen the life championed by Norbert of Magdeburg; and at a deeper level, it was Norbert's choice that was being criticized by the abbot of Huysburg. Norbert had studied and experimented with many forms of religious life and chosen the path of service over that of withdrawal. In the *Epistola apologetica*, Anselm says that as a contemplative, the apostle Paul would have contributed little to the church but that as an apostle, he had spread the Gospel far and wide.[25] For Anselm the apostolic life was thus inextricably associated with service. While he does not mention Norbert, whose name would have had little impact on Egbert, it is clear that when he wrote the *Epistola*, Anselm was defending the way of his mentor. The paradox is that the *Epistola* and its scathing inditement of monasticism had no chance of furthering the peace Norbert had held so dear; moreover, it was written by a man who was having a difficult time finding for himself any position of active clerical service at all.[26]

Anselm was soon drawn into yet another controversy, this time between Archbishop Conrad of Magdeburg and Wigger, Conrad's suffragan bishop of Brandenburg. This controversy showed him a possible way out of the seeming impasse of being an exiled bishop and moved him toward supporting the Hohenstaufen Conrad.

Wigger of Brandenburg was an early companion of Norbert and former provost of the Church of Our Lady in Magdeburg. He had recently gone to great lengths to free himself from the dependent position of an exiled bishop. Brandenburg itself lay beyond his grasp, controlled like Havelberg by the Wends; but Wigger did have some control of the edge of his diocese across the Elbe, and in 1139 he established a Norbertine foundation at Leitzkau (south-west of Brandenburg) as a first step toward becoming bishop in fact as well as in name. Wigger even went so far as to give the foundation the right to elect the bishop of Brandenburg, making of Leitzkau what Hans-Dietrich Kahl has called "a provisional cathedral."[27] Finances, how-

---

[25] *Epist. apol.*, 1136-37.

[26] For my analysis of the *Epistola apologetica* see Part Two, Chapter One below.

[27] Kahl, *Slawen und Deutsche* 1:124-66, esp. 141, 151-55, 160.

ever, remained a major stumbling block in this quest to gain a small hold on his diocese. Unfortunately for Wigger, the right to tithes from that small area of his diocese free of the Wends was claimed by the abbey of St. Moritz in Magdeburg under a grant from Otto I given according to old proprietary church law;[28] and St. Moritz's assignee since 968 had been the archbishop of Magdeburg. Wigger asserted his right to the income from this area on the basis of canon law, which gave a bishop full control of his diocese. In so doing and going against the claims of his own archbishop, Wigger was asking for trouble.[29]

In the spring of 1139, the bishop made his way to Rome for the Lateran Council, there to lay his case before Pope Innocent II. On April 20, the pope issued a bull ordering that Brandenburg be recompensed by Magdeburg with money and land if the latter were to continue collecting tithes from the Leitzkau area.[30] The pope named a commission of three men to select the land for Brandenburg: Anselm of Havelberg, Provost Gerhard of Magdeburg, and Abbot Arnold of Berge.[31]

Innocent's bull is the only evidence for Anselm's participation in Wigger's struggle for control of his diocese. It does not indicate who first suggested Anselm for the commission, but Archbishop Conrad was not in Rome to influence the selection. The point of the commission was to enforce Innocent's bull, and both the pope and Wigger surely wanted men who would do just that. Anselm had much in common with Wigger and probably sympathized with his plight. Both were not only suffragan bishops of Magdeburg but bishops in exile from their dioceses; and they were both followers of Norbert. In Wigger, Anselm found a colleague committed to a missionary church on Germany's eastern frontier[32] and unwilling to accept the subser-

---

[28] Claude, *Geschichte des Erzbistums Magdeburg* 1:34.

[29] On Wigger and the control of tithes in his diocese, see Kahl, *Slawen und Deutsche* 1:168-178, who describes the problem as "dieses heisse Eisen" (p. 170); also Claude, *Geschichte des Erzbistums Magdeburg* 2:47-49.

[30] A third of the income went to the support of parish priests. It was money which, as Kahl says, "Wigger bei dieser Gelegenheit gleichfalls für den Aufbau seiner Diözese hatte sicherstellen können." *Slawen und Deutsche* 1:171.

[31] *UB Erzstifts Magdeburg* 1:246, pp. 307-9, stating clearly that Wigger and Gerhard were at the Lateran but only that Anselm and Arnold were to participate on the commission, not that they were present in Rome. Kahl, *Slawen und Deutsche* 1:173, suggests that Anselm was the leader of this commission.

[32] Kahl, *Slawen und Deutsche* 1:166, 410-11.

vient position of an exiled bishop or to let his own archbishop hinder his designs for Brandenburg without a fight. The evidence indicates that in Wigger's struggle, Anselm saw possibilities for himself as bishop of Havelberg.

The two disputes, the narrow one between Brandenburg and Magdeburg and the broad one between the Welfs and the Hohenstaufen, merge here and reveal if not Anselm's sympathies at least his calculated attempt to give some teeth to his powerless position as a bishop in exile. For in order to achieve success, Wigger needed more than a decree from a distant pope and a three-man commission,[33] and the individual he turned to for help was Duke Albert the Bear of Saxony, a loyal supporter of Conrad III.

Just before his death, Lothar III gave Saxony to the Welf Henry the Proud who was already duke of Bavaria. Henry, who had hoped to succeed Lothar as king, saw his plans for the crown fade with the election of Conrad III and, injury added to insult, his duchies taken from him. Conrad insisted that a duke could not hold two duchies. When Henry refused to relinquish control of either Saxony or Bavaria, the ruler declared them both forfeit and then granted Saxony to Albert the Bear and Bavaria to Leopold IV of Austria. With this outrage, Henry raised the standard of rebellion.[34] Albert the Bear was already margrave of the North March (the land between Saxony and the Havelland) and interested in extending his power east to Brandenburg and Havelberg.[35] As such he was a natural ally for Wigger and, one might add, Anselm. However, by April of 1139 (when Innocent issued his bull on the tithes of Brandenburg), Archbishop Conrad had shown himself a firm supporter of Henry the Proud,[36] and

---

[33] Wigger's difficulties in carving out an independent position for himself were far from over. Archbishop Conrad continued to resist Brandenburg's claims and turned over no land. Kahl, *Slawen und Deutsche* 1:172-85. There is no evidence, however, that the commission worked to this end.

[34] Bernhardi, *Konrad*, pp. 82-83; Friedrich Hausmann, "Die Anfänge des staufischen Zeitalters unter Konrad III.," *Vorträge und Forschungen* 12: *Probleme des 12. Jahrhunderts* (Constance, 1968), 56-59; Fuhrmann, *Germany in the High Middle Ages*, pp. 126-27; Karl Jordan, *Henry the Lion: A Biography*, trans. P. S. Falla (Oxford, 1986), pp. 19-21, 23.

[35] See p. 49 above for Albert's 1136 expedition. In 1137-38 he also attacked the Slavs: *Annales Patherbrunnenses*, p. 165, *Regesten der Markgrafen von Brandenburg* 1, 57, p. 14; Petke, *Kanzlei*, pp. 356 n. 57, 359-60.

[36] Claude, *Geschichte des Erzbistums Magdeburg* 2:44-45, referring to Archbishop Conrad as belonging "zu den erbittertsten Gegnern des Staufers" (p. 45).

Henry had attacked Albert forcing him to abandon both the North March and (along with Conrad III) Saxony.[37]

The situation was a critical one for the king, and in May he called his supporters together in Strasbourg to determine what measures could be taken against the rebel Henry. The attendance at this meeting helps us to determine who was supporting the king at this juncture and who was not. As would be expected, Albert the Bear was there while Archbishop Conrad of Magdeburg stayed away. As for Wigger (newly returned from Rome with Innocent's bull on Brandenburg) and Anselm, both of them did attend the Hoftag in Strasbourg.[38] Wigger's motives are clear: he was pushing for independence from Archbishop Conrad and wanted the support of Albert the Bear in Brandenburg. The alliance with Albert meant supporting King Conrad. As for Anselm, Archbishop Conrad was hardly the man to assist him in taking control of the diocese of Havelberg, and even if he were, his dealings with Wigger indicated that he might try to control the Havelland himself. If anyone was to going to help Anselm, it was Albert the Bear; and as in Wigger's case, the bishop of Havelberg was drawn toward the Hohenstaufen camp.

The problem for Anselm was that his first attendance at the court of Conrad III had much to do with his friendship with Wigger and via Wigger with Albert the Bear. That still left considerable distance between himself and the king, and the likelihood is that Conrad did not fully trust a man who had waited more than a year to display any loyalty.

The admittedly meager evidence for Anselm's whereabouts after the Strasbourg *Hoftag* indicates that he was unable to gain King Conrad's confidence and had possibly offended Archbishop Conrad by siding with the Hohenstaufen whose fight with the Welfs had not yet been resolved. Henry the Proud's death in October 1139 had not simplified the situation, for Richenza took up the cause of Henry's son and her grandson, Henry the Lion, who continued the feud. Early in 1140, Conrad called a *Reichstag* in Worms. While the Saxon princes who supported Henry the Lion and his grandmother, along with the still obdurate Archbishop Conrad of Magdeburg and most

---

[37] Kahl, *Slawen und Deutsche* 1:459; 2:918 n. 12; Claude, *Geschichte des Erzbistums Magdeburg* 2:45;

[38] *UK* 21, pp. 35-37, dated May 28, 1139.

of his suffragans, stayed clear of the *Reichstag*, many bishops did attend.[39] Among them was Anselm, who appears only as a witness to a charter of Archbishop Adalbert II of Mainz to the Augustinian cloister of Hönigen.[40] He was not a witness to any of Conrad's charters, perhaps a hint that while he may have been trying to ingratiate himself with the ruler, he was not successful. In October, Anselm was once again at Conrad's court, this time in Nuremberg, where he may have assisted Count Guido of Biandrate in attaining confirmation of his possessions in Italy and lands held in fief from the king:[41] Anselm is not a witness to any more royal charters until the end of 1144.

During this period, there is no evidence that Anselm attended, little less served at, Conrad's court. Neither is there evidence that he returned to Magdeburg, for he did not witness any charters for Archbishop Conrad until shortly before the latter's death in 1142. Far from filling the Norbertine role of peacemaker, Anselm had apparently played the political game so poorly as to lose the trust of both his king and his archbishop.

It is only in March of 1142, that Anselm appears again at Archbishop Conrad's court along with Bishop Wigger of Brandenburg.[42] The two may have come with the knowledge that the archbishop, who died on the second of May, did not have long to live. They were surely aware of some dramatic changes in the political situation and perhaps hoped that a new archbishop would be more able and willing to help them.

The changes that Conrad's successor, Archbishop Frederick, faced concerned a settlement between the Welfs and the Hohenstaufen. Henry the Lion had reconciled with the king in exchange for Saxony which Albert the Bear had agreed to give up. Already at Archbishop Conrad's funeral, the erstwhile enemies of the Welfs had come to meet the new archbishop. They included Albert, the Saxon nobility,

---

[39] Bernhardi, *Konrad*, pp. 130-31. The only other bishop from the archdiocese of Magdeburg in attendance was Udo of Zeitz: *UK* 40, p. 66; 42, p. 69. A relative of Conrad, Udo was always loyal to the king. He died while accompanying Conrad on the Second Crusade. Bernhardi, *Konrad*, p. 680.

[40] *Mainzer UB* 2, *Die Urkunden seit dem Tode Erzbischof Adalberts I. (1137) bis zum Tode Erzbischof Konrads (1200)* 1: *1137-1175*, ed. Peter Acht (Darmstadt, 1968), 14, pp. 22-24, dated to Feb. 2-13, 1140; Bernhardi, *Konrad*, pp. 131-32 n. 8.

[41] *UK* 51, pp. 85-87. Perhaps Anselm had met Guido in Italy. He is one of only four witnesses which include the chancellor and the notary of the charter.

[42] *UB des Erzstifts Magdeburg* 249, pp. 314-15; *Regesta archiepiscopatus Magdeburgensis* 1156, pp. 454-55, dated March 29, 1142.

and several of the suffragan bishops, Anselm among them.[43] For his part, Archbishop Frederick took advantage of this pause in the Welf-Hohenstaufen quarrel to gain the favor of the king.[44] The possibility for Anselm to move into Conrad's court was again open.

However, if it was Anselm's intention to ingratiate himself with the king or the new archbishop, or with both, he appears to have failed. Again the evidence is sparse, but none of it places him with either Conrad or Frederick. What we find is a good indication that the bishop of Havelberg was trying somewhat desperately to carve out a position of episcopal service in which he would be dependent on neither the king nor the archbishop of Magdeburg. A hint of how he went about this is found back in 1140 when Anselm was in the company of Archbishop Adalbert II of Mainz at Conrad's *Reichstag* in Worms. There Anselm may have established a friendship with Adalbert's provost Henry.[45] In September 1142, Henry himself became archbishop of Mainz, and by March of the following year Anselm was in the company of the new archbishop. From March of 1143 to July of 1144, the documentary evidence for Anselm's whereabouts places him in the company neither of his ruler nor of the archbishop of Magdeburg but rather in that of Archbishop Henry.[46] Most significantly, on the June 16, 1143, the two men were together when Anselm dedicated the altar of St. Stephen in the south trancept of the abbey church of St. Peter in Erfurt.[47]

In dedicating an altar Anselm was exercising a level of authority which marks him as something more than Henry's traveling companion. In Anselm's time there was no office of auxiliary bishop, but

---

[43] *UB des Klosters Unser Lieben Frauen zu Magdeburg*, ed. Gustav Hertel, GQPS 10 (Halle, 1878), 10, pp. 10-11.

[44] Bernhardi, *Konrad*, p. 302; Claude, *Geschichte des Erzbistums Magdeburg* 2:55-56.

[45] Henry was in Worms in 1142. He is a witness, along with Anselm, to *Mainzer UB* 14 (see p. 59 with n. 40 above) and is also mentioned in the document as having helped with the arrangements for bringing the Augustinian foundation of Höningen under the archbishop of Mainz's protection.

[46] Mainz, Mar. 19-20, 1143, Anselm at Henry's first provincial synod: *Mainzer UB* 2.1, 36-39, pp. 64-76; Heinrich Büttner, "Erzbischof Heinrich von Mainz und die Staufer (1142-1153)," *ZKG* 69 (1958), 251. June 1143 in Erfurt: *Mainzer UB* 2.1, 40, pp. 76-78. The evidence can conveniently be followed in *Regesten zur Geschichte der Mainzer Erzbischöfe von Bonifatius bis Uriel von Gemmingen 742-1514* 1, *Von Bonifatius bis Arnold von Selehofen 742?-1160*, ed. Johann Friedrich Böhmer and Cornelius Will (Innsbruck, 1877), 5-10, 23, 37, pp. 319-22, 324-25.

[47] *Notae dedicationum Montis S. Petri Erfordensis*, ed. O. Holder-Egger, MGH SS 30.1:483.

bishops of dioceses held by pagans could act as unofficial assistants to archbishops. This had, of course, been the case for bishops of Brandenburg and Havelberg since 983; but while it might be expected that they would serve the archbishops of Magdeburg, this was far from always the case. Often, these bishops moved west to exercise their episcopal authority under an archbishop other than their own.[48] Anselm's association with Archbishop Henry indicates a man looking for a place where he could serve some episcopal function, however modest. That association continued well into 1144, though again the evidence is scanty.[49] It is only late in that year that Anselm is found in the company of Archbishop Frederick. This was in Merseburg where Frederick had come to meet King Conrad, himself probably on the way to Magdeburg.[50]

Two points can be made on this evidence: First, Anselm, so often portrayed as an adviser of kings, played no role in imperial politics and no role at Conrad's court for almost a decade after the death of Lothar III; and second, his relationship with Henry of Mainz was one which, unlike that with Norbert of Magdeburg, had little chance of furthering a career at court. The archbishop of Mainz fought hard for the political and economic interests of his diocese; and Conrad III, who had gone along with Henry's election in 1142, found himself strapped with an archbishop who had no background of Hohenstaufen loyalty and who felt that good relations with the Welfs would best serve his ambitions for his diocese.[51] By attaching himself to Henry, Anselm gives some indication that he had given up on the possibility of returning to royal service and had turned his back on Magdeburg as well.

---

[48] For example, Bishop Hartbert of Brandenburg (1102-1122/25) spent far more time assisting the archbishop of Mainz than accompanying the archbishop of Magdeburg. Curschmann, *Die Diozese Brandenburg*, pp. 71-74; Kahl, *Slawen und Deutsche* 1:169. Bishop Erich of Havelberg (1008-1028) went into imperial service and ended up at the court of the bishop of Verden; Bishop Hezilo (before 1096-1110) also went west for a time and served Bishop Gebhard of Constance, ending his life in the service of Bishop Cuno of Strasbourg. Buchholz, "Die Havelberger Bischöfe," pp. 13, 16-17. The bishops of Havelberg who followed Anselm also frequently served the archbishop of Mainz. Wentz, *Bistum Havelberg*, pp. 26, 35, 41-46.

[49] Before Feb. 4, 1144, no location given: *Mainzer UB* 2.1, 48, pp. 93-95; Erfurt, June 18, 1144: *Mainzer UB* 2.1, 53, pp. 101-2; Heiligenstadt, July 1144: *Mainzer UB* 2.1, 57, pp. 110-11.

[50] *UK* 119, pp. 212-14. For the dating to November 1144, Bernhardi, *Konrad*, p. 392.

[51] Büttner, "Erzbischof Heinrich von Mainz," pp. 248-53.

Anselm eventually got his chance to devote himself to the way of life he had defended in the *Epistola*, not by returning to court but rather by aiding in the advancement of the Norbertines into the Havelland. Events having a direct bearing on Havelberg virtually forced the diocese's bishop into the camp of Conrad III and Archbishop Frederick of Magdeburg, the latter of whom had both the ear of the king and a desire to further missionary efforts across the Elbe.

In 1144 Anselm's diocese was touched by a quarrel between the provost of Bremen and Henry the Lion. In March of that year, Count Rudolf of Stade, a firm ally of Henry, was killed by revolting peasants.[52] Rudolf had been a man of great wealth holding much of the area around Bremen, the Dithmarsch, and lands near Magdeburg as well. Since he had no children, his wealth fell to his brother Hartwig, the cathedral provost of Bremen and a canon of Magdeburg. That so much land in Saxony should be inherited by Hartwig, who openly desired to become archbishop of Bremen, was immediately resisted by Henry the Lion; and the provost began looking for allies. In return for financial support and the promise of a close alliance between Bremen and Magdeburg should he receive the archiepiscopal pallium, Hartwig along with his mother Richardis donated or sold to Magdeburg the nearby family lands.[53] Here was Anselm's chance, for those lands included the town of Jerichow about twenty-five miles south of Havelberg and within his diocese. It was a settled and thriving town to which Rudolf of Stade had already sent colonists.[54]

Some time after Hartwig began parcelling out the family patrimony, he decided to found a religious house in Jerichow dedicated to Norbert. Whether the idea for such a foundation originated with

---

[52] On Rudolf, Richard G. Hucke, *Die Grafen von Stade, 900-1144. Genealogie, politische Stellung, Comitat und Allodialbesitz der sächsischen Udonen*, Einzelschriften des Stader Geschichts- und Heimatvereins 8 (Stade, 1956), pp. 49-50, 107-12. Hucke points out that Rudolf had good relations with Archbishop Conrad of Magdeburg and had been a firm supporter of Richenza and Henry the Proud.

[53] Claude, *Geschichte des Erzbistums Magdeburg* 2:55-58, Hans Patze, "Kaiser Friedrich Barbarossa und der Osten," *Vorträge und Forschungen* 12: *Probleme des 12. Jahrhunderts* (Constance: 1968), 342-45; Hucke, *Die Grafen von Stade*, pp. 51-52; Jordan, *Henry the Lion*, pp. 27-29; Bernhardi, *Konrad*, pp. 395-402; Wentz, *Bistum Havelberg*, pp. 191-92.

[54] *UB Erzstifts Magdeburg* 268, p. 337 says that when the canons moved into the church in Jerichow, "propter tumultum forensis populi propositum sue religionis ibidem minime conservare poterant." See also Schlesinger, "Bemerkungen zu der sogenannten Stiftungsurkunde des Bistums Havelberg," p. 23.

Hartwig, with the Norbertines in Magdeburg, or with Anselm himself is difficult to say. Historians have, nevertheless, followed the lead of Gottfried Wentz in assuming that Anselm had little or no interest in the foundation, indeed, little interest in his diocesan duties at all.[55] Actually, at the time the possibilities for the Havelland opened up, Anselm had little else with which to interest himself, and a closer scrutiny of the documents involved in the establishment of Jerichow lends no support to Wentz's accusation of indifference.

It is clear that part of the financial support Hartwig received from the sale of his inheritance came from the Norbertine foundation of Our Lady of Magdeburg. The brothers there paid Hartwig nineteen talents for the village of Wulkau near Jerichow. While the charter in which this purchase is mentioned says that Our Lady did this "for the brothers who are in Jerichow," the document goes on to say that Richardis had added two farms in Erxleben to Hartwig's grant, and finally, that Anselm, who is identified as the bishop not only of Havelberg but of the church in Jerichow, had turned the farms in Erxleben over to Our Lady "in restoration of their loss." Whether Anselm initiated the idea for the foundation or not, he was at this point clearly concerned that the new establishment should not have strings

---

[55] Initially, Wentz did point to Anselm as initiating the Jerichow foundation: "Die Staatsrechtliche Stellung des Stiftes Jerichow," *Sachsen und Anhalt: Jahrbuch der Historischen Kommission für die Provinz Sachsen und Für Anhalt* 5 (1929), 270-71. Later, he changed his position: "Eine Beteiligung des Havelberger Bischofs Anselm an diesen Erwägungen [for a Norbertine foundation in Jerichow] ist vermutlich nur gering gewesen, zumal die speziellen Angelegenheiten seiner Diözese ihn in seiner Stellung als vielbeschäftigter Diplomat im Dienste des Reiches immer nur wenig in Anspruch genommen haben." Here he points to the Norbertine Foundation of Our Lady as the driving force behind the new foundation (*Bistum Havelberg*, pp. 187, 191-92; also idem, "Havelberg, Jerichow, und Broda," pp. 331-38, where Wentz suggests that Walo, the first provost of Havelberg, was the man behind the plans for the new foundation—see p. 67 below). However if Our Lady took all of the initiative in Jerichow and Anselm had little interest in his own diocese, it may be argued against Wentz that when Hartwig gave Jerichow itself and all its appurtenances to Magdeburg rather than to Havelberg, Our Lady could have made the foundation under the auspices of Magdeburg and there was no need to involve Anselm in the new foundation at all. Wentz goes on to portray Anselm as a man who had no interest in his own diocese and who always put service at court above all else, a view which has continued to cloud his reputation. As Wentz admits, it was a stroke of luck, Rudolf of Stade's death and the grants of Hartwig of Bremen, that provided the opportunity for creating a Norbertine foundation in Jerichow ("Havelberg, Jerichow, und Broda," p. 333). Before that, as has been shown, Anselm hardly attended, little less served at, the royal court. It was his service to Conrad that was "gering." See also Hucke, *Die Grafen von Stade*, p. 186.

attached to Our Lady.[56] He could, of course, have expected no financial support from his diocese and would have been in a difficult
position to buy Wulkau. It is certainly possible that he sought the
necessary financial backing from Our Lady and then moved to eliminate any claims that might be made to the income of the new foundation by turning over the farms in Erxleben to the Norbertines in
Magdeburg. With these negotiations completed, Anselm followed the
example of Wigger in Leitzkau by creating an episcopal chapter in
Jerichow which would serve as his residence until such time as Havelberg was again in Christian hands.

The foundation charter of Jerichow shows Anselm's hand. It is
concerned very little with defining the duties of the brothers or the
mission of the new church. Instead, the issue addressed in this charter
is that of where the controlling power of the new foundation would
reside. The life the brothers in Jerichow were to lead is given short
shrift: Hartwig and Richardis simply give land for a group of canons
who would follow the Augustinian Rule as observed by Archbishop
Norbert of Magdeburg. The greater concern is for the ability of the
new foundation to securely hold its lands, for without the controlling
strong arm of Rudolf of Stade, a chaotic struggle among his former
vassals for the Jerichow lands was a real possibility. No mention is
made of the jurisdiction of any secular lord; rather the foundation is
identified as part of the episcopate of Havelberg. Hartwig relin-
quishes all control so that neither he nor anyone else may transfer
outside of the episcopate any of the lands attached to Jerichow's
church.

A considerable part of the foundation charter is given over to
limiting the powers of whomever should represent Jerichow as its
advocatus in secular concerns. The office of advocate was one rife with
possibilities for abuse, especially so in a situation such as that in
Jerichow where authority was no longer focused on one man; and it

---

[56] The charter in question here is *UB Erzstifts Magdeburg* 255, pp. 320-21 (also *UB
Unser Lieben Frauen* 15, pp. 14-15) in which Archbishop Frederick of Magdeburg
recognizes all of these transactions. The charter has no date but must have been
issued before December 31, 1144, when Conrad III himself recognized the new
establishment (*UK* 122, p. 218) and Our Lady's possession of the two farms (*UK* 123,
p. 221). The transactions given in *UB Erzstifts Magdeburg* 255 must also antedate
Jerichow's also undated foundation charter (n. 58 below) which stresses Jerichow's
independence from outside influence, calls Wulkau a "donation" from Hartwig, and
makes no mention of any claims on the part of Jerichow to lands in Erxleben.

was important to keep that office out of the hands of any of Rudolf's *ministeriales* who might misuse it to alienate Jerichow's possessions for personal gain. The donation charter goes so far as to say that the foundation will have no advocate unless the brothers themselves elect one in time of need and then only for a designated period of time [*pro statu temporis*]. Those who substitute for the brothers of the foundation in administering secular justice over their possessions are to be supervised by the advocate or members of the foundation. The congregation itself is subject to no law except that of God and his saints; as for canonical justice, the brothers will defer to the bishop. If the advocate should act contrary to the will of the foundation, the brothers may replace him; and if he refuses to abide by their decision, he is to be coerced by synodal justice and episcopal authority. Hartwig grants his vassals, *ministeriales* and freemen of the district the unencumbered right to make donations to the church, and after listing the properties of the foundation,[57] takes care to corroborate his grant with his seal "together with that of Anselm, bishop of this same church."[58]

There is a clear echo here of Wigger's attempt to carve out independent jurisdiction in Leitzkau,[59] but no less of the strategies of Norbert of Magdeburg, who had been careful to keep the first houses of his order free from all outside control.[60] With Jerichow's foundation charter, Anselm had, at least on parchment,[61] taken the reins from Hartwig, paid off Our Lady of Magdeburg, eliminated secular claims to the new church, assumed legal jurisdiction, and provided for the possibility of new donations. However, from his involvement in the Leitzkau foundation, the message must have rung clear to Anselm that the archbishop of Magdeburg could pose just as much of a threat as a secular lord. A charter of Conrad III's confirming Hartwig's grants reveals Anselm's problem: the *castrum* of Jerichow, with

---

[57] The brothers received land in Jerichow along with the villages of Wulkow, Nizinthorp and Slavic Wulkow (or Minor Wulkow). See Schlesinger, "Stiftungsurkunde," p. 23.

[58] "Stiftungs Urkunde von Jerichow vom Jahre 1144," ed. Winter, *Die Prämonstratenser*, pp. 350-51; for a more exact dating of the charter to between April and August 31, 1144 see Arthur Bierbach, ed. *UB der Stadt Halle, ihrer Stifter und Kloster* 1, *806-1300*, *GQPS NR* 10 (Magdeburg, 1926), 34, p. 37.

[59] Kahl, *Slawen und Deutsche* 1:259-60; Hucke, *Die Grafen von Stade*, p. 70.

[60] Weinfurter, "Norbert von Xanten—Ordensstifter," pp. 66-98; idem, "Norbert von Xanten als Reformkanoniker," pp. 159-83.

[61] The office of *advocatus* would later fall to Albert the Bear and his son Otto or to their designates. Wentz, "Die staatsrechtliche Stellung des Stiftes Jerichow," pp. 274-75; Kahl, *Slawen und Deutsche* 1:402, 456.

all its appurtenances except the few specifically set aside for the new foundation, was given by Hartwig "to Frederick the venerable archbishop of Magdeburg and his successors."[62] In contrast, the foundation charter makes no mention of the archbishop but rather contains a striking repetition of the idea of episcopal authority: The church (*locum*) is "in the episcopate of Havelberg," its lands cannot be transferred "outside the episcopate of Havelberg," ecclesiastical justice resides "with its bishops," recalcitrant advocates will be dealt with "by episcopal authority." Anselm himself is mentioned three times in the charter, in each instance with the designation "bishop of this same church [of Jerichow]" or "bishop of this same Jerichontine church."[63] The charter, in short, cut two ways by setting up a legal defense against the encroachments of both secular and ecclesiastical authorities.

Curiously, there is no provision made for the election of a new bishop after Anselm, something which Wigger put in the hands of the brothers in Leitzkau.[64] However, among the witnesses to the charter

---

[62] *UK* 123, p. 220.

[63] The reference to Anselm as *ejusdem ecclesie [i.e. Jerichow] episcopus* (which, by the way, in this first instance does not add the designation *Havelbergensis*) is repeated both with Anselm's name as a witness to the charter and in the dating of the charter to the sixteenth year "ordinacionis domini et venerabilis Anselmi Havelbergensis Episcopi et ejusdem Jerichontine Ecclesie" ("Stiftungs Urkunde von Jerichow," Winter, *Die Prämonstratenser*, p. 352). Wentz uses this as evidence that Anselm was, in effect, creating a provisional cathedral church out of Jerichow by taking this as his official title until Havelberg could be retaken ("Die staatsrechtliche Stellung," p. 271; "Havelberg, Jerichow und Broda," pp. 332-35; cf. Hucke, *Die Grafen von Stade*, pp. 168-69). While admitting the striking nature of the title, Kahl says that "die Wendung soll wohl nur [Anselms] Zuständigkeit als *episcopus loci* betonen" (*Slawen und Deutsche* 2:757 n. 21). Kahl is probably right. However, the title is also used in *UB Erzstifts Magdeburg* 255, p. 321 in which Anselm gives the farms in Erxleben to Our Lady in Magdeburg, and Kahl's "wohl nur" moderates what I see as a real concern on Anselm's part that at Jerichow's inception he be recognized as the authority of the new foundation.

[64] On Leitzkau see p. 55 above. The brothers in Jerichow did, in fact, claim the right of participation in the election of bishops of Havelberg. A sixteenth-century register for Jerichow lists a charter from 1276 in which "Guilielmus Havelbergensis episcopus [1220-1244] protulit laudum inter ecclesiam Havelbergensem et Hierichontanam super iure, quod habent Hierichontani in electionibus episcopi Havelbergensis." H. Krabbo, "Ein Verzeichnis von Urkunden des Prämonstratenserstifts Jerichow," *Geschichts Blätter für Stift und Land Magdeburg* 56-60 (1924), 102 nr. 14; Wentz, *Bistum Havelberg*, pp. 195-96; idem, "Die Staatsrechtliche Stellung," pp. 271 and 293 nr. 13. This right of election must go back to before the bishops were established in Havelberg, that is to Anselm. Wentz, *Bistum Havelberg*, p. 192; idem, "Havelberg, Jerichow und Broda," p. 332.

is one Walo, identified as the provost of Havelberg.[65] There was as yet no chapter in Havelberg in need of a provost, and yet in spite of this, documents issued soon thereafter show that Anselm clearly wanted his diocese defined in terms of the as yet inaccessible Havelberg rather than of Jerichow. Provost Walo appears as the first indication of Anselm's creation of his diocesan staff.

In December of 1144, Conrad III came to Magdeburg and issued several charters confirming Hartwig's gifts for the new foundation and those made to Archbishop Frederick.[66] The brief charter concerned specifically with the lands attached to the Jerichow foundation is for the most part copied from the list of gifts in the foundation charter and was probably drawn up by Anselm himself and presented for Conrad's seal.[67] There are, however, several important distinctions between the foundation charter and Conrad's. Most important, the foundation charter is concerned with what the lands are given for—a Norbertine foundation, whereas Conrad's charter is concerned with to whom the lands are given—*ad Havelbergensem ecclesiam*, a phrase which does not appear in the earlier charter. If the foundation charter identified Jerichow as being "in the episcopate of Havelberg," so too, it could be argued, were the lands given to Magdeburg. In Conrad's charter, the Norbertine foundation is not even

---

[65] A provost of Jerichow is not listed among the witnesses while Lambert, provost of Leitzkau, is. On Walo, who would succeed Anselm as bishop of Havelberg in 1155, see Wentz, "Havelberg, Jerichow und Broda," pp. 331-38 with the caveat that Wentz's assertion that Walo was behind the plan for Jerichow (pp. 334, 337-38) depends on reading his later career as bishop back into the story of the founding of Jerichow. In the documents relevant to the founding itself, his appearance among the witnesses to the foundation charter is the single mention of his name. Also Kahl, *Slawen und Deutsche* 1:456-57; 2:684-85 n. 53, 757-58 n. 21.

[66] *UK* 122, pp. 217-18 for the lands given to Havelberg; *UK* 123, pp. 219-22 and 125, pp. 223-26 for those given to Magdeburg, all dated December 31, 1144. Anselm is a witness to 123 and 125 as well as to 121, pp. 215-17 dated December 29, 1144.

[67] *UK* 122 has no witnesses and is dated "per manum Arnoldi cancellarii," a formula used generally for documents not actually drawn up by the imperial chancellery. See the editorial notes to *UK* 122, p. 218. Another charter issued to Anselm by Conrad in 1150 (p. 93 n. 87 below) uses this same formula instead of the usual "Ego Arnoldus cancellarius... recognavi." On the "Data per manum" formula in these documents, Bernhardi, *Konrad*, pp. 403 n. 25, 857 n. 48; Dombrowski, *Anselm*, p. 28; cf. Schlesinger, "Bemerkungen," p. 33. On the formula during Conrad's reign, Bernhardi, *Konrad*, p. 465 n. 1; in general, Julius Ficker, *Beiträge zur Urkundenlehre* 2 (1878, reprint: Aalen, 1966), pp. 221-37. One may note an example of this formula in a famous document sealed but most certainly not drawn up by King John of England: "Data per manum nostram in prato quod vocatur Ronimed."

mentioned; it is the Havelberg church that clearly gets the lands.[68] A further donation is also recorded in Conrad's charter, the village of Rogätz given by Otto of Hillersleben, again "to the Havelberg church," along with Conrad's confirmation of "whatever the three Ottonian emperors or Emperor Henry II gave to the aforementioned church."[69] Whereas the foundation charter emphasizes Anselm's power within the new foundation, Conrad's charter nicely conveys the claims of a bishop of Havelberg to his entire diocese and suggests, moreover, that Anselm had been working to extend his claims through negotiations with Otto of Hillersleben.[70] Though Anselm's name does not appear in Conrad's charter, it is perhaps significant that neither in the charters he witnessed at this time nor in those he witnessed thereafter does he use the ambiguous title *episcopus eiusdem Jerichontine ecclesie*. *Episcopus Havelbergensis* was enough.

The king spent the winter in Magdeburg, and for the first time Anselm was near Conrad's court for an extended period of time. What contact Anselm had with Conrad is not known. The Byzantine emperor, Manuel I Comnenus, had opened negotiations with Conrad and sent a delegation to arrange a marriage with Conrad's sister-in-law, Bertha of Sulzbach,[71] and it is within the realm of possibility that Conrad sought Anselm out to question him about the Byzantines.

Through a rather round-about process, Anselm had been forced off the fence separating the Welfs and the Hohenstaufen and had arrived back at the king's court. The provost of Bremen had donated lands meant to establish an anti-Welf alliance with Magdeburg and those lands included the new foundation at Jerichow. To become more than a bishop in exile, Anselm had to support the Hohenstaufen and their allies. Between March 13 and April 1145, Anselm appears as a witness to a charter drawn up in the king's chancellery

---

[68] In Conrad's charter the list of lands is prefaced with "Possessionum [of the Havelberg church] vero nomina hec sunt..." (*UK* 122, p. 218). Cf. to the foundation charter: "Hec est descriptio et denominatio bonorum et villarum, que illi Ecclesie [i.e. Jerichow] contulimus..." ("Stiftungs Urkunde von Jerichow," Winter, *Die Prämonstratenser*, p. 351).

[69] *UK* 122, p. 218.

[70] When Otto made his donation is not known (see the editorial comments to *UK* 122, p. 218); however, I strongly suspect the donation was fairly recent, namely sometime after the founding of Jerichow. Otherwise, Otto would have been giving land to a virtually nonexistent diocese.

[71] Bernhardi, *Konrad*, p. 412.

in which Archbishop Frederick promises to support Hartwig.[72] There is no reason to doubt Anselm's wholehearted concurrence. At any rate, in the coming months, Anselm would spend considerable time at the royal court.

---

[72] *UK* 125, p. 223-25, dated between March 13 and April 15 in Magdeburg; Dombrowski, *Anselm*, p. 29.

CHAPTER FIVE

THE WENDEN CRUSADE
AND EXILE TO HAVELBERG
1145-1152

While rendering valuable if brief assistance to Conrad III, for the most part Anselm would show himself far more committed to his now accessible diocese than to the Hohenstaufen. When the call for a crusade to the Holy Land took his ruler to Damascus, Anselm would throw his lot in with those German nobles who moved into the pagan lands east of the Elbe. Then, in a dramatic turn of the wheel of fortune, he would lose his standing at Conrad's court and find himself banished to Havelberg, a threatened outpost, there to live a quasi-monastic life and write the *Antikeimenon*.

The establishment of some authority in his own diocese meant that Anselm was no longer a bishop in exile. That authority was, however, limited and precarious, and Anselm did not have the means single-handedly to expand it. Conrad, Archbishop Frederick of Magdeburg, Hartwig of Bremen and Albert the Bear were now allied against Henry the Lion, and the evidence for Anselm's whereabouts in 1145 places him in the company of his archbishop[1] and his king. In May and again in August 1145, he was with his ruler and then remained with the court for the next seven months.[2]

What dealings he had with Jerichow during this time are unknown. However, this reemergence at court did not necessarily bring with it the full confidence of the king, and Anselm probably saw his best chance for future advancement in the new inroad into the Havelland and the possibilities it opened for expanding episcopal control

---

[1] *UB des Erzstifts Magdeburg* 258, pp. 326-28, after Feb. 15 and before Sept. 1, 1145.

[2] Anselm's movements with Conrad: in Worms, May 1145: *UK* 130, pp. 234-36; in Corvey, Aug.: *UK* 133, pp. 241-43; in Werden, Sept.: *UK* 135, pp. 244-45; in Kaiserwerth, Sept.: *UK* 136, pp. 245-47; in Elten, Oct.: *UK* 137, p. 247; in Utrecht, Oct.: *UK* 139-41, pp. 249-55; in Aachen, Dec.-Jan. 1146: *UK* 143-45, pp. 257-66; possibly into Mar.: *UK* 148, pp. 270-72. The last document is dated April 3, 1146, but Bernhardi calls this a scribal error and dates it to Jan. 3 (*Konrad*, p. 449). Dombrowski would date it to Mar. 5 (*Anselm*, p. 31).

over the rest of his diocese.[3] For one thing, Anselm apparently left the court early in 1146, after which his name appears on only a single document for the rest of the year. Moreover, that document is very much concerned with Jerichow.

The document in question was one which Anselm himself drew up, and it shows that he turned his attention to the Jerichow Norbertines. Already in the charter obtained from Conrad for Jerichow, Anselm had made the claims of his diocese clear by mentioning the donations of the Ottonian rulers and Henry II to Havelberg.[4] Now, sometime before Christmas 1146, he donated certain of those lands to the new foundation in Jerichow. His charter making these grants is a public document, not a private letter to a friend. Still, there is nothing formal about the opening lines. Touched, perhaps, with a hint of wry humor, they capture Anselm's situation as an exiled bishop so nicely that it is difficult to believe that they do not capture his feelings as well:

> Although my heart has often been moved to penance by pious and divine inspiration concerning whether I would ever be able to reform the episcopate of Havelberg, which bristled all over with the barbarism of pagan inhabitants and was almost nonexistent because of the destruction of the Christian religion, omnipotent God, who always deems it worthy to consider pious prayers, gave more than the longings of my soul and mind.

He expresses his deep appreciation to Our Lady of Magdeburg for helping with the foundation in Jerichow and to Hartwig for his donations. Then he is very explicit about defining Jerichow's purpose:

> Surely, [Hartwig] created this [foundation] with the intention that brothers from [the order of] our father Norbert of blessed memory should be gathered together there in an institution of regulars by whose holy way of life that vicious and perverse generation may be corrected.[5]

Actually, the foundation charter, which more than anything should have made Hartwig's intentions clear, says nothing at all about the Slavs, that *generatio prava atque perversa*, but only that Jerichow is to be

---

[3] The archive of Jerichow, which might have provided documentation for Anselm's activities, was, after considerable peregrination, lost in the Thirty Years War. Wentz, "Staatsrechtliche Stellung," pp. 266-67.

[4] See p. 68 above. On these early donations, Schlesinger, "Stiftungsurkunde des Bistums Havelberg," pp. 2-6.

[5] *Hamburgisches UB* 180, pp. 169-70; Winter, "Zur Geschichte," pp. 150-51; Dombrowski, *Anselm*, pp. 31-32.

a memorial to Norbert of Magdeburg. In Anselm's charter, Jerichow is the answer to the prayers of the bishop of Havelberg; and if it memorializes Norbert, it is Norbert the preacher, for the brothers are there to help their bishop re-Christianize his diocese.

Anselm then proceeds to grant the town of Marienburg (Kablitz) and its eleven villages to Jerichow, saying that these had been given to the episcopate of Havelberg by Emperor Otto, which is to say sometime in the latter part of the tenth century.[6] This was Anselm's only legal claim, one perhaps hallowed by age but undoubtedly somewhat obscure to those presently in possession of those villages which had survived the past century and a half. Still, aside from Hartwig's recent grant, the old charters were all Anselm had at hand to establish a territorial claim beyond the town of Jerichow, and he made the best of them.[7]

Finally, in this charter Anselm creates the archpresbyterate of Jerichow, its borders defined as the Elbe on the west, the Havel on the east, the Strume on the south, and Klitzsee and the province of Schollene on the north, in short an administrative district covering that territory to which Anselm had access.[8]

Far from showing no interest in his diocese, Anselm had deliberately moved toward creating a secure position for himself as bishop of Havelberg, and the charters concerned with the Norbertines in Jerichow show his tracks. In the foundation charter, it is clear that An-

---

[6] Which Otto is not stated. See Wentz, *Bistum Havelberg*, p. 192.

[7] Five of the eleven villages listed in Anselm's charter can be identified (Wentz, *Bistum Havelberg*, p. 107). For three of these Wentz finds evidence that Jerichow did not acquire them until much later, and he suggests that an 1159 confirmation charter of Pope Hadrian IV describes Anselm's donation in more realistic terms: "curtem de Burward Kobelitz, que et Marienburgk dicitur, intra vallum antiquum sitam cum stagno et villa, que similiter Cabelitz vocatur." Wentz concludes by calling Anselm's use of the imperial charter an "Archaismus, der vielleicht zur gelegentlichen Verwendung bei Verfechtung bischöflicher Prätensionen beabsichtigt worden ist" ("Die staatsrechtliche Stellung," pp. 271-72).

[8] The Havel River could have served as the northern border as well as the eastern since it runs north of the artificial Klietz-Schollene line and then turns west to the Elbe. Wentz says the course of the Havel was not used in order to leave the land north of the artificial border and below the Havel free for Provost Walo of Havelberg ("Havelberg, Jerichow und Broda," p. 333). Again, Wentz is making more of Walo's involvement than the sources permit (see p. 67 n. 65 above). On the one hand, the land north of the Klietz-Schollene line may have been threatened or held by Wends (as was Havelberg). On the other hand, if there was some access to this area, Anselm would have been just as interested as his provost in keeping the land close to Havelberg unattached to Jerichow.

selm, as bishop, is to have authority in the Jerichow foundation; in Conrad's confirmation charter, the bishop's authority over his entire episcopate is stressed; and in Anselm's grant to Jerichow, a full-fledged bishop emerges taking care of a foundation within his diocese. It is, moreover, a diocese with a purpose: to "correct" the Slavs. Anselm says this will be due to the holy life of the brothers, which can only mean he expected missionary work to begin. Events beyond his control, however, were moving things toward a rather less peaceful form of conversion.

In December 1146, Anselm was again with the king, this time in Weinheim on the way to a large meeting of the king's court in Speyer. At this *Hoftag* he met with his old friends Wibald and Arnold. In earlier months Anselm had come in frequent contact with these two men since they both served at the royal court. Conrad had chosen Wibald as the new abbot of Corvey, and he was invested with this office on December 12. Wibald, whose health was poor, had hoped to avoid the onerous responsibility of Corvey and had asked Arnold and Anselm to try to dissuade Conrad from proceeding with the investiture.[9] That he asked this of his friends shows that he thought they had some leverage with the king, but it may be suggested that Anselm's was influence by association rather than his own. As Conrad's chancellor and close adviser, Arnold was obviously someone who might influence the king, but the most that can be said of Anselm is that Wibald did not think his bishop friend would detract from Arnold's ability to persuade. It is doubtful that Anselm could have added to it. While Anselm did accompany Conrad's court for several months, Wibald's request for his assistance and Conrad's own choice of Anselm to serve on a delegation to the pope shortly thereafter are the only times anything like a close relationship is found between the bishop and the ruler. On both occasions Anselm's participation may have been due to his own friendship with a friend of the king (he went with Arnold on Wibald's behalf and with Wibald to see the pope). Later events would show that however close Anselm's relationship with Conrad may have appeared, below the surface it was shallow and precarious.

---

[9] Wibald, 150, p. 241. See Jakobi, *Wibald von Stablo*, p. 82; Wolter, *Arnold von Wied*, pp. 23-24. The situation in Corvey was by no means clear. Henry, the deposed abbot, was on his way to Rome to have his case reviewed. For a summary of these events see Hausmann, *Reichskanzlei*, pp. 191-92.

In Speyer, Anselm met Bernard of Clairvaux who had come with a very definite mission in mind. On March of the previous year, the famous abbot had stood before a huge crowd in Vézelay and read the declaration *Quantum praedecessores* of Pope Eugenius III declaring a new crusade to the Holy Land. The French were caught up in a spirit of excitement for the new venture, and many nobles threw in their lot with their pious King Louis to set forth after a year of planning.[10] Never one to do things by halves, Bernard began preaching the crusade far and wide. In November this brought him to Conrad's court in Frankfurt where his attempts to get the king to join the crusade were unproductive. Then in December at Speyer with Anselm in attendance,[11] Bernard performed Mass and preached before the court. At the end of his sermon, he pictured Conrad not as king but as a man standing before Christ at the Judgment and being asked: "O man! What should I have done for you which I did not do?" Through his tears, Conrad proclaimed himself ready to show his thanks and serve his God. As the crowd gave voice to its joy, Bernard thrust the banner from the altar into Conrad's hands to take with him to the Holy Land.[12]

In Bernard's entourage were several men eager to prove the sanctity of their master and the validity of his call for a crusade. To this end they recorded hundreds of miracles performed by Bernard as he moved from place to place calling for volunteers to go to the Holy Land. Anselm is named among those whom Bernard healed. As reported, Anselm was suffering from a headache and a sore throat and asked Bernard to cure him. To this Bernard responded jokingly (*jocunde*): "If you had the faith of little girls, perhaps you could cure yourself." "And if I do not have faith," Anselm said, "your faith will make me whole." And Bernard healed him.[13]

---

[10] Virginia G. Berry, "The Second Crusade," in Marshall Baldwin, ed., *The First Hundred Years*, 2nd ed, vol 1 of Kenneth Setton, ed., *A History of the Crusades* (Madison, 1969), pp. 467-69.

[11] Anselm's presence in Speyer: *UK* 164-165, pp. 295-300; n. 13 below.

[12] *Sancti Bernardi vita prima* 6.1.4.15, PL 185:382; Berry, "Second Crusade," p. 474; Bernhardi, *Konrad*, p. 531.

[13] *Sancti Bernardi vita prima* 6.1.5.19, PL 185:384AB. On this incident see Berges, "Anselm von Havelberg," p. 43; Morrison, "Anselm of Havelberg: Play and the Dilemma of Historical Progress," p. 229; for the recording of Bernard's miracles at this time: Benedicta Ward, *Miracles and the Medieval Mind: Theory, Record and Event 1000-1215* (Philadelphia, 1987), pp.180-83. Miracles are a realm difficult for a historian to enter. Thus, I relegate my interpretation to a footnote: Given the number of

But however great Bernard's faith may have been, the problems which beset his crusade were not so easy to cure. For one thing, Pope Eugenius III, like Innocent II before him, had come north of the Alps looking for help. In Rome, a republican commune held sway; and once again, a pope needed a German army to get him back into the city of St. Peter. Eugenius was none too happy that, due to Bernard's persistence, Conrad had decided to take his army elsewhere. For his part, Conrad needed papal approval of his decision to join the crusade, and he decided to send a delegation to the pope.[14] As a first step in this direction, he called Wibald to meet him in Fulda.[15] Anselm also joined the court and accompanied it to Frankfurt where preparations were made for the coming crusade.[16]

As more and more nobles made their decision to join the expedition, dissent was voiced by the Saxons who saw this as an opportunity to attack the Slavs on their eastern border.[17] While the motives

---

miracles recorded by Bernard's scribes, I suspect the recorders saw any change in anyone who came into contact with him as a miracle. Anselm is said to have suffered pain in the head and the throat about which Bernard joked. I would suggest that Bernard would not joke about real pain but that he would have scorned anyone whose head was so muddled as to think the crusade was not a good idea or whose throat would not open to lend a voice of support for it. Bernard's "miracle" may have been one of persuasion.

[14] Berry, "Second Crusade," pp. 475-77.

[15] The *Chronographus Corbeiensis* says that a man who had taken the crusader's cross was sent to fetch Wibald (Jaffé, *Bibliotheca rerum Germanicarum* 1, *Monumenta Corbeiensia* (Berlin 1864), pp. 53-54. Jaffé identifies the man as Anselm, saying he is referred to as a crusader because of his vow to go on the Saxon campaign against the Slavs (p. 54 n. 3; see also Hausmann, *Reichskanzlei*, p. 193; Bernhardi, *Konrad*, p. 351 n. 35). If Jaffé is right, then the Saxons must have decided on a campaign into the Wendenland when Conrad took the cross in December 1146. The passage is, however, far from clear. The first certain mention of Saxons deciding to attack the Slavs rather than the Moslems is at the *Reichstag* held in Frankfurt in late February 1147, and the crusade against the Slavs was not proclaimed publicly by the pope until April. In short, the insignia of a crusader speaks for someone other than Anselm in January 1147. Was it perhaps Arnold of Wied, also Wibald's close friend and a man who did go with Conrad to the Holy Land?

[16] Anselm in Fulda: *UK* 167-68, pp. 302-5; in Regensburg: *UK* 172, pp. 311-12; 174, pp. 314-15; on the call for the crusade in Regensburg: *Gesta Friderici* 1.42, p. 60; Anselm in Bishofsheim on the Tauber: *UK* 175, pp. 15-16; in Frankfurt: *UK* 178, pp. 320-21; 182, pp. 328-30. See also Bernhardi, *Konrad*, pp. 543, 546-47; Dombrowski, *Anselm*, p. 23.

[17] *Gesta Friderici* 1.42, p. 61; *Annales Palidenses*, ed. Georg Heinrich Pertz (Hanover, 1859), MGH SS 16:82. Critical of the goals of the crusaders is Vincent of Prague: "Sed quia Saxones potius pro auferenda eis terra, quam pro fide christiana confirmanda tantam moverant militiam," *Annales*, ed. Wilhelm Wattenbach (Hanover, 1861), MGH SS 17:663. This critical estimation has been accepted by many histo-

of the Germans were not untouched by a sense of the religious nature of a crusade, some were interested in seizing land, others viewed the Wends as friends and were less enthusiastic about, if committed to, the venture.[18] Even Archbishop Frederick was apparently thinking of expanding Magdeburg's sway into Pomerania at the expense of supporting his own suffragan bishops.[19] Bernard was aware that the enterprise could get sidetracked, and he did his best to prevent this. In a letter written to win support for the crusade, he promised those who moved against the Wends the same remission of sins as had been granted the main body of crusaders, but he added that "they should on no account enter into a pact with [the pagans] either for money or tribute until either their cult or their nation is destroyed."[20]

Bernard may have overstepped his bounds in giving consent for this northern crusade, and Conrad had himself accepted the cross

---

rians, e.g. Eric Christiansen, *The Northern Crusades: The Baltic and Catholic Frontier 1110-1525* (Minneapolis, 1980), p. 52. For an opposing view, emphasizing spiritual motives, Hans-Dietrich Kahl, "Zum Ergebnis des Wendenkreuzzugs von 1147. Zugleich ein Beitrag zur Geschichte des sächsischen Frühchristentums," *Wichmann-Jahrbuch* 11/12 (1957/58), 99-120; idem, *Slawen und Deutsche* 1:222-227; Friedrich Lotter, "Bemerkungen zur Christianisierung der Abodriten," in *Festschrift für Walter Schlesinger* 2, ed. Helmut Beumann, Mitteldeutsche Forschungen 74/2 (Cologne, 1974), pp. 395-442. The best treatment is Lotter's *Die Konzeption des Wendenkreuzzugs. Ideengeschichtliche, kirchenrechtliche und historisch-politische Voraussetzungen der Missionierung von Elb- und Ostseeslawen um die Mitte des 12. Jahrhunderts, Vorträge und Forschungen*: Sonderband 23 (Sigmaringen, 1977), pp. 70-75. For a succinct account, see Bernard Töpfer and Evamaria Engel, *Vom staufischen Imperium zum Hausmachtkönigtum: Deutsche Geschichte vom Wormser Konkordat 1122 bis zur Doppelwahl von 1314* (Weimar, 1976), pp. 41-43.

[18] Lotter, *Die Konzeption des Wendenkreuzzugs*, pp. 70-75, pointing out that the ill-defined nature of a crusade in which the participants held such different views of its goals led to constant bickering. See also Giles Constable, "The Second Crusade as Seen by Contemporaries," *Traditio* 9 (1953), 224-26, 237-44; Johannes Schultze, "Der Wendenkreuzzug 1147 und die Adelherrschaften in Prignitz und Rhingebiet," *JGMOD* 2 (1953), 95-98; Margret Bünding-Naujoks, *Das Imperium Christianum und die deutschen Ostkirche vom Zehnten bis zum zwölften Jahrhundert*, Historische Studien 366 (Berlin, 1940), pp. 38-42; Curschmann, *Die Diozese Brandenburg*, pp. 53-59.

[19] Jürgen Petersohn, *Der südliche Ostseeraum im kirchlich-politischen Kräftespiel des Reichs, Polens und Dänemarks vom 10. bis 13. Jahrhundert: Mission-Kirchenorganisation-Kultpolitik*, Vergangenheit und Gegenwart 17 (Cologne, 1979), pp. 344-49.

[20] Ep. 457, PL 182:652. On Bernard's apparent call to convert or kill the Slavs (the "Taufe oder Tod" referred to by German historians) see Lotter's study, *Die Konzeption des Wendenkreuzzugs*. Lotter argues that Bernard meant not the massacre of unbaptized Slavs but their destruction as a national entity, which would be preserved should they convert. I must say that Bernard was asking a lot of the crusaders if he expected them to follow the niceties of this distinction. For the older opinion that Bernard was out for Slavic blood, see Helmut Beumann, "Kreuzzugsgedanke und Ostpolitik im hohen Mittelalter," *HJ* 72 (1953), 125-27.

without the pope's permission.[21] It was therefore imperative that all this be cleared up with Pope Eugenius, who was with King Louis VII of France in Dijon. To that city Conrad sent a delegation comprised of Anselm, Wibald, Bishop Bucco of Worms, and other churchmen[22] with a letter explaining the king's decision to take the cross and describing his preparations for the expedition to the Holy Land. Conrad also invited the pope to a diet in Strasbourg and presented his three legates as having the power to act in his behalf.[23]

The legates arrived in Dijon at the end of the month and were received *benigne et honorifice* by the pope.[24] It must have been from this delegation that Eugenius first heard of the idea for a northern crusade, and this by word of mouth for the letters the delegates brought from Conrad do not mention it. Wibald could have found some motive for advocating the idea in an old claim of Corvey's to the Slavic held island of Rügen, but his main concern in meeting with the pope was to get support for his two abbeys and to secure Eugenius' approval of Conrad's decision to go to the Holy Land.[25] Anselm, on the other hand, was confronted with the fact that an army was going to march into the very lands he had hoped to convert through the spiritual life of his fellow Norbertines, and he had every

---

[21] Berry, "Second Crusade," p. 479 n. 15; cf. Lotter, "Bemerkungen," pp. 403-4; Constable, "The Second Crusade," pp. 256-75 with n. 222. Constable is of the opinion that Bernard's letter was written after Eugenius had issued *Divina dispensatione* in which he approved the Saxon expedition (see p. 78 below). Constable cites "Bernard's extreme deference in taking up the preaching of the crusade" as evidence that Bernard would have been careful neither to extend the crusade to include the Wends nor to grant indulgences to these crusaders without the approval of the pope. While Constable may be right about when Bernard wrote the letter, it must be noted that the saint showed no deference at all to the pope when he preached the crusade to the Holy Land to Conrad in Speyer, for Conrad was careful to apologize for taking the cross without papal permission in a letter sent to the pope in Dijon (*UK* 184, see n. 23 below). Even if Bernard was not willing to go so far as to grant indulgences to the Saxon crusaders in Frankfurt, I doubt whether this enthusiastic supporter of the crusade to the Holy Land placed a barrier of caution in front of the Saxons.

[22] Peter Acht, "Die Gesandtschaft König Konrads III. an Papst Eugen III. in Dijon," *HJ* 74 (1955), 668-73. Acht has edited a papal charter from Dijon giving the names of the delegates, pp. 672-73.

[23] *UK* 184, pp. 332-33.

[24] Wibald, 35, p. 114. The only accounts of this meeting are given in this letter and letter 150, pp. 242-43. Constable, "The Second Crusade," pp. 278-79; Bünding-Naujoks, *Das Imperium Christianum*, pp. 39-40; Acht, "Die Gesandtschaft."

[25] Jakobi, *Wibald von Stablo*, pp. 95-96, 100; Curschmann, *Die Diozese Brandenburg*, pp. 5-7, 66-67.

reason to be concerned about defining the role a military force would assume in this missionary effort.[26]

On the whole, Eugenius was being presented with a *fait accompli* and was hardly in a position to refuse permission to either Conrad or the Saxons to go on their respective crusades. His hoped for support against the Roman commune was not to be had, and now the Germans were showing themselves unable even to mount a concerted effort against the Muslims. Whether Eugenius found this discouraging or took heart in the idea that he was now at the head of a great crusade against pagans on all the borders of Christendom,[27] he did not show any inclination to better his relations with Conrad (whom he had not met), for he turned down the legates' invitation to visit the German king in Strasbourg. Moreover, the pope viewed the Saxon crusade with a wary eye. Eugenius' bull *Divina dispensatione* concerning the crusade against the Slavs and issued shortly after meeting with Conrad's delegation, reveals a pope troubled by a sense that the crusaders might end up quarreling among themselves or that the crusade would not be used primarily to advance Christianity in these pagan lands. These misgivings must have come from Anselm whom Eugenius chose as his legate specifically to help maintain peace within the army and to keep that army from realizing mere secular ambitions. The bishop was not, then, simply acting as the mouthpiece of the Saxons. He gave the pope his honest and accurate appraisal of their attitudes about the Slavs. His reward was to be made the legate of the pope himself with orders to keep the Saxons in line. Undoubtedly he took pride in Eugenius' description of him:

> Because we judge it to be expedient that some spiritual, discerning, learned person be among you [i.e. the Saxon crusaders] who will provide for your peace and tranquillity, preserve unity among you, and impress upon you [the need] to further the Christian religion, we have provided for this our venerable brother A[nselm], bishop of Havelberg, a spiritual, discerning and learned man; and this responsibility we have given to him.[28]

---

[26] Kahl, *Slawen und deutsche* 1:229-33.

[27] The crusade also included Spain. See Constable, "The Second Crusade," *passim*, esp. pp. 221-22, 227-35.

[28] Eugenius III, *Epistolae et privilegia* 166, PL 180:1203CD. This bull was issued on April 11 in Troyes. On the possibility that Anselm went with Eugenius to Troyes see Kahl, *Slawen und Deutsche* 2:751 n. 250. The evidence is far from conclusive.

The pope then went with King Louis to Clairvaux to see Bernard, and the delegation returned to the King Conrad's court, which was by then in Nuremberg.[29]

And what of Anselm's relationship to King Conrad and his court? The delegation to Dijon was the culmination of Anselm's service to Conrad III, and it was only superficially successful. Even the explanations of Conrad's decision to go on the crusade had not been enough to get the pope to visit the ruler. A pope suspicious of Conrad could not but make Conrad suspicious of that pope. Moreover, this separate Saxon campaign into the Havelland robbed Conrad of part of the army he was preparing to take to the Holy Land. With which expedition would his counselors go? There was nothing in a northern crusade to tempt Arnold of Wied, and he joined his ruler. Wibald had just been made abbot of Corvey by Conrad, and so was serving his ruler by staying home and even joining the Saxon crusade to defend territorial claims of Corvey to Rügen. And Anselm? If the bishop of Havelberg had been uninterested in his diocese, if he had been the close friend of his king, and if service at the court of that king had been all important to him, he should have been able to bargain that friendship and his earlier experience as a legate to Constantinople into a place of prominence among those going to the East with the ruler.[30] By becoming a papal legate and going to the Havelland rather than to the Holy Land, Anselm hardly communicated allegiance to his ruler. Should anything go wrong, the bishop of Havelberg had inadvertently set himself up as the scapegoat.

From Nuremberg, Anselm and Wibald made their way to Magdeburg, where the army for the northern crusade was assembling. In July, 1147, the Wenden Crusade began.[31]

The crusaders' plan of attack was to advance into Pomerania in two armies.[32] One army, under Henry the Lion, moved north against the forces of the Slavic Prince Niclot. This army managed to besiege the prince in the fortified town of Dobin and forced these Wends to accept baptism; but this was merely a diplomatic way to end hostili-

---

[29] *UK* 189, pp. 342-45, dated April 24, 1147.

[30] Constable, "The Second Crusade," p. 264 n. 263.

[31] Schultze, "Die Wendenkreuzzug 1147," p. 114.

[32] On the Wenden Crusade see the works referred in notes 10, 17, 18, 19, 20 above; also Bernhardi, *Konrad*, pp. 563-78; Brüske, *Untersuchungen*, pp. 106-12.

ties, for the besiegers apparently never expected the Wends to leave their pagan cult for longer than it took the Saxon army to disperse.[33]

Anselm himself remained with the second army.[34] Its goal was Niclot's second stronghold at Demmin, a town lying some seventy miles north-east of Havelberg. This army, under the command of Albert the Bear and Conrad of Meissen, crossed the Elbe and captured Havelberg. As far as the record shows, it was the first time Anselm had visited the town.[35] The army then made its way to Malchow near Lake Moritz and burned a nearby pagan temple.[36] Moving on to Demmin, the crusaders broke into two groups. One, including Wibald, stayed to besiege the town. The other, under Albert, continued on to Stettin at the mouth of the Oder River.

Anselm almost assuredly went with Albert. There are two interpretations of the advance on Stettin. One is that, in effect, Albert turned his back on the spiritual ideals of the crusade and went off to grab land for himself.[37] If this was the case, Anselm's duty was to stay close to Albert and in so far as possible, try to keep his actions in line with

---

[33] Helmold, *Cronica Slavorum*, 65, ed. Bernard Schmeidler (Hanover, 1909), MGH SrG 32:122.

[34] Anselm among participants of the crusade: *Annales Magdeburgenses*, MGH SS 16:188; *Annales Palidenses*, MGH SS 16:82; *Chronicon Montis Sereni*, MGH SS 23:147. See also the *Regesta archiepiscopatus Magdeburgensis* 1143, p. 449; 1219, p. 489.

[35] Bernhardi, *Konrad*, p. 575 n. 35. In 1157 Archbishop Wichmann of Magdeburg issued a charter concerning a donation which it describes as having been confirmed by Archbishop Frederick "penes Havelberch" in the presence of secular lords "cum collecti essent ibi in expeditione versus Dimin" (*UB Erzstifts Magdeburg* 294, p. 366). This is not to say that Havelberg was the assembly ground for the army or that it had been in German hands before the crusade. Wibald of Stablo speaks of the entire army crossing the Elbe: "Intraveramus cum armata milicia et exercitu christianorum principum terram Leuticiorum transmisso Albi flumine" (Wibald 150, p. 244). Schultz suggests that once the army had arrived at Havelberg, the opportunity was seized "zur Einsetzung Anselms in seinem Bischofssitz, Errichtung einer Kapelle und zur Säuberung der Umgebung." ("Die Wendenkreuzzug 1147," p. 115). As Wentz points out, there is no direct evidence of this; but he goes further by contending that "der Umstand, dass Erzbischof Friedrich 'bei' Havelberg und nicht 'in' der Stadt urkundet, lässt es zweifelhaft erscheinen, dass die Truppe in Havelberg Quartier bezogen hat" ("Havelberg, Jerichow und Broda," p. 335). Apparently this is supposed to mean that Anselm still could not get into the town. This is hard to accept. If anything, Havelberg was too small for the army. The church itself probably offered the only defensible position for the Wends, and the crusaders would have made short work of it if, as is most probable, it and the town had not already been abandoned.

[36] *Annales Magdeburgenses*, MGH SS 16:188.

[37] Berry, "Second Crusade," p. 494; Bernhardi, *Konrad*, pp. 576-77; Christiansen, *The Northern Crusades*, p. 53; Bünding-Naujoks, *Das Imperium Christianum*, p. 49; Brüske, *Untersuchungen*, p. 109.

the exhortations of the pope. The second interpretation is that the capture of Stettin was part of the crusader's original plan for their campaign.[38] In this case, again Anselm would probably have stayed with Albert in the capture of one of the major goals of the crusade.

Anselm could be grateful that the crusade brought him to Havelberg. Still, it is questionable whether this student of Norbert of Magdeburg thought that the armed knight could or should replace the poor man of Christ in converting the Slavs, and he may have had doubts about the entire expedition.[39] As papal legate, his job was to keep the crusaders unified and to make sure that whatever they accomplished would, in some way, lend itself to advancing Christianity. Perhaps he hoped that in contrast to what had happened in the Holy Land, the strongholds taken or built by the crusaders in Slavic territory would not serve ambitious men in increasing their power but rather constitute secure places from which real missionary work could proceed. Had things gone properly, at least Anselm's diocese should have been made a secure place for the missionary work of his brother Norbertines.

Things did not go properly. At Demmin the crusaders bickered among themselves. Wibald gave up on the possibility of success and, after little more than a month in the field, returned home.[40] At Stettin the crusaders surrounded the city and prepared to attack. Then, to their astonishment, crosses appeared on the walls. Two men emerged from the city gates to speak with the leaders of the army. One was Ratibor, the prince of the Liutizians, and the other presented himself as Albert, the bishop of the city since its conversion some twenty years before by Otto of Bamberg! The bishop had some questions for these unexpected and now rather embarrassed visitors: Why had they come with weapons drawn? If they wanted to strengthen the faith of the inhabitants of the city, would preaching not be better than swords? The report of this meeting says that because the Saxon princes had come to conquer rather than for the sake of the Christian religion, Ratibor and Albert spoke with the

---

[38] Kahl, "Zum Ergebnis des Wendenkreuzzugs," pp. 117-18. Kahl suggests that Anselm himself first called for the attack on Stettin (p. 118). There is no evidence for this. A far more likely candidate is Archbishop Frederick of Magdeburg, as Petersohn forcefully argues, *Der südliche Ostseeraum*, pp. 343-49.

[39] Kahl thinks Anselm saw the crusade as "eine Katastrophe" for missionary work across the Elbe (*Slawen und Deutsche* 1:231). Forced conversion had been officially rejected by the church; see Lotter, *Die Konzeption des Wendenkreuzzugs*, pp. 34-38.

[40] Wibald, 150, p. 245; Bernhardi, *Konrad*, p. 576.

Saxon bishops and concluded a peace.[41] Most likely, Bishop Anselm played a leading role in this council for the next summer Ratibor came to Havelberg to parley with the Saxon princes. The peace concluded at Stettin took the wind out of the crusade, and the invading army withdrew. The Wenden Crusade was over.[42]

Havelberg was now in German hands, and less than a year later, in the summer of 1148, Prince Ratibor came there to meet the Saxon leaders. Some indication of Anselm's presence is found in the oath Ratibor took in Havelberg. The Slavic prince professed his faith and promised "always to defend and spread the Christian religion with all his strength."[43] In that oath is a clear echo of Eugenius' injunction to Anselm to guide the crusade toward advancing Christianity.

Not that Anselm thought that much had been accomplished by the military expedition across the Elbe. In the *Antikeimenon*, written shortly afterwards, he mentions Liutizia among the areas into which Norbert's order had spread;[44] but he says not a word about the crusade—and this in a work dedicated to Pope Eugenius III and to be read by Anselm's brothers, who would have noticed the omission. Anselm's and the pope's fears about the crusade had proven accurate, and in a work meant to tout Christianity's successes, the bishop apparently thought it best to pass over the Wenden Crusade in silence.

In 1148, Anselm also visited his old companion Henry of Mainz in Erfurt,[45] and he participated in a commission called to mediate the disputed election of a new provost at Gratia Dei, southeast of Magdeburg and founded by Norbert apparently as a step toward organizing his diocese for missionary work.[46] The brothers there had fallen

---

[41] Vincent of Prague, *Annales*, MGH SS 17: 663.

[42] Vincent of Prague ends his description of the crusade by saying: "Ubi etenim Deus non fuit in causa, bono fine terminari difficillimum fuit" (*Annales*, MGH SS 17:663). Perhaps the best summation of the expedition is found in the *Magdeburger Schöppenchronik*, p. 16: "Van disser vart sint ganze bose gemaket und geschreven. We dat weten wil, de mach dar lesen, wat jammers do in der werlde was." On the secular success of the crusade see Kahl's article, "Zum Ergebnis des Wendenkreuzzugs;" also Christiansen, *The Northern Crusades*, pp. 53-54.

[43] *Annales Magdeburgenses*, MGH SS 16:190 Riedel, "Nachrichten," p. 240; Winter, *Die Prämonstratenser*, pp. 162-63; Petersohn, *Der südliche Ostseeraum*, pp. 347-48.

[44] *Antik.* 1.10, 1155B.

[45] *Mainzer UB* 2.1, 106, pp. 202-5, dated to February, 1148; probable presence at a meeting of Saxon bishops and princes in July: *Regesta archiepiscopatus Magdeburgensis* 1228-29, pp. 492-93; Dombrowski, *Anselm*, p. 36.

[46] Grauwen, *Norbertus Aartsbisschop*, pp. 438-69, esp. pp. 439-41; Claude, *Geschichte des Erzbistums Magdeburg* 2:338.

to quarreling among themselves over the selection of a provost and had asked Anselm "and other fathers" to assist them. One Lambert from Our Lady was chosen, but "with Bishop Anselm resisting for some time because [Lambert] had a shallow knowledge of the Scriptures." Anselm's criticism is interesting, coming as it does from a disciple of Norbert whose leadership depended far more on personal charisma than on learning. While Lambert did end up providing the leadership necessary to end dissension among the brothers of Gratia Dei, Anselm's doubts may have been prompted by a concern that the new provost be able to lead his brothers into the mission field as well. For this, piety alone was apparently not enough.[47]

Anselm also paid attention to Jerichow. The Norbertines whom he had established there were having a problem with, of all things, noise. The old cloister was on the main thoroughfare of this lively, little town, and the good brothers found that the noise of the market-place interrupted their devotions. To give them a quiet place to worship, Anselm arranged to exchange some land held by Havelberg for a piece of property on the quiet north-western side of town where a new church could be built.[48] The land was purchased from Magdeburg, and Archbishop Frederick's confirmation charter of the transaction shows that Anselm had moved to secure his position in Havelberg. The donation of Hartwig of Bremen, made originally for a foundation of canons regular in the diocese of Havelberg, is referred to as a donation "to St. Mary's in Havelberg," the first mention of Anselm's newly acquired cathedral. Beyond Havelberg itself, however, the material possessions of the diocese had apparently not grown, for Anselm traded land from Hartwig's original donation for the property on which the new church in Jerichow would be built.[49]

Late in 1148, Anselm was visited by a papal delegation on its way to Poland. Its leader brought a letter from the papal chancellor,

---

[47] *Fundatio monasterii Gratiae Dei* 11, MGH SS 20:690; Claude, *Geschichte des Erzbistums Magdeburg* 2:390-91.

[48] *UB des Erzstifts Magdeburg* 268, pp. 336-37. Since Hartwig of Bremen had given the town of Jerichow itself to Magdeburg, the exchange was made with Archbishop Frederick. See the *Regesta archiepiscopatus Magdeburgensis* 1230, p. 492 and pp. 65-66 above. To this day and in spite of the Elbe having changed course to the west, the town of Jerichow has hardly spread beyond the church.

[49] *UB des Erzstifts Magdeburg* 268, p. 337. Anselm gave up eleven *mansi* in the village of Nizinthorp. The limits of Anselm's authority in Jerichow are also quite clear. Frederick was careful to state that the exchange would not effect his claims to the fortifications and village of Jerichow. Anselm retained control of the congregation and church.

Guido, whom Anselm had met in Dijon. Writing to his "dear brother and friend," he requested that Anselm write him in return and wished him well.[50] The letter is a sign of the extent of Anselm's circle of contacts which reached as far as Italy and the papal court; and Margrave Conrad of Meissen may have had this in mind when, early in 1149, he asked Anselm to visit the pope. Here was Anselm's chance to do a good turn for a powerful secular lord, renew his contact with Chancellor Guido and the pope, and reaffirm his good relations with Our Lady in Magdeburg, for Gerhard, its provost, was chosen for the trip, as well. The business to be conducted did not pose serious problems: The cloister of Niemegk, which had been founded by Conrad's parents, was unable to support itself; and Conrad wanted to transfer ownership to nearby Monte Sereni. Anselm and Gerhard's task was to get papal permission for this transaction. As far as is known, this is the only business Anselm had to conduct on his trip to Italy, a trip which was to cost him a lot of trouble and more than a little despair.[51]

Anselm dashed off a letter to Wibald, showing some aggravation with his friend for not writing. To goad him into sending a letter in return, Anselm says that he is leaving to see the pope *in dominica esto mihi* (February 13), and "if there is anything you want to ask [the pope], you can do it through your me [*per me tuum*] as if through yourself."[52] Wibald responded warmly with a letter in which he asks for help. Abbot Ado of Harsefeld had been forced out of his monastery by the monks and had come to Wibald for help. Taking Anselm at his word, Wibald requests that the bishop intercede with the pope on behalf of Ado. Not to be outdone in the game of meshing identities, he goes on:

---

[50] Wibald, 121, p. 195. A second letter from Guido to "karissimo fratri et speciali amico Anselmo" saying much the same thing is probably from this same period, Wibald, 122, p. 196. Dombrowski, *Anselm*, p. 37. For Guido's presence in Dijon see Acht, "Die Gesandtschaft," p. 672.

[51] Anselm was probably in Magdeburg when Conrad asked him to go to Italy: *UB des Erzstifts Magdeburg* 269, pp. 337-39, dated Jan. 15, 1149. Conrad's request that Anselm go to Italy: *Chronicon Montis Sereni*, MGH SS 23:147; see also Claude, *Geschichte des Erzbistums Magdeburg* 2:400-1. On Niemegk and Conrad, Willy Hoppe, "Markgraf Konrad von Meissen der Reichsfürst und der Gründer des wettinischen Staates," in Hoppe, *Die Mark Brandenburg Wettin und Magdeburg: Ausgewählte Aufsätze*, ed. Herbert Ludat (Cologne, 1965), p. 199.

[52] Wibald, 158, p. 263; Morrison, "Anselm of Havelberg," p. 229. See also pp. 19-20 above.

Whatever you do for [Ado], you do for me. You see how unmindful I am of you! This does not say "I was," because it speaks of the present and the future. Thus it is "I am," which is the present that is eternal.[53]

He closes saying that he would appreciate Anselm's work on the creation of the angels for his own study of the subject.[54]

Anselm made the trip to Italy in the company of Hartwig, the man who had donated the lands for the Jerichow foundation and now the archbishop elect of Bremen going to receive the pallium of his new office from the pope. The delegation met with Eugenius in March or April 1149 in Tusculum.[55] A Greek delegation had recently visited the curia. Its leader was a very learned man who spoke at length about the differences between Greek and Latin beliefs and rites. Since these differences were almost the same ones Anselm had debated with Nicetas in 1136, the pope asked that he write about what he thought could be said to the Greeks. Thus, Anselm received his commission to write the *Antikeimenon*.[56] Then on May 3, the pope granted Conrad of Meissen's request concerning Niemegk.[57] Anselm had fulfilled his mission.

The bishop of Havelberg did not, however, return to Germany. Perhaps it was Hartwig who wanted to stay with the curia in hopes of winning support for expanding Bremen's territorial claims;[58] but for whatever reason they stayed, the two men soon found themselves in the middle of a quagmire of changing alliances. They had come expecting to find the pope closely allied with their ruler. However, since his election, Eugenius had, on more than one occasion, been forced to flee Rome because of its independent-minded commune. The pope had thought that Conrad III would help him regain Rome

---

[53] Wibald, 159, p. 265. The outcome of Ado's problems is not known. See Jakobi, *Wibald von Stablo*, pp. 128-29.

[54] No manuscripts of this work have been found.

[55] Anselm says that he was in the presence of the pope in "mense Martio apud urbem Tusculanam" (*Antik.* prologus, 1139B). The *Regesta Pontificum Romanorum* 2, ed. Philip Jaffé (1888; repr. Graz, 1956), 9330-31 shows that the pope was in Viterbo on Mar. 25 and in Tusculum on Apr. 8. Anselm probably met him in Viterbo and accompanied him to Tusculum.

[56] Anselm's is the only account of this Greek delegation and of his meeting with the pope. *Antik.* prologue, 1139-42.

[57] Eugenius III, *Epistolae et privilegia* 348, PL 180:1390-91; Claude, *Geschichte des Erzbistums Magdeburg* 2:401.

[58] Günter Glaeske, *Die Erzbischöfe von Hamburg-Bremen als Reichsfürsten (937-1258)*, Quellen und Darstellungen zur Geschichte Niedersachsens 60 (Hildesheim, 1962), pp. 150-56.

only to see that ruler go off to the Holy Land; and now Arnold of Brescia was putting himself at the head of the commune and openly calling for a limitation of the pope's power in the papal city.[59] Eugenius, ever more desperate for help, moved to Viterbo where he entered into negotiations with Roger II of Sicily. This was to stand former papal policy on its head and run a terrible risk of completely losing Conrad III's support. Since the beginning of Conrad's reign, Roger had backed the Welfs in their struggles against the German ruler. Count Welf VI, who had gone along with Conrad on the crusade, returned early, stopping to visit Roger on the way to Germany; and the Norman king promised to give financial assistance for a Welf rebellion against Conrad.[60] Meanwhile in the Treaty of Thessalonica, the German ruler had formed his own alliance against Roger with the Byzantine Emperor Manuel I Comnenus. Eugenius was not aware of the treaty[61] and even less of the fact that while his legates negotiated with Roger, Conrad was drawing the disastrous Second Crusade to a close and preparing to sail for Italy with plans for a Greco-German assault on Roger's kingdom.[62] The pope's legates concluded a four year truce with the Norman ruler, and Roger responded by sending troops to join in what turned out to be an unsuccessful attack on Rome.[63] So, when Conrad III arrived in Aquileia at the beginning of May, committed to attacking Roger of Sicily

---

[59] *Gesta Friderici* 2.28, p. 133; John of Salisbury, *Historia Pontificalis* 31, ed. and trans. Marjorie Chibnall (London, 1956), pp. 62-65; George William Greenaway, *Arnold of Brescia* (Cambridge, 1931), pp. 123-25; Peter Partner, *The Lands of St Peter: The Papal State in the Middle Ages and the Early Renaissance* (Berkeley, 1972), pp. 182-83.

[60] Wibald, 147, pp. 228-29; Bernhardi, *Konrad*, pp. 751-52; Caspar, *Roger II.*, pp. 397-98. As Caspar points out (p. 35), Roger thought the Germans were barbarians (John of Salisbury, *Historia Pontificalis* 32, p. 65) and on Conrad's death in 1150, the Germans suspected Roger of having had him poisoned (Otto of Freising, *Gesta Friderici* 1.70, p. 98). On Roger's support of the Welfs, Caspar, pp. 356-57 with 357 n. 1.

[61] As late as October 1149, Cardinal Guido was writing to Wibald about rumors of a treaty between Conrad and Manuel. Wibald, 198, pp. 316-17; Bernhardi, *Konrad*, pp. 681-82 n. 45.

[62] Berry, "Second Crusade," pp. 510-12; Peter Rassow, *Honor Imperii: Die neue Politik Friedrich Barbarossas 1152-1159* (Munich, 1940), pp. 31-32; Paolo Lamma, *Comneni e Staufer: Ricerche sui rapporti fra Bisanzio e l'occidente nel secolo XII* 2 vols (Rome, 1955-57), 1:90-96; Bernhardi, *Konrad*, pp. 680-84. The *Continuatio Praemonstratensis*, ed. D. L. C. Bethman (Hanover, 1844), MGH SS 6:454, indicates that Conrad planned to move on Roger immediately upon his arrival in Italy.

[63] Wibald, 147, p. 229; Romoald of Salerno, *Annales*, ed. Wilhelm Arndt (Hanover, 1866), MGH SS 19:425; John of Salisbury, *Historia Pontificalis* 27, pp. 60-61. Caspar, *Roger II.*, pp. 400-1; Bernhardi, *Konrad*, p. 748 with n. 35; H. Gleber, *Papst Eugenius III. (1145-53)* (Jena, 1936), pp. 109-13.

and perhaps helping the pope take Rome, he was met with bewilder-
ing news: The pope was now dealing with Roger and Roger was
financing the rebellion of Welf of Bavaria.[64] Conrad wrote his sister-
in-law at the Byzantine court:

> When word of this atrocious thing [i.e. Welf's Norman financed rebel-
> lion in Germany] was received, and since rumor, as is so often the case,
> multiplies everything for the worse, I hastened to prevent and suppress
> it, and went quickly and unexpectedly to Germany.[65]

The last is an understatement. Conrad did not delay even long
enough to write the pope of his return. Eugenius immediately and in
a very understandable fear of losing Conrad's support hastened to
make contact with the king by sending several cardinals to meet him
in Aquileia. They returned alone. Conrad had already gone.[66]

The situation was an awkward one for Eugenius. While Conrad's
precipitous departure spared him from an embarrassing meeting with
the German ruler, he did not want to make an enemy of Conrad or
push him into the camp of the rebellious Roman senate, which for its
part was delighted to see fissures splitting ruler and pope and more
than ready to try to widen the breech. Eugenius did, however, have
two men at his court who might be able to clear a way out of this
dilemma: Hartwig of Bremen and Anselm of Havelberg. Particularly
with Anselm, Eugenius had a known quantity. This was the man who
had debated with the Greeks without apparently arousing their ire,
the man who had served both pope and ruler by winning Eugenius'
support for Conrad's crusade and then acting as the pope's legate
with the Saxon army that attacked the Wends. And so it was that
Eugenius sent Anselm and Hartwig scrambling after the German
ruler. They had no written message[67] but were left to explain this
very messy situation as best they could.

---

[64] Gleber, *Papst Eugenius III.*, p. 113.

[65] Wibald, 243, p. 364.

[66] Eugenius, *Epistolae et privilegia* 354, PL 180:1393-94.

[67] Fina, "Anselm von Havelberg," *AP* 33 (1957), 213, says that Anselm delivered
Eugenius' *epistola* 354 (PL 180:1393-94) to the king. This is the pope's first letter to
Conrad after his return from the crusade. While it tells us that Anselm and Hartwig
were sent after the king when it became known that he was going back to Germany,
it makes it quite clear that they were not the bearers of the letter, which is dated June
24—that is after Conrad was back in Germany—but that they had spoken to him
earlier ("...sicut per venerabiles fratres nostros Artwicum Bremensem archiepisco-
pum, et Anselmum Hamelburgensem [sic] episcopum tibi significavimus"). Moreover, the deliverer of the letter is named, one Franco, to whom the king was to give
his reply.

There is no record of what was said to the ruler, but Anselm was in a delicate position requiring all of his diplomatic skills. Beyond defending the pope, he had, as well, to consider his own standing in the eyes of his ruler. His relationship with Conrad had never been as close as that of his friends Wibald and Arnold, and defense of the pope might easily rebound against Anselm himself. However, no matter how diplomatically Anselm may have put things, for Conrad he was explaining the inexplicable. The crusade had been a failure, there was rebellion at home, and now things had gone so amuck in Italy that one could scarcely sort them out. The furious king was already making plans for some double-dealing of his own. In June, the king's notary wrote Wibald of Stablo a private letter: "What I say is secret. In an assembly of his trusted followers, the lord king intends to send delegations both to the Romans and to the lord pope."[68] If Eugenius could negotiate with Conrad's enemies, then the king could negotiate with the pope's! But such a delegation would take time. For the moment it was Anselm, standing before his king and defending his pope, who became the lightening rod for the ruler's anger.

Anselm felt like Christ at the court of Pilate. "There, standing before the prince," he later wrote Wibald,

> the Jews cry, "Crucify Him! Crucify Him!" ....[standing] in the palace with mocking soldiers, whipping, spitting, and beating one down with insults, and fashioning a crown of thorns. Thorns! Yes, thorns! Withered thorns, dry of the sap of eternal life! Slanderous barbs! After having been praised, the sun of divine contemplation darkens, the foundation of the body trembles, the rock of the faith splits, the veil of the temple is rent.[69]

The Havelland and Havelberg, which Anselm had apparently hoped would open more possibilities for him than attendance at court, suddenly became a place of semi-confinement. From the time of Conrad's return to Italy in May of 1149 to August of 1150, Anselm's name is not to be found on any royal document. The king had banished him.

Anselm returned to Havelberg to take up his duties as bishop. There he wrote a letter (since lost) to his friend Arnold, the chancellor of the king. Arnold passed it on to Wibald, who mentioned it

---

[68] Wibald, 182, p. 302; Wolter, *Arnold von Wied*, pp. 40-41; Hausmann, *Reichskanzlei*, pp. 148-49.
[69] Wibald, 221, pp. 340-1.

when he wrote "to Anselm, the bishop of a poor town": "I read the letter you sent to our communal friend [Arnold] as your petition to be excused from the offense to the lord our king." But the abbot could offer little hope: "I expect [that you will receive] neither very long lasting nor very great favor."[70]

Anselm responded with a long letter. If only he could sit down with Wibald and Arnold for a few days and talk things over "so that together we could share those thoughts which each must now keep to himself." On his recent mission to the papal curia he had seen the straits the pope was in and had, perhaps with some trepidation, probably thought that in "mutual conversation" with Conrad, the king would understand the pope's actions. But at the royal court, he had had a rude awakening, and in his letter he gives vent to his bitter feelings. "We've played around long enough," he writes as if his time at court had been but a futile game. "For the rest, let serious matters receive our attention." He pictures Havelberg as the cradle of Christ compared to the terrors of a court like Pilate's: "Believe me, dearest brother, it is safer in the cradle than in the palace. Consolation in the one, terrors in the other." Anselm's reception at court had hurt him deeply, and so he expresses to Wibald his acceptance of the contemplative life in the cradle of Christ at Havelberg: "I have withdrawn into the cloister of my heart," and "I will remain in my cradle of Havelberg, a poor man of Christ with my brothers in Christ."[71]

Wibald had learned something of "the very secret poison" in Conrad's court and had told Anselm that "your fault, if it is indeed a fault, is also shared with you by us and certain bishops."[72] In fact, Wibald had found himself out of the king's grace for a brief time,[73]

---

[70] Wibald, 211, p. 330.

[71] Wibald, 221, pp. 339-41; also printed with a German translation by Karl Pfändtner, "Ein Brief des Praemonstratenserbischofs Anselm von Havelberg," *AP* 7 (1931), 95-107.

[72] Wibald, 211, p. 330.

[73] Jakobi, *Wibald*, p. 136. One should be careful, however, of the often repeated idea that there was a "curial party" in Germany at this time which included Wibald, Arnold, and Anselm and which Conrad attacked on his return to Germany. See for example Bernhardi, *Konrad*, pp. 774-76; Hausmann, *Reichskanzlei*, pp. 107-9, 149-50, 210; and Jakobi, *Wibald*, pp. 135-36. Freya Stephan-Kühn is, I believe, quite accurate in her contention that "es ist also nicht erlaubt, Wibald, Anselm und der Kanzler Arnold auf Grund ihres Fernbleibens vom Königshofe generell einer kurialen Partei zuzuordnen, deren Einfluss Konrad auszuschliessen versuchte. Der Grund für das Fernbleiben ist bei allen dreien verschieden. Fraglich ist, ob es überhaupt eine offen kuriale Partei gab." *Wibald als Abt von Stablo und Corvey und im Dienste Konrads III.* (Cologne, 1973), p. 341.

but whereas the abbot could tell his friend that he was confident of seeing the king again in the near future,[74] Anselm had no such hope. His diocese was in a most precarious situation, and he could ill afford this lack of royal support. The picture he paints for Wibald of life in Havelberg is one of preparing for the Wends to attack and overrun the church:

> Some of us build a fortified tower in the face of the enemy; others stand guard against the onslaught of the heathens; others, giving themselves over to divine services, daily expect martyrdom; others cleanse their souls with fasting and prayer as preparation for a return to God; others busy themselves in their free time with the liturgy and apply themselves to holy meditation and imitate the lives and examples of the saints; and thus all of us, naked and poor, follow the naked and poor Christ as well as we can.[75]

The old church itself was transformed into a kind of castle keep. The sides of the massive front tower were given doors cut high above the ground, accessible only by ladders which could be drawn up in an emergency. The tower was further topped with fortress-like battlements either to provide cover for the church's defenders from attackers below or at least to give the impression of a fortress.[76] For Anselm, after the long years of hoping to get to Havelberg to engage his diocese in the *vita activa* of missionary work, the defensive and military position in which he found his church must have been discouraging. The life now imposed on him by circumstances was hardly compatible with the *vita contemplativa* nor was it the kind of *vita activa* he had envisioned; and on the whole, his letter to Wibald rings the discouraging note of a man powerless to work even for his own diocese.

Still, and in spite of all his protestations of having withdrawn into this "cradle of Havelberg," Anselm was not going to allow himself to be cut off from the world. He must finish in haste, he writes Wibald, because the messenger of the archbishop of Mainz had arrived with a letter for him and will leave within the hour. No doubt Anselm also

---

[74] Wibald, 211, p. 330, closes with mentioning Conrad's invitation to attend court in Bamberg in Dec. 1149.

[75] Wibald, 221, p. 340.

[76] Though the tower has been built up above Anselm's defensive work, today the lines of the crenels and merlons are easily visible in the mortar. The doors in the tower are still there. Whether this fortress-like appearance was meant to be serviceable in the case of an actual assault is a matter of continuing debate.

had a message for his old friend Henry of Mainz with whom he was obviously staying in correspondence. At the end of his letter, Anselm shows his concern for the king who had treated him so shabbily by telling Wibald:

> Diligently guard my and your august and most humble lord [Conrad] whenever you are near him; and because God has made you faithful and wise, do what is in your power and ability to accomplish as much as is permitted you. Greet our chancellor [Arnold] from your Anselm and his.[77]

These are not the words of a man who had turned his back on the court but of one who despaired over the way things were handled there. In spite of the bitter tone of the letter, there is nothing in it to indicate that, given the chance, Anselm would not return to royal service. Because Anselm did return to court early in the reign of the next ruler, Frederick Barbarossa, scholars have seen hypocrisy in his assertion that he had given up the court life for humble Havelberg. However, the letter to Wibald is not an indication of some sort of feigned personal conversion to a life of quasi-monastic withdrawal in Havelberg; it is a reaction to political and military circumstances over which Anselm had no control.

For over a year, Anselm was either in Havelberg or with his archbishop in Magdeburg. He gave some of his time over to literary endeavors. The *Antikeimenon* was composed at this time, and Archbishop Frederick asked Anselm to write a standard litany for the diocese of Magdeburg. To this, Anselm responded with his *De ordine pronuntiandae letaniae*, a work which contains an echo of the *Antikeimenon* and its patient search for common ground with the Greeks. In his brief discussion of the *Kyrie eleison* of the litany, Anselm emphasizes the fact that the words are Greek as a reminder of a unity of Christendom beyond that of the Latin West: "The Greek names [*Kyrie eleison, Christe eleison*] are allowed in the first invocation of the Holy Trinity in order to show that the Greeks and the Latins hold the same catholic faith."[78]

Anselm was not, however, asked to write this litany to address problems with the East, but because there seemed so little organiza-

---

[77] Wibald, 221, p. 341.
[78] Ed. Winter, "Zur Geschichte," pp. 144-55; here p. 145.

tion or uniformity in the litanies used in the dioceses of Magdeburg.
The problem, as Anselm relates it, was that such confusion had
arisen in the litany that some thought there was no order to it at all,
others guessed that there might be a correct order but did not know
it, and those who knew it were slothful about reciting it properly or
emphasized patrons and local saints rather than the most important
ones. In writing his litany, Anselm says, "I have done that which the
urgency of such confusion was seen to demand."[79]

De ordine pronuntiandae letaniae was Anselm's chance to help his archbishop unify the worship service of an entire archdiocese, but in it he
has managed to slip in the hint of a special prayer for his own
church. In his letter to Wibald about life in Havelberg, Anselm borrowed a line from the sixtieth psalm, saying that some of the brothers
were building "a fortified tower in the face of the enemy;" and the
last prayer of his litany is the same line, now as a plea to God: "Be,
O Lord, for us a fortified tower in the face of the enemy."[80]

Anselm remained in Havelberg until August of 1150 when he was
again at the king's court in Rothenburg on the Tauber.[81] By this time
there were many factors which favored royal forgiveness. His good
friend Wibald of Stablo stood high in Conrad's favor once again[82]
and may have put in a good word for him, though the abbot was not
in Rothenburg with the court. With or without Wibald's influence,
Conrad himself had good reason to try to eliminate any enmity between himself and the bishop of Havelberg. Between 1146 and 1150,
Albert the Bear had taken every opportunity to expand his power
east of the Elbe not only with the sword, as in the Wenden Crusade,
but with diplomatic alliances which created serious possibilities for
conflict with his erstwhile friend and ally King Conrad. When Conrad asked Albert to come to a *Hoftag* in April 1150 to resolve mutual
difficulties, Albert stayed away.[83] The duke had, moreover, established close ties with the Wendish Prince Pribislav of Brandenburg,

---

[79] Winter, p. "Zur Geschichte," p. 145.
[80] Winter, "Zur Geschichte," p. 155; Psalm 60:4 and p. 90 above.
[81] *UK* 237, pp. 415-16.
[82] On Wibald's relationship with the king: Jakobi, *Wibald von Stablo*, pp. 136-49;
Hausmann, *Reichskanzlei*, pp. 106-11, 149-50, 205-20; idem, "Die Anfänge des staufischen Zeitalters," pp. 72-73.
[83] Tadeusz Manteuffel, *The Formation of the Polish State: The Period of Ducal Rule, 963-
1194*, trans. Andrew Gorski (Detroit, 1982), pp. 118-28; Bernhardi, *Konrad*, pp. 801-
2; Kahl, *Slawen und Deutsche* 1:374-75; Schlesinger, "Bemerkungen," pp. 34-35.

who went so far as to make Albert his heir. When the prince died in 1150, Albert claimed his inheritance and moved on Brandenburg where he stationed a garrison.[84] Meanwhile, in June of that same year, Pope Eugenius III sent Conrad a desperate plea for help; and the following month, Conrad responded by asking Wibald to go to Italy with Chancellor Arnold.[85] While Anselm's importance in all of this should not be overestimated, he was nevertheless a man who had moved in the circles of both the pope and the Bear. His reappearance at court came at a time when Conrad was reconciling himself with Eugenius and needed allies in Albert's camp.

Nevertheless, it is probable that Conrad remained at least somewhat wary of Anselm. Certainly, the bishop of Havelberg took up no permanent position at his ruler's court. There is documentary evidence of his presence there on only two other occasions after August 1150, and on both of them he was representing the specific interests of either Havelberg or Magdeburg.[86] On December 3, Anselm met with the king, this time in Würzburg. There he presented Conrad with a charter concerning Havelberg to which the ruler gave his official sanction.[87] If the king had hoped to win Anselm's support, he would have gone a long way toward achieving his goal in sealing this charter.

Behind this document stands a bishop who has emerged from "the cloister of [his] heart" and done his best to make that "cradle of Havelberg" into a functioning diocese. He shows himself to be a bishop who wants that diocese legally defined and the tools to build it up. Given the problems he had recently had with Conrad, his first concern was to leave no doubt about his loyalty to his ruler or his commitment to his episcopal charge:

---

[84] Kahl, *Slawen und Deutsche* 1:30-32, 327-28, 340; von Heinemann, *Albrecht der Bär*, pp. 180-81; Bernhardi, *Konrad*, pp. 834-35.

[85] Eugenius III, *Epistolae et privilegia* 395, PL 170:1422; *UK* 236, pp. 414-15.

[86] Bernhardi's sarcastic remark that Anselm "sein geliebtes Havelberg, wo er sich so wohl gefühlt haben wollte, verliess, um das Verderben des Hofes aufzusuchen" (*Konrad*, p. 849) is unfounded. For Schlesinger's suggestion that after August 1150 Anselm "scheint nun bei Hofe geblieben zu sein," ("Bemerkungen," p. 32) there is no evidence. After Aug. 20, 1150 and before Conrad's death, Anselm's name appears in only two of the ruler's charters, one of which is the confirmation charter to Havelberg which has no witnesses. Thus, Anselm witnessed only one of the fourteen royal charters with lists of witnesses from this period.

[87] The eschatocol is "Data per manum Arnoldi cancellarii." See p. 67 n. 67 above.

> With pious devotion we [i.e. Conrad] wish to help Anselm, the vener-
> able bishop of this church, who has labored most fervently to rebuild
> and restore it, because we have found him both devoted to the religious
> life and steadfast and true in his loyalty to us and our kingdom.[88]

The possessions of the diocese are listed, most going back to grants of
the Ottonians and Henry II. The grants of Hartwig of Bremen and
Otto of Hillersleben are also confirmed; and in speaking of the
church of Jerichow, Anselm adds with a bit of pride, "in which
Anselm the venerable bishop of Havelberg recently instituted a
priory of devout canons."[89] A grant of Henry the Lion to Havelberg
is also mentioned, an indication that Anselm had not been inactive in
strengthening his diocesan holdings.[90]

This all echoed Anselm's earlier efforts to create a legal framework
for his episcopal office; however, in the 1150 document Anselm took
the next steps by frankly describing the sad condition of the towns
and villages of his diocese as "devastated by pagan attacks and so
depopulated that they are rarely or never inhabited," and obtaining
permission freely to seek out colonists to repopulate the land.[91] As
with the foundation of Jerichow, Anselm was particularly concerned
that his authority in the diocese of Havelberg not be circumvented.
He makes it clear that secular power whether that of duke, margrave,
count, vicount, advocate, or subadvocate, "be subject only to the
bishop of Havelberg in all things."[92] The document is not the work of
a man hoping to abandon his episcopal duties to travel with the court
of Conrad III. On the contrary, it shows Anselm taking further steps
to control and strengthen his diocese by defining its borders, emphasizing that its episcopal government was not to be interfered with by
secular authorities of any kind, opening it for colonization, and placing it under royal protection.

A virtue of Conrad's grant of royal protection was that the king
was in no position to turn that protection into control. The charter
does, however, make passing reference to "a power like unto monarchical authority" which might try to control the episcopate. The only

---

[88] *UK* 241, p. 420. Note Schlesinger's comment: "Mit Selbstlob wird also nicht
gespart, zugleich aber doch ein offenbar echtes Anliegen Anselms hervorgehoben."
"Bemerkungen," p. 33.

[89] *UK* 241, p. 421.

[90] Schlesinger, "Bemerkungen," pp. 24-26, 37.

[91] *UK* 241, p. 421.

[92] *UK* 241, p. 421.

person who could threaten Anselm and whose power might be described as quasi-monarchical was Albert the Bear.[93] Perhaps Conrad was trying to use Anselm as part of a plan to counterbalance Albert's growing strength,[94] but if so Anselm turned it very much to his advantage for within a year he was dealing with Albert himself.

Anselm's relationship with Albert the Bear had met no setback like that with Conrad. The two had known each other since Norbert's tenure as archbishop of Magdeburg, served on the Wenden Crusade together, and most likely, helped negotiate the treaty with Prince Ratibor. Albert had experienced firsthand the difficulty of eastward expansion as an enterprise of war; and while Anselm had always supported expansion, he stood on the side of using missionaries and colonists. Now ensconced in Brandenburg, Albert moved to secure the lands he had inherited from Pribislav by granting considerable privileges to those willing to colonize them.[95] These efforts were in complete accord with Anselm's plans for Havelberg.

In May of 1151, Anselm attended a provincial synod in Magdeburg, and it may have been at this time that he discussed Havelberg with Albert.[96] The margrave showed himself more than willing to assist the bishop. He issued a charter in which he affirmed the bishop's unencumbered authority in his diocese, donated land to Havelberg's growing possessions, committed himself to restore Havelberg, and gave his full support to Anselm. Neither the canons of Havelberg nor the bishop was to pay any secular duties encumbering their ability to work "for the expansion of Christianity and the conversion of the gentile, and that the church of Havelberg may prosper."[97]

---

[93] *UK* 241, p. 421; Schlesinger, "Bemerkungen," pp. 34-35.

[94] Schlesinger ("Bemerkungen," p. 35) says that Conrad may also have created a *Burggraf* for Brandenburg at this time who, as the king's man, "würde...ein Gegengewicht gegen die Aufsteigende Landesherrschaft des Askaniers gebildet haben, ebenso wie Bischof Anselm selbst, dessen Herrschaft von die Markgräflichen *potestas* völlig gelöst wurde." There are several problems with this. As Schlesinger himself points out, the first evidence of a *Burggraf* comes only in 1157. Moreover, Albert had just taken Brandenburg and stationed troops there (Bernhardi, *Konrad*, p. 836). That a *Burggraf* would have had any authority in these circumstances or acted as a "Gegengewicht" to Albert's power is doubtful, and Conrad would have been running a serious risk of antagonizing Albert.

[95] Bernhardi, *Konrad*, p. 836; Heinemann, *Albrecht der Bär*, pp. 181-83; Hauck, *Kirchengeschichte* 4:634; Erich Freiherr von Guttenberg, "Albrecht der Bär," *Neue Deutsche Biographie* 1 (Berlin, 1953), pp. 160-61. See n. 98 below.

[96] Both are witnesses to *UB des Erzstifts Magdeburg* 272, pp. 341-43. Dombrowski, *Anselm*, p. 45; Kahl, *Slawen und Deutsche* 2:873-74 n. 62.

[97] *Codex diplomaticus Anhaltinus* 1, 368, pp. 277-78.

Anselm's freedom of action in his own diocese was secure. Conrad considered the bishop to be a man whose assistance might be valuable in patching up his differences with Albert the Bear. Albert, for his part, found in Anselm a valuable instrument for helping colonize his eastern possessions. Anselm made the most of the decrees of both parties and at no cost to himself.[98]

In November, Anselm was at the king's court in Altenburg to witness Conrad's grant of protection to the Norbertines of Gratia Dei.[99] It was the last documented time he saw the ruler, who died on February 14, 1152, having accomplished nothing against either Roger of Sicily or Henry the Lion.[100] In the fourteen years of Con-

---

[98] Schlesinger ("Bemerkungen," p. 35 n. 133) says that Albert's charter to Anselm shows "dass Anselm mit dem Privileg Konrads wirklich gegen die Askanier operiert hat, mit dem Erfolg, dass nun auch diese sich genötigt sahen, dem Bistum wichtige Zugeständinisse zu machen. Vor allem ist von der Restituierung unrechtmäßig entzogenen Besitzes die Rede." This may not, however, take fully into account the state of the diocese of Havelberg at the time of the charter. That diocese had virtually disappeared after 983, and any control Germans might have gained there in the years that followed was not at the expense of the bishop but of the Slavs. While the document does say that donations made by Slavs to the episcopate must be confirmed by the authority of King Conrad, Schlesinger himself points out that German donations (which is to say most donations) would apparently have needed only the approval of the margrave. Even concerning Slavic donations, Albert has specifically referred to Conrad's, not royal, approval, indicating this was not to last beyond that king's death. Albert was facing the task of restoring the missionary church of Havelberg from the bottom up. It was a church which was to colonize and Christianize his newly won territory, and it would not have been in his best interest to erect barriers to its bishop's effectiveness in carrying out these endeavors. One does not have to read the evidence in terms of a contest between Conrad and Albert. Rather, as so often in the past, the two were pursuing the same policy; and it was from this, not from their enmity, that Anselm benefitted. Albert did not look to Havelberg alone for help. He made donations of formerly Slavic lands along with their tithes (though he held on to the *vogtei*) to Our Lady in Magdeburg (*UB Unser lieben Frauen* 20, pp. 19-20; Heinemann, *Albrecht der Bär*, pp. 185-86); and he looked far and wide for colonists. Stressing Albert's use of settlers from Holland, Zeeland, and Flanders, Helmold of Bosau praised Albert's success: "Et confortatus est vehementer ad introitum advenarum episcopatus Brandenburgensis necnon Havelbergensis, eo quod multiplicarentur ecclesiae, et dicimarum succresceret ingens possessio." *Cronica Slavorum* 1.89, pp. 174-75.

[99] *UK* 265, pp. 458-60, dated Nov. 13, 1152, but should be dated to 1151 (Conrad was dead by Nov. 1152). There is some indication that it was drawn up in haste and dated later. See Bernhardi, *Konrad*, p. 902 n. 41; Hausmann, *Reichskanzlei*, p. 152; editorial comments, *UK* 265, p. 459; *UB des Hochstifts Naumberg (967-1207)*, ed. Felix Rosenfeld, GQPS NR 1 (Magdeburg, 1925), 196, p. 179 n. 1.

[100] Critical of Conrad's reign: Karl Hampe, *Deutsche Kaisergeschichte* (1969; repr. Darmstadt, 1981), pp. 141-42; Töpfer and Engel, *Vom staufischen Imperium zum Hausmachtkönigtum*, pp. 35; sympathetic: Hausmann, "Die Anfänge des Staufischen Zeitalters," pp. 53-78.

rad's reign, Anselm of Havelberg served less than twelve months at
the royal court, and historians should be wary of thinking of him as
one of the ruler's closest advisers. It was the new possibilities for his
diocese east of the Elbe that brought him into contact with the king;
and during Conrad's reign more than at any time before or after,
Anselm was bishop of Havelberg in fact as well as in name.

CHAPTER SIX

ADVISER TO BARBAROSSA AND
ARCHBISHOP OF RAVENNA
1152-1158

The death of Conrad of Hohenstaufen ended an important phase of Anselm's life, namely his attachment to Havelberg. From 1144 and the foundation of Jerichow to Conrad's death in 1152, virtually all of the documentation for Anselm's life shows a bishop energetically furthering the interests of his diocese. After Conrad's death, there is no evidence of Anselm's presence in Havelberg; but since the archive of his church has been lost, we should be careful about assuming that Anselm had no interest in his diocese after 1152. Nevertheless, during the last three years of his tenure as bishop of Havelberg, he moved into the circle of the close advisers of the new ruler, Frederick Barbarossa; and he probably spent none of this time in Havelberg. Then in 1155, he again took up episcopal duties, this time as archbishop of Ravenna, a position he held until his death in 1158.[1]

Anselm's attachment to the court of Frederick Barbarossa was precipitous. Conrad died on February 15, 1152, leaving the *regalia* in the hands of his nephew, Frederick of Hohenstaufen. The German nobility sealed Conrad's choice of a successor by electing Frederick king on March 4, and he was crowned in Aachen within a week.[2] A mere two months later, Anselm attended the king's court in Goslar,[3] marking his reemergence as a royal adviser. That Anselm was so quickly taken into the king's confidence may have resulted from his having made a favorable impression on the frequent occasions he

---

[1] For following Anselm's association with the court of Frederick Barbarossa, see Hans Patze, "Friedrich Barbarossa und die deutschen Fürsten," in *Die Zeit der Staufer* 5, ed. Reiner Haussherr und Christian Väterlein (Stuttgart, 1979), pp. 35-75, esp. pp. 64-65 and the maps by Herbert Reyer. It should be noted that Reyer has mistakenly shown Anselm instead of Arnold of Wied accompanying Frederick to Paderborn in 1152. In general for Frederick's itinerary, Ferdinand Opll, *Das Itinerar Kaiser Friedrich Barbarossas (1152-1190)* (Cologne, 1978).

[2] Simonsfeld, *Friedrich I.*, pp. 19-44; Ferdinand Opll, *Friedrich Barbarossa* (Darmstadt, 1990), pp. 41-42.

[3] *UF* 9-10 (May 8 and 9, 1152), pp. 16-19.

had met Frederick during Conrad's reign.[4] Just as important, if not more so, was his friendship with Wibald and Arnold, who moved rapidly to secure the new king's trust.[5] At the same time, they found growing opposition to their influence. In April 1152, Wibald wrote Frederick's notary complaining that since ignorant and inexperienced men had entered Frederick's service, "my service and that of certain other princes of the realm have either completely ceased or are considered superfluous." Wibald's description of the new men at court, men "who serve the majesty and the dignity of the Empire with neither knowledge nor experience," rings a note of alarm about this king, his court, and the direction they might take.[6] While an exile in Havelberg, Anselm himself had expressed this same concern about the counselors of Conrad III,[7] and the return to court of this kindred spirit at the beginning of Frederick's reign was something Wibald and Arnold surely welcomed. Anselm would later express some deep reservations about his new ruler, reservations that he may have had from the beginning of Frederick's reign,[8] for soon after he met the ruler in Goslar, the king moved onto a collision course with the papacy.

Anselm probably came to Goslar with another of Magdeburg's suffragan bishops, Wichmann of Zeitz-Naumburg.[9] The two accompanied the court to Regensburg[10] where Anselm saw his new ruler create a confrontational situation that would draw a clear line between those who supported the ruler and those who supported the

---

[4] Mutual witnesses to *UK* 130 (Worms, May 1145), p. 237; 164 (Speyer, Jan. 4, 1147), p. 297; 175 (Tauberbischofsheim, Mar. 2, 1147), p. 316; 178, 182 (Frankfurt, Mar. 19-23, 1147), pp. 321, 330; 188 (Nuremberg, Apr. 24, 1147), p. 342.

[5] Simonsfeld, *Friedrich I.*, pp. 22-25; Jakobi, *Wibald von Stablo*, pp. 163-65; Wolter, *Arnold von Wied*, pp. 84-89; Hausmann, *Reichskanzlei*, pp. 117-18, 220; Peter Munz, *Frederick Barbarossa: A Study in Medieval Politics* (Ithaca, 1969), pp. 46-47. It was Arnold who crowned Frederick in Aachen.

[6] Wibald, 377 (dated to April 1152), p. 507. The other *principes* certainly included Arnold. Hausmann, *Reichskanzlei*, pp. 231-32; Wolter, *Arnold von Wied*, p. 87.

[7] See p. 91 above. It may be noted that after Anselm met Wibald at court in Goslar (May 8-9, 1152), the two went on to Merseburg for the Reichstag of May 18. After this Wibald left court until October. Still, Anselm and Wibald had at least eleven days together to discuss the new king and his advisers.

[8] See pp. 105-7 below.

[9] On Wichmann, Willy Hoppe, "Erzbischof Wichmann von Magdeburg," *Geschichtsblätter für Stadt und Land Magdeburg* 43 (1908), 134-294; Claude, *Geschichte des Erzbistums Magdeburg* 2:71-175. There is also a set of articles in the catalog of an exhibition devoted to Wichmann: Matthias Puhle, ed., *Erzbischof Wichmann (1152-1192) und Magdeburg im hohen Mittelalter: Stadt-Erzbistum-Reich* (Magdeburg, 1992).

[10] En route in Merseburg: *UF* 11 (May 18, 1152), pp. 19-22.

pope. Archbishop Frederick of Magdeburg had died just as Conrad's reign came to an end. His office, however, had remained vacant because of a dual election by the cathedral chapter in Magdeburg, the majority party choosing the cathedral provost Gerhard, while a minority chose the deacon Hazeko. There can be no doubt of where Anselm stood in this matter. Gerhard was a loyal Norbertine and a friend of Anselm's with whom he had served on both the Leitzkau commission and the ill-fated trip to Italy in 1149.[11] Hazeko, on the other hand, had once been accused of treason by Archbishop Norbert himself and then gone over the archbishop's head by appealing his case to the pope.[12] However, Anselm's choice in this matter was complicated by the emergence of yet a third candidate. When the two sides came to Frederick and he was unable to reconcile them, he seized the opportunity to gain influence in an important archdiocese by putting forth Bishop Wichmann as his own candidate. After winning the support of Hazeko's minority party, the king invested Wichmann with the *regalia* of the archbishop's office.[13] This smooth dealing relied on an extremely liberal view of a secular ruler's right to decide split elections,[14] and Frederick could never have expected the pope to let it pass, particularly since Gerhard was furious over the proceedings and on his way to Italy to complain.[15] With this in mind, it was probably the king himself who constrained the prelates who were with him in Regensburg into writing the pope in support of

---

[11] See pp. 56, 84 above.

[12] Grauwen, *Norbertus Aartsbisshop*, pp. 300-1, 369-70, 400-9. The accusation of treason came in 1130. Hazeko appealed to the wrong pope: Anacletus II.

[13] Otto of Freising, *Gesta Friderici* 2.6, pp. 106-7. On Wichmann and on Frederick's treatment of the German episcopacy: Simonsfeld, *Friedrich I.*, pp. 88-94; Hoppe, "Erzbischof Wichmann," pp. 3-8; Claude, *Erzbischof Magdeburg* 2:71-82; Opll, *Friedrich Barbarossa*, pp. 42-45; Munz, *Frederick Barbarossa*, pp. 55-58; Hauck, *Kirchengeschichte* 4:199-200; Benson, *The Bishop Elect*, pp. 284-91; Michele Maccarrone, *Papato e impero: Dalla elezione di Federico I alla morto di Adriano IV (1152-1159)* (Rome, 1959), pp. 30-35; Bernard Töpfer, "Kaiser Friedrich I. Barbarossa und der deutsche Episkopat," in Alfred Haverkamp, ed., *Friedrich Barbarossa. Handlungspielräume und Wirkungsweisen des staufischen Kaisers*, Vorträge und Forschungen 40 (Sigmaringen, 1992), pp. 389-433.

[14] Otto of Freising, *Gesta Friderici* 2.6, pp. 106-7; Simonsfeld, *Friedrich I.*, pp. 92-94. While Otto of Freising uses the Concordat of Worms as the legal justification for Frederick's action, Pope Eugenius (n. 19 below) avoided bringing the Concordat into the dispute by saying the transfer of a bishop from one see to another (here Zeitz-Naumburg to Magdeburg) without just cause was uncanonical. On this point see Claude and Benson, cited in n. 13 above.

[15] Eugenius told the cathedral chapter in Magdeburg not to accept Wichmann as archbishop: *Epistolae et privilegia* 522, PL 180:1543.

Wichmann's election. Among the three archbishops and eight bishops present was Anselm.[16]

Anselm was in an extremely unpleasant situation. On one side of the line Frederick was drawing stood Anselm's friend Gerhard, the Norbertines of Magdeburg, and Pope Eugenius III. On the other side were Wichmann with pretensions to being Anselm's archbishop and Frederick who was apparently not above exerting some pressure on the gathered prelates. Thus, Anselm was faced with either offending both the Norbertines in Magdeburg and the pope himself or risking a repetition of his falling out with Conrad. Anselm knew full well what the lack of royal support could mean, and he along with all the other prelates at Regensburg signed, as Otto of Freising put it, "out of love for the king."[17] Frederick, in short, got his way. At best, Anselm had saved his own position at court, a position without which he would have had no influence on Frederick. As will be seen, he used that position again and again to obscure the line of loyalty Frederick was trying to draw.[18]

---

[16] *UF* 14 (end of June-beginning of July, 1152), pp. 26-27. The letter the bishops wrote to Eugenius has been lost, but their names are given in Eugenius' response (n. 19 below). The letter was probably written in Regensburg. Of the eleven archbishops and bishops to whom the pope's response is addressed, seven are witnesses to *UF* 13, pp. 24-25, or to *UF* 14: Archbishop Eberhard of Salzburg and the bishops Eberhard of Bamberg, Herman of Constance, Henry of Regensburg, Otto of Freising, Conrad of Passau, and Anselm. Of these only Anselm appears in the charters from May 1152 drawn up in Goslar (n. 3 above) and Merseburg (n. 10 above). Of the remaining four men mentioned in Eugenius' letter, Archbishop Hartwig of Bremen and Bishop Daniel of Prague were with the court in Merseburg (n. 10 above) and may have continued on to Regensburg. Archbishop Hillin of Trier went with Bishop Eberhard of Bamberg to Rome to inform the pope of Frederick's election and was likely with Eberhard in Regensburg on their return (Simonsfeld, *Friedrich I.*, pp. 52, 102, 107). Burchard of Eichstatt is not mentioned in any charters from this period, but see Hauck, *Kirchengeschichte* 4, pp. 184 n. 9, 205 n. 2; Munz, *Frederick Barbarossa*, p. 68; Simonsfeld, *Friedrich I.*, p. 185. The authenticity of charter 14 has been questioned (Simonsfeld, *Friedrich I.*, pp. 105-7). However, the similarity between its list of witnesses and the list of bishops who wrote Eugenius is, I feel, hardly coincidental. See the introduction to *UF* 14, p. 26 and *UB des Hochstifts Naumberg*, p. 184 n. 1. I must take exception to Peter Rassow's assertion that the bishops wrote the letter to Eugenius as a matter of course and without knowing of the pope's opposition (*Honor Imperii*, pp. 19-20). The latter may be true to the extent that they had not yet received any news from the pope, but the fact that they wrote the letter at all indicates some uneasiness about Wichmann's elevation which papal approval could dispel.

[17] *Gesta Friderici* 2.8, p. 108.

[18] Again (see p. 89 n. 73 above), the notion of a "curial party" has been used to assess royal advisers with the assumption that these men either were part of or in opposition to it, there being no middle ground. This has frequently been the basis for evaluating Anselm, eg. Simonsfeld, *Friedrich I.*, p. 108; Lauerer, *Anschauungen*, p. 5. I

Eugenius immediately saw the threat Frederick's action posed to papal control of church affairs in Germany. He wrote the German bishops expressing his astonishment that they had sided with Wichmann and exhorting them to use their influence to dissuade Frederick from what the pope saw as "opposition to God."[19] In pushing Wichmann's candidacy, Frederick was testing the pope; Eugenius' letter proved his mettle. For the moment Wichmann held to his claim to be the archbishop of Magdeburg, and Anselm once again saw Christian unity threatened by an issue which forced men to choose sides.[20]

By October 1152, Frederick's attitude toward the papacy was shifting. At a large meeting of ecclesiastical and secular princes in Würzburg, the ruler showed himself willing not only to honor the promises of Conrad III and render the pope military assistance but also to send a delegation for the purpose of drawing up a formal treaty with Eugenius. Among its members were two churchmen: Bishops Herman of Constance and Anselm of Havelberg.[21]

The delegation met with the pope's representatives in Rome sometime in December 1152 or January 1153,[22] and drew up what with some alterations would become the Treaty of Constance.[23] This

would suggest that one will not get far in understanding the post-Concordat of Worms royal advisers such as Norbert, Wibald, Arnold and most certainly Anselm by taking this either-or position. See the apt comments of Berges, "Anselm von Havelberg," pp. 40-41.

[19] Eugenius III, *Epistolae et privilegia* 523, PL 180:1544B.

[20] Rassow, *Honor Imperii*, pp. 46-47, who sees the bishops as having freely sided with the ruler (see n. 16 above).

[21] Anselm presence at court in Speyer, Aug. 1152: *UF* 27 (Aug. 1152), pp. 46-47; at Würzburg: *UF* 30-31 (Oct. 16-17), pp. 50-54; 34 (Oct. 20), pp. 58-59; 36 (Oct.), pp. 60-62; Frederick's decision to campaign in Italy: Otto of Freising, *Gesta Friderici* 2.7, p. 108. The names of those who made up the delegation are derived from the resulting Treaty of Constance. See n. 23 below and Simonsfeld, *Friedrich I.*, p. 136 n. 425; Gerhard Dunken, *Die politische Wirksamkeit der päpstlichen Legaten in der Zeit des Kampfes zwischen Kaisertum und Papstum in Oberitalien unter Friedrich I.*, Historische Studien 209 (Berlin, 1931), pp. 12-13.

[22] Maccarrone, *Papato e impero*, pp. 43-44.

[23] There are many editions of the Treaty of Constance, e.g. *UF* 51, pp. 85-86; *Variorum ad Eugenium Papam epistolae* 14, PL 180:1638-40; Wibald, 407, pp. 546-47; Rassow, *Honor Imperii*, pp. 115-21; Maccarrone, *Papato e impero*, pp. 50-51. The last two of these give the treaty as it was probably put together in Rome by the representatives of the pope and the king. The first three give the treaty as it appeared after having been reworked in Germany, probably by Wibald of Stablo. See Rainer Maria Herkenrath, "Regnum und Imperium in den Diplomen der ersten Regierungsjahre Friedrichs I.," in *Friedrich Barbarossa*, ed. Gunther Wolf (Darmstadt, 1975), pp. 323-59, esp. pp. 331-35.

treaty guaranteed that Frederick would not sign a truce or make peace with either the Romans or with Roger of Sicily without the pope's consent, and that he would strive to subjugate the Romans and the Roman church as they had been in the past; he would preserve and defend the pope's honor and allow no territorial concessions in Italy to be made to the Greeks but rather would repel any Byzantine invasion. On his side, the pope agreed to crown Frederick emperor should he come to Rome, lend him aid in supporting and spreading the honor of his kingdom,[24] and excommunicate those who persisted in opposing it; further, he also would not concede land to the Greeks and would oppose any invasion they might launch. These were provisions with which Anselm would assuredly have been in agreement. Conrad III's Treaty of Thessalonica with Manuel Comnenus and Eugenius' alliance with the Normans had created tensions between king and pope by making it difficult to tell friend from foe (and one might add, had caused personal misfortune for Anselm). The Treaty of Constance addressed these problems by identifying the forces which worried the pope—the Normans, the Romans, and the Greeks—and placing the German ruler in the position of defending the papacy against all three. At the same time, it left Frederick a free hand to deal with the Greeks on any other basis than territorial concessions in Italy, and it left the pope an opening for peaceful negotiations with the Normans. Here was a treaty which allowed pope and ruler to perceive of each other as allies while forcing neither the pope to view the Normans nor the Germans to view the Greeks as enemies. This was a master stroke of avoiding divisive lines for which Anselm would readily have worked.[25]

---

[24] This would be changed from *honor regni* to *honor imperii* in the revised version. See Rassow, *Honor Imperii*, esp. pp. 45-65, Munz, *Frederick Barbarossa*, p. 64 n. 2; Heinz Zatschek, *Beiträge zur Geschichte des Konstanzer Vertrages vom Jahre 1153* (Vienna, 1930); Maccarrone, *Papato e impero*, pp. 41-81; Odilo Engels, "Zum Konstanzer Vertrag von 1153," in *Deus qui mutat tempora. Festschrift für A. Becker zu seinem 65. Geburtstag*, ed. E.-D. Hehl, H. Seibert and F. Staab (Sigmaringen, 1987), 235-58; Simonsfeld, *Friedrich I.*, pp. 158-67; Gleber, *Papst Eugenius III.*, pp. 153-58; Gunther Wolf, "Der 'Honor Imperii' als Spannungsfeld von Lex und Sacramentum im Hochmittelalter," in Wolf, *Frederick Barbarossa*, pp. 297-322.

[25] Rassow (*Honor Imperii*, p. 56) says that the fact that Frederick had to have papal consent to negotiate with the Normans while the pope did not need imperial consent to do the same is not important because the pope would not have risked an alliance with the Normans and Frederick's legates knew it. However, if this were so, the legates—including Anselm!—were ignoring Eugenius' recent, flirtatious alliance with Roger while Conrad was crusading (see pp. 86-87 above) and would have soon been proven wrong by the Treaty of Benevento (see p. 117 below). Is it not more likely

Between Frederick and Eugenius there still remained the problem of Wichmann and his claims to Magdeburg; and it is significant that Anselm and Herman of Constance, two of the signatories of the letter written in Wichmann's defense, were sent to Rome. Given the correspondence between the pope and the German bishops concerning Wichmann, it is inconceivable that the two men did not expect to be asked about Frederick's position, not to say their own, on Wichmann's candidacy. For Frederick to have remained obstinate in this matter and then to have dispatched to Rome two bishops who had given written proof of siding with the ruler would have been consciously to undermine the negotiations. Anselm's own earlier and good relationship with Eugenius must have played some role in his being chosen to go to Rome; but if that were to be of any real use, he had to assure Eugenius that Frederick was not trying to defy the pope. While the evidence is not crystal-clear, Wichmann, who had been using the archiepiscopal title, did revert to using that of bishop of Zeitz-Naumburg; and one may suggest that, ever the mediator, Anselm asked Frederick to moderate his position and went to Rome in the knowledge that for the moment his ruler was willing to back away from a confrontation.[26]

that the legates of both sides realized that, short of an imperial-papal expedition into southern Italy which was by no means certain, the pope would have to negotiate with the Normans alone? See Opll, *Friedrich Barbarossa*, 45-46.

[26] In Sept. 1152, Pope Eugenius wrote to Wibald asking for help in dealing with Frederick concerning ecclesiastical problems in Germany and Italy (Wibald, 403, p. 538). While the letter does not specifically mention Wichmann, Maccarrone demonstrates that this was "per prudenza" (*Papato e impero*, pp. 33-37). For Eugenius, Wibald was the man who might do something about the Wichmann problem. Nevertheless, in Würzburg, before Anselm left for Italy, Wichmann was witnessing charters as *Magdeburgensis archepiscopus* (*UF* 34, 36, pp. 58, 62), a practice he started in Regensburg after receiving the *regalia* from Frederick (*UF* 13 as *Magdeburgensis episcopus*, p. 25; 14, p. 27; also *Hamburgisches UB* 201, p. 186 witnessed as *Magdeburgensis electus*, dated only 1152). Wichmann himself issued one charter on Jan. 6, 1153 as bishop of (Zeitz-)Naumburg (*UB des Hochstifts Naumberg* 213, p. 192), that is before the delegation returned from Italy. In April 1153, he witnessed two of Frederick's charters as bishop of (Zeitz-)Naumburg (*UF* 54, 55, pp. 94, 95). Obviously, someone had persuaded Frederick to moderate his position, something which would certainly have helped his legates in their deliberations with the curia had they known about it when they left for Rome sometime after the court met in Würzburg in Oct. 1152. Wibald was not in Würzburg at that time, and Anselm, both as Wibald's confidant and one who would negotiate for Frederick with the pope, is the likely man to have advised the ruler in this matter. Rassow, *Honor Imperii*, pp. 20-23; Claude, *Geschichte des Erzbistums Magdeburg* 2, 76-80; Simonsfeld, *Friedrich I.*, p. 177. Wichmann only resumed the use of the archiepiscopal title in late May or early June 1154 (*UF* 80, p. 134), that is after he had received the pallium in Rome. See n. 56 below.

On his return, Anselm appears to have remained fairly close to Frederick's court.[27] Nevertheless, there is good indication that he was uneasy about his ruler. The evidence for this derives from Frederick's dealings with the Burgundian abbey of Baume-les-Messieurs. On June 11, 1153 in Worms, Anselm witnessed Frederick's confirmation of Cluny's ownership of this abbey.[28]

The monks of Baume-les-Messieurs were Benedictines and proud of a long and for the most part radiant past. In recent times, however, the abbey had lost some of its spiritual luster and there were complaints that the brothers needed more discipline, especially after they physically assaulted a representative of the bishop of Autun in 1147. By 1151 Pope Eugenius III was moving to attach Baume to Cluny and thus place it under the guiding hand of Abbot Peter the Venerable. In doing this, Eugenius took the further step of degrading the status of Baume from an abbey to a priory. This did not sit well with the brothers in Baume, but Cluny's possession of the monastery was recognized and confirmed by Frederick in Worms.[29] It was at this time that Anselm wrote a brief letter to Peter the Venerable expressing his love and admiration for the abbot of Cluny. The letter also gives a remarkably candid look at Anselm's feelings about Frederick Barbarossa.

In the letter, Anselm says that he has received news of Peter "through Brother Go., prior of the community of Baume." This must be a certain Guigo, who would be mentioned in another document concerning the abbey some years later. Apparently, he had come to participate in the negotiations over Frederick's confirmation of Cluny's possession of the abbey.[30] Was Guigo one of the Benedictine monks of Baume or someone Peter the Venerable had put in charge to guide the priory in the ways of Cluny? Anselm says he has heard

---

[27] Feb. 1153, in Besançon: *UF* 49, pp. 81-83; Mar., in Constance (Frederick's acceptance of the treaty with Eugenius) and *UF* 52-53, pp. 87-92; Apr. in Bamberg: *UF* 55, pp. 94-95.

[28] *UF* 58, pp. 98-99.

[29] For the history of Baume from 1147 through 1157, René Locatelli, *et al*, *L'abbaye de Baume-les-Messieurs* (Dole-du-Jura, 1978), pp. 48-60; Giles Constable, "Baume and Cluny in the Twelfth Century," in *Tradition and Change: Essays in honour of Marjorie Chibnall*, ed by Diana Greenway, Christopher Holdsworth, and Jane Sayers (New York, 1985), pp. 35-61.

[30] *Recueil des chartes de l'abbaye de Cluny* 5.4176, pp. 526-27. For the dating of the letter to June 1153, see Lees, "La lettera di Anselmo di Havelberg a Pietro il Venerabile: Federico Barbarossa e Baume-Les-Messieurs," *Benedictina* 40 (1993), 49-56; for the later document in which Guigo is named see n. 31 below.

about Peter's piety and discretion from Guigo, some indication that Guigo was Peter's man. But the story of Baume and Cluny did not end in 1153. By 1157 Frederick had married Beatrice, heiress to Burgundy, and was more than willing to help the monks of Baume break their ties to Cluny in return for allegiance to him. In November of that year, he removed all Cluniac control of Baume, reestablished it as an abbey under royal protection, and allowed the monks to elect their own abbot. It appears that the monks had proceeded to throw off the yoke of Cluny by holding their first election before Frederick issued this grant of protection, for the charter speaks of the present abbot of Baume: Guigo. His tenure of office lasted until 1170.[31] In spite of any kind words about Peter to Anselm, this former prior was on the side of the Benedictine monks of Baume and in opposition to Cluny.

This same two-faced attitude can also be seen with Frederick, who, in 1153, appeared to have fallen in line with Peter's desires to reform Baume by bringing it under the sway of Cluny. Anselm says in his letter that Frederick had the highest regard for Peter: "Ever since [the king] saw you once, he has retained a sweet memory of you."[32] But as has been shown, Frederick turned around some four years later and took the side of the Benedictines of Baume in opposition to Cluny.

When Anselm met Guigo in 1153, he met a man who had probably come to Frederick to plead on behalf of Baume's continued independence from Cluny; and in Frederick, Anselm may very well have perceived a ruler looking for ways to use the royal prerogative to create allies out of religious institutions. Twice in the letter, Anselm indicates that in spite of the friendly words of Guigo and Frederick, Peter should be careful. The first instance is just a hint: After speaking of Guigo, Anselm says that since he recognizes that Peter is engaged in the affairs of the empire, he would like to come to the

---

[31] *UF* 193, pp. 323-325, dated November 18, 1157. Locatelli, *L'abbaye de Baume-les-Messieurs*, p. 81-86, esp. p. 85, for the election of abbots of Baume. Locatelli points out how scarce the evidence is and does not deal with Guigo. Guigo is identified in Locatelli's list of abbots as Guy or Guigues whose abbacy lasted from 1157 to 1170 (p. 242), though he is not shown on the list of priors where none are identified for the period 1146 to 1191 (p. 244).

[32] *Recueil des chartes de l'abbaye de Cluny* 5.4176, p. 527. Frederick's meeting with Peter was in Frankfurt in 1147. Peter was granted a charter by Conrad III to which Frederick is a witness, *UK* 176 (March 13, 1147), p. 318. Anselm was also in Frankfurt at this time (see p. 75 n. 16 above) and may have met Peter.

abbot's attention with his letter, and he hopes "at some time to see you and enjoy conversation with your holiness."[33] There is an echo here of the cautious Anselm who, as an exile in Havelberg, wrote Wibald expressing a desire to speak with his friends face-to-face rather than put his thoughts in writing.[34] The second caveat is at the close of the letter when he comes as close as he dares to spelling out his fears. After mentioning the esteem in which Frederick holds Peter, Anselm writes:

> It concerns you, therefore, that you conduct those affairs which must be done carefully and prudently according to the wisdom given you by God, since you realize that man's nature is tortuous and as changeable and slippery as a cunning snake. In other words, 'I know not how to hold fast the changing countenance of Proteus.' Pray for us and all men, beloved father.[35]

This friendly letter is, then, a warning, and not about human nature in general but about Frederick and Guigo in particular: Be careful, for behind the cordiality these men might offer now, their expression can change in an instant. The problems with Baume touched concerns about the spiritual lives of monks and clerics and the control of ecclesiastical offices, concerns that were central to the great reform movement of the eleventh and early twelfth centuries. A heavy-handed ruler could upset the gains reformers had made as well as the fragile balance between spiritual and lay authorities. Anselm had already seen Frederick move willfully to get the archiepiscopate of Magdeburg for his man Wichmann, and this willfulness apparently presented itself again in the deliberations over Baume. One does not have to attribute to Anselm a clear prescience of what would happen in 1157 to suggest that he saw a disturbing willfulness in Frederick in 1153. Even if for the moment Peter the Venerable got what he wanted, for Anselm the one who granted the abbot's wish was "as cunning as a snake."

The sources have left little more than a suggestion of Anselm's

---

[33] *Recueil des chartes de l'abbaye de Cluny* 5.4176, p. 527.

[34] See p. 89 above.

[35] *Recueil des chartes de l'abbaye de Cluny* 5.4176, p. 527: "Vestra igitur interest, ut juxta sapientiam vobis a Deo datam caute ac prudenter ea que tractanda sunt tractetis, quoniam hominem tortuosum et serpentina astucia volubilem et lubriosum reperietis, et de quo dici potest: 'Nescio quo teneam mutantem Prothea wultus.' Orate pro nobis et hominibus, amabilis pater." Anselm is using Horace, epist. 1.1.90: "Quo teneam vultus mutantem Protea nodo."

movements from mid-1153 to May 1154.[36] Then his name disappears completely from the court records for another year, during a considerable part of which he was once again in Constantinople as the legate of his ruler. Whatever his problems had been with Conrad III, there is little better evidence that Anselm stood high in Frederick's estimation than the fact that the ruler looked to him for assistance in repairing the damage the Treaty of Constance—the very treaty Anselm himself had helped negotiate—had done to relations with the Greeks. While the Treaty of Constance carefully left the door open for negotiations between Frederick and Byzantium, it also destroyed the alliance Conrad III and Manuel I Comnenus had created in 1149, and in that sense it could only have hurt relations between the two powers. In 1153 Frederick had divorced his first wife, Adela;[37] and as a means of renewing the alliance with Byzantium, he sought the hand of a niece of Emperor Manuel I Comnenus. If such an alliance could be formed, a joint attack on Sicily was yet within the realm of possibility.[38] Negotiations with the Greeks concerning the marriage had begun the previous year, and now with the advice of his counselors, Frederick chose Anselm and Alexander, the count of Apulia who had been deposed by Roger of Sicily, to undertake the mission.[39] It did not meet with much success. Manuel

---

[36] Fall, 1153, Anselm at church court in Aachen on behalf of Wibald: Wibald, 421, pp. 557-60, Simonsfeld, *Friedrich I.*, p. 196 n. 156, Dombrowski, *Anselm*, pp. 47-48; Jan. 17, 1154, with Frederick in Speyer: *UF* 69, pp. 114-15; Feb. in Bamberg: *UF* 70, pp. 116-17; Apr. in Quedlinburg: *UF* 73, pp. 121-23; May, in Göppingen: *UF* 77, pp. 128-29.

[37] Simonsfeld, *Friedrich I.*, pp. 157-58, 167-69; Munz, *Frederick Barbarossa*, pp. 66-67.

[38] Rassow, *Honor Imperii*, p. 57; Lamma, *Comneni e Staufer* 1:141-47; Maccarrone, *Papato e impero*, pp. 68-70; Peter Classen, "La politica di Manuele Comneno tra Frederico Barbarossa e le città italiane," *Popolo e stato in Italia nell'età di Federico Barbarossa: Alessandria e la Lega Lombarda*, Relazioni e communicazioni al XXXIII Congresso storico subalpino (Turin, 1970), p. 267; Opll, *Friedrich Barbarossa*, pp. 46-47.

[39] There has been a great deal written on the possibility that Anselm made two trips to Constantinople, one in the fall of 1153, the second in the spring of 1154. The problem stems from a passage in Otto of Freising's *Gesta Friderici* (2.11, pp. 111-12): "Rex tamen, quia non multo ante haec per apostolicae sedis legatos ab uxore sua ob vinculum consanguinitatis separatus fuerat, pro ducenda alia pertractans, ad Manuel Grecorum imperatorem tam pro hoc negotio quam pro Gwilhelmo Siculo, qui patre suo Rogerio noviter defuncto successerat, utriusque imperii invasore, debellando in Greciam legatos destinandos ordinat, sicque primatum suorum consilio Anshelmus Havelbergensis episcopus et Alexander Apuliae quondam comes." Since the diet of Regensburg took place in Sept. 1153 and Roger died in Feb. 1154, the reference to

was as set on territorial gain in Italy as Frederick was on denying it to him;[40] and no matter what Anselm's talents were, this was an impasse he could not overcome.[41]

In the fall of 1154, Anselm set off for Italy to join Frederick in his efforts to obtain the imperial crown. On this journey, he may have stopped in Thessalonica to meet the Greek Archbishop Basilius of Achrida and debate much the same issues as those addressed in Constantinople in 1136. The debate was amicable, but little progress

---

overthrowing William has been taken to show some confusion on Otto's part about when Anselm was first sent to Constantinople. Simonsfeld says that Otto, writing after the event, mistakenly mentioned William and that Anselm went to Constantinople in September, returning by January 17, 1154 at the latest (*Friedrich I.*, pp. 200 n. 173, 211-12). Then he would have Anselm leave again for the East in the spring of 1154 with Otto making no mention of this departure and see Otto's reference to Anselm's return in 1155 as referring to this second trip (*Gesta Friderici* 2.27, p. 132). Simonsfeld's argument hinges on a letter from Manuel to Wibald dated November 22, 1153, in which he speaks of the negotiations for a Greek bride (Wibald, 424, p. 561). That negotiations had been going on before this is certain (Lamma, *Comneni e Staufer* 1:141-45), but there is no evidence that Anselm was part of them. Wentz supports Simonsfeld, saying that "der Umstand, dass der griechische Kaiser einen Brief an den Abt Wibald mitgibt spricht für A[nselm] als Überbringer des Schreibens" (*Havelberg*, p. 36). Manuel had had other correspondence with Wibald, and there is no reason to believe that he would be particular about the bearer of this letter. In fact, the letter itself refers to Manuel's own *nuntii*. The most persuasive argument that Anselm made this earlier trip has been that his name, so frequently found among the witnesses to Frederick's charters, is not to be found between June 1153 and January 1154 (Lamma, *Comneni e Staufer* 1:145 n. 1; Ferdinand Chalandon, *Les Comnène: Etudes sur l'empire byzantin au XIe et au XIIe siècles* 2.1: *Jean II Comnène (1118-1143) et Manuel I Comnene (1143-1180)* (Paris, 1912), pp. 344 n. 2, 346 n.1.) This point, however, becomes meaningless when one recognizes that between July 12, 1153 (*UF* 67, pp. 110-111) and Jan. 17, 1154 (*UF* 69, pp. 114-15, to which Anselm is a witness—n. 36 above), no charters were issued. I agree with Lamma's statement: "Non si può imputare ad Ottone un'esposizione confusa, perchè egli non dice affatto che l'invio dell'ambasceria sia contemporaneo alla Dieta di Ratisbona." *Comneni e Staufer* 1:145 n. 1. See also Dräseke, "Bischof Anselm von Havelberg," pp. 181-82.

[40] Rassow, *Honor Imperii*, p. 75; Lamma, *Comneni e Staufer* 1:145-46; Werner Ohnsorge, "Zu den Aussenpolitischen Anfängen Friedrich Barbarossas," *Quellen und Forschungen aus Italienischen Archiven und Bibliotheken* 32 (1942), p. 32; Chalandon, *Les Comnène* 2.1:344-347.

[41] Manuel's rejection of a Latin delegation is mentioned by John Kinnamos, *Deeds of John and Manuel Comnenus*, trans. Charles M. Brand (New York, 1976), 4.1, p. 106. Lamma suggests that Frederick responded to this by sending Anselm's delegation. Lamma, *Comneni e Staufer* 1:146. See also Wolfgang Georgi, *Friedrich Barbarossa und die auswärtigen Mächte: Studien zur Aussenpolitik 1159-1180*, Europäische Hochschulschriften, Reihe 3, 442 (New York, 1990), pp. 17-19.

toward reconciliation was made. It should be said that the fragmentary surviving account of these debates comes from Basilius and does not give the name of his Latin opponent.[42]

Anselm returned to find Frederick already in Italy. Making good on his promise to assist the pope, the ruler had assembled his army and come south. After aiding the citizens of Pavia in besieging and eventually leveling Tortona, he moved along the Po River and then south toward Bologna, stopping near Modena in early May. By this time Anselm had returned to the king's court.[43] Frederick does not seem to have been bothered in the least by the failure of Anselm's mission, for he bestowed on him a great honor. According to Otto of Freising:

> Around this time, Bishop Anselm of Havelberg, having returned from Greece, received from the prince by election of the clergy and people the archiepiscopate of Ravenna as well as the exarchate of that same province, a magnificent reward for his labors.[44]

There is an echo here of the Wichmann affair. Anselm, completely unknown to "the clergy and people" of Ravenna, was Frederick's candidate. Whatever dissent clergy and people may have expressed has been covered by Otto's description of a perfectly legal election. Otto gives the sense that Anselm's "election" came soon after his return from Greece. However, where Wichmann had immediately assumed the title of archbishop, Anselm (who, like Wichmann, was switching from one episcopal office to another without papal permission) proceeded with caution. On June 4, he witnessed a charter for

---

[42] The debate has been edited by Joseph Schmidt, *Das Basilius aus Achrida, Erzbischofs von Thessalonich, bisher unedierte Dialoge: Ein Beitrag zur Geschichte des griechischen Schismas* (Munich, 1901). On the probable date of the debate (October 1154), V. Grumel, "Notes d'histoire et de littérature Byzantines," *Echos d'Orient* 29 (1930), 336. Lamma tends toward identifying the Latin as Anselm but shows how speculative this is. *Comneni e Staufer* 1:169 n.1. On Basilius of Achrida see Hans-Georg Beck, *Kirche und Theologische Literatur im Byzantinischen Reich, Handbuch der Altertumswissenschaft* 12, 2.1: *Byzantinisches Handbuch* 2.1 (Munich, 1959), p. 626, who, however, wrongly identifies Anselm as the "Abgesandten des Papstes."

[43] *UF* 103 (to May 5-13, 1155), pp. 174-76.

[44] Otto of Freising, *Gesta Friderici* 2.27, p. 132. It is possible that Frederick considered Havelberg to be an unimportant diocese and Anselm's service as its bishop a waste of talent. The ruler generally did his best to influence episcopal elections, but apparently showed no interest in the election of Anselm's successor. See Töpfer, "Kaiser Friedrich I. Barbarossa und der deutsche Episkopat," p. 412.

Frederick still using the title "bishop of Havelberg."[45] The archiepiscopal title could wait until the new pope, Hadrian IV, had bestowed the pallium.

Frederick proceeded toward Rome to meet the pope, who, in the meantime, had himself traveled to Sutri and thence to Viterbo. To arrange the details of the meeting, delegations from each camp were sent to the other. Anselm and his old friend Archbishop Arnold of Cologne, led the German delegation.[46] The pope, who wanted to be certain of Frederick's willingness to help him deal with the Normans and the Romans, had withdrawn to Civita Castellana to start negotiations from a distance. There Anselm and Arnold met with him and expressed Frederick's good will toward Hadrian and the church. Still, Hadrian was unwilling to confer in detail about a meeting with Frederick, and on the advice of his court, decided to await his own delegation's return. This was no help, for Frederick had taken the same position and sent the Italians back no wiser than when they started. The two unsuccessful delegations met on the road returning to their respective camps and decided to make arrangements on the spot to avoid further confusion. Both groups returned to Frederick, who, realizing Hadrian's fears, took an oath to hold to the terms of the Treaty of Constance and not to harm the pope or his cardinals in any way.[47] Anselm's exact role in all of this is not known, but one may be certain that he and Arnold saw it as their duty to remove any stumbling blocks in the way of an alliance between Frederick and Hadrian, and in this they were successful.

---

[45] *UF* 110, pp. 186-87. Moses, the previous archbishop, died on Oct. 26, 1154. Ferdinand Ughelli, *Italia sacra sive de episcopis Italiae* 2 (1717; repr. Nendeln, 1970), pp. 77, 368; Giorgio Orioli, "Cronotassi dei vescovi di Ravenna," *Felix Ravenna* 127-30 (1984-85), 330. See p. 100 n. 14 above.

[46] Boso, *Adrien IV, Liber Pontificalis* 2, ed. L. Duchesne (1882; repr. Paris, 1955), p. 390. Wolter gives as one of the reasons Anselm and Arnold were chosen "dass sie...als Stellvertreter für den deutschen und italienischen Episcopat angesehen werden konnten" (*Arnold von Wied*, p. 100). However, Anselm still used the title *episcopus Havelbergensis* at this time. To have assumed the archiepiscopal title would have created an unnecessary problem; to have acted as the representative of the Italian episcopate would have been asking for trouble. Boso did describe Anselm as the archbishop of Ravenna but wrote after Anselm received the pallium (an event Boso does not record).

[47] Boso, *Adrien IV*, pp. 390-91; Maccarrone, *Papato e impero*, 110-17; Munz, *Frederick Barbarossa*, pp. 78-80; Hausmann, *Reichskanzlei*, pp. 119-20; Simonsfeld, *Friedrich I.*, pp. 327-29.

The meeting of pope and ruler took place on June 9 at Sutri. Arnold of Cologne led the most important men in Frederick's army to greet the pope and escort him to the king.[48] The meeting, however, did not live up to the expectations of either side. Frederick held back, waiting while the pope dismounted and was seated. Then the ruler prostrated himself and rose, expecting the papal kiss of peace. Now Hadrian held back. He had expected Frederick to honor him by acting as his *strator* or groom by taking the bridle of his horse and helping him to dismount, that is to give him the honor "which your predecessors the rightful emperors were accustomed to show my predecessors the Roman pontiffs out of reverence for the apostles Peter and Paul." Until such honor was shown, said Hadrian, there would be no kiss of peace.[49] This, however, was an act of submission that Frederick would not perform. Not yet off the ground, the negotiations had already broken down.

In assessing Anselm's role in the negotiations at Sutri, it should first of all be admitted that his name is not specifically mentioned in the sources. Nevertheless, we are told that when Frederick refused to act the part of *strator*, he retreated to discuss the situation with his advisers "and especially those who went with King Lothar to Pope Innocent." One of these, almost certainly the most important, was Anselm. He had not only worked hard to bring the pope and the ruler together, but he is the only man in Frederick's entourage for whom there is documentary evidence of his being both with Lothar III in Liège to witness that king act as groom to Innocent II in 1131 and with that ruler on the Italian expedition in 1132-1133.[50] When Frederick asked what happened when Lothar went to the pope, Anselm could and almost assuredly did respond that in Liège, when the pope went to Lothar, the ruler had acted as *strator*. Beyond this, however, Frederick must have been interested in what Lothar had done in a situation which more closely resembled his own at Sutri, that is what Lothar had done when he had gone to Italy, with An-

---

[48] Simonsfeld, *Friedrich I.*, pp. 682-83; Wolter, *Arnold von Wied*, p. 100.

[49] Boso, *Adrien IV*, p. 391.

[50] Lothar was in the company of Innocent in Liège in 1131 and on the Italian expeditions of 1132/33 and 1136; Anselm was with the ruler on all three occasions. Though there is no documentation, Simonsfeld suggests that both Arnold of Cologne and Hillin of Trier (who were with Frederick at Sutri) were in Liège in 1131. *Friedrich I.*, pp. 683-84; see also Maccarrone, *Papato e impero*, p. 120; Wolter, *Arnold von Wied*, pp. 100-1; and pp. 34, 35 n. 55, 50-53 above.

selm in accompaniment, to meet the pope.[51] While there is no evidence that Lothar again acted as *strator*, he and Pope Innocent
clashed when the ruler insisted on the full right of investiture. It was
Anselm's mentor Norbert who had found a way through the impasse
by moving the focus away from Innocent and onto St. Peter, saying
that because of his (Norbert's) duty to St. Peter, he would have to
oppose Innocent should the pope surrender to Lothar's demands.[52]
According to the accounts of Hadrian and Frederick's first meeting,
Hadrian refused to give the kiss of peace because Frederick had not
shown him honor "out of reverence for the Apostles Peter and Paul"
or "from reverence for the Prince of the Apostles."[53] These same
sources go on to say that Frederick was finally persuaded to take the
part of Hadrian's groom precisely by emphasizing that he would be
acting, as one source puts it, "out of reverence for the blessed apostles," and another, "out of reverence for the prince of the apostles
and the apostolic chair,"[54] part of the pope's original demand. It is
not, then, that someone among Frederick's advisers introduced into
the negotiations a phrase concerning the apostles, but that someone
saw that by emphasizing the reverence due the apostles over the
honor Hadrian felt he was owed in his somewhat clichéd demand,
the pretensions of the ruler would not be set against those of the
pope. One may suggest that Anselm, the student of Norbert and the
sole member Frederick's entourage at Sutri who had been with Norbert and Lothar in Italy, is the likely candidate to have grasped this.[55]

---

[51] Boso (*Adrien IV*, p. 391) and a second account of the meeting by Albinus-
Cencius, *Liber Censuum, Pontificum Romanorum vitae* 2, ed. J. M. Watterich (Leipzig,
1862), pp. 342-43, say Frederick was especially interested in talking to those who
went with Lothar to Innocent. Boso: "Tandem requisitis antiquioribus principibus,
et illis precipue qui cum rege Lotario ad Innocentium papam venerant..." Albinus-
Cencius: "Tandem vero antiquioribus principum et illis qui cum imperatore Lotario
ad domnum papam Innocentium venerant, requisitis...." (These sources are compared by Simonsfeld, *Friedrich I.*, pp. 679-80.) By using the title *rex* rather than
imperator for Lothar, it appears Boso thought Frederick's concern was for the Liège
and 1132/33 meetings whereas Albinus-Cencius is either generalizing or focusing on
the period after Lothar's coronation. Boso is almost certainly correct.

[52] See p. 36 above.

[53] Boso, *Adrien IV*, p. 391; Albinus-Cencius, *Liber*, p. 342.

[54] Boso, *Adrien IV* 391-92: "pro beatorum Apostolorum [principis?] reverentia;"
Albinus-Cencius, *Liber*, p. 342: "pro apostolorum principis et sedis apostolice reverentia." Simonsfeld, *Friedrich I.*, p. 680.

[55] On Sutri: Maccarrone, *Papato e impero*, pp. 117-21; Simonsfeld, *Friedrich I.*, 677-
88 with an evaluation of the sources giving Albinus-Cencius precedence over Boso;
Holtzmann, *Der Kaiser als Marschall des Papstes*, pp. 44-49, arguing against Simonsfeld;

On June 18, 1155, Frederick was crowned emperor by the pope in St. Peter's in Rome. Anselm had avoided the pitfalls of the Wichmann affair, and on this same day, Hadrian IV bestowed on him the pallium of the archbishop of Ravenna.[56] As such his name appears in Frederick's grant of protection to S. Maria in Portu in Ravenna issued shortly afterwards.[57] For the next two months Anselm stayed with the imperial court as Frederick, unable to draw his princes into an attack on William, the new ruler of Sicily, began the march back to Germany.[58] After stopping in Faenza,[59] Frederick himself went with Anselm to Ravenna, where he made arrangements for his new archbishop to procure a statue of the Virgin for S. Maria in Portu.[60] The ruler was apparently concerned enough about his control of the city to leave an imperial official in Ravenna as the captain or prefect of the city, one Conrad the German to whom Anselm gave the usufruct of an estate.[61] If Conrad's presence in Ravenna is an indica-

---

and Munz, *Frederick Barbarossa*, pp. 80-83. Munz argues (p. 82 n. 1) that a third source for the incident is consistent with Boso, namely Helmold of Bosau's *Cronica Slavorum* 1.81, pp. 152-54. Helmold says that Bishop Eberhard of Bamberg tried to placate the pope, a point accepted by Maccarrone (p. 118). Helmold's account is, however, extremely confused, saying that the pope was upset that Frederick had taken the wrong bridle, not that he had been unwilling to act as *strator*. Munz cites the response to the charge of taking the wrong bridle attributed to Frederick by Helmold ("Dicite [papae], quia defectus hic non fuit devocionis, sed scientiae") as if it applied to Frederick's not having served as *strator* at all (p. 82   with n. 1). In short, I do not think the two accounts are as consistent as Munz would have it.

[56] *Regesta Pontificum Romanorum Italia Pontificia* 5: *Aemilia sive provincia Ravennas*, ed. Paul Kehr (1911; repr. Berlin, 1961), 219, p. 64; *Annales Palidenses*, MGH SS 16:89; *Chronicon Montis Sereni*, MGH SS 23:150. By way of comparison with Wichmann, one may note that while Anselm received the pallium directly from the pope as was customary, Wichmann had stirred up such animosity in the curia that Anastasius IV refused to bestow it on him personally. Instead, he laid it on the alter in St. Peter's, telling Wichmann to go and get it if he felt he had been canonically elected. According to this wonderful story, when Wichmann hesitated, two of his companions picked it up for him and died soon after. *Chronicon Montis Sereni*, MGH SS 23:149.

[57] June 18-19, 1155, *UF* 111, pp. 187-90.

[58] *UF* 115-116, pp. 195-99, dated respectively July 7, 1155 near Tusculum and to shortly after July 7 near Tivoli.

[59] Aug 25. 1155, *UF* 119, pp. 200-2.

[60] Marco Fantuzzi, *Monumenti Ravennati* 2.63 (Venice, 1802), p. 124; Ferdinand Opll, "Amator ecclesiarum: Studien zur religiösen Haltung Friedrich Barbarossas," *Mitteilungen des Instituts für Österreichische Geschichtsforschung* 88 (1980), 79.

[61] Hieronymus Rubeus, *Historiarum Ravennatum* 6 (Venice, 1572), p. 369. This charter is not in MGH DD 10.1. Conrad, called *Conradus Alemannus* by Rubeus, has been identified as Conrad of Swabia by Riedel ("Nachrichten," p. 262) and Dombrowski (*Anselm*, p. 52). By this they may mean Frederick's half brother Conrad who accompanied him to Italy. Rubeus is probably referring to one *Conradus Teutonicus* men-

tion that Frederick was unsure of the loyalty of Ravenna, events were to prove his fears well founded.

Anselm spent the remainder of his life as the archbishop of Ravenna and never returned to Germany. As Otto of Freising says, he was not only archbishop but *exarchus* of the province.[62] The use of the title exarch was rare in the West. In Ravenna, the archbishop does not seem to have used it since at least the early part of the eleventh century,[63] making Anselm unique in calling himself Archbishop of the church of Ravenna and exarch of the same city (*Sancti Ravennatis ecclesiae archiepiscopus et eiusdem civitatis exarchus*).[64] While the archbishop's pallium came from the pope, the office of exarch was a secular one presumably granted by Frederick before he had met with Hadrian. Here Frederick was attempting to create or revive an office for Anselm in which his dependence on the emperor rather than on the pope would be clear.[65] But what authority did this office have? Otto says Anselm was made exarch of the province of Ravenna. It is difficult to say exactly what was meant by this. Apparently, Frederick wanted Anselm to have jurisdiction over the whole of the Romagna extending north to Ferrara, west to Reggio and south to Rimini.[66] If

---

tioned in several documents of the period: *Regesto di S. Apollinare Nuovo, Regesta chartarum Italiae*, ed. V. Federici (Rome, 1907), 89, pp. 78-79; *Regesto della chiesa di Ravenna: Le carte dell'archivio Estense 1, Regesta chartarum Italiae*, ed. V. Federici and G. Buzzi (Rome, 1911), 46-47, pp. 33-34. See Augusto Torre, "La Romagna e Federico Barbarossa," *Popolo e stato in Italia nell'età di Federico Barbarossa: Alessandria e la lega Lombarda*, Relazioni e comunicazioni al XXXIII congresso storico subalpino per la celebrazione del'VIII contenario della fondazione di Alessandria (Turin, 1970), p. 598; Ferdinand Opll, *Stadt und Reich im 12. Jahrhundert (1125-1190)*, Forschungen zur Kaiser- und Papstgeschichte des Mittelalters, Beihefte zu J.F. Böhmer, Regesta imperii 6 (Vienna, 1966), pp. 407-8.

[62] See p. 110 above.

[63] The *Regesto della chiesa di Ravenna* gives only twenty-nine charters for the period 896-1155 (only one from before the eleventh century). In none of these charters does the archbishop refer to himself as the exarch.

[64] *Regesto della chiesa di Ravenna* 30-36, pp. 23-28.

[65] Augusto Torre, "La Romagna e Federico Barbarossa," 597-98.

[66] John Larner, *The Lords of Romagna: Romagnol Society and the Origins of the Signorie* (Ithaca, 1965), p. 23: "From the end of the tenth century, 'the Exarchate of Ravenna,' which included the whole of Romagna, was within the medieval Empire." On the difficulty of defining the borders of the Romagna, see Larner, pp. 205-8. Some light on Frederick's use of the office of exarch is found in an imperial charter of 1157. On Nov. 18, Frederick invested Archbishop Heraclius with the city of Lyon and with full legal jurisdiction both in and outside of the city and throughout the archiepiscopal see. Finally, he granted Heraclius the title *gloriosissimus exarchon* of the Burgundian Palatinate (*UF* 192, pp. 321-23). Here is a much clearer attempt than in

so, Anselm must have rapidly become aware that his authority outside of the city of Ravenna was limited, indeed;[67] and it is noteworthy that in his charters he never refers to himself as the exarch of a province but only as exarch of the city.[68] The limits of Anselm's authority only become apparent with Frederick's second Italian campaign in 1158.

In the intervening years, the evidence for Anselm's activities is found exclusively in the charters he issued as archbishop. However, whereas the charters for Jerichow and Havelberg can be placed firmly within the context of a bishop establishing episcopal authority and defining the borders and possessions of a newly won diocese, the context of those issued in Ravenna remains vague. Whether they show an archbishop acting authoritatively or merely reacting to the pressures of long established forces is impossible to determine.[69] It is,

the case of Anselm to create a secular office dependent on the emperor out of an ecclesiastical one. This use of the office of exarch north of the Alps was possibly an extension of Frederick's intentions for Ravenna. However, shortly after Anselm's death, Frederick abandoned the idea of a combined spiritual and secular office and placed control of the city in the hands of his secular official. See Alfred Haverkamp, *Herrschaftsformen der frühstaufer in Reichsitalien* 2, Monographien zur Geschichte des Mittelalters 1 (Stuttgart, 1970), pp. 337-41.

[67] On the limits of archiepiscopal authority in Ravenna and Frederick Barbarossa's efforts to control the city, see Torre, "La Romagna e Federico Barbarossa," pp. 595-607, specifically on Anselm as archbishop, pp. 597-99. Opll (*Stadt und Reich*, pp. 406-7) points to the attempts of German rulers to counterbalance the power of the local nobility, above all the family of Traversarius, by controlling the archbishop and placing royal officials in the city. Larner (*The Lords of Romagna*, pp. 17-18) says that from the time of the Investiture Controversy, the communes of the province claimed independent jurisdiction and the contado came under the control of the nobility.

[68] See n. 69 below; also Lamma, *Comneni e Staufer* 1:193.

[69] Charters issued by Anselm: Confirmation of possessions of S. Maria in Porto: Wolf Gehrt, *Die Verbände der Regularkanonikerstifte S. Frediano in Lucca, S. Maria in Reno bei Bologna, S. Maria in Porto bei Ravenna und die cura animarum im 12. Jahrhundert*, Europäische Hochschulschriften series 3, 224 (New York, 1984), p. 146. Lease of church land near Argenta, Mar. 12, 1156: *Regesto della chiesa di Ravenna* 30, pp. 23-24. Confirmation of possessions of the parish of Pulianello: Ughelli, *Italia Sacra* 2, pp. 370-71; Ludovico Antonio Muratorio, *Antiquitates Italicae medii aevi* 6 (Milan, 1742), 441-44; Francesco Milani, "Le pievi rurali di Reggio Emilia," *Ravennatensia* 4 (1974), 627. Grant of lands in Cinque Taverne to S. Apollinare Nuovo, Feb. 3, 1157: *Regesto di S. Apollinare Nuovo* 86, p. 77. Purchase of villages near Cesena, June 1157: Riedel, "Nachrichten," p. 53; Dombrowski, *Anselm*, p. 53, relying on later editions of Rubeus than the one available to me. Confirmation of predecessors' grants of land to the bishop of Modena, July 26, 1157: *Regesto della chiesa cattedrale di Modena* 1, *Regesta chartarum Italiae* 16, ed. Emilio Paolo Vicini (Rome, 1931), 470, pp. 364-65. Lease of land near Ferrara, Feb. 1158: *Regesto della chiesa di Ravenna* 31-35, pp. 24-28.

however, worth noting that in February 1158, Anselm confirmed the rights of the cardinal archdeacon of the church of Ravenna and those of his fellow cardinals and their successors in the churches of the city and its suburbs.[70] These were the men on whom Anselm depended to govern his exarchate,[71] and they were also the men who should have played a leading role in an archiepiscopal election,[72] a right which in Anselm's case had been usurped by Frederick. Perhaps, Anselm feared resistance from those closest to him and wanted to remove any fears that, in acting as Frederick's agent, he would undermine their prerogatives. On the other hand, the powerful families of the Romagna soon demonstrated that the archbishop and his ruler did not command their unconditional loyalty, and Anselm was securing the support of those whose services he would need in any confrontation. Such a confrontation was in the offing, for when Frederick decided on a new campaign in Italy, the loyalty of the Ravannese came very much into question.

By 1158, events in Germany and elsewhere in Italy had rapidly precipitated a second campaign by Frederick and his army. As long as the emperor was at his elbow, Pope Hadrian had remained true to the spirit of the Treaty of Constance in his opposition to William of Sicily; and at Frederick's departure, the pope was allied with the barons of southern Italy who were in rebellion against their king. Within a year, however, William successfully defeated his enemies; and Hadrian, who had already sought help from the Byzantines,[73] came to terms with the Norman king in the Treaty of Benevento. The message was clear: Frederick and the Treaty of Constance had not given Hadrian the protection he needed; henceforth, the pope would look south. Frederick was furious.[74] Hardly in a position to

---

[70] In Angelo Duranti, "Il collegio dei cardinali di Ravenna," *Ravennatensia* 4 (1974), 593-95.

[71] See Duranti, "Il collegio," pp. 529-618, on the offices of cardinal in Ravenna. The author comments: "Ora per indicare la differenza tra il clero del vescovo e quello delle chiese private non vi era termine che meglio si prestasse della voce cardinale. E' quindi in tal senso che deve intendersi l'appellativo di *cardinale* dato al collegio dei presbiteri, dei diaconi e dei subdiaconi delle varie cattedrali diocesane, collegio formante un sol corpo con il vescovo, con cui conviverva, ufficiava e sbrigava le cose più importanti, agendo in sua assenza e rappresentando, lui morto, la sua chiesa" (p. 533).

[72] Duranti, "Il collegio," pp. 575-76.

[73] This was done secretly and was clearly a violation of the Treaty of Constance. Maccarrone, *Papato e impero*, pp. 144-45.

[74] Chalandon, *Histoire de la domination Normande* 2:233-35; Maccarrone, *Papato e impero*, pp. 141-58, 162; Lamma, *Comneni e Staufer* 1:244.

expect papal support for a campaign against William, he turned his gaze on the Lombard cities and in particular on Milan, which had resisted imperial control and oppressed its neighbors in defiance of the emperor.[75] If the pope would not give him ecclesiastical control in Lombardy, Frederick would enforce his secular rights with a vengeance.

Before beginning his second Italian campaign, Frederick sent his close adviser Rainald of Dassel with Otto of Wittelsbach into Italy early in 1158 to cities loyal to Frederick to get assurance of support for the operation against Milan.[76] The two men made their way from Verona to Bologna and then to Ravenna.[77] There Anselm met them with all honors, having assembled fourteen bishops for their reception.[78] While Anselm's allegiance was never in question, it rapidly became obvious to Frederick's ambassadors that the loyalty of the city was very much in doubt. The *podestà*, William Traversarius, had taken some three hundred men including many of the nobility of the city to Ancona to meet with representatives of the Greek emperor Manuel.[79] These had come officially to recruit men to fight William of Sicily, but rumor had it that their true mission was to bring the cities of the Adriatic coast over to the Greeks.[80] Ever the diplomat, Anselm tried to keep Rainald and Otto in the city to await the *podestà*'s return. In his account of the ensuing events, Rainald says

---

[75] Frederick wrote Wibald of Stablo: "Mediolanensis dumtaxat populi superbiam ac temeritatem, qua aecclesiae et civiates Lonbardiae, sicut optime nosti, multifarie destructae sunt et cotidie ad contumeliam imperii destruuntur" (Wibald, 456, p. 589); also Rahewin, *Gesta Friderici* 3. 29, pp. 203-4). Lamma, *Comneni e Staufer* 1:248-49; Gina Fasoli, "Federico Barbarossa e le città lombarde," *Vorträge und Forschungen* 12: *Probleme des 12. Jahrhunderts* (Constance, 1968), pp. 128-29; Maccarrone, *Papato e impero*, p. 162; Hampe, *Deutsche Kaisergeschichte*, p. 163. For a useful overview extending beyond the period dealt with here, see David R. Carr, "Frederick Barbarossa and the Lombard League: Imperial Regalia, Prescriptive Rights, and the Northern Italian Cities," *Journal of the Rocky Mountain Medieval and Renaissance Association* 10 (1989), 29-49.

[76] The oath the cities were to give is found in Rahewin, *Gesta Friderici* 3.20, p. 191.

[77] There are two accounts of Rainald and Otto's journey through northern Italy: Rahewin, *Gesta Friderici* 3.20, pp. 190-94; and Rainald's own report in *Registrum, oder merkwürdige Urkunden für die deutsche Geschichte* 2, ed. H. Sudendorf (Berlin, 1851), pp. 131-32. For the general itinerary of their travels, I have used Rainald. For a comparison of the two accounts see Simonsfeld, *Friedrich I.*, pp. 716-19; Lamma, *Comneni e Staufer* 1:292-306.

[78] Sudendorf, *Registrum* 2:131.

[79] Sudendorf, *Registrum* 2:131. For William Traversarius, see Lamma, *Comneni e Staufer* 1:292-94.

[80] Rahewin, *Gesta Friderici* 3.20, p. 192.

that both he and Otto were full of anger and indignation;[81] but most likely, the brash Otto, who would shortly display dashing and almost foolhardy bravado, insisted on going after the Ravennese.[82]

Anselm accompanied them, but if he had hoped to avoid an armed clash, he did not reckon with Otto's fast sword. Just outside of the city, the archbishop and the ambassadors with their small force of no more than ten knights met the returning citizens of the city, some three hundred strong. Furious that they could have made a pact with the Greeks and in spite of being outnumbered some thirty to one, Otto drew his sword and charged. One can only imagine Anselm's horror upon witnessing an event which, no matter what the outcome, must have appeared diplomatically unsalvageable. Fortunately for the archbishop, Otto managed to grab William Traversarius and hold him at sword's point. The others drew back, and Otto led William, his son, and six other men away captive.[83] With no blood spilled, Anselm now had time to work out a peaceful solution.

Anselm accompanied Rainald and Otto, who continued to Ancona where they forced the Greeks to return home. After this, according to Rainald, the archbishop asked for the release of William and the other hostages. At first, Rainald was unwilling to agree but finally gave in to Anselm's pleas that the archbishop would be unwelcome in his own city should he return alone. On condition that they swear allegiance to Frederick, the German ambassadors let their prisoners take their valuables and go.[84] Anselm's fears indicate that he had made little headway in winning the affection of his city and its nobility,[85] and there is evidence that the Traversarius family had created earlier difficulties for the archbishop, as will be seen. Still, Rainald's account smacks of an attempt to cast the Ravennese in the

---

[81] Sudendorf, *Registrum* 2:131.

[82] Note Rahewin's description of the two ambassadors: "Etas iuvenilis, eloquentia mirabilis; prope moribus equales, preter quod uni ex officio et ordine clericali mansuetudo et misericordia alteri, quem non sine causa portabat, gladii severitas dignitatem addiderat. Aput alterum miseris profugium erat, aput alterum malis pernicies." *Gesta Friderici* 3.19, p. 190.

[83] The above draws on both Rainald's and Rahewin's accounts. Though Simonsfeld seems to feel that Rahewin can be discounted, I do not entirely agree. Rainald speaks of himself as acting with Otto in initiating the action, thus allowing himself to share in the glory. Rahewin's reliance on others for his story may have caused him to make errors of time and place, but he is much more willing to give credit where it was due. See Lamma, *Comneni e Staufer* 1:295-300.

[84] Sudendorf, *Registrum* 2:132-33.

[85] Simonsfeld, *Friedrich I.*, p. 627.

role of the enemy and Otto and himself in that of victors willing to release their prisoners only to maintain the archbishop's safety. Surely Anselm's own position in Ravenna was not the only argument he could have brought forward. The ambassadors' job was not, after all, to make enemies but allies; and Otto's verve had rapidly convinced the Ravennese that these Germans were not the sort to antagonize. Anselm played the role of mediator in convincing the ambassadors that Ravenna was on the side of the emperor.

With an imperial army moving into Italy, Anselm gained some control over the Ravennese nobility. On June 30, 1158, one of the nobles turned over to the archbishop a string of castles and towns stretching from the Adriatic coast to Forli,[86] and the archbishop resolutely pressed the leading family of Ravenna to lend its aid in the campaign against Milan. A story related some forty years later by an eyewitness and confirmed by others tells how Duke John Traversarius met with Anselm in the cloister of S. Maria de Vado. There Anselm insisted that a reluctant John accompany him to Milan. When John resisted, Anselm accused him of pledging lands to Venice which he held in tenure from the archbishop.[87] This is a good indication of the limits of Anselm's authority before Frederick's return: not only had John been dealing with the Venetians but he had used church land to do it. Finally, when Anselm threatened to "seize your whole duchy," John admitted that he was the tenant of the archbishop and agreed to go on the campaign.[88] He would die during the siege of Milan.[89]

---

[86] Ugelli, *Italia Sacra* 2:368-70; later confirmed by Frederick, *UF* 2.315 (Apr. 16, 1160), p. 137.

[87] The reason Anselm gives for his disapprobation is John's dealings with the Venetians. Still, it is possible that John was among the three hundred who treated with the Greeks and, as a relative of the *podestà*, one of the captives taken by Otto of Wittelsbach.

[88] *Regesto della chiesa di Ravenna* 126, pp. 85-86, dated 1197, giving two versions of this exchange which are almost identical. The exact date of the incident is not given, but the fact that John had been using church lands for his own purposes but was now willing to go along with Anselm in aiding the emperor indicates that it occurred sometime after Otto and Rainald's stay in Ravenna (middle of May) and the beginning of the siege of Milan (early Aug. 1158). Frederick's later confirmation of the possessions of the archiepiscopate of Ravenna (*UF* 315, MGH DD 10.2:137) reiterates a grant of Otto III at the end of the tenth century which names the *comitatum Trauesarie*. No doubt John felt the lands were his, and Anselm would have been in a weak position to enforce his claims without Frederick's army close at hand.

[89] *Regesto chiesa di Ravenna* 126, p. 85. That troops from Ravenna served in the siege of Milan is borne out by Vincent of Prague, *Annales*, MGH SS 17:673.

Anselm played an important role in the siege of Milan. It may have been because of him that there was a siege to begin with, and again because of him, or rather his death, that the siege was lifted. Exactly when and where he joined the imperial army is not known. The army began the march south in the middle of June. Rainald and Otto had done their job well, and men from imperial cities including Anselm and the Ravennese joined the Germans on the march through the Lombard plain. Brescia, Milan's erstwhile ally, submitted; and on July 23, Frederick's forces crossed the Adda River and moved on Milan.[90] The Milanese were not ignorant of the danger confronting them and sent representatives of the city to Frederick in an attempt to reach an agreement. They approached Frederick with a promise to pay a large sum of money to avoid a siege. The German princes were impressed and advised the emperor to accept the offer. At this point, Anselm spoke out:

> You do not know the slyness of the Milanese. They give you pleasant and humble words while carrying a wicked fox in their hearts. They should be judged by the standard with which they have judged others. They have destroyed the churches of God and the free cities of the emperor. They have not shown mercy, and so should be shown none.[91]

These are the last known words of Anselm of Havelberg. Here at the end of his life this man whose *Antikeimenon* has been noted for compromise showed no compromise at all. The communes of Italy, with their jealousies, competitive feuds, civil strife and complexities of government unheard of on the banks of the Havel, may have struck him as so intractable that the rebellious ones were beyond peaceful mollification. At any rate, after three years in Italy, Anselm had had time to assess the situation.[92] Frederick listened and then made his deci-

---

[90] Rahewin, *Gesta Friderici* 3.27-29, pp. 199-204.

[91] Vincent of Prague, *Annales*, MGH SS 17:671. According to Vincent, this meeting took place after Frederick crossed the Adda River. Without mentioning Anselm, Rahewin says the Milanese met with Frederick before he crossed the river (*Gesta Friderici* 3.30-31, pp. 204-5). Peter Munz has apparently taken both at face value and describes two meetings between representatives of Milan and Frederick (*Frederick Barbarossa*, pp. 160-61). However, it is clear that both Vincent and Rahewin are describing the same meeting for each says that afterwards Frederick placed Milan under his ban. Vincent, who was present, is probably the more reliable.

[92] Lamma, *Comneni e Staufer* 2:7-8.

sion. Throwing his gauntlet to the ground, he declared Milan under his ban.[93] On the next day, August 6, the siege began.[94]

During the next few days, the courageous resistance of the towns-people demonstrated that victory for the besiegers would come hard. Then, on August 12, Archbishop Anselm, the man who had convinced the emperor to carry out the siege, suddenly died.[95] His death took Frederick's army by surprise, and rumors began to circulate through the imperial camp that it was God's judgment on the archbishop of Ravenna for having advised the emperor to begin the siege.[96] This idea apparently had some impact on Frederick, for within a month a settlement was arranged which let the city off very lightly: The Milanese paid a fine and swore an oath of loyalty to the emperor.[97] But Anselm's warning about the Milanese was to be justified. In 1160 Frederick put the city under siege once again, this time for nearly two years; and when the city finally surrendered, Frederick had it destroyed.[98]

And so Anselm died in a camp of battle surrounded by the paraphernalia of war. Whatever his faults, he had often worked on the side of peaceful compromise whether between Greeks and Latins, monks and canons, rulers and popes, or Ravennese citizens and imperial ambassadors. At the very end of his life, before the walls of Milan, he took a position of uncompromising hostility; and because of this, it was thought that God had struck him down.[99]

---

[93] Vincent of Prague, *Annales*, MGH SS 17:671.

[94] Gian Luigi Barni, "La lotta contro il Barbarossa," *Storia di Milano* 4 (Milan, 1954), p. 32; Lamma, *Comneni e Staufer* 2:1-11.

[95] *Annales Colonienses Maximi*, ed. Karl A. F. Pertz, MGH SS 17:267-68; *Chronicon Montis Sereni*, MGH SS 23:151.

[96] Vincent of Prague, *Annales*, MGH SS 17:674.

[97] Fasoli, "Federico Barbarossa e le città lombarde," p. 129.

[98] Barni, "La lotta contro il Barbarossa," pp. 57-70.

[99] Anselm's burial place, often said to be in Ravenna, is unknown. See Walter Edyvean's letter in "Chronicon," *AP* 49 (1973), p. 174.

PART TWO

DEEDS INTO WORDS

INTRODUCTION

Anselm of Havelberg's life may be divided into several phases. The career path he chose was that of the court bishop, so aptly described in the recent work of C. Stephen Jaeger, and the first part of his life followed that path with considerable success: Educated at Liège, he moved into the circle of Archbishop Norbert of Magdeburg, became a bishop (if only one in exile) and went to the court of Lothar III, whom he continued to serve after Norbert's death. But with Lothar's death the contacts for advancement were gone, and the second phase of Anselm's life was one in which he failed to establish close associations with the men who followed Norbert as archbishops of Magdeburg and particularly with the new ruler, Conrad III. This left him the single option of serving another archbishop (Henry of Mainz) until, in the next phase of his life, fortunate circumstances permitted him to carve out a modest position of power in the Havelland by virtue of which he was permitted into Conrad's court. The next phase was the disastrous one of banishment to Havelberg in which, once again, his contact with the court was severed. Finally, he managed to move into the service of Frederick Barbarossa, capping his life off with a prestigious archbishop's position obtained by a tenacious commitment to the active clerical life in the face of often very adverse circumstances.

Anselm's written works were produced during those phases of his life when he was out of favor at court, which is to say, at those times when the desired role of a court bishop was least open to him. The **Epistola apologetica** was written in 1138 between Lothar III's death and Anselm's service to Henry of Mainz, a period in which he had no clerical role to play at all, little less that of a bishop at the royal court. The **Antikeimenon**, with its **De una forma credendi** and description of the debates with Nicetas, was produced during Anselm's period of exile in Havelberg. These works all reveal an author committed to precisely the sort of clerical action denied him by his current circumstances. They constitute Anselm's denial of failure in that they reflect an image of him that stands at odds with the reality of his situation.

Jaeger has said that the teachers of the eleventh and early twelfth centuries educated their students by presenting living models of the qualities necessary for advancement in the clerical hierarchy and at court. After his formal education, Anselm served Norbert of Magdeburg, a man with the same charismatic image of success presented by the teachers of the time. This concept of the model to be emulated plays a crucial role in Anselm's writings. At those times in his life when he was least capable of demonstrating success in emulating the great teacher or Norbert, he constructed a written image of himself which did fit his model. This will be important for understanding that aspect of Anselm's writings for which he is most renowned: his idea of history.

As was pointed out at the beginning of this work, the exegetical imagination in the Middle Ages focused on allegorical interpretations meant to inspire meditation on the mysteries of God and spiritual understanding. What we find in Anselm's writings, however, is something quite different. In the Scriptures, Anselm sought images which could be used both to define the active life being denied him and make it appear that he himself was participating in that life. Thus where others drew allegories from Scripture, Anselm described images of men in action, images which captured past deeds that were meaningful as models in their own right rather than as symbols. By emphasizing a historic rather than a symbolic meaning in the deeds communicated by Scripture, he was able to interpret his own deeds and those of his contemporaries on the same level as Scripture and as having a similar value.

In the following chapters, we will turn our attention to the connections among Anselm's written works. In brief, we shall see that in the **Epistola apologetica**, he addresses the narrow issue of whether a canon can, without permission, become a monk. Beyond this, however, he deals with what Karl Morrison has identified as the hermeneutic dilemma: the disparity between words and the things to which they refer, whether they be words of Scripture or post-biblical words like "monk" and "canon regular." In the **Epistola**, Anselm attempts to solve the dilemma by maintaining his distance from mystical and categorical meanings and focusing on the literal meanings—that is, on the individuals and actions to which words refer. Then he unashamedly uses biblical figures to argue that the canon regular (thus Anselm himself) is more important to the church than the monk. This approach to biblical exegesis forged a link between past and present quite at odds with traditional allegorical interpretation. Then, in **De una forma credendi**, Anselm organizes the deeds of the past to demonstrate a progressive development leading to his own time.

Within this scheme, he departs from his contemporaries by portraying Christ as the historic model for further action rather than the climax of previous developments. Finally, in the second part of the **Antikeimenon** and its debates with Nicetas we find a literary tour de force inadvertently underrated by historians who have viewed it as an act of historical reportage. Through words, Anselm recreates an event from his own life and reshapes the "deed" of the debates of 1136 into a model for his brothers who are committed to a unified Christendom. The model is the great teacher, and it is Norbert of Magdeburg, and it is Anselm himself.

CHAPTER ONE

THE *EPISTOLA APOLOGETICA*

A. *Monks, Canons, and the* optima pars

The early twelfth century was a time of extraordinary experimentation with different forms of religious life. This occurred within a mental framework which viewed these forms in a hierarchical fashion. The individual life took on meaning in so far as it participated in one of the forms of life on the hierarchy. That at the top was deemed closest to God, and nearness to God meant moving away from the world. Since monasticism incorporated ideas of withdrawal from the world in meditative devotion to God, its adherents could defend it as taking a position at the pinnacle of the hierarchy. However, whether the followers of the monastic life should draw a line of separation between themselves and the laity or promote their ideals in the world at large was an open one.[1]

By Anselm's time this question was hotly argued, and it formed one aspect of a debate the importance of which was not confined to the members of religious orders, new or old. For in wrestling with defining the monastic life, the clerical life also came into question: what was it and what were the duties of its adherents? These questions came as a result of the efforts of the eleventh century papacy to grapple with the issues of clerical celibacy and simony. Whatever the success or failure of the papacy to impose clerical celibacy and stamp out the purchase of ecclesiastical offices or sacramental rites, the formerly nebulous line between clergy and laity was made much more distinct. The result was nothing less than a redefinition of "the church" by which the broad sense that it embraced all Christendom was narrowed drastically by equating it with the clerical hierarchy and the pope at its head. Anselm's contemporary, Otto of Freising, expressed this clericalization of the church by noting that he would

---

[1] The monastic ideal is succinctly described by Gerd Tellenbach, *The Church in Western Europe from the Tenth To The Early Twelfth Century*, trans. Timothy Reuter (New York, 1993), pp. 101-34.

speak of the church as "the ecclesiastical personages, that is the priests of Christ and their attendants."[2] Here the issue was that of a line being drawn between clergy and laymen.

On one level, the *Epistola apologetica* is a defense of a new religious order against the old Benedictines. However, Anselm followed a career path that, aside from any debate concerning the monastic and canonical lives, moved solidly in the direction of active involvement in the political and ecclesiastical institutions of his time. While in the *Epistola*, he chose to defend his life within the narrow context of being a canon regular, a glance at that life reveals him as bishop, archbishop, and court bishop, positions which did not require him to be a regular at all. Even his close association with Norbert is best seen as that of a suffragan bishop. Using a narrow context and an ill-defined term like canon regular allowed Anselm to create a special definition of what amounts to the clerical life in general. In a sense, he brought together the two issues of the quarrel over the highest form of spiritual life and the struggle to divide the clergy from the laity, and he gave voice to a view of the clerical life that was no longer willing to accept a position on the spiritual hierarchy below that of the monk.

Anselm's teachers in Liège had provided models of action for courtly service to the empire. His mentor, Norbert of Magdeburg, had spent considerable time investigating and experimenting with various ways of religious life. As was pointed out earlier, Norbert instructed his early followers in a way of life that was at odds with the one he himself was leading.[3] While they were required to move into a monastic-like seclusion, Norbert devoted himself to the active life of the preacher, a life that rapidly led to promotion into the ecclesiastical hierarchy. In effect, his early followers did as Norbert said, not as he did. For Anselm, however, Norbert was like a schoolmaster of the time, teaching by his actions as well as by his words; he was the charismatic mentor to be emulated. Anselm pursued the political career of a court bishop; and Norbert, as archbishop and adviser to rulers and popes, stood as an example for him in a way that was

---

[2] Otto of Freising, *Cronica sive Historia de duabus civitatibus*, ed. Adolf Hofmeister, *MGH SS r. G.*, Hanover, 1912. See Johannes Laudage, *Gregorianische Reform und Investiturstreit* (Darmstadt, 1993), pp. 4-5; also Tellenbach, *The Church in Western Europe*, pp. 166-67, 334-47; Gerhardt B. Ladner, "The Concepts of 'Ecclesia' and 'Christianitas' and Their Relation to the Idea of Papal 'Plenitudo Potestatis' from Gregory VII to Boniface VIII," in Sacerdozio e regno da Gregorio VII a Bonifacio VIII (*Miscellanea Historiae Pontificiae* 18, Rome, 1954), 49-77.

[3] See pp. 22-25 above.

simply out of the question for those who laid their emphasis on withdrawal. In Anselm's view, the "deed", the action in the world which had the result of strengthening Christendom was the earmark of success. Even the periods of inactivity in Anselm's own life were forced on rather than embraced by him. While he may have given lip-service to withdrawal in his "cradle of Havelberg" after being banished there by Conrad III, he devoted himself during this time to attempting to conceptualize the active life that was being denied him.

This was no easy task. In the realist philosophy of the day, the concept meant everything. It was the reality toward which the individual aspired. The orderliness of the monastic life, with its cycle of prayer and ritual making each day much the same as the one before and the one that followed, was formulated around the concept "monk." This lent meaning to the pattern of carefully repeated daily activities. Individual monks, whole monastic orders, might argue about how best to live according to that concept, but they had no doubt that the ideal was there to be emulated. A man was a monk by virtue of his oath of commitment to that ideal even if his life was an eventful one. The debate over the extent to which a monk might engage in pastoral activities such as preaching revolved around a broader or narrower definition of the concept "monk" and the extent to which such activities could be accommodated to a life of withdrawal and meditation. However, while Anselm certainly had a lot to say about monasticism, his *Epistola* was not an effort to refine its meaning. Rather, it was in contrast to the definition "monk" as contemplative that Anselm sought to move the debate away from monasticism and over to the issue of defining the clerical life; and herein rests part of his importance to scholars.

In attempting to conceptualize the way of life to which Anselm had dedicated himself, he had at hand a number of terms: *vita activa*, *clericus*, and *canonicus regularis*. To call his life an active one would be true enough, but this term could be applied by monks to all those who were not monastic advocates of the *vita contemplativa*. This negative definition of the active life was communicated through an allegorical interpretation of biblical stories where, for example, the favored sister Rachel became a symbol of contemplation and the less favored Leah, of action;[4] Jacob, limping away from wrestling with an

---

[4] On Rachael and Leah see Giles Constable, *Three Studies in Medieval Religious and Social Thought: The Interpretation of Mary and Martha; The Ideal of the Imitation of Christ; The Orders of Society* (New York, 1995), pp. 10-11.

angel, revealed in his hurt leg the active life, in his good leg the contemplative.[5] Most influential of all was the story of Christ's visit to the contemplative Mary and the busy Martha. The contrast was an imposing one: the bleary-eyed Leah and the beautiful Rachel; Jacob's gimpy leg and his sound one; Martha fussing with her chores and the silent Mary sitting in rapt attention at her Lord's feet. Good they might all be, but there was little doubt where the best part lay.[6]

The term *clericus* certainly also applied to Bishop Anselm, but it failed to distinguish his life as something special and deserving of the highest position on the spiritual hierarchy. In so far as Norbert defined the life of his followers, it was by choosing for them the Augustinian Rule, a rule which did not restrict them from engaging in pastoral duties and identified them as canons regular. The term *canonicus regularis*, was, however, ill-defined, nebulously allowing those who claimed it to pursue lives of either monastic contemplation or clerical action.[7] Monks were quick to point out and joke about the difficulties with the term. The Benedictine Idung of Prüfening found the whole notion of a *canonicus regularis* to be nonsense. The two words both meant a rule, and so, he quipped, one might as well talk about a regular regular. Those who called themselves canons regular followed a rule, and for Idung that was enough. "Whether they wish it or not," he said drily and with specific reference to Norbert's followers, "they are monks."[8] Anselm of Havelberg could not have disa-

---

[5] So for example, Gregory I, *Homiliae in Hiezechihelem prophetam*, 2.2; 2.13, ed. Marc Adriaen, CC 142 (Turnhout, 1972), pp. 231-32, 233-34; idem, *Moralia in Iob*, CC 143, ed. Marc Adriaen (Turnhout, 1979), 4.33, p. 221; and Anselm's contemporary Rupert of Deutz, *De Sancta Trinitate et operibus eius*, ed. Hrabanus Haacke, CCCM 21-24 (Turnhout, 1971-72), *In Genesim* 8.9, CCCM 21:494.

[6] Monks could apply the term *vita activa* in a more restricted sense to other monks whose activities seemed to warrant it (see n. 11 and p. 155 below); but at least through Anselm's time, however much value individual writers may have assigned the *vita activa*, they almost always saw it as in some way subordinate to or preceding the *vita contemplativa*. See pp. 155-56 below.

[7] On the difficulties both for contemporaries of Anselm and modern scholars of defining the canonical spirituality as something different from monastic spirituality see Caroline Walker Bynum, "The Spirituality of Regular Canons in the Twelfth Century," in *Jesus as Mother: Studies in the Spirituality of the High Middle Ages* (Berkeley, 1982), 22-58; Bynum, *Docere verbo et exemplo: An Aspect of Twelfth-Century Spirituality*, Harvard Theological Studies 31 (Missoula, 1979).

[8] Idung of Prüfening, *Dialogus duorum monachorum* 2.32 and 42, in *Le moine Idung et ses deux ouvrages: "Argumentum super quatuor questionibus" et "Dialogus duorum monachorum"*, ed. R. B. C. Huygens, Biblioteca degli "Studia Medievali" 11 (Spoleto, 1980), pp. 138, 142-43. That the problems of definition were not resolved is seen in Jean Leclercq's classic *The Love of Learning and the Desire for God: A Study of Monastic Culture*, trans.

greed more and stated his contrary position unequivocally: "I am not a monk."[9]

Anselm's denial shows that the concept *monachus* communicated a standard for the spiritual life that he could reject but not ignore. Monks had firmly defended the notion that their life stood above that of the clergy on the scale of perfection. They could point to Christ's statement to the busy Martha upset that Mary, listening at Jesus' feet, would not help her: "Martha, Martha, thou art anxious and troubled about many things; and yet only one thing is needful. Mary has chosen the best part, and it will not be taken from her" (Luke 10:38-42). To choose a life of withdrawal and contemplation was to choose this same best part. So it was that Abbot Peter the Venerable of Cluny urged the archbishop of Narbonne to give up his episcopal position by comparing the labors of Martha to the peaceful repose of Mary.[10] Ailred of Rievaulx compared Martha to the bishops, priests and clergy who distribute alms to the poor but who, nevertheless, envy those who have chosen the way of Mary.[11] And while the Benedictine Rupert of Deutz was willing to say that Mary and Martha, taken together, signify the church of Christ,[12] he succinctly expressed the monks' view of their respective ranking:

> The active life is indeed truly blessed, but the contemplative life is more blessed, as seen in the testimony of the Lord Who acclaims the one while not rejecting the other when He says: "Mary has chosen the best part, and it shall not be taken from her."[13]

Catharine Misrahi (New York, 1961). Near the beginning of his book, Leclercq cites a comment of the twelfth century canon Godfrey of St. Victor on the life he and his brother canons were leading. Leclerq uses the canon's comments as a means of defining the monastic life (p. 4).

[9] *Epist. apol.*, 1120D.

[10] *The Letters of Peter the Venerable* 1, ed. Giles Constable (Cambridge, Mass., 1967) 105, p. 268.

[11] Ailred of Rievaulx, *De institutione inclusarum* 28, in *Aelredi Rievallensis opera ominia* 1, *Opera ascetica*, ed. C. H. Talbot, CCCM 1 (Turnhout, 1971), pp. 660-61. The distinction between Mary and Martha could be used by monks of various orders to determine which order was most contemplative and which had allowed for elements of the *vita activa*. Ailred defended total seclusion so that monks with duties such as taking care of widows and orphans resembled Martha (*ibid.*, p. 661). See also Constable's *Three Studies*, pp. 68, 74.

[12] *Commentaria in Euangelium Sancti Iohannis*, ed. Hrabanus Haacke (Turnhout, 1969), CCCM 9, p. 569.

[13] *De Sancta Trinitate, Quattuor Euangelistarum commentariorum* 31, CCCM 23:1822. Like Anselm and many others, Rupert also used Rachel and Leah as symbols of the two lives. For example *De Sancta Trinitate, In Genesim* 7, CCCM 21:466-467.

If, as sometimes happened, a member of the clergy did as Peter the Venerable suggested and withdrew into a monastery, it was a change for the better. As Peter put it: "From the good, the better; from the cleric, the monk."[14]

Such a change in religious vocation occurred in Saxony, probably in 1138, when an Augustinian canon of Hamersleben named Peter decided to leave his order to become a monk at Huysburg.[15] Hamersleben had been founded by the reform minded Bishop Reinhart in 1107/8, and the foundation's first provost, Thietmar, was an energetic man who offered his foundation to advance the reform of the church.[16] Peter was not just a canon but a successor to Thietmar's position of provost, and for him to turn his back on Hamersleben was a serious blow to the regulars. For the monks of Huysburg, on the other hand, Peter had simply moved up the ladder of perfection, closer to Christ's feet to sit in undisturbed contemplation; and Egbert, the abbot of Huysburg, penned several tracts defending Peter's change of vocation.

In response to a since lost tract of Egbert, Anselm wrote his *Epistola apologetica*. Here he combats monastic claims of superiority, and he employs the terms *vita activa*, *clericus*, and *canonicus* to describe his own way of life as not just equal but superior to that of the monks. The weapons for his attack on the monks and defense of his own way life are the words of Scripture of which the monks had made such good use. But Anselm and the monks looked at those words and saw different things, and as we shall see, the Bishop of Havelberg went so far as boldly to place the Mary-Martha story itself at the heart of the *Epistola*.[17]

---

[14] *Letters of Peter the Venerable* 1, 104, p. 267. For further examples see Constable, *Three Studies*, pp. 26-28, 35, 47, 74-79.

[15] See pp. 54-55 above.

[16] For Hamersleben in this period see Karlotto Bogumil, *Das Bistum Halberstadt im 12. Jahrhundert: Studien zur Reichs- und Reformpolitik des Bischofs Reinhard und zum Wirken der Augustiner Chorherren* (Cologne, 1972), pp. 107-13; Walter Zöllner, *Die Urkunden und Besitzaufzeichnungen des Stifts Hamersleben (1108-1462)*, Studien zur katholischen Bistums- und Klostergeschichte 17 (Leipzig, 1979), pp. 8-14. On Reinhart, whose episcopacy lasted from 1107 to 1123, see. Bogumil, passim; Zöllner, p. 9; Karl Bosl, *Regularkanoniker (Augustinerchorherren) und Seelsorge in Kirche und Gesellschaft des europäischen 12. Jahrhunderts*, Bayerische Akademie der Wissenschaften, philosophisch-historische Klasse, Abhandlungen-NF, Heft 86 (Munich, 1979), pp. 43- ; and for Thietmar, Bogumil, pp. 113, 141, 173-76; Zöllner, pp. 10-11.

[17] On the problem of individuals changing from one order to another see Gert Melville, "Zur Abgrenzung zwischen Vita canonica und Vita monastica: Das Übertrittsproblem in kanonistischer Behandlung von Gratian bis Hostiensis," in *Secundum*

B. *Allegorical and Historical Interpretation*

When an exegete found action and contemplation in the wives or legs of Jacob, he derived a not readily recognizable meaning from the words of Scripture. By the early twelfth century, the prolific exegete Rupert of Deutz worried that the symbolic meaning had been emphasized out of hand; and he sent a warning that the places, people and events to which Scripture literally refers were at risk of being completely forgotten or ignored "as if the visible and corporal things did not exist."[18] Rupert was not alone in this concern for the historical referents of Scripture. His contemporary Hugh of St. Victor compared the interpretation of Scripture to an architectural plan in which the historical sense formed the foundation, and he warned students not to trust that "you will be able to become perfectly sensitive to allegory unless you have first been grounded in history."[19] However, for both of these exegetes discovering the historical sense was a means to that spiritual end all exegetes sought. While Rupert chastised those who viewed Scripture only as a vehicle for spiritual meaning, it was nevertheless spiritual meaning to which he ultimately wanted to lead his readers.[20] For him, the historical meaning could be compared to a mother hen who keeps her chicks warm. What he sought was the chicks; the hen could be left behind "because clearly in certain places it is necessary to pass over the history so that only the mother's chicks, that is the faculty of spiritual understanding, may be our food, that the chicks, not the mother, may refresh us."[21] And in what amounts to a biblical allegory for historical interpreta-

---

regulam vivere: Festschrift für P. Norbert Backmund O. Praem. (Windberg, 1978), 205-43, esp. 205-18;; Kurt Fina, "'Ovem suam requirere': Eine Studie zur Geschichte des Ordenswechsels im 12. Jahrhundert," *Augustiniana* 7 (1957), 33-56; Philipp Hofmeister, "Der Übertritt in eine andere religiöse Genossenschaft," *Archiv für katholisches Kirchenrecht* 108 (1928), 419-81, esp. 424-30.

[18] *De Sancta Trinitate, In Genesim* 2.24, CCCM 21:212.

[19] *Didascalicon* 6.4; 6.3, PL 176:801A; trans. Jerome Taylor, *The Didascalicon of Hugh of St. Victor: A Medieval Guide to the Arts* (New York, 1961), p. 136; see also Spicq, *Esquisse*, pp. 94-97.

[20] *De Sancta Trinitate, In Genesim* 4.16, CCCM 21:300: "Historiam omnes nouimus, mysteria requiramus." See de Lubac, *Exégèse Médiévale* 2.1, p. 222: "Bref, partout dans l'ouvrage de l'Esprit Rupert cherche l'Esprit." See also Leo Scheffczyk, "Die heilsökonomische Trinitätslehre des Ruperts von Deutz und ihre dogmatische Bedeutung," *Kirche und Überlieferung*, ed. Johannes Betz and Heinrich Fries (Freiburg, 1960), p. 100.

[21] *De Sancta Trinitate, In Deuteronomium*, 1.15, CCCM 22:1034-35.

tion, Hugh pointed to Isaiah's description of the wings of the sera-
phim which cover their bodies. These wings "are the historical sense,
which covers mystical meanings beneath the veil of the letter."[22]
Correct historical understanding was the foundation, not the edifice.
For the latter, the spiritual meanings of the words of God were the
brick and mortar.

What then did Anselm of Havelberg see when he read the words
of Scripture? The bishop has given a thorough answer to this question in his *Epistola apologetica*. The opening arguments of Anselm's
tract to Abbot Egbert revolve around the meaning of words not
found in Scripture, the terms *monachus* and *canonicus regularis*. For Egbert, the concept *monachus* was sacred and gave meaning to his life.
When the canons of Hamersleben insisted that their Prior Peter return to them from what they felt to be an inferior way of life in the
monastery of Huysburg, Egbert expressed concern that the whole
idea "monk" had been threatened. Wrote the abbot: "That which
until now was held in veneration and praise, our name, that is the
name of monks, is reproached by [the canons]."[23] Egbert assumed an
inherent goodness in the concept *monachus*, a goodness above that
inherent in those of *canonicus regularis* and *clericus*, and in which the
individual could participate by becoming a monk. Like the words of
Scripture, the concept *monachus* led to a higher reality beyond the
individuals to which it might be applied. Since that reality was not
time-bound, Egbert was not constrained in his application of the
concept. He could look at the description in the Book of Acts of the
first Christian community as "of one heart and one mind," and call
its members "monks." Indeed, he could find "monks" throughout the
Scriptures.[24] Like the words of Holy Writ, the concept *monachus*
pointed both to individuals in this world and to eternal spiritual
ideals. The first were time-bound; the second reached beyond this
world into the realm to which the Christian aspired, and that they

---

[22] *Arca Noe morali*, PL 176:624C, 628D.

[23] Egbert 2, ed. Walter Zöllner, "Ekbert von Huysburg und die Ordensbewegung
des 12. Jahrhunderts," *Forschungen und Fortschritte* 38 (1964), 27. This is from the extant
fragment of one of two responses to the canons written by Egbert, both edited by
Zöllner. A fragment of Zöllner's Egbert 1 is also found in *Die Reinhardsbrunner Briefsammlung*, ed. Friedel Peeck, MGH Epp. sel. 5 (Weimar, 1952), pp. 8-9. Neither of
the tracts edited by Zöllner is the specific work addressed by Anselm in his *Epistola*.

[24] *Epist. apol.*, 1119C; see also C. H. Lawrence, *Medieval Monasticism: Forms of Religious Life in Western Europe in the Middle Ages* 2nd ed. (New York, 1989), p. 149 citing
contemporary monks.

should be emphasized is not surprising. What is surprising about Anselm of Havelberg and important for an understanding of his thought is that he almost abandoned this dual interpretation and firmly emphasized the time-bound or historical referent as giving the key to what was expected of the dedicated Christian.

Anselm begins his commentary on the term *monachus* by attacking the notion that this word has a timeless reality and could therefore be applied to individuals who lived before the term was in use. The community of Acts was made up of the apostles and their followers, he says, "among whom the name of the monks of the present time was not even known;" and he not so gently points out that Luke wrote the Acts of the Apostles, not the Acts of the Monks. Anselm makes this a point of exegesis, accusing Egbert of twisting the Scriptures into saying things contrary to what Anselm calls "divine Scripture's own sense." There is no notion here of multiple stages of exegesis with the historical meaning being only the first, but rather of one clear meaning to Scripture. Anselm goes so far as to say that this single meaning should be "adopted" as if the words were so clear as not to require interpretation.[25]

"Scripture's own sense" and the sense of words like *monachus* are, for Anselm, to be found in what the words refer to in this world, not in a timeless world of ideas. Thus where Egbert could go from *monachus* to "the good," Anselm moves from *monachus* to the individuals who claim the name "monk." If he is willing to defend the monastic order because "so many blessed men...are read to have served in that rule,"[26] it is because the way these men lived their lives has brought luster to the name *monachus*, not because the name has brought heavenly luster to them. Anselm is at pains to make the implications of his position clear:[27] Within time one does not find *monk* but rather individuals who describe themselves with the term *monk*; so if one is going to determine good from bad, one must look at the individual, not just at the term used to categorize the individual. As Anselm puts it:

> I do not call a monk good because he is a monk; but because he is good, I praise the good. Neither do I say a cleric is good because he is a cleric; but because he is good, I call him good and I love the good. Neither do

---

[25] *Epist. apol.*, 1119BD.

[26] *Epist. apol.*, 1120D-21A.

[27] *Epist. apol.*, 1121B: "Pauca duntaxat volo praemittere, in quibus judicium meum clarius tibi possit illucescere."

> I judge a layman either good or bad because he is a layman, but
> because he is good or bad, I either approve of the good or disapprove of
> the bad. Truly, "God is not a respecter of persons, but in all people, he
> who fears God and does what is just is acceptable to Him."[28]

The individual, not the category, determines whether that individual
is bad or good. This was nothing less than a page out of the living
book presented by the models of action given by the teachers of Liège
and Norbert of Magdeburg; and in trying to understand his world
and the value of his own life in it, Anselm concentrates on the individual whose actions give reality to, rather than reflect the reality of,
generalized concepts. Indeed, the *Epistola* is for the most part devoted
to assessing the actions of specific individuals.

C. *The Attack on the Monks*

In the debate over the definition of the monastic life Anselm stood on
the periphery. Where most concerned themselves with the subtleties
of defining that life, Anselm simply equated it with withdrawal and
made no mention of the possibility that monks might engage in the
vita activa as well. Not only was this a very simplistic position to take,
but it is hard to excuse Anselm on the grounds of ignorance. His own
friend Abbot Wibald, was as active as any cleric at the royal court,
and Anselm would later tell this monk to guard the king.[29] But in the
Epistola, the bishop chooses to ignore the subtleties of the monastic
profession. His plan of attack and defense comes clear: He will hold
the monk to a standard of complete withdrawal, and it is alongside
that standard that he will create another one defending the canon
and cleric.

This unwillingness to admit that the realities of the world might
impinge on the lives of monks allowed Anselm an easy, one might
even say cheap, means of attacking them. An unfortunate and prevalent aspect of his presentation of monasticism is the use of arguments
ad hominem in which he makes outrageously uncharitable assaults on
Egbert and his monastic brothers for perverting or not maintaining
the standard. In fact, the tenor of the entire *Epistola* is brutally aggres-

---

[28] *Epist. apol.*, 1121B (with citations from Acts 10:34-35 and Tim. 2:4).
[29] See p. 91 above.

sive as Anselm tries to build the canons up by tearing down the monks.[30] Thus the Benedictine Abbot Rupert of Deutz, whose work Egbert had used to buttress his arguments, is subjected to a vitriolic attack: "Perhaps," says Anselm, "[Rupert] is considered among you [monks] to be someone great, not because he wrote anything great but because he was an abbot of monks." Anselm claims to have read some of Rupert's work "as a curious novelty," and to have known the abbot himself. And then, in the most famous slur of the *Epistola*, "I discovered that the proverb told among the Greeks fits him perfectly: 'A fat belly does not engender a fine mind.'"[31] In this flurry of jabs, Anselm has managed to hit the categories "monk" and "abbot" as having no value in assessing Rupert and to accuse Rupert of a lack of intellect and of being indulgently inactive, as well. Egbert himself is dealt with harshly as Anselm accuses him of creating a meaningless controversy, defending the monastic order when no one attacks it, and pursuing personal ambition to make a name for himself. Denouncing Egbert for passing bombast off as enlightened thought, Anselm fires off another proverbial dart, accusing the abbot of attempting "to sell bladders for lanterns." It is Egbert who is teaching "new things" which stir up the undiscerning so that a useless controversy spreads; Egbert who, by uselessly and superfluously defending

---

[30] On this point and historians' attempts to ameliorate Anselm's attack, see Lees, "Charity and Enmity in the Writings of Anselm of Havelberg," *Viator: Medieval and Renaissance Studies* 25 (1994), pp. 53-62.

[31] *Epist. apol.*, 1120B; Ber. 2, fol. 253r: "Ego sane quaedam scripta illius, fateor, curiosa novitate legi, ipsum etiam vidi et novi, sed pulchre dictum apud Graecos proverbium in illo verum reperi: 'Pinguis venter non gignit tenuem sensum.'" The saying "pinguis venter..." is from St. Jerome's *Epistolae* (52.11), the work Anselm claims to have been reading when Egbert's tract arrived (see p. 54 above and p. 227 below). Hans Walther, ed., *Carmina medii aevi posterioris Latina* 2.3, *Proverbia sententiaeque Latinitatis medii aevi, Lateinische Sprichwörter und Sentenzen des Mittelalters in alphabetischer Anordnung* (Göttingen, 1965), 21505b, p. 825. Some scholars have said that Anselm praised Rupert elsewhere in his writings, e.g. M.-D. Chenu, *La theologie au douzième siècle*, p. 236 n. 1; Wolfgang Beinert, *Die Kirche—Gottes Heil in der Welt: Die Lehre von der Kirche nach den Schriften des Rupert von Deutz, Honorius Augustodunensis und Gerhoch von Reichersberg*, Beiträge zur Geschichte der Philosophie und Theologie des Mittelalters, Neue Folge 13 (Münster, 1973), p. 29 n. 94, both citing the praise of Rupert found in the *Liber de ordine canonicorum*, PL 188:1111D. This work, once attributed to Anselm, has been shown to be that of Arno of Reichersberg. See Classen, *Gerhoch von Reichersberg*, pp. 445-46; H. Silvestre, "La tradition manuscrite des oeuvres de Rupert de Deutz: A propos d'une étude récente de Rhaban Haacke," *Scriptorium* 16 (1962), 339 n. 16.

"the venerable tunic of monks" which only a fool would criticize, risks losing the tunic of Christ, the garment of charity, "by wishing to cut it in two."[32]

Here again, Anselm takes issue with the notion that membership in a particular order or possession of a particular office is what determines goodness. For Anselm, the category is a call to action of some sort, and the individual will be judged by how well the demands of that life or office are met. While monks claimed "the best part" in their contemplative life, Anselm insists that the reality of the lives of individual monks be considered; and it is constantly to the individual example that he turns when he deals with the term "monk." What he finds are monks in the market place, monks contending over material goods, monks entering into secular negotiations, monks extorting money from their *coloni*, monks disrupting the silence of the monastery with gossip, monks debating the whole Christian religion.[33] Whatever the standard monks may be trying to maintain, they have failed.

While Anselm's assessment of the monks of his own time is, for the most part, critical, it also reveals that the standard he seeks is a historical one. Egbert had apparently cited the early monks such as St. Benedict and St. Anthony as incorporating the goodness in which he thinks all monks participate, and argued syllogistically that because Benedict and Anthony were monks and were good, all monks are good. Anselm will not allow this reasoning. For him, Benedict and Anthony were good because they were good men, not because they participated in the concept "monk." Their actions and the actions of other early monks are the stuff of the concept "monk," and it is against this standard of action that the actions of Egbert and his brothers will be judged. Here Egbert falls short. Says Anselm:

> I am absolutely astounded at the shamelessness, the temerity with which you say that these [monks of old] are your masters. Indeed, you would boast yourself to be their disciple, when, in fact, neither do you seem to have anything in common with them nor they with you except the common law of Christianity by which we are all one in Christ.

---

[32] *Epist. apol.*, 1120CD; Ber. 2, fol. 253r: "Dum monachorum venerabilem tunicam, quam nemo Christianus, nisi amens impugnat, incassum et otiose defendis, tunicam Christi vestem scilicet charitatis scindere volendo amittas." Here, Anselm comes close to comparing Egbert to the soldiers who cast lots for Christ's garments at the crucifixion. Cf. Matt. 27:35; John 19:23-24.

[33] *Epist. apol.*, 1135AB.

The comparison Anselm draws is explicitly one of historic action to present action:

> These ragged men [the first monks], though scarcely able to cover the shame of their flesh, were content to deal with bitter cold howsoever they could; you, however, behave differently. These famished men, seeking food with their own hands, depended on mattocks and hoes; you, however, do not act in this way. They were destitute, you have a superabundance; they were afflicted, you have consolation; they were tormented, you lead a tranquil life; they wandered in the desert..., you sit secure on your lofty throne in the middle of what is yours.[34]

Here, Anselm has drawn on the apostle Paul's description of the faithful of the Old Testament (Hebrews 11:37-38), a description which lumps those persecuted for the faith together with the likes of Samson and David and which, in fact, had been used by the earliest monks to describe their own life.[35] If Egbert could seek out "monks" in Scripture, then Anselm could use Scripture to show how Egbert did not reflect his own ideals.

D. *The Defense of the Canons*

The bishop turns this method to the defense of the canons regular. Egbert, charges Anselm, had condemned the term *canonicus regularis* as a novelty unsanctified by age by saying that the name of canons regular "is a new name and thus contemptible, as if the major premise were evident: If new, then contemptible."[36] This centuries-old tradition that antiquity lent sanctity[37] reflected the notion that

---

[34] *Epist. apol.*, 1121D-22A.

[35] *The Life of Pachomius (Vita Prima Gaeca)* 1, trans. Apostolos N. Athanassakis, Society of Biblical Literature: Texts and Translations 7, Early Christian Literature Series 2 (Missoula, Montana, 1975), p. 5.

[36] *Epist. apol.*, 1122CD; Ber. 2. fol. 253v: "Causaris etiam hoc nomen regularis canonicus, et dicis illud esse nomen novum, et ideo contemptibile, quasi necessaria sit illa consequentia, si novum, tunc contemptibile." Anselm calls this syllogism itself contemptible. See Fina, "Anselm," *AP* 32 (1956), 207 n. 49.

[37] Johannes Spörl traces the tradition back to St. Vincent of Lerins (d. 450), "Das Alte und das Neue im Mittelalter. Studien zum Problem des mittelalterlichen Fort-schrittsbewusstseins," *HJ* 50 (1930), 297-341, 498-524; esp. pp. 297-309. Elizabeth Gössmann has pointed out that both Cassiodorus and Bede resisted this tradition. *Antiqui und Moderni im Mittelalter: Eine geschichtliche Standortsbestimmung*, Veröffentlichun-gen des Grabmann-Institutes, NF 23, (Munich, 1974), pp. 21-31. Gössmann's work (with extensive bibliography) shows how complicated the use of terms like *modernus* and *novus* could be. See also Walter Freund, *Modernus und andere Zeitbegriffe des Mittel-*

reality was distant, if not in the spiritual realm then in the historical one; and in the twelfth century, the adjective *novus* was often one of disapprobation.[38] The bishop of Havelberg was himself not above using it against Egbert by condemning him for teaching foolish things to those who marveled "at anything new."[39] But just as Anselm had tried to undermine the notion that "good" was a necessary attribute of "monk," so he attacks the idea that "bad" should always be associated with "new":

> Whether something is old or new, it ought rightly to be acceptable to all good men if it is nonetheless good and useful. Truly there are old things that are good and new things that are good, and there are old things that are bad and new things that are bad, and certainly, just as the antiquity or novelty of evil things brings no authority to them, so no less does the lack of antiquity or novelty in good things take their worthiness from them.

Terms like "old" and "new" were for Anselm no less time bound than "monk" and "canon regular." As he puts it: "Not because something is new or was new is it more or less contemptible, nor because it is old or will be old is it more or less acceptable."[40] The terms are relative to the flow of time, not outside of it: What is now new will become old; what is now old was once new.

But what does *canonicus regularis* mean? And what is the difference between a canon and a monk or a canon and a cleric? Here again, Anselm does not present ideals as existing apart from the deeds of men; it is the deeds themselves which give meaning to the concepts. In the narrow context of the case of Peter of Hamersleben, the *Epistola* is, as would be expected, a defense of the superiority of the canon. In the broader context of Anselm's attempt to conceptualize a meaningful life and of the scriptural exegesis on which that conceptualization is based, the *Epistola* is Anselm's attempt to create a standard by which the actions of monks, clerics, and canons regular can be compared and evaluated, a standard which would, one may

---

alters, Neue Münstersche Beiträge zur Geschichtsforschung 4 (Graz, 1957), pp. 63-66; Beryl Smalley, "Ecclesiastical Attitudes to Novelty c. 1100-1250," in *Church and Society*, Papers read at the Thirteenth Summer and the Fourteenth Winter Meeting of the Ecclesiastical History Society, ed. Derek Baker (Oxford, 1975), pp. 113-31.

[38] So for example Hugh of St. Victor, *De vanitate mundi*, PL 176:710C; Orderic Vitalis, *Ecclesiastical History* 4.8.2, ed. and trans. Marjorie Chibnell (Oxford, 1973), pp. 331-35. See also Gössman, *Antiqui und Moderni*, pp. 40-41, citing other examples.

[39] *Epist. apol.*, 1120C.

[40] *Epist. apol.*, 1122D-23A.

add, reflect his own chosen life as a court bishop and follower of Norbert.

The first indication of the design for this standard is found in Anselm's praise of the early monks whom he finds the more worthy of celestial life in so far as they humbly subordinate themselves to the clerical order "through which the church of God is governed."[41] As the monk claims that the *vita contemplativa* draws a line between himself and everyone else, so Anselm gives a positive definition to the clergy which puts the monk on the negative side of the line *per quem Ecclesia Dei regitur.*

Anselm's definition of clerical action is, thus, created at the expense of the monk. One of his first arguments that Peter of Hamersleben could not become a monk without permission is that church law forbids it. Along with citing various ecclesiastical pronouncements to this effect, he admits that there are indeed examples of clerics who have legitimately become monks. These, however, have done so only with a grant of permission. With some glee, he describes these men as clerics who have become useless, haughty, lax in discipline, deceitful, or injurious to members of the church and themselves: "Such like are, indeed, not prohibited from becoming monks." While this is said somewhat tongue-in-cheek (though no less biting for that), the distinction that is emerging here is between a way of life which is directed toward administering the church and one which is not. Anselm is explicit about what this should mean for those who would compare the canonical and monastic orders: "No one with a sound mind can doubt that the order of canons is more exalted in the church than that of monks."[42] He is not going to argue for the equality of the two ways of life but for the superiority of the life of the canons, a life of active involvement in the ecclesiastical hierarchy.

In doing this, Anselm turns from those *criminosi et infames* clerics who become monks to their opposite, monks who become clerics. Such a one is for Anselm the monk who "presents himself as useful to the church of God" (*utilem se Ecclesiae Dei praebuerit*)[43] and can therefore advance to the priesthood and up the ladder of ecclesiastical offices. Here we must look once again at Anselm's education.

In his study of the development of cathedral schools, C. Stephen

---

[41] *Epist. apol.*, 1121CD.
[42] *Epist. apol.*, 1125AC.
[43] *Epist. apol.*, 1126A.

Jaeger points to a change in their educational goal from the "correction and reformation of the religious life" to transmitting "knowledge to be applied in the practical duties of running the empire."[44] As an example of this change, Jaeger cites the tenth-century schoolmaster Meinhard of Bamberg's definition of the new instruction as being given *pro ecclesiastico usu*. This phrase, says Jaeger, "makes sense only if we understand that instruction as combining the moral and ethical improvement of the individual with a preparation for service to the church."[45] In effect, in the *Epistola* Anselm applies the educational raison d'etre of the cathedral school to the entire clergy. The model of service presented by the teacher to the student, the model to which Anselm had dedicated himself, becomes the standard against which various forms of religious life can be judged.

Anselm pays considerable attention to describing the ordination of a monk into the clerical order as a time of rebirth into a new life in which the monastery will be left behind. This description deserves some analysis, for if the bishop is looking for actions performed in the past to give meaning to the word *clericus*, we may well ask who the model for this description is. It may be suggested that the *Epistola* was meant to be read not only by Egbert but by Anselm's fellow canons as well, and that his description of the ordination of a monk addresses these two audiences. For his brothers, the individual whom he means to bring to mind as worthy of imitation is Norbert of Magdeburg.

Before dealing with the monk who becomes a cleric, Anselm writes about the cleric who imitates the life of the apostles and of the primitive church. In describing that life, Anselm chooses words which, while certainly having more general connotations, would have evoked Norbert in the minds of his followers who called themselves *pauperes Christi*.[46] The cleric, says Anselm, takes his place among the disciples of Christ "if he sold everything and gave it to the poor, and then, naked, follows Christ...[and] carries his own cross and is prepared to imitate Christ and his apostles in everything."[47] Here is the ideal of Norbert's *pauperes Christi*; here, in fact, is Norbert, who, says

---

[44] "Cathedral Schools and Humanist Learning," pp. 569-616, here p. 574.

[45] Jaeger, "Cathedral Schools and Humanist Learning," pp. 578, 580. Jaeger also points out that Meinhard writes his own former teacher to thank him for instruction in a way of living that was *ad utilitatem efficacius* (p. 586).

[46] See p. 31 above.

[47] *Epist. apol.*, 1124C.

one of his *vitae*, sold his inheritance, gave the proceeds to the poor and then decided that "naked, he should follow the naked cross."[48]

When Anselm turns to the issue of a monk who becomes a cleric, he cites the example of Pope Gregory I, a monk who moved to the very pinnacle of the ecclesiastical hierarchy.[49] But Gregory's name is merely mentioned. A comparison of Anselm's description of the ordination of a monk with the ordination of Norbert described in his *vitae* shows that, again, the unstated example behind Anselm's description is Norbert, who had also worn the habit of the monk. The monk who becomes a cleric is described by Anselm as having proven himself by serving obediently under the Rule of St. Benedict and by devoting himself to the study and understanding of Holy Scripture that he may be promoted to the priesthood.[50] Norbert's *vitae* say that in his early quest for the religious life, he went to the monastery of Siegburg for instruction from the learned Abbot Cuno.[51] Anselm describes the ordination of a monk to the priesthood by saying that the monk does not cast off his monastic habit but conceals it under his vestments,[52] the contemplative and active lives symbolically coming together. One of the *vitae* says that Norbert sought to build within himself "a new grace of interior virtue" and at the same time to shed the exterior trappings of his old secular life. He wanted "at once to put on the garment as well as the adornment of the new man, the former in the habit of the monk, the latter in the office of the priest."[53] Says Anselm:

> In all things, in his habit just as in his office, [the newly ordained cleric] regularly and manifestly shows himself to have become a cleric with, it is true, the black garment hidden within and below as a sign of sorrow for the human condition, its fragility and mortality, and always with the linen and white garment showing."[54]

At his own ordination, Norbert "exchanged his worldly clothing for one which appeared that of a monk and wore over it the sacred vestments."[55] For Anselm the vestment is white "on account of the

---

[48] *Vita Norberti* B 4.22, p. 827. Note also Anselm's letter to Wibald cited p. 90 above.
[49] *Epist. apol.*, 1125C-26B; 1127B.
[50] *Epist. apol.*, 1126AB.
[51] *Vita Norberti* A 1, p. 671; *Vita* B 1.8, p. 822.
[52] *Epist. apol.*, 1126B.
[53] *Vita Norberti* B 1.8, p. 822.
[54] *Epist. apol.*, 1126C.
[55] *Vita Norberti* A 2, p. 672.

newness of life and the radiance of the resurrection" and because white is the color of the garment of a preacher;[56] and Norbert, while showing some impatience with the issue of the color of habits, had, indeed, chosen white for his followers. This, his *vitae* say, was on account of the white-clad angels who appeared as witnesses to the resurrection.[57]

Finally, in describing the time of change when a monk becomes a cleric at his ordination, Anselm says the initiate moves from singing the *canticum graduum* (psalms of degrees), which as a monk he had intoned mournfully to the Lord, to singing psalm 119 (118), *Beati immaculati*, which is divided into octaves. With this, says Anselm, he crosses into "the true *octava*" to perform the Divine Offices with the clergy.[58] Psalm 119 apparently had a personal resonance for Norbert with its pilgrim's cry to the Lord for guidance; and when in the year 1119 he studied for a brief time in Laon, he chose this psalm as the subject of exegesis.[59] For those who had followed Norbert, Anselm's mention of psalm 119 could not but have evoked their mentor.[60]

Anselm has used specific individuals and their actions to give a sense of the progress of a good man from being a monk to being a cleric. Earlier, he had said that things should not be judged by their age but according to whether they are "good and useful."[61] He now begins to emphasize the latter term *utilis* clearly in the sense of Meinhard's *pro ecclesiastico usu* to distinguish the monk from the cleric. Thus, the monk who has kept his vows, served obediently, and been schooled in the study of the Scriptures, may prove himself "useful" to the church by becoming a cleric. He may then "usefully" be promoted up the ecclesiastical hierarchy, for he can now "usefully" speak to Christians.[62] The focus is on the individual whose actions meet the clerical needs of the church.

By way of contrast, the monk Rupert of Deutz emphasized neither the idea of a new life for an ordained monk—certainly, not that the monk would leave the monastery—nor the qualities necessary to en-

---

[56] *Epist. apol.*, 1126C.
[57] *Vita Norberti* A 12, p. 683; *Vita Norberti* B 9.24, p. 836.
[58] *Epist. apol.*, 1126BC.
[59] *Vita Norberti* A 9, p. 678.
[60] I have drawn here on the provocative article by Grauwen, "De crisissituatie van Norbert begin november 1119 en zijn belangstelling voor psalm 119 (118)," *AP* 64 (1988), 5-18.
[61] See p. 144 above.
[62] *Epist.* 1126AB.

gage in the *vita activa*. Rather, he started with a definition of the term *clericus* as one who performs a sacramental function and has the right to preach. Turning the definition onto individual monks, he could conclude that the ordained monk may naturally function as a clergyman. "What does it mean," the abbot of Deutz asked clerics, "for a monk to be tantalized by a longing for holy orders, as the blessed Jerome says, unless it is to wish to perform the sacred rites of the altar...and preach the word of God in church?"[63] Here Rupert was thinking in functional terms: priests perform a sacramental function, and therefore a monk with priestly orders must be allowed to perform that function. Accusing clerics of paying too much attention to externals and of distinguishing between the monk and the cleric with the bovine eyes of the common crowd, Rupert shot at the cleric: "A bishop legally invested me as well as you with the same insignia," and, "It is permitted to many of us [monks]...that we may be clerics because we hold holy orders."[64] The ideals "cleric" and "monk" were unchanging, and personal worthiness was found in participating in those ideals. As one monk, borrowing on Rupert's ideas, wrote to a cleric:

> We do not belittle the blessed Bishop Augustine, but we confidently put Martin [of Tours, who was both] bishop and monk, before him, and even the more Gregory [I], who was a pope and a monk.[65]

Service to the church—the "usefulness" of which Anselm speaks—has no bearing on the ranking of these men. The emphasis here is

---

[63] *Super quaedam capitula Regulae Divi Benedicti Abbatis* 4.8, PL 170:532AB, the reference is to Jerome, Epistola 125.8.

[64] *Super quaedam capitula Regulae Divi Benedicti Abbatis* 4.11, PL 170:534CD. It is possible that Egbert of Huysburg relied on this work to defend Peter of Hamersleben's change of orders. See van Engen, *Rupert of Deutz*, pp. 313 n. 47, 333. See also Rupert's *Altercatio monachi et clerici quod liceat monacho praedicare*, PL 170:539D: "Ego clericus sum;" and his *Epistola ad Everardum*, PL 170:544A: "Ego autem et clericus et monachus sum." The issue of whether the monk who becomes part of the clerical hierarchy nevertheless remains a monk is one which Anselm ignores, though Egbert rallied to this cause in one of his tracts: "Et quidem plures...post susceptum habitum pontificatus honorem susceperunt, quidam post susceptam episcopatus dignitatem habitum monachicum suscipientes nihilominus episcopi permanserunt." Egbert 2, Zöllner, "Ekbert von Huysburg," p. 28. See also Zerfass, *Der Streit um die Laienpredigt*, pp. 160-71.

[65] *Epistola ad Liezelinum*, ed. R. Vander Plaetse, "Notities betreffende Wazelinus abt van Saint-Laurent," *Sacris erudiri* 24, 260. This letter, often attributed to Rupert himself, was written by Wazelinus, a student of Rupert's. See van Engen, *Rupert of Deutz*, p. 309.

not on clerical office, little less on the contribution of its holders to the church, but on participation in the ideal "monk." Thus, when Anselm suggests that "usefulness to the church" is the defining feature of the cleric, he is taking the monastic view by the horns: The clerical service of Gregory I was what was useful to the church, not that he was a monk.

Anselm's image of the clergyman contrasts sharply with monastic ideas about clerical office, such as those of Rupert of Deutz. In the latter, clerical office allows one to function in certain sacramental ways but does not define the individual in the way that "monk" does. For Gregory I to become pope did not effect the essence of his being a monk; he was a monk who performed a sacramental function by virtue of his priestly office. For Anselm, that office allows one access to and participation in the ecclesiastical hierarchy. The defining feature of the cleric was not the reception of priestly orders but the point at which he engages those orders in the offices of the ecclesiastical hierarchy. Thus Anselm emphasizes a distinction between the monk-priest and the priest who holds an office in the clerical hierarchy. It is the hierarchy with its implication of upward movement that is important to him.

This is seen when Anselm addresses Egbert's use of St. Benedict as an example of a monk exercising ecclesiastical authority. Egbert had pointed to two cases of this from the *Dialogi* of Gregory I, arguing that in one Benedict had exercised juridical authority by forbidding a cleric to take holy orders, in the other that he had exercised the authority of ecclesiastical censure to excommunicate two sisters. From this Egbert concluded that the ordained monk could officiate as part of the ecclesiastical hierarchy. This hit at the heart of the regulars' claim to a particular way of life in the integration of monastic commitment to a rule with active participation in the affairs of the church. If monks could do the same, then Idung of Prüfening was right: The regulars were monks.

Anselm's response to this is to look at authority in the church and distinguish between that which comes with an office in the ecclesiastical hierarchy and that which is exercised only in unusual circumstances and when permission has been granted by someone with the legal right to do so. Egbert's examples do not, says Anselm, demonstrate the authority of an office in the church hierarchy. In telling the cleric not to assume holy orders, Benedict did not exercise an authority to pass judgement (*auctoritas iudicandi*) but simply gave useful council (*utilitas consulendi*). Authority did not come into play at all, for Benedict did not tell the cleric that he could not take orders, only that he should not. In the second story, Anselm points out that Benedict only made known that the sisters could be excommunicated but did not pass the sentence. After their deaths, Benedict forgave the sisters, but while he did this with *auctoritas sacerdotalis*, it was accomplished by prayer that God would absolve them, not by passing an ecclesiastical sentence. The important contrast Anselm makes here is between sacerdotal authority and ecclesiastical authority. Benedict possessed the former, but since he held no position in the church hierarchy, he did not possess the latter: Priestly office allowed entrance to, but was not the same thing as ecclesiastical office. Thus while examples of monks taking action "sometimes by useful dispensation, sometimes by discrete permission, sometimes by special mandate" could be found, such, according to Anselm, should not be confused with those acts which "derive their strength from unalterable law and invincible authority."[66]

Anselm fastens on this issue of authority to make the distinction between a monk and a canon clear. He gives two examples of papal grants of permission to preach before the curia—one to a monk-priest, Bernard of Clairvaux, and one to a canon-bishop, himself. Though he uses both to illustrate his point that there are extraordinary mandates which allow one to act beyond one's office, he nevertheless contrasts Bernard's office as a monk with his own as a bishop. While Bernard preached in obedience to the pope "more than in accordance with his sacerdotal office," Anselm preached more in obedience to papal authority than "by my authority allowed me as a bishop." Here is precisely the distinction he had made in dealing with St. Benedict: Bernard's office was merely sacerdotal; Anselm's authority derived from possession of an office in the ecclesiastical hierarchy. This office gave Anselm authority beyond that of a priest and distinguished him from Bernard, that is to say, distinguished the canon from the monk.

Anselm has shaped his view of the cleric out of ideas of individual commitment to action in the service of the church, and of a church that gives form, meaning, and authority to that action by means of

---

[66] *Epist. apol.*, 1127D-28C. Cf. Gregory, *Dialogi: Libri IV*, ed. Umberto Moricca, Fonti per la Storia d'Italia (Rome, 1924), 2.16; 2.23, pp. 103-4; 114-15. Anselm's interpretation does fit the stories.

ecclesiastical office. This attitude toward ecclesiastical authority can most certainly be seen in Anselm's own life. In Italy in 1137, he had argued that the sole ground necessary for removing Abbot Rainald of Monte Cassino from his office was that he had not been ordained to it by one in authority. To allow Rainald's claim to office, said Anselm, was to build on sand. In 1143-1144 when he could neither serve at the royal court nor get to his diocese, he attached himself to the archbishop of Mainz in order to exercise this authority if only in a auxiliary capacity. And when he later had an opportunity to build a foundation of canons regular in Jerichow, his first concern was to make clear that authority in the new foundation resided with him as bishop and then to emphasize that authority extended to an entire diocese.[67] In Egbert, however, Anselm found someone who, like Idung of Prüfening, held that canons were monks and should therefore not serve in the church hierarchy. Much of the insulting tone of the *Epistola* can be understood by realizing that Egbert's assumption that a canon regular was a monk would be read by Anselm as an attack on his own authority and that of Norbert of Magdeburg.

Through Anselm's anger, however, one can see that action in the world, the deeds of men, is the focus of his attention. "It has come to my attention," he says, "that you are not afraid to fill the ears of some—nay, that you do not blush sometimes to tell them that canons regular ought not to hold dioceses nor direct the care of souls among the people." Anselm's ecclesiastical office is one of providing the *cura animarum* to the ordinary Christian, and he finds outrageous Egbert's suggestion that such service should be denied the regulars. He tells the abbot that any right-minded person would invite all priests to become canons regular rather than try to remove the regulars from pastoral duties among the Lord's flock. Such service is, in fact, performed all the better by canons regular, for living in obedience to a rule makes them more mindful of the bad conduct of others and thus more diligent in its correction. Moreover, it distinguishes them both from the monks and to the people. Whereas monks have no diocesan function, canons serve in ecclesiastical courts, participate in synods, administer the care of souls, and are not barred from any ecclesiastical office or dignity. "In fact, often demanded by the common people, [a canon] is elected and raised up, so that, shining like a lamp in the fog and teaching by word and example, he is loved and

---

[67] See pp. 64-68, 71-73, 93-95 above.

honored."[68] Here is what the ecclesiastical office bestows on a good man: a position above the people where he can become an example to them in word and deed, where he becomes, like Norbert and the teachers of Liège, a model for others. This is "useful" to the church, and on a scale of values in which usefulness replaces goodness, Anselm is demonstrating the canonical to be more important than the monastic life.

E. *Images of Action*

Anselm's exegesis proceeds with the intent of proving usefulness to the church to be the valid criterion for evaluating the monastic and canonical lives. At the beginning of the *Epistola*, he accuses Egbert of abandoning the sense of sacred Scripture and looking for monks in the Bible when there are none. He then gives what he believes are the proper referents (Scripture's "own sense") of the Scriptures Egbert has used: When the words of the Old and New Testaments speak of the faithful and Luke points to the single mindedness of the members of the Christian community, they refer to the individuals of a time before the society of monks existed. Otherwise, says Anselm, one will end with the absurdity of calling the five hundred who saw Christ after the resurrection or the hundred and twenty gathered on the day of Pentecost "monks."[69] After using historical individuals as the referents of Scripture, he deals with individuals who have lived since the Scriptures: Egbert the author of a tract against the canons, Rupert of Deutz the author of some *scripta curiosa*, the first monks in comparison to Egbert, Peter of Hamersleben and his attempt to change orders, Pope Gregory I, and St. Benedict. He has, in effect, placed these individuals within the framework of historical scriptural exegesis. Thus when he returns to Scripture to use it to defend the value of the canonical life, he can remain firmly committed to a historical level of interpretation, looking for people, rather than symbols, whose actions, like those of clerics, are useful to the church.

The problem remains of distinguishing the canons regular from the secular clergy. Here, for all his emphasis on contemplative withdrawal as the distinguishing feature of monasticism, Anselm will not

---

[68] *Epist. apol.*, 1128C-29A.
[69] *Epist. apol.*, 1119BC-20A.

allow it to be preempted by the monks. He stakes a claim for the canons to the contemplative life as well as to clerical action. In treating biblical figures, Anselm employs terms applicable to both Scripture and contemporary life, namely *vita contemplativa* and *vita activa*; and he looks to the Scriptures for examples of contemplative withdrawal from and active engagement in the affairs of the church. He tries not to equate the former *vita* with the monk or the latter with the canon, but would like to see the canons as men

> who are both contemplative and active, so that they scorn neither the one nor the other, but rather in a time of holy contemplation, they love good active men, and likewise in a time of good action, they esteem the holy contemplatives.[70]

Though in his commitment to a notion of usefulness to the church, he emphasizes action, nevertheless, it is its combination with contemplation that he seeks to find in the actual lives of people named in Scriptures which could then be used to distinguish the canon from both the monk and the secular cleric. Pointing to scriptural descriptions of individuals who had clearly lived active lives, he asks whether they "were in any way devoid of that which is called the contemplative [life.]," whether, in short, they led their lives as a combination of the two *vitae* in the way contemporary canons claimed to be living theirs.[71]

Anselm starts with a series of Old Testament figures to demonstrate contemplation in the lives of those noted for active service to God. His exegesis is firmly grounded on *historia*—person and deed, and though he does not scorn symbolism,[72] he shows little interest in moving into allegorical interpretations. Scripture's "own sense" is in its description of what people did: Abel must have had a share in divine contemplation for he made sacrifice acceptable to God; Noah must have been contemplative for God entrusted the safety of the

---

[70] *Epist. apol.*, 1129B; Ber. 2, fol. 256v; Wolf. 2, 9r: "...qui ut, praestante Domino, aut sic essent contemplativi ut contra activos non murmurarent aut sic essent activi, ut contemplativos non calcarent, aut sic essent et contemplativi et activi, ut nec illos nec istos spernerent, sed potius tempore sanctae contemplationis bonos activos amarent, et rursus tempore bonae actionis sanctos contemplativos diligerent."

[71] *Epist. apol.*, 1129CD.

[72] Abel, for example, is described as "typum gerens pastorum animarum," Noah as "rector arcae ecclesiasticae." Exegetes had seen in Jacob's wives Rachael and Leah symbols of the *vita activa* and the *vita contemplativa* (p. 131 above), an exegesis which Anselm plays on by having their husband symbolize both. *Epist. apol.*, 1129D, 1130A.

ark's passengers into his hands; Abraham, the father of nations, spoke with and contemplated the Lord. The allegory of Jacob's legs got the exegete to the active and contemplative lives but at the expense of Jacob the man. Anselm ignores the allegorical interpretation completely; what is important is that Jacob "saw God face to face and the angels ascending and descending the ladder [of heaven]" (Gen. 32:30, 28:12).[73] God appeared to Moses the shepherd in the burning bush on Mount Herob: "Just as the loyal active man pastured his father-in-law's sheep, so the great contemplative saw on the mountain of the Lord a great vision in a flame of fire."[74]

Anselm proceeds to cite example after example of active men who were contemplative, as well. Perhaps strained is that of Joshua and Caleb who "went forth to explore and survey [*contemplendam*] the Promised Land" (cf. Num. 13:21). But then there is David, king and prophet, who could administer his lands and prophesy with equal grace; and Daniel, Shadrach, Meshach and Abednego, and Ezekiel, the last of whom preached to the people and then withdrew "to preserve spiritually the cloistered joy of life within himself through contemplation."[75]

While Anselm calls several of his examples images or figures of the two lives, this is not to say the he makes symbols of them in the same way other exegetes had of Jacob's feet. For Anselm, the biblical character himself produces (*gerit*) the image.[76] Like *bonus*, the states *contemplativus* and *activus* are made manifest by the individual, not through some general category like "monk." As Anselm puts it to Egbert, "Behold, you see that with no ambiguity the ancient fathers have sometimes followed the contemplative, sometimes the active life with complete perfection."[77]

The image or figure is, however, more than one of the two ways of life. It is also that of the Christ to come. In allegorical fashion, Anselm represents the Old and New Testaments with the biblical de-

---

[73] *Epist. apol.*, 1129D-30A.

[74] *Epist. apol.*, Wolf. 2, fol. 9v: "Sicut fidelis actiuus oues soceri pauit, sic magnus contemplatiuus in monte domini in flamma ignis magnam uisionem uidet." This passage is found neither in Migne nor in the Berlin ms. It would follow "Vadam, et visionem hanc magnam videbo," PL 188:1130B.

[75] *Epist. apol.*, 1130C-31A.

[76] *Epist. apol.*, 1131B; also 1129A (Abel); 1130A (Jacob); 1130C (Joshua and Caleb).

[77] *Epist. apol.*, 1131A.

scription of two men carrying a bunch of grapes on a pole from the Promised Land back to the Israelites.[78] The grapes symbolize Christ on the wine press of the cross; the man walking in front is the Old Testament because he is unable to see Christ; the one walking behind is the New, having seen the crucified Savior. Even this allegory is turned toward history, showing the reader that over and above person, place and thing, the *historia* of Scripture has a dimension of time in which action before Christ is different from action after Christ.

The centrality of Christ in human history was unquestioned in Anselm's time. Jesus' conquest of death had created a great dividing line symbolically captured by the bunch of grapes carried by the two men.[79] Anselm's aim, however, is not to repeat this commonplace which, so to speak, focused attention on the grapes, but rather to emphasize the relationship to the bunch of grapes of the men on either side of it, a relationship created by what they are able to see. The man who can see the grapes has not only a knowledge that death has been overcome but an image or model of how he is supposed to behave. In other words, Anselm explains the centrality of Christ in terms of the perfection of words and deeds which Christ presents to the world; for in Christ, says Anselm, we find the combination of action and contemplation which is to be imitated. From this perspective, the dividing line Christ presents is one of knowledge of how one is to act in this world. Those who came before Christ had a likeness—a *figura*—of the two lives; and *figura* is a term Anselm has used in reference to several of his Old Testament examples of lives lived actively and contemplatively.[80] Then comes Christ Himself, openly teaching these things so that the earlier *figura* is now revealed and those coming after can see its true nature. *Ea...istos revelata jam facie videre*: they can, literally, look into the face of Christ.[81] The *figura*,

---

[78] It should be noted that in dealing with Joshua and Caleb as examples of men who were both active and contemplative, Anselm does not use the allegory of the two Testaments but remains close to the *historia*. The two are among those who go out to reconnoiter and return to encourage the Israelites to occupy the fertile land (Num. 13:23-27). The allegory comes later in the *Epist. apol.* to introduce Anselm's discussion of the New Testament and without reference to Joshua and Caleb. Cf. 1130CD to 1131B.

[79] E.g. Augustine, *Exposition on the Book of Psalms* 8.2; Jerome, Letter 108.11; Ambrose, *De fide* 4.168.

[80] *Epist. apol.*, 1130A (Jacob), 1130C (Joshua and Caleb). On *figurae*, see Constable, *Three Studies*, p. 5.

[81] *Epist. apol.*, 1131B: "Dei scilicet Filius in torculari crucis calcatus aliquando dixisse legitur: 'Beati oculi, qui vident quae vos videtis, multi' reges et 'prophetae'

multiple and varied, becomes the *facies*, the single manifestation of how one's life should be lived. Of course, the model of the teacher instructing by presenting the image of how the student should behave is precisely what Anselm had before him as a student in Liège and as a follower of Norbert. In the *Epistola*, he has, in effect, projected his own education for the role of court bishop onto his understanding of the mission of Christ. This ideal Anselm most profoundly attempts to demonstrate by using that very biblical story often cited by monks in defense of their way of life, the story of Jesus' visit to Mary and Martha.

Giles Constable has recently written at length about the various interpretations of the Mary and Martha story. While he provides examples of a great variety of interpretations, usually subtle in their differences, he finds that in general one can speak of several phases of interpretation. The church fathers saw contemplation as a fleeting state, impossible to maintain over time since even, its closest adherents would inevitably be thrown back into activity of some sort. In this interpretation, Mary and Martha showed two sides of the life of a spiritually committed individual. By the tenth century, exegetes were making an ever clearer association between Mary's contemplative life and the life of withdrawal of a hermit or monk, while seeing in Martha the active life of the clergyman or layman. In this view, the story showed alternative ways of life and could thus become a justification of the monk's claims of superiority. In the second half of the eleventh century with its new emphasis on clerical reform and "the growing prestige of action," Constable finds the first inklings of an attempt to turn the story around and praise those who had chosen the active path.[82]

The interpretation of any given exegete would, of course, depend on the particular issue he was addressing. Thus, for example, if the goal were to distinguish between the different duties of monks, one could find both Marys and Marthas in a monastic community;[83] or if the issue were to distinguish the clergy from the laity, the clerical life could be viewed as a reflection of Mary rather than of Martha.[84] It

---

voluerunt 'videre quae videtis, et non viderunt; et audire quae auditis et non audierunt' [Cf. Matt. 13:16-17], manifeste docens ea quae illis in figura contingebant, istos revelata jam facie videre."

[82] Constable, *Three Studies*, pp. 40-42, 44.

[83] Constable, *Three Studies*, pp. 35-37, 80-83, 86-87.

[84] Constable, *Three Studies*, p. 50.

was more difficult, however, to use Mary and Martha to demonstrate that clerical service was as valuable if not more so than monastic withdrawal. Mary's position at Christ's feet and Christ saying that she had chosen the best part formed a potent image, and those trying to move the emphasis over to Martha tended either to use the notion of a mixed life propounded by the church fathers with the Virgin Mary or Christ embodying this combination,[85] or to speak of an honorable and necessary decent from the heights of contemplation to the service of one's fellow Christians.[86] Only with Innocent III, says Constable, was Mary made to appear "in almost a selfish light" and these arguments were "brought together...more powerfully, and the part of Martha defended more openly, than in previous works."[87] Anselm, as we have seen, used the notion of a combined life to distinguish the canon regular from the monk in an effort to show the former's superiority. That superiority rested on action for it is what made the canon useful to the church. His interpretation of the Mary and Martha story may continue to give lip service to the combined life, but it is only as a cover for a blistering attack on monastic withdrawal.

When Anselm presents the story of Mary and Martha, he appears to be emphasizing a mixed life with Christ as the example. While he concedes that Martha may suitably signify the active life and Mary the contemplative, he goes on to ask whether when Christ speaks of Mary choosing the "best part," He means this in comparison to Martha alone or to both Himself and Martha:

> Sitting, Jesus Christ taught; teaching He exhibited the character of the doctors. Sitting silently and devotedly, Mary heard his words. Martha solicitously ministered to the disorderly crowd. Let your love hear this, [Egbert]: Christ teaching, Mary listening, Martha ministering are three people.[88]

Then comes the allegory as Anselm asks the rhetorical question:

---

[85] Constable, *Three Studies*, pp. 40, 48, 61-65, 70-72, 96-97, 179.

[86] Constable, *Three Studies*, pp. 40-41, 63, 68-69. Constable also gives examples of canons who attempted either to demonstrate that Martha was Mary's equal or praised Martha without making an explicit comparison with her sister (pp. 87-89). In the latter half of the eleventh century, he sees "a turning point not only in the interpretation of Mary and Martha but also in the history of medieval spirituality" as Martha's active life finds its proponents (p. 41).

[87] Constable, *Three Studies*, p. 99.

[88] *Epist. apol.*, 1131D-32A.

"There are three offices. Which of the three seems to you the most worthy?" Mary's choice of the best part refers, says Anselm, to those who are the listeners (*in ordine auditorum*) in the church. They elect to listen but are taught by those who are chosen as being worthy to teach.[89] Christ, then, is the highest example to be followed.

But what sort of example is the Christ Anselm presents to his readers? Constable has shown a movement from a concern in the early church for understanding the divinity of Christ to a vast interest by Anselm's time in imitating His humanity where emphasis was placed on Christ's suffering, obedience, humility, compassion, charity, purity, simplicity, poverty, etc.[90] All of these, including the oft used notion of imitating Christ in word and deed or, for that matter, the ideas of a *vita contemplativa* or *vita activa*, were means to an end. But with Anselm we find a definition of the end itself, for the defining feature of his Christ is that He teaches; He is actively engaged in instructing the listening Mary. Where Anselm's contemporary Hugh of St. Victor could speak of imitating "the Master like disciples, the Lord like slaves, and the King like soldiers,"[91] Anselm is speaking of imitating the Teacher by teaching. The idea of choosing the best part is nicely turned around: the *optima pars* is no longer Mary's choice to sit in silent contemplation but rather the object of her contemplation, the teacher. When Anselm concludes his discussion by speaking of an office of listening (Mary), one of serving (Martha), and one of teaching (Christ), his intent is clear: to impose silence on the monk, to leave the loaded image of an inferior Martha behind, and to associate Christ with the clergy.

Anselm proceeds along precisely these lines, moving from allegory to the historical level of exegesis to find Christ in states of contemplation and action. However, if it were really his intention to show a mixed life, one would expect to find him moving back and forth between examples of Christ in contemplation and Christ in action. He does not. First he turns to contemplation, citing Christ's sojourn in the desert, the night of Gethsemane, and the transfiguration. Then he turns to action pointing to Christ's preaching and the miracles of

---

[89] *Epist. apol.*, 1132AB.

[90] Constable, *Three Studies*, pp. 145-93.

[91] Cited by Constable, *Three Studies*, p. 184. As Constable points out, Hugh described the end with a list of possible Christs: pastor, guard, merchant, soldier, exile, pilgrim, etc.

healing and driving out demons.[92] The sequence here is worth mentioning, for in the traditional interpretation of the Mary and Martha story, action was seen to precede contemplation, the latter forming a kind of summit toward which one moves or from which one descends through action.[93] While Anselm is not explicit about his intentions, the way he presents his examples of the two ways of life at least suggests the opposite interpretation.

Anselm gives a nod to the notion of a mixed life as Christ's "standard of right living," saying it was applied particularly to the apostles, and thus may be termed the *vita apostolica*. He cites the examples of the active Paul, who had time for contemplation, and the contemplative John, who could nevertheless engage himself in the affairs of the church.[94] But in spite of this, the weight of Anselm's definition of the apostolic life comes down solidly on the side of action, and that action is defined in terms which identify it absolutely with the clerical hierarchy. He gives little room to defining contemplation, but he lists the elements of the active life with ease, elements which, taken together, exclude the monk entirely: preaching, healing, founding churches, ordaining bishops, and appointing priests.[95] Anselm's notion that the two lives should merge is not a concession to the monks. The canon regular is a member of the ecclesiastical hierarchy who, by following a rule, participates in the contemplative life. By doing the latter, he becomes a better person and thus a better clergyman, for adherence to a rule further distances him from bad conduct, and he is thus better able to recognize it in others. The more he devotes himself to improving the lives of others, the more obligated he is to improve his own.[96] Whatever Anselm may have said about the meshing of lives, his answer to the question of why the canon regular is better than the monk revolves around the active side of the canonical life.

Anselm had spoken of the monk who becomes a priest and moves into the clerical hierarchy by proving himself "useful" to the church. With the word *utilis*, Anselm weights the scales in favor of the canons,

---

[92] *Epist. apol.*, 1132D-33B. After "paralyticos sanabat" (1133B), Ber. 2, fol. 258r and Wolf. 2, fol. 10v add "claudos et curuos erigebat, turbas populorum mirabiliter faciabat."
[93] Constable, *Three Studies*, p. 37-39.
[94] *Epist. apol.*, 1133B-1134A.
[95] *Epist. apol.*, 1133C, 1134A.
[96] *Epist.* 1136CD.

asking Egbert whether the canonical or monastic order is the more "useful and necessary" to the church of God.[97] The formulation of his answer is instructive for it shows a definition of the church as an institution dependent on the ecclesiastical hierarchy that can claim to be its most essential part by virtue of its leadership of all Christians. It is a claim the contemplative monk, living his life of withdrawal, has no business making.[98]

For the sake of argument, Anselm asks Egbert to imagine the monastic order existing by itself "naked and without ecclesiastical orders" in a world without any clergy at all:

> I beg you tell me, brother, in what way will the church remain, which cannot be called or be a church without archbishops, without bishops, without presbyters, without deacons, without the lower clerical orders?[99]

If the reverse were true and there were only clerics, Anselm says that the church "would still be able to exist well and orderly without monks," for it would have "some prophets, some apostles, some evangelists, and some pastors and teachers, and some orders of clerics." He gives here Paul's list of spiritual officers (Eph. 4:11-12) with the significant addition of *alios clericorum ordines* and concludes by citing the apostle: "Are they not sufficient 'in order to perfect the saints for a work of ministry for building up the body of Christ, which is the church?'" Anselm attempts to place not just Egbert but all monks in a corner as he pushes inexorably to his logical conclusion: If the church is able to stand without monks but "with different orders of the elect," then "just as a good and perfect monk should be loved and imitated more than an unfit cleric, so a cleric living well and regularly should doubtlessly be preferred to the best monk." This reduces monasticism to the individual monk whose goodness, as Anselm pointed out earlier, does not depend on the fact that he is a monk but on whether he is good. The cleric is judged harshly if he is unfit (*ineptus*)

---

[97] *Epist. apol.*, 1136AB. See Severino, "La discussione degli 'Ordines'," p. 87.

[98] Constable cites several examples of writers referring to Martha as "useful" to the church (*Three Studies*, pp. 42-43, 71). Particularly interesting is that of Anselm's contemporary, Robert Pullen (d. 1146) who used this argument, though in a much gentler way, to find the active life of Martha to be superior to the contemplative one of Mary (pp. 89-90). Constable also shows Innocent III's use of this argument (pp. 97-99).

[99] *Epist. apol.*, 1136B; Ber. 2, fol. 259v: "Dic, quaeso, frater, quomodo stabit Ecclesia, quae sine archiepiscopis, sine episcopis, sine presbyteris, sine diaconibus, sine inferioribus clericorum ordinibus nequidem vocari nec esse potest Ecclesia?"

to perform his duties, and while this does not free him from a general standard of goodness,[100] it is his contribution to helping the church function that raises him and his whole order above the monk, no matter how good. Whereas Otto of Freising had taken the word "church" to refer to the clergy almost as a concession to common usage,[101] Anselm equates the clergy with the church in such a way as to make them its essence. To demonstrate this he turns once again to the *historia* of Scripture.

Anselm refers to Paul whom he had earlier used as an example of the apostolic life of both contemplation and action. This time, however, it is not the apostolic unity of the two that Anselm chooses to emphasize or even to mention. Rather, he considers Paul first as an active apostle and then as a contemplative monk. Again, it is not an allegory that Anselm draws; he seeks to evaluate the importance of the historical personage Paul for the church. Paul the apostle, says Anselm, was God's instrument to carry the Gospel to kings and rulers; his sermons and letters helped gather believers to the faith from among Jews, Greeks and Romans; and he fought not for his own glory, but to spread and build God's church. Moreover, Paul's influence continues through his writings. But while Paul the apostle suffers persecution and martyrdom, Paul the monk withdraws to busy himself with devotions and wear himself out with vigils. Against Anselm's standard of usefulness to the church, Paul the monk is found wanting. While he might seek nothing but Christ, he is *sibi soli utilis*, useful only to himself. "Now," Anselm tells Egbert, "weigh the labor of both and the fruit or reward of both."[102] Anselm's exegesis has given the follower of Paul the active apostle the clear advantage. The weight not of allegory but of historical deeds which nourish the church rests completely on the side of the follower of the active life.

The active life that Anselm defends is, in a very real sense, his own life of devotion to active engagement in the affairs of Christendom. This is not the life of contemplation to which men like Hugh of St. Victor and Rupert of Deutz committed themselves. Yet, scholars

---

[100] Here again, Anselm says the canon who does not live properly should be corrected by his own order or permitted to become a monk. *Epist. apol.*, 1136BD. See p. 143 above.

[101] See p. 129 above. Otto says: "Porro ecclesiam ecclesiasticas personas, id est sacerdotes Christi eorumque sectatores, tam ex usu locutionis quam consideratione potioris partis diximus...."

[102] *Epist. apol.*, 1136D-37AC.

have tended to interpret Anselm's most well known work, his *De una forma credendi*, by comparing its schemes of periodization with those formulated by these contemporary contemplatives. Valuable as this has certainly been, both Anselm's own devotion to the active life and the *Epistola* as a source for Anselm's ideas about history need to be taken into consideration. In the *Epistola*, we find the elements Anselm will use to fashion his history: the sense of a church which needs to be defended and built up; the as yet undeveloped but implicit and concomitant notion that the church is not a static entity but is still maturing in some way; the use of Scripture to study the deeds of men in the past; the emphasis on Christ as the perfect image of action which needs to be imitated, and on Christ who, by giving the world that image, has created a distinction between time before Him and time after. All of these ideas would be used by Anselm to formulate his *De una forma credendi*.

F. *The* Epistola *and Charity*

There is one element of the *Epistola apologetica* that Anselm would abandon in the *Antikeimenon*: the former's acerbic tone. The importance of the *Epistola* as a contemporary statement of the clericalization of the church in the twelfth century should not obscure its author's lack of love or even consideration for a fellow Christian.

The *Epistola* ends as it began, with the claim of brotherly love for Egbert, a pretension supported by precious little of what Anselm says in between. The uncharitable tenor of the entire *Epistola* is, in fact, all the more glaring in a work meant to praise clerical service to the church. There was little to be gained in the cause of Christian unity by declaring Egbert to be ignorant of proper scriptural exegesis and full of bombast, a man who cuts the garment of charity, whose writings are "muddy water" stirring up useless controversy, and whose arguments are contemptible and sly.[103] Just as impossible to reconcile with Anselm's pretensions to charity is his description of the monastic community. He gives but passing praise to those monks who labor for the good of the monastery (and even here in the sense of active

---

[103] *Epist. apol.*, 1121C, 1123A. Other examples of Anselm's disparaging comments about Egbert: 1122C, 1125A, 1127D, 1129AB, 1132BC, 1133A, 1134AC, 1134C-35A.

Martha rather than contemplative Mary), and then describes the others as *simplices*: monks who enjoy a leisurely and secure life of strolling around the monastery, sitting in their cells clapping their hands, gossiping, exercising their office with a perplexing sign language, and calling this the contemplative life. Anselm's description of them fairly drips with contempt:

> If they should ever see the course of their personal desire impeded, they are immediately incensed and either grumble in private or stubbornly raise a racket in the open. Often, as well, it happens that they fain patience by hiding in their cells, choosing for themselves a haughty silence under the guise of sanctity, for which occasion they fruitlessly impose on themselves fasts of perverse displeasure rather than of pious devotion. And while they let the misery and unfairness of their trial boil within and do not reveal these things openly by confessing and doing penance, they drink the cup of their own bitterness.[104]

Against this, Anselm's claim to be the charitable teacher has the hollow ring of rhetorical convention.

The uncharitable tenor of the *Epistola* can, perhaps, be attributed to Anselm's own commitment to the canonical life and his indignation that its worth had been attacked. Nevertheless, this ill-tempered response rings a shrill note as Anselm attempts to shout his opponent down with arguments that, in a quieter setting, would not appear so strong. His tight association of the canon with the cleric serving in the church hierarchy and, even more so, his lack of charity only serve to undermine the union of lives he would claim for canons. The taunting, insulting, and self-righteous slander he levels at monks cannot help but appear as criticisms of contemplative withdrawal and make sharp its distinction from the active clerical life. Again and again, Anselm himself keeps the two lives apart by comparing and contrasting them rather than emphasizing their unity in the canon. Egbert, he says, must choose between the two; he must put them on either side of a balance and decide which is better. Paul is not the one, good man, but is cut in two as Anselm presents Egbert with "your Paul" (the monk) and "our Paul" (the apostle) and insists that the abbot compare them as if they were two separate entities. Paul the monk he finds guilty of "vain silence by abandoning his apostolate and neglecting his ministry which he received from the Lord and honored among men." Paul the apostle, on the other hand,

---

[104] *Epist. apol.*, 1135BD.

abandoned solitude and, in a "more useful" fashion, worked "for the cultivation of the vineyard of God" and "brought forth and nourished so many sons of the church."[105]

The *Epistola apologetica* is a work of passion, but passion that has gotten in the way of charity. Moreover, in defining the active canonical life in terms of Norbert's ordination, Anselm emphasizes the importance of clerical office to the point of forgetting his own dictum that a man is good because he is good, not because he is a cleric. The ecclesiastical office brought power to build and strengthen the church. It allowed a man "usefully to open his mouth, which before was humbly closed, in the middle of the church."[106] In assuming that office, Anselm could claim to be imitating Norbert, but this was the same superficial kind of imitation for which he condemns the monks. Anselm has missed the essence for the trappings. However much he would like to come across as the loving Christian teacher, his instruction is at bottom an attack on Egbert and the monastic profession. On the whole, Anselm conveys the unsettling impression of a boxer who ducks his opponent's jab, lands his own punch, and then draws back to apologize while nevertheless demonstrating that he wants to deliver the knockout blow. His constant affirmations of Christian charity ring hollow. This is not a work of love.

Some years after writing the *Epistola*, Anselm discovered how little his own church office could mean and found himself exiled to Havelberg. There he wrote the *Antikeimenon*, trying once again to grasp what made Norbert a good man.

---

[105] *Epist. apol.*, 1137BC.
[106] *Epist. apol.*, 1126A.

CHAPTER TWO

THE *ANTIKEIMENON*

Anselm of Havelberg's *Antikeimenon* is not an extension of the truculent debate with Egbert over the relative merits of different religious lives. Instead, Anselm refrains from all uncharitable attacks in the *Antikeimenon* and concentrates on one of the ideas presented in the *Epistola apologetica*: the career of the clerical teacher instructing by word and deed to the benefit of the church. It is precisely in Anselm's view of teaching by example that an intimate integrity is found between the *Antikeimenon*'s two parts: *De una forma credendi* and the debates.

A. *The Prologue and the Proem*

1. *The circumstances of composition*

Anselm wrote the *Antikeimenon* during his years of exile from the court of Conrad III. The loss of royal favor marked a major reversal of Anselm's fortune. His earlier life had been a success story, that of a man who found a model for his life in Norbert of Magdeburg, learned at Norbert's side, saw how his mentor served a united Christendom by advising popes and rulers, and imitated that model himself by serving both secular and ecclesiastical leaders as bishop, legate and adviser. In the space of just the last two years of this part of Anselm's life, from the spring of 1147 through the spring of 1149, he served on a delegation from Conrad III to Eugenius III, was the pope's legate on the Wenden Crusade, went on a mission to the papal court in Italy, and was Eugenius' messenger to Conrad at the end of the Second Crusade. The break in Anselm's life came when he arrived at Conrad's court and was sent to Havelberg in disgrace. "Thorns, thorns, thorns!" he wrote, "After such service."

In the *Epistola apologetica*, Anselm had emphasized that by serving in the church hierarchy, the canon regular showed himself "useful" (*utilis*) to the church. In his position as archbishop, Norbert had shown Anselm time and again a man who proved his usefulness by standing between opposing parties. While each side saw only that it was right and the opposing camp wrong, Norbert perceived the problem as one of threatened disunity and gave his attention to finding that common ground on which dividing lines would disappear. Anselm also held an official position in the church hierarchy and tried to prove himself *utilis*. When in 1149, Conrad returned to Europe from his failed campaign in the Holy Land, the situation could hardly have been more threatening to papal-imperial harmony; but standing in Conrad's court, Anselm found that his office meant little. Everything depended on the man and whether he, not the office, was *bonus*. In looking for an explanation for his banishment, Anselm could bitterly try to blame his king by comparing him to Pilate or find fault with Conrad's advisers by telling his friend Wibald to guard the king, but it was on Anselm that the responsibility for maintaining the papal-German alliance rested. He had been the one who had to find the middle ground, the man on whom unity and harmony depended. And he had failed.

There is perhaps a hint of desperation beneath the surface of Anselm's prologue to the *Antikeimenon*. There he makes much of his close friendship with Pope Eugenius III, saying that he will respond to the pope's request for an account of the debates he had held in Constantinople on the legation of Lothar III. The reality, however, was that he was writing at the command of a pope whom he had failed about service to a king long dead and of debates which had come to nothing. For all the eminence with which Anselm tried to surround himself in that prologue, the bishop's situation was far better captured by Wibald when he called Anselm "the bishop of a poor town."[1] Withdrawn into his "cradle" in Havelberg, Anselm set about writing the *Antikeimenon* a much sobered man.

Anselm had tried in the *Epistola apologetica* to convey the sense that he was leading a life both active and contemplative. But here he had failed as well, for in both the tract and his own life it was active engagement with the world which had been given far and away the greater emphasis. In banishment there was time for contemplation. "We've played around long enough," he wrote, as if the active life would now be set aside. And yet, the *Antikeimenon* is very much about the active life. In it Anselm confronts his own failure and, one might

---

[1] See p. 89 above.

say, contemplates action to find what, beyond clerical office, makes it good.

2. *Divisions*

More than anything else about the bishop of Havelberg, the *Antikei-menon* has captured the attention of scholars of the twelfth-century. Nevertheless, that attention has for the most part been focused on one or the other of what has been perceived as two separate works (*De una forma credendi* and the debates with Nicetas). There remain questions, however, which should be pursued more forcefully: Who is the *Antikeimenon*'s intended audience(s)? And more profoundly, is it best to treat the *Antikeimenon* as having two loosely connected parts or should we see it rather as an integrated whole?

By accepting the division into two parts, historians have provided an excuse for dealing with the one or the other but at the cost of oversimplification. I would suggest that for an understanding of the entire work, it is best to consider it as having five parts:

First, a prologue addressed to Pope Eugenius III which says the account of the debates with Nicetas has been written at the pope's behest and that Anselm has added *De una forma credendi* at the request of certain brothers.

Second, *De una forma credendi*, a history of the faithful which is designated Book One and addresses the brothers' concern about the proliferation of new religious orders.

Third, a proem addressed to the brothers who have read Book One. This functions both as a conclusion to the history and as an introduction to the debates.

Fourth, the first debate with Nicetas, which deals in its entirely with the question of the *Filioque*. This is designated Book Two.

Fifth, the second debate with Nicetas, which is concerned with differences in sacramental ritual. During this debate, the further issue is raised of whether the Roman pope has a sovereign rather than an honorary primacy in the church and can thus determine proper ritual. This is designated Book Three.

The common approach to the *Antikeimenon* has been to consider the prologue addressed to Eugenius as Anselm's statement of the purpose and the audience of his work: The purpose is to fulfill Euge-nius' request for a work showing how Latins can respond to Greek attacks on their beliefs and rituals; the audience is the pope. Since *De una forma credendi* addresses neither of these and Anselm says in this prologue that he has written it at the request of certain brothers, it has seemed preferable to disassociated it from the debates as having a different audience and purpose. From this perspective, the entire work is tenuously held together only by the common theme of Christian unity: Book One deals with the unity of the faithful; Books Two and Three with Latin-Greek unity.

A major problem with this approach is what I have pointed to as the third part of the work: the proem to the brothers. This has been the most overlooked part of the *Antikeimenon*. And yet, once it is considered, it becomes difficult to maintain that the *Antikeimenon*'s primary audience is Pope Eugenius III. The prologue and the proem give rather different versions of why the *Antikeimenon* was written, versions which require close scrutiny and comparison if we are to determine the purpose of the work in its entirety.

3. *Audience*

In his prologue, Anselm addresses the *Antikeimenon* to Pope Eugenius III with a rhetorical flourish of titles: "Lord and always revered and esteemed, most blessed pope of the sacrosanct Roman church." He then gives a description of the circumstances under which he received Eugenius' request to write about the Greeks and explains why that request was made of him in particular. If Eugenius is the specific audience to whom the work is addressed, this is a polite introduction, perhaps nudging the pope's memory. If, on the other hand, Anselm was thinking of other readers, he establishes some important groundwork for what follows. He indicates first of all that his relationship with the pope is a close one. His first words after the salutation are "when I was in the presence of your Holiness," made concrete in time (March) and place (Tusculum). Moreover, this meeting does not take place because Eugenius has heard of Anselm's experiences in Constantinople. Rather, the two know each other well for the disagreements with the Greeks were discussed "among many things which it pleased your holiness to confer about with me." Eugenius' request for the *Antikeimenon* comes, says Anselm, on the heels of the pope's meeting with a learned Greek who has twisted Scripture to support his views. Was Eugenius able to prove the Greek wrong?

Anselm does not say, subtly leaving himself in the position of one to whom the pope has turned not just for information but for help.[2] More than Anselm's relationship with the pope is touched on. He lets drop that he went to Constantinople as "the legate of Lothar the Great, august emperor of the Romans." He indicates that he was held in esteem by the Greeks, for they discussed religious matters with him "sometimes in private, sometimes in public" and he debated with "the most learned and venerable Archbishop Nicetas," the first of a board of twelve Greek theologians to whom all difficult theological question where brought.[3] The prologue of the *Antikeimenon* is about Anselm himself, and he introduces himself as a man who travels in high circles, a man of eminence, a man whose words should be heeded.

At the end of this prologue, Anselm expresses a deep sense of humility in fulfilling Eugenius' command to write the *Antikeimenon*. The learned pope, he says, has no need of his help to answer the Greeks and if need be, has abundant scholars who can offer arguments more valid than the bishop's. This can be interpreted as a tactful way of framing the delicate situation of schooling a pope, but be that as it may, Eugenius is cast as the judge of what Anselm has written, not its student.[4] If anyone is going to learn from the *Antikeimenon*, they are "some humble people" (*aliqui humiles*) who,

> not having such a nimble ability to learn something quickly, are perhaps going to read these things gladly that they may both more truly understand those things which the Greeks say and, to some extent, discover here those things which can be said to them in return.[5]

Throughout the prologue and particularly in its conclusion, Anselm emphasizes the he writes out of obedience to the pope that "whoever

---

[2] Anselm makes much of writing only out of obedience to the pope, yet when he describes how the pope asked him to write the *Antikeimenon*, he says: "...placuit sanctitati vestrae et praecipiendo rogare, et rogando praecipere" (*Antik.* prol., 1140C). It is impossible to tell how formal this request was, but it may well have been a passing suggestion, much more important to Anselm than to Eugenius. If so, Anselm has managed to give the opposite impression.

[3] *Antik.*, prol., 1139-41.

[4] *Antik.*, prol., 1140C-41A.

[5] *Antik.*, prol., 1142AB; Ber. ms., fol. 208v; Wolf. 1, fol. 3r: "...ad aliquid inveniendum subito non adeo agiles sensus habentes, ista libenter lecturi sunt, ut et quae Graeci dicunt, verius cognoscant; et quae illis responderi possunt aliquatenus hic inveniant."

may read this may know that I have not written these things in order
to teach anyone or publicize something by way of boasting."[6] Whoever reads Anselm's prologue may note his tone of obedience and
humility, but just as important the prologue tells the reader again and
again that this is a work written under papal auspices. Anselm has
lent the *Antikeimenon* an aura of authority which could only be accepted by an audience other than the pope.

He passes over the addition of the first book very quickly in the
prologue, but he is explicit about its position in the work as a whole:
"I have given in advance [*praemisi*] a book on the unity of the faith
and the many ways of living from Abel to the last of the elect."[7] By
placing *De una forma credendi* between the prologue addressed to the
pope and the debates themselves, Anselm has brought it under the
umbrella of papal sanction and is able to put it forward as just as
worthy of consideration as the books that follow. It is not so much
that Anselm wants to bring the history to the attention of the pope as
that he wants a larger audience to consider it thoughtfully before
reading about the debates.

Between the first book and the debates, Anselm has given a proem
to Book Two.[8] This stands in marked contrast to the prologue.
Whereas the latter emphasizes the papal authority by which the *Antikeimenon* has been written, the proem is addressed specifically to the
brothers who have already read the first book and accepted its teachings, Pope Eugenius receiving only passing mention. In considering
the integrity of the *Antikeimenon*, it should be emphasized that this
means that the prologue to Eugenius, usually interpreted as an introduction to the debates, has been placed by Anselm in such a way as
to lead immediately into the history. The proem to the brothers, who
are usually considered the audience of the history, has been placed as
the introduction to the debates.

In the proem, Anselm gives a somewhat different account of how
and why he came to write the second two books. Here, as in the
prologue, he says that he wrote *De una forma credendi* because he was
plagued by questions about the variety of religious lives in the
church. But, he sighs, the questions kept coming, this time about the

---

[6] *Antik.*, prol., 1142A; see also *Antik.*, prol., 1139A (the *salutatio*); 1140C; 1141A.
[7] *Antik.*, prol., 1141B.
[8] *Antik.* 2. proemium, 1159-62.

differences between the Greek and Latin churches. Anselm claims that he does not feel adequate for the task of answering these questions properly and would prefer to have remained quiet on the subject. Then he mentions that he has been commanded by the pope to respond to the very questions asked him by those who have read the first book. A happy conjunction of circumstances! But Anselm goes further than this. It is precisely *because* they have read and accepted the first book that his readers are ready for the ones which follow. The first book has changed them:

> What earlier they apparently did out of zeal rather than because it was good, now, changed for the better, they are seen to inquire about in a pious and humble spirit.[9]

The *Antikeimenon* is not, then, an attempt to satisfy a papal demand for an account of what happened to Anselm in Constantinople in 1136. Anselm clearly will have his audience learn something from the first book that will form the basis for comprehending the message of the latter two, and his opening address to the pope is a *causus scribendi* which lends authority to all three of the following books. Anselm meant the *Antikeimenon* to be appreciated as a unified work of pedagogical value which would lead its reader from one level of understanding to a higher one.

The designation "certain brothers" for the intended audience of the *Antikeimenon* requires some elaboration. In the *Epistola apologetica*, Anselm was very clear about identifying his opposition: Abbot Egbert of Huysburg. Egbert was, in fact, framed not only as the opponent but as the problem. Anselm treated the issues Egbert had raised with contempt—"muddy water," "empty cisterns," "bladders"—and focused on Egbert himself: If the abbot would only keep quiet, there would be no problem. "Why are you stirring up contention where there is none?" Anselm demanded. He then tried to shout Egbert into silence at no matter what cost to the monastic way of life by delivering broadside after broadside of abuse with little concern that he was hitting monks in general as well as Egbert. But to what end? As an attempt to instruct, this work is a failure. No monk was going to read Anselm's tract, feel himself properly chastised, meekly withdraw into his cell, and allow the value of the entire monastic way of

---

[9] *Antik.* 2. proemium, 1159D-60D.

life to be determined by the bishop of Havelberg. For Anselm to cast his argument in terms of the superiority of one way of life was to create opposition from those he designated inferior, and his defense of the superiority of the canons could only push opposing sides further apart.

The attitude of Anselm toward those introduced in the prologue of the *Antikeimenon* as having provoked him into writing *De una forma credendi* is distinctly different from his attitude toward Egbert in the *Epistola*. The issue Anselm says his history is meant to address is the criticism of new religious orders; but rather than identifying a specific critic with whom he can do combat, he maintains considerable distance between himself and those who attack the new orders and the Latin church. He says that he has written his history "on account of the prayers of certain brothers" for an answer to the criticisms of "many child-like and even learned men."[10] This would indicate two very different audiences. On the one hand, one might say that Anselm is writing for members of the new orders, presumably Norbertines, who had been criticized, and that he wants to assuage their concerns; on the other, one could say that Anselm is by-passing these worried brothers to confront directly their critics. But in defining Anselm's audience, one must note that the bishop draws the criticized and the critics together. First, he gives no more concrete definitions of them than that they are "certain brothers" and "child-like and learned men"; and second, at the end of *De una forma credendi* and in the proem to the debates, he says that on the basis of his preceding arguments, "no one" (*nemo*) should be startled by the changing variety of forms of religious life.[11] Twice he says that he has responded "to those who would complain about such variety in the holy church,"[12] which would suggest that the work was written for the critics themselves. However, he proceeds to identify the critics and those disturbed by the criticisms as one and the same. It is those who raised the criticisms in the first place who, he says, are now content with his answers and come to him *again* with questions—not criticisms—concerning the rites and beliefs of the Greeks. These are called "brothers."[13]

---

[10] *Antik.*, prol., 1141B.
[11] *Antik.* 1.13, 1160A.
[12] *Antik.* 1.13, 1160C; proemium, 1159D.
[13] *Antik.*, proemium, 1162B.

Thus, whatever definitions the shadowy terms "child-like and learned men" and "certain brothers" receive will come from the reader rather than the author of the *Antikeimenon*.[14] Modern scholars have often identified the audience with Egbert's monks, making of Anselm's history another polemic tract much like the *Epistola apologetica* in the debate between canons and monks or old orders and new. This can only be done by squeezing from Anselm's words things he avoids saying. In this work, canons are not set against monks nor new orders against old; nor are the "child-like and learned men" ever identified as monks or the "brothers" as canons.[15] Most profoundly, the terms *vita contemplativa* and *vita activa*, around which so much of the *Epistola*'s argument is made, never appear in the *Antikeimenon*. For Anselm's contemporary readers, the question of the identity of the brothers and the critics can only be asked of themselves: are they "brothers" or critics? Here one may suggest that Anselm did precisely this by turning the question on himself. If the "certain brothers" had acted "out of zeal rather than because it was good" and then learned "to inquire in a pious and humble spirit," then perhaps they had originally expressed more than concern for the criticism of the new orders. Perhaps, they had returned that criticism by mounting an attack of their own on their critics. Such was the attack mounted by the author of the *Epistola apologetica*. The author of the *Antikeimenon* has, indeed, changed. Here he will teach rather than condemn.

B. *De una forma credendi*

1. *Anselm and the critics*

Anselm created a literary situation in which he cast himself as a teacher teaching under papal patronage. For Anselm, a teacher taught others by serving as an example of how to be useful to the

---

[14] Note Walter Berschin's attempt to define the brothers: "Wer [Anselm] veranlasst hat [*De una forma credendi*] zu schreiben, sagt Anselm nicht direkt. Jedenfalls war es nicht der Papst, vielmehr *fratres quidam*—Amtsbrüder", "Ordensbrüder", Glaubensbrüder", etwa sogar griechische?...." "Anselm von Havelberg," p. 228.

[15] The "brothers" are only identified as *fratres* and not as *fratres meorum* which Anselm uses to refer to the canons of Havelberg in his letter to Wibald (ep. 221, p. 340). *Frater* is a very neutral term which Anselm has used elsewhere to refer to both Egbert (*Epist. apol.*, 1120A, 1124B, 1127A, etc.) and Wibald (ep. 158, p. 263). See Lees, "Charity and Enmity," pp. 58-62.

church. The task Anselm thus set himself in the *Antikeimenon* was not merely to give learned responses to the arguments of the critics of the new orders in *De una forma credendi* and to the Greeks in the debates, but to present himself as a model for his readers.

This is shown even in the title Anselm gives his history. The printed edition and several manuscripts use the title "On the unity of the faith [*De unitate fidei*] and the multiplicity of ways of life from the just Abel [*ab Abel iusto*] to the last of the elect." However, in the prologue to the *Antikeimenon*, Anselm says he has written a book "on the single form of believing [*de una forma credendi*] and the multiplicity of ways of life from the time of the just Abel [*a tempore Abel iusti*] to the last of the elect."[16] This alternative title makes the thrust of his book much clearer than does the commonly used *De unitate fidei*, for the book is not so much about what is believed as it is about the believers. The faithful should fit a single *forma*, a form, mold, or model, regardless of when they live. This issue is raised immediately by Anselm. He begins the book by presenting an array of rhetorical questions leveled by critics of the new ways of religious life in the church. Among these, they ask: "Who is not scandalized and tormented by disgust and scandal among so many and such different forms [*formas*] of religious life disputing among themselves?"[17] Confronting change they are driven to despair. "Oh!," they sigh, "If only we could find some secure place where we could confidently rest our head in the expectation of eternal salvation."[18] The newness of everything overwhelms them as the new orders elect "a new way of life, ... invent a new kind of psalmody, a new way of abstinence; [they make] everything new according to their own caprice." The task the critics present Anselm is how to demonstrate that the many forms of religious life nevertheless reflect the "single form of believing."

---

[16] "Liber Primus de unitate fidei et multiformitate vivendi ab Abel justo usque ad novissimum electum" is the title of the first book as given in Migne (1141-42), Ber. 1 (fol. 209r), and Mun. (fol. 2v). It is not in Wolf. 1. Anselm gives the title in the prologue as "Lib[er] de una forma credendi et multiformitate vivendi a tempore Abel justi usque ad novissimum electum" (*Antik.*, prologus, 1141B). While most scholars use the title *De unitate fidei*, Anselm is ambiguous enough about the title that Peter Classen once referred to the work as *Liber de una forma credendi et multiformitate vivendi* without further comment. "*Res Gestae*, Universal History, Apocalypse," p. 407.

[17] *Antik.* 1.11, 1141C.

[18] *Antik.* 1.1, 1143A.

Anselm's response is to affirm that a changeless unity untouched by time is, indeed, what the faithful seek. But he takes the quest for that final resting place and turns it into a time-measured and progressive line of development, suggested by the word *tempus* in the title of his book.

The notion of the church extending from Abel to the end of time did not originate with Anselm.[19] Augustine, on whom Anselm shows some reliance,[20] speaks of time going from Abel "to the end of time [*usque in finem saeculi*]."[21] However, Anselm's *usque ad novissimum electum*[22] bears a closer comparison to a phrase of Gregory I which refers to time going "from the just Abel to the last of the elect [*usque ad ultimum electum*]."[23] While both *ultimus* and *novissimus* may be translated as "last," Anselm's *novissimus* carries the connotation of "newest," "latest" or "youngest" and in effect plays on the concern he had shown in the *Epistola apologetica* for criticism of something new merely because it is new. Here, however, he avoids evoking a separation into camps of "new" and "old." *Novus* is presented in a positive light that should be acceptable to the critics. While faith has a single form (*una forma*), the expression of that faith is multiple and varied (*multiformitas*) and constantly made new in the elect, the last of whom will also be the "newest" (*novissimus*). Anselm's title emphasizes not just a series of faithful Christians from Abel to the end of time, but a series that can be understood by following the changes in the expression of the one, unchanging faith.

The critics have, then, not imagined the changes they find disturbing but have failed to understand them. Should they be willing to

---

[19] Yves Congar, "Ecclesia ab Abel," in *Abhandlungen über Theologie und Kirche: Festschrift für Karl Adam*, ed. Marcel Reding (Düsseldorf, 1952), pp. 79-108.

[20] Cf. *Antik.* 1.2, 1143D, Ber. 1, fol. 209v; Mun., fol. 3r; Wolf. 1, fol. 7r: "Ecclesia Dei...filios suos...diversis modis at diversis etatibus generavit et generat et quos diversis legibus et institutis informavit et informat a sanguine Abel justi usque ad novissimum electum" with Augustine, *Sermones ad populum* 341 9.11, PL 37:1159: "Ex Abel justo usque in finem saeculi quamdiu generant et generantur homines, quisquis justorum per hanc vitam transitum facit...totum hoc unum corpus Christi...adjungitur ista Ecclesia."

[21] Augustine, *Sermones ad populum* 341.9.11, PL 39:1499-1500; *Enarrationes in Psalmos* 61.6 and 90.21, CC 39, pp. 777, 1266; *De civitate Dei* 18.51, CC 48, p. 650. See Congar, "Ecclesia ab Abel," pp. 83-86 with further examples.

[22] Found both in the common title and the title Anselm gives in the prologue. See n. 16 above. Anselm also uses the phrase twice in *Antik.* 1.2, 1143D-44A and 1144C.

[23] Gregory I, *Homiliarum in Evangelia* 1.19.1, PL 76:1154.

relax their rhetorical stance and take their own questions seriously, Anselm will guide them to answers so that "all that they now find in scandal and ruin shall turn to their correction and edification."[24] Their questions answered, they will find themselves to be "religious men with the truly religious, inside with us, not outside against us."[25] Anselm's goal is not to defeat an opponent as it was in the *Epistola*, but to protect the unity of the faith by demonstrating that it is not threatened by the changes the critics disparage.

We must, however, be careful not to view these critics as the only or primary audience intended for Anselm's work. If we are to grasp the connection between *De una forma credendi* and the debates with the Greek archbishop that follow, it is important to remember that Anselm has said in his prologue that he is addressing an audience of brothers who are disturbed by the critics and want to know how to deal with them. As Pope Eugenius wants Anselm to show how Latins can respond to Greeks, so the brothers want Anselm to show how they can respond to their critics. In each case, Anselm's audience observes him addressing a third party: Nicetas or the critics. In the latter case, Anselm shows his brothers that he does not attack the critics but rather obscures the line between himself and them by drawing attention to how much they have in common.

The issue raised by the critics is the disparity between the ideal of a church unified and immutable and the experience of disunity and change. Anselm's answer is that the faithful make the one faith manifest, but that they can only do this in so far as their knowledge of it allows. That knowledge—not the faith itself—is what has changed over time. Knowledge will form or shape the believer who must stay within its mold. As Anselm puts it: "The church of God...has produced and produces [its sons] in different ways and in different times, and it shaped and shapes them by different laws and institutions."[26] In other words, the faith is, for Anselm, something that is lived and made manifest by the believers. This, he hastens to add, does not demonstrate a lack of unity in the church. Here he takes pains to show himself in agreement with the critics by emphasizing the word *unus*: The church "is one, one in faith, one in hope, one in charity,

---

[24] *Antik.* 1.1, 1143BC; cf. 2 Cor. 10:8.
[25] *Antik.* 1.2, 1143D.
[26] See n. 20 above.

one of a kind," and there is "one generation of the just" and "one body of the church."[27]

Having established this common ground between himself and the critics, Anselm moves toward dealing with variety and change by referring to the Holy Spirit. The Spirit governs the one church and is "unique, manifold, discriminating, changeable [*mobilis*], eloquent, unspotted, sure, pleasant, loving good deeds," etc. In spite of this multifaceted nature, the Spirit is nevertheless one.[28] Anselm has drawn here on Scripture (Wisdom 7:22-23) to describe the Holy Spirit as not only multifaceted but *mobilis*. Earlier, he had said that the critics complained that "the more changeable [*mobilior*] a spiritual way of life is, the more contemptible."[29] Rather than slashing out at them for this, he has subtly put *mobilis* forward as an aspect of the Holy Spirit supported by Scripture.[30]

Anselm goes on to cite the apostle Paul's assertion that the gifts of the Spirit are given in different measure to the faithful for the good of the whole.[31] Thus, the one church reflects the multifaceted but nevertheless one Spirit, and he concludes this chapter by linking that variety to historical development:

> Behold! The one body of the church is seen to be vivified by the one Holy Spirit, Who is unique unto Himself and multiplied in the diverse distribution of His gifts. Truly, this body of the church, vivified by the Holy Spirit and divided and separated through its different members in different ages and times, begins with the just Abel and is consummated in the last of the elect, always one in the one faith, but greatly separated by the manifold variety of ways of living.[32]

---

[27] *Antik.* 1.2, 1144A; Ber. 1, fol. 209v; Mun., fol. 3r; Wolf. 1, fol. 6v: "Una est [Ecclesia], una fide, una spe, una charitate, una unius....et est una generatio justorum." This follows Anselm's quotation of Song of Songs 6:9: "Una est columba mea, perfecta mea, una est matris suae...."

[28] *Antik.* 1.2, 1144A.

[29] *Antik.* 1.1, 1142C.

[30] Perhaps Anselm assumed his readers would know the verse which follows those he cites: "Omnibus enim mobilibus mobilior est sapientia" (Wisdom 7:24).

[31] *Antik.* 1.2, 1144B, citing 1 Cor. 12:4, 7-11.

[32] *Antik.* 1.2, 1144BC; Ber.1, fol. 210r: "Ecce manifeste apparet unum corpus Ecclesiae uno Spiritu sancto vivificari, qui et unicus est in se, et multiplex in multifaria donorum suorum distributione. Verum hoc corpus Ecclesiae Spiritu sancto vivificatum, et per diversa membra diversis temporibus et aetatibus discretum et distinctum, a primo Abel justo incoepit, et in novissimo electo consummabitur, semper unum una fide, sed multiformiter distinctum multiplici vivendi varietate."

The faithful seek to emulate the Spirit; those He favors become themselves images of faithfulness, images that change through time as the Spirit reveals more of His multifaceted nature. The goal of Christians, including both the critics and Anselm's brothers, is to comprehend their position on this developmental line and the image their particular time requires of them.

Implicit in Anselm's discussion of the operation of the Spirit in time is the sense that he wants his readers to understand themselves as participants in a progressive historical development rather than as passive observers of the unfolding of God's plan for the world. It is the faithful themselves through whom that plan is brought to fruition and who show the various aspects of the Spirit to the world. From this perspective, it is not hard to see why Anselm ignores the traditional Augustinian divisions of time into the six ages of man going from *infantia* to *senectus* which could give only a pessimistic view of the present "old age" of the world.[33] The point of Anselm's work is not to show his readers that their world has passed its prime and that they are living in decrepitude, but to convince them that they are at the pinnacle of a progressive line of development which they can help to advance.

2. *The schemes of periodization*

In plotting the changes in the church, Anselm uses a variety of schemes of periodization and then compares the different periods of time to demonstrate both the overriding unity of the faith and a variety of expression of that faith which purposefully changes over time. In brief, the schemes of periodization are as follows:

First scheme: A five part division of time before Christ which runs 1) Adam to Noah, 2) Noah to Abraham, 3) Abraham to Moses, 4) Moses to David, 5) David to Christ (*De una forma credendi* 3-4).

Second scheme: A two part division of this same time before Christ into a period of natural law (from Adam to Moses) and of written law (Moses to Christ) (*De una forma credendi* 3-4).

Third scheme: A three part division created by two great changes (*transpositiones*), called testaments or earthquakes. These divide the

---

[33] For a comparison of Anselm to Augustine see Edyvean, *Anselm of Havelberg*, pp. 14-15.

time of idolatry from that of law and the time of law from that of the Gospel (*De una forma credendi* 5-6).

Fourth scheme: A seven part division that uses the seven seals of the Apocalypse to divide the history of the church from Christ to the end of time into a series of states: They are the states of 1) Christ and the primitive church, 2) persecution of the saints and conversion of the gentiles, 3) heresy and church councils, 4) false brothers and new religious orders, 5) plaintive waiting, 6) the Antichrist, 7) the end of time (*De una forma credendi* 7-13).

None of these schemes originates with Anselm.[34] Indeed, perhaps the most often used approach to studying Anselm has been to compare his schemes with the similar ones of his contemporaries in an attempt to discover how the medieval mind saw past, present and future time and related them to each other; and in particular to determine the extent to which thinkers in the Middle Ages can be said to have had a "consciousness of history."[35] The medieval sense of historical time operated within the context of the relationship of God to man and fashioned past events into a narrative with its focus, in one way or another, on salvation. A fruitful way of looking for this consciousness of history in those who, like Anselm, made use of the periodization of time is to ask what they thought important to salvation: Is the emphasis on God's relation to the faithful in which periodization is used to understand God? Or is the emphasis on the faithful's relation to God in which periodization is used to chart their progress toward God? I would suggest that the more salvation is seen to hinge on the latter, the more we find a consciousness of history; for in this view the past will be interpreted to understand the distinctness of the present and ourselves existing in it, rather than to fathom a divine force operating on us.

To better understand Anselm's consciousness of history, I would like to look briefly at some of those contemporaries most often com-

---

[34] In general on medieval periodization see Roderich Schmidt, "Aetates mundi: Die Weltalter als Gliederungsprinzip der Geschichte," *ZKG* 57 (1955-1956), 288-317; Edyvean, *Anselm of Havelberg*, pp. 12-35; also Matthäus Bernards, "Geschichtsperiodisches Denken in der Theologie des 12. Jahrhunderts," *Kölner Domblatt* 27 (1967), 115-24.

[35] Hans-Werner Goetz, "Die Gegenwart der Vergangenheit im früh- und hochmittelalterlichen Geschichtsbewußtsein," *Historische Zeitschrift* 255 (1992), 61-97; Herbert Grundmann, *Geschichtsschreibung im Mittelalter: Gattungen—Epochen—Eigenart* (Gottingen, 1978), p. 72.

pared to Anselm and who attempted a full-fledged periodization of history: Rupert of Deutz and Hugh of St. Victor; as well as Eberwin of Steinfeld and Bernard of Clairvaux.

a. *Rupert of Deutz*

We know that Anselm "saw and knew" Rupert of Deutz, presumably when he was a student and Rupert a teacher in Liège, and that he had no very high opinion of the abbot of Deutz from his jab about Rupert's "fat belly."[36] Anselm's criticism of Rupert probably has more to do with the latter's aversion to Norbert of Xanten than to Rupert's ideas of history.[37] Certainly, in Rupert's writings, Anselm could have found a massive periodization of the past. However, Rupert's view of salvation very much emphasizes God's relation to man and is not particularly concerned with the present. The goal of Rupert's masterpiece *De Sancta Trinitate* and other of his works is the apprehension of the Trinity as it is revealed in the narrative of Holy Scripture.[38] While Rupert felt that the narrative was not to be ignored[39] and saw Scripture as dealing with the human race "for which God fought and through which he conquered,"[40] it was a spiritual meaning to which he wanted to lead his readers.[41] In the deeds of God among men Rupert saw the means of contemplating the Divine Mystery and understanding the Trinity.[42] It is through Scripture, the "book of the wars of the Lord," that one witnesses the combat be-

---

[36] See p.139 above. For Rupert's biography see van Engen, *Rupert of Deutz*; van Engen, "Rupert von Deutz und das sogenannte Chronicon sancti Laurentii Leodiensis. Zur Geschichte des Investiturstreites in Lüttich," *DA* 35 (1979), pp. 33-81; Maria Lodovica Arduini, "Contributo all biografia di Ruperto di Deutz, *Studi Medievali* 16 (1975), 537-582 with extensive bibliography.

[37] Van Engen, *Rupert of Deutz*, pp. 311-12.

[38] "Le propre de Rupert, c'est de considérer les oeuvres admirables de la Trinité dans son peuple, plûtot que les effects de la grâce en chaque fidè." Jean Gribomont, intro. to Rupert de Deutz, *Les Oeuvres des Saint Esprit* 1, ed. and trans. Elisabeth de Solms, Sources Chrétiennes 131 (Paris, 1967), p. 25.

[39] See p. 135 above.

[40] *De Victoria Verbi Dei*, MGH QzG 5:51-52.

[41] *De Sancta Trinitate, In Genesim* 4.15, CCCM 21:300: "Historiam omnes nouimus, mysteria requiramus." See Henri de Lubac, *Exégèse Médiévale: Les quatre sens de l'écriture*, 2 vols. (Paris: 1959-1964), 2.1, p. 222: "Bref, partout dans l'ouvrage de l'Esprit Rupert cherche l'Esprit." See also Leo Scheffczyk, "Die heilsökonomische Trinitätslehre des Ruperts von Deutz und ihre dogmatische Bedeutung," *Kirche und Überlieferung* (Freiburg, 1960), p. 100.

[42] *De Victoria Verbi Dei* 6.24, MGH QzG 5:207; see also Scheffczyk, "Trinitätslehre des Ruperts von Deutz," pp. 66-67.

tween the Lord and Satan and the former's victory and triumph.[43] The central figure is Christ in whose incarnation, death and resurrection the victory is consummated.[44] For Rupert, the Scriptures helped one to understand God who stood outside of time, not man within time.

In *De Sancta Trinitate* time was divided by Rupert into three parts: from the creation to the fall, from the fall to the passion, and from the passion to the resurrection of the dead. The first of these periods (*creatio*) is the "personal work" of the Father, the second (*redemptio*) of the Son, the last (*renovatio*) of the Holy Spirit.[45] Thus almost the whole of the Old Testament and the gospels falls within the period of redemption or of the Son. This period is itself divided into six states corresponding to the six days of creation with a seventh state paralleling the day of rest. But whereas the deeds of the days of creation are accomplished through nature, those of the six ages are doctrinal.[46] The first, from Adam to Noah, prefigures Christ in deeds; the second, to Abraham, again prefigures Christ and is the time of the covenant between God and man; the third, to David, promises the Lord's birth; the fourth, to the Babylonian captivity, reflects Christ as king; the fifth, to the Incarnation, shows Him as priest; and in the sixth, Christ enters the world.[47] This exegesis is highly Christocentric as each period is treated as a means of revealing a different aspect of Christ rather than showing different stages of human development.

Rupert's trinitarian scheme and the pattern of sevens shaped his view of the time after Christ. He tied the revelation of the Trinity to numbers (3 and 6 or 7) and then the numbers to time. With the first of his tripartite division, the time of the Father, the seven days of creation emerged naturally as a means of periodization. With the time of the Son, Rupert drew on Augustine's division of history into

---

[43] *De Victoria Verbi Dei* 2.18, MGH QzG 5:66-67.

[44] De Lubac, *Exégèse Médiévale* 2.1, pp. 222-226.

[45] *De Sancta Trinitate, Epistola ad Cuoneum* and prologus, CCCM 21:122, 126; also *De diuinis officiis* 11.17, CCCM 7:390-391. See Joseph Ratzinger, *Die Geschichtstheologie des Heiligen Bonaventura* (Munich, 1959), p. 100; Grundmann, *Studien über Joachim von Fiore,* p. 91; Scheffczyk, "Trinitäteslehre des Ruperts von Deutz," pp. 93-99.

[46] *De Sancta Trinitate, In Genesim* 3.36, CCCM 21:279: "Istae sex aetates sex primis diebus respondent, de quibus hactenus dictum est; sed quae in illis diebus facta sunt naturalia, quae autem in istis aetatibus doctrinalia sunt."

[47] *De Sancta Trinitate, In Genesim* 3.36, CCCM 21:279; also *De diuinis officiis* 4.3, CCCM 7:104.

six ages.[48] But if the third member of the Trinity were also to be understood through His works then a period had to be assigned to Him as well.[49] Rupert did just that, completing his recurring pattern of sevens by using the seven gifts of the Holy Spirit (Isaiah 11:2-3). As the seven ages of the world correspond to the seven days of creation, so do they both reflect the gifts of the Holy Spirit. In the first day of creation and expulsion from Eden is fear; in the second day and the ark is piety; and so forth until the seventh day and the assumption which demonstrates wisdom.[50] In this way the three parts come together to reveal the Trinity to man in a recurring pattern of seven. On the seventh day of the first part, God rests and the first age of the Son begins. Likewise at the beginning of the seventh age Christ rests in the tomb[51] and in his passion and resurrection embodies the first and greatest of the gifts of the Holy Spirit, wisdom.[52] The third part of Rupert's division of time then reflects the gifts of the Spirit working from *sapientia* back again to *timor* through seven further stages of history. In the first, *sapientia*, the sacraments are established and the devil defeated. In the second, the apostles receive a clear understanding of Scripture through *intellectus*. In the third, the gospel is spread and taken to the gentiles through *consilium*. In the fourth, paganism is defeated by the *fortitudo* of the martyrs. In the fifth, the Scriptures are interpreted by the fathers through *scientia*. From here Rupert skips to the future when in the sixth stage the Jews will bring *timor*.[53]

In his trinitarian scheme Rupert was quite revolutionary.[54] He gave history tremendous theological importance as the tool for un-

---

[48] See for example Augustine's *De Civitate Dei* 22.30.

[49] Scheffczyk, "Die Trinitätslehre des Ruperts von Deutz," pp. 110-111.

[50] For the ages of the world as reflecting the gifts of the Spirit see *De Sancta Trinitate, In Genesim* 3.36, CCCM 21:280. For the days of creation see *In Genesim* 1.21, p. 150; 1.24, p. 153; 1.39, p.167; 1.48, p. 175 (4th and 5th days); 2.12, pp. 197-98; 2.18, p. 204.

[51] *De Sancta Trinitate, Quattuor evangel.* 30, CCCM 23:1821.

[52] *De Sancta Trinitate, De operibus Spiritus Sancti* 2.11, CCCM 24:1905.

[53] *De Sancta Trinitate, De operibus Spiritus Sancti* 1.31, CCCM 24:1860-1861. For this and other schemes of periodization in Rupert's writings see Beinert, *Kirche*, pp. 322-327.

[54] Rupert's division of history bears some comparison with Augustine's three part division *exortus, excursus, sine ullo temporis fine* (*De Civitate Dei* 15.1; Grundmann, *Studien über Joachim von Floris*, p. 88) in so far as the first, *exortus*, refers to the time before the fall and the *excursus* to man's history. But Augustine's division is not trinitarian nor is the third of his divisions part of history but rather the time after the last judgment.

derstanding God's relation to man,[55] and by relegating the period after Christ to the third member of the Trinity, Rupert elevated it above the sixth day of the world week to a position of equal importance with the periods of creation and salvation. But the factor of time as the distinguishing element in determining the borders of the seven parts of that final period is very vague. There is no use of an *ab...usque* formula; the first three divisions (the granting of spiritual understanding to the apostles, the conversion of the gentiles, and the suffering of the martyrs) are hardly to be distinguished from each other chronologically, and Rupert gave the time between the fathers and the conversion of the Jews (which would include the present) no consideration at all. He was not concerned with comparing the events of earlier times with later and much less with trying to understand the present by studying the past. He used events since Christ to reflect the Holy Spirit whose gifts were to be seen in the earlier periods as well. Still, the time after Christ was no longer simply one of the six ages. The possibility of looking for stages of historical development within it was opened.[56] In fact, Rupert himself pointed the way in his commentary on the Apocalypse.

In his *In Apocalypsim Joannis Apostoli*, Rupert again makes use of the seven gifts of the Spirit. There he explains each of the gifts through the seven letters written to the seven churches of Asia Minor (Apoc. 2-3). In his treatment of the period of the Spirit in *De Sancta Trinitate*, Rupert dealt with the gifts in descending order: "Here [in the period of the Spirit] we descend from wisdom to fear, having at the end of time what we would always fear, however perfect we may be and however much we seem to have already attained."[57] In dealing with the seen churches of the Apocalypse, he reverses the order and goes from fear to wisdom.[58] While he does not couple the ascending order of gifts with history and no periodization emerges from his exegeses of the seven letters,[59] nevertheless the idea of ascension is joined with

---

[55] Rupert's three ages were "nicht also reine Geschichtsepochen, sondern Studien der Weltprocesses." Grundmann, *Studien über Joachim von Floris*, p. 94.

[56] Ratzinger, *Geschichtstheologie*, pp. 101-2.

[57] *De Sancta Trinitate, De operibus Spiritus Sancti* 1.31, CCCM 24:1861.

[58] *In Apocalypsim* 2, PL 169:865C.

[59] In books 3-11 of *In Apocalypsim*, John's seven visions are also interpreted through the seven gifts, this time from *sapientia* back again to *timor* (prologus, PL 169:903-4). In this work, Rupert does often bring historical events into his exegeses but without any chronological order. See Kamlah, *Apokalypse und Geschichtstheologie*, p. 102.

that of the *ecclesia*, and that of the *ecclesia* with the imitation of Christ: "Surely when the church imitates Christ, it begins with fear and by ascending arrives at wisdom."[60] Rupert's goal remained the understanding of the Trinity, but he gave a schema which, in other hands, could be equated with historical progress toward an institutional imitation of Christ.

In looking for a consciousness of history in Rupert, it can hardly be overemphasized that he was primarily concerned with how a twelfth-century Christian could intellectually comprehend the revealed Godhead through scriptural study, and not with how much those in, say, the period Adam to Noah understood as compared to those in the period Noah to Abraham, nor with what relative limitations this placed on them. In his tripartite scheme, Rupert's first period is *creatio* in which the Father is revealed before man has even begun his sojourn on earth. Thus, were one to ask Rupert to whom the Father is revealed, he would surely have replied that He is revealed to the pious student of Scripture. Rupert's period of *redemptio*, which is broken up into ages, lasts from the fall to the crucifixion, setting up the history that precedes the latter as a reflection of Christ's coming. While Rupert tried to show that the seven gifts of the Holy Spirit are revealed in a series of states from Christ to the end of the world, it was only after showing how these same gifts are revealed both in the days of creation and in the states of the period of redemption—again demonstrating that his interest was not in showing when these things were revealed historically but rather how they are revealed to the student of Scripture. Moreover, when Rupert gets to the time after Christ, he ignores the present entirely.

b. *Hugh of St. Victor*

There is no evidence that Anselm knew another great twelfth-century exegete, Hugh of St. Victor, but their visions of history are in some ways similar.[61] Still, Hugh's view of history was, like that of Rupert of Deutz, very much colored by theological concerns for understanding

---

[60] *In Apocalypsim* 2, PL 169:865C.

[61] See R. W. Southern, "Presidential Address: Aspects of the European Tradition of Historical Writings: 2," ser. 21 (1971), p. 175, who suggests a greater dependence of Anselm on Hugh then I see. For Hugh in general, see Joachim Ehlers, *Hugo von St. Viktor: Studien zum Geschichtsdenken und zur Geschichtsschreibung des 12. Jahrhunderts* (Wiesbaden, 1973).

Divine Mystery rather than man. And as with Rupert, though not so severely, those concerns tended to confound the development of an idea of historical progress.

The work in which Hugh most fully developed his ideas of historical periodization is his masterpiece *De sacramentis Christianae*. There he went well beyond the historical-literal level of Scripture in order that his readers "might fix their minds on the foundation of knowledge of the faith," for it is allegory which teaches right faith.[62] Hugh proceeded to discuss the mysteries of the faith and its sacraments. In doing this, he wrote in several places of the periods *sub naturalem legem, sub lege, sub gratia*. However, trying as he was to understand the sacraments, his use of this tripartate division depended on the particular sacramental question he was addressing rather than on an attempt to understood the present; and Hugh exhibits no sense of any incongruity in giving his periods different, even contradictory, interpretations.

In *De sacramentis*, Hugh says that the sacraments were instituted as weapons to do battle with Satan and his followers. The three divisions serve to define the combatants: The first, that of natural law, is made up mainly of men guided solely by natural reason who are openly evil, pagan, and to be compared with Magog. The second, that of imposed law, is composed largely of those who live according to exterior precepts, are falsely good and serve out of fear. Among them are the Jews, and their sign is Gog. In the third period, those living under grace are Christians and have felt the Holy Spirit.[63] While the three periods are given chronological boundaries (Adam to Moses,[64] Moses to Christ, Christ to the end of the world), these are not sharp distinctions, for Hugh further asserts that the three kinds of men are found in all three periods.[65] His point is that there have always been men of grace, and that as the devil's sacraments have bound his followers to him, so from the beginning of time have God's followers chosen His sacraments.[66] Only those having grace follow Christ, and so to live by natural reason or by law is not only not enough but it is to side with the devil. Natural reason, law, and grace

---

[62] *De sacramentis* prologus, PL 176:183-85.

[63] *De sacramentis* 1.8.11, PL 176:312-13. See also *De sacramentis legis naturalis et scriptae dialogus*, PL 176:32BC.

[64] Hugh could give different ends for the period of natural law. Cf. *De sacramentis* 1.12, PL 176:347 with *De arca Noe mystica* 5, PL 176:683AB.

[65] *De sacramentis* 1.8.11, PL 176:313B; also *De arca Noe mystica*, PL 176:688D.

[66] *De sacramentis* 1.8.11, PL 176:312.

are not a means of plotting the progress of Christians. Rather the first two are opposed to grace not so much as historical periods but as ways of living without God's sacraments.[67]

Shortly after this, Hugh asks whether faith changes with the passage of time. He answers in the negative; but he thinks that faith, while not changing, does increase, and the divisions for plotting that increase are again the times before the law, under the law and under grace. This time the divisions take on a historical character as man's understanding of God and the Savior grows from one period to the next.[68] Hugh goes little further than to point out this increase which is all that his initial question demands of him, and his skeletal periodization is not fleshed out.[69] But while the faith may not have changed, Hugh admits that the sacraments—"the signs of sacred things"—have.[70]

Later in *De sacramentis*, the three part division becomes the means of plotting, defining, and explaining changes in the sacraments. Here natural and written law refer not to a reprehensible way of living which excludes grace, but to certain types of sacraments which did indeed have the effect of sanctification.[71] The sacraments of natural law included tithes, oblations, and sacrifices; and they increased in number under the law.[72] The former were a shadow of truth; the latter were its image or figure, and both led to the body of truth under grace.[73]

Hugh's concern is for sacramental unity. All men who fight for Christ, whether they precede or follow the incarnation, are members of the same army, serving under the same banner.[74] But the unity of Christ's followers is expressed, indeed created by the sacraments at least as an expression of interior commitment.[75] It is not an under-

---

[67] A similar treatment of the three periods is given by Hugh in *De arca Noe mystica* 5, PL 176:688-91. Here, however, the main motif is the ark-church, and it is the relationship of the three kinds of people to the church which is discussed. While men of natural and written law may be "partim in Ecclesia," they are nonetheless "nullo modo de Ecclesia."

[68] *De sacramentis* 1.10.6, PL 176:339CD.

[69] See also *De sacramentis* 1.8.3, PL 176:307BD.

[70] *De sacramentis* 1.11.6, PL 176:345D.

[71] *De sacramentis* 1.11.1, PL 176:343BC. See also *De sacramentis legis naturalis*, PL 176:35A.

[72] *De sacramentis* 1.12.4, PL 176:351D.

[73] *De sacramentis* 1.11.6, PL 176:346CD.

[74] *De sacramentis* prologus.2, PL 176:183CD.

[75] *De sacramentis* 1.12.1, PL 176:347-48.

standing of past people whose rites were different from present sacraments that Hugh is aiming at, nor an understanding of present rites
through studying those of the past. If anything, the opposite is true. It
is the perception of the "body of truth" under grace through which
past sacraments can be understood and the unity of all sacraments,
past and present, seen. The tripartite division of time is a tool of
interpretation where the goal is an understanding of the means of
grace given to mankind. While the three periods may refer to actual
divisions of time, this is subsumed under the issue of sacramental
grace.

If Hugh's periodization comes in some ways closer to a consciousness of history than Rupert's, he nevertheless shows the same lack of
interest in the present as does the abbot of Deutz. When Hugh says
that "through times faith grew in all things but it did not change so
as to be different,"[76] he hints at the idea of some kind of historical
development; but again, he associates this change closely with the
sacraments. The change he seeks in the past is sacramental, for a
change in the sacraments is visible evidence of increasing spiritual
cognition. Living in the present, when the Redeemer Himself is
"manifestly proclaimed and believed by all,"[77] he can look to the past
with this knowledge and understand the sacraments of the past. Like
Rupert's, Hugh's is a Christocentric interpretation of Scripture. Increasing spiritual cognition is, for him, increasing awareness of Christ
as mankind's Redeemer. Hugh's works, unlike Rupert's, are not ori-
ented toward an understanding of the Trinity, and so far as I am
aware, nowhere does he interpret the periods of natural law, written
law, and grace as showing a progressive understanding of the Father,
Son, and Holy Spirit.[78] Much more important to Hugh is the two
part division of time into the work of establishing (*opus conditionis*) and
the work of restoration (*opus restaurationis*). The former, treating the
creation of the world, has the lesser dignity and needed only six days
to be completed. The latter tells of man's redemption and has the

---

[76] *De sacramentis* 1.10.6, PL 176:339C.

[77] *De sacramentis* 1.10.6, PL 176:339C.

[78] The only passage I have found in which Hugh speaks of the Trinity as being
revealed to man is *De sacramentis* 1.3.21, PL 176:225BC, but even there Hugh's point
is not that man's understanding of the Trinity is a historical development, but that in
the consciousness of one's own rational being the individual may first look for the
Trinity: "In hoc ergo primum Trinitatis vestigium inventum est cum agnoscere
coepit ipsa quod erat in se, et ex eo consideravit quod erat supra se."

higher dignity, needing six ages for its fulfillment.[79] In the present—
the third period—the spiritual cognition of Christ as Redeemer is
complete; and in the second book of *De sacramentis*, Hugh moves from
a description of the changes in man's understanding of the redemption to a delineation of the ways in which the present sacraments
reflect that cognition. Whatever one may say of Hugh's attitude
about the past, he lends virtually no support to a notion of historical
progress in the time after Christ,[80] and the church is shown as a static
institution—namely the body of the faithful—held together by the
sacraments through which the Redeemer is recognized.

The lack of interest in the present as a period of development or
change is shown in others of Hugh's works. In an oft quoted passage
from *De arca Noe morali*, he says that the order of time or the succes-
sion of events parallels the order of place and that this order of place,
beginning in the East in the Garden of Eden, has proceeded to its
climax in the West, "from which we may perceive that the end of
time approaches, because the course of events has now reached the
end of the world." He shows this movement by pointing out that
power shifted among the kingdoms of the world in a westerly direction from the Assyrians to the Chaldaeans, Medes, Greeks, and "finally towards the end of time to the Romans in the West, living as it
were at the end of the world."[81] The course of events has moved to its
geographical conclusion. By linking time with geography, Hugh can
see himself as living at the end of time. There is no more development to be made; and as a consequence, there is in Hugh's theology
no room for historical change after Christ which would create an
interest in development since then. For Hugh there is no development to be probed.

c. *Eberwin of Steinfeld and Bernard of Clairvaux*

While Rupert of Deutz and Hugh of St. Victor showed little concern
for the present, other writers did. The seven seals of the Apocalypse
were often explained in ways so similar to Anselm's that one may
speak of a tradition going back to Bede that interpreted particularly

---

[79] *De sacramentis* prologus 2, PL 176:183-84.
[80] Christian Schütz, *Deus Absconditus, Deus Manifestus: Die Lehre Hugos von St. Viktor über die Offenbarung Gottes*, Studia Anselmiano 56 (Rome, 1967), p. 234; Ehlers, *Hugo von St. Viktor*, pp. 144-45.
[81] *De arca Noe morali* 4.9, PL 176:677D-78A.

the second, third, and fourth seals in terms of attacks on the church, an exegesis picked up by twelfth-century writers.[82]

In a stimulating article, Guntram Bischoff discusses a letter of the Premonstratensian canon Eberwin of Steinfeld to Bernard of Clairvaux.[83] In this letter, Eberwin uses the seven jugs of water Christ turned into wine at Cana to symbolize six attacks on the church from Christ through the Antichrist, namely those of the scribes and Pharisees, the gentiles, the heretics, the false Christians, the heretics "who come at the end of time," and the Antichrist.[84] Bischoff says, "[The] amazing agreement between Eberwin's and Anselm's views, even to the point of identity, can hardly be accidental."[85] Since Anselm's work (ca. 1149) was written after Eberwin's (1143), the bishop would have been the one to have been influenced. Still, one wonders how this could have proceeded. Did Anselm somehow come upon a copy of this letter? Or did he at some time actually meet with Eberwin, a fellow Premonstratensian, and—over a jug of wine?—discuss the

---

[82] Walter Edyvean has pointed to the *Glossa ordinaria* as having an influence on Anselm. (*Anselm of Havelberg*, pp. 22-24). While the *Glossa* does interpret the seals of the Apocalypse to show the church running through a series of states similar to Anselm's, it should be pointed out that the passages in the *Glossa* which Edyvean cites show no verbal similarity to Anselm's exegeses. See Sieben, *Konzilsidee*, p. 223 n. 20. In this context, one may also mention Rupert of Deutz, who gives a vaguely similar interpretation of the first four seals in his commentary on the Apocalypse, which is, however, very ahistorical (*In Apocalypsim*, PL 169:942-43). For Rupert each seal takes on multiple meanings. Thus, for example, the second seal—the red horse —is construed to symbolize Christ's passion, the city of the devil, the blood of the just, and persecution from Christ to the last of the elect. Rupert also reverses the order of heretics and false brothers or hypocrites, the exegesis found in Bede, *Explanatio Apocalypsis*, PL 93:147BC. Honorius Augustodunensis divides history into a series of wars, six before and six after Christ. *Expositio in Cantica Canticorum* 2, PL 172:451-54. Those after Christ parallel Anselm's divisions very closely, except that Anselm adds a fifth state of waiting. On the interpretation of the Apocalypse in the Middle Ages, see Kamlah, *Apokalypse und Geschichtstheologie*.

[83] "Early Premonstratensian Eschatology: The Apocalyptic Myth," *The Spirituality of Western Christianity*, ed. Rozanne Elder (Kalamazoo, 1976), pp. 41-71.

[84] Bernard, ep. 472, PL 182:676-80

[85] "Early Premonstratensian Eschatology," p. 57. Bischoff also suggests that Eberwin drew on Rupert's *In Euangelium Iohannis* 2.12, CCCM 9:112-15 (Bischoff's citation of PL 169:805-26—p. 193 n. 14—must be a misprint for PL 169:286-90) for his interpretation of the jugs of wine, but unfortunately does not elaborate. In the twelfth century there were certainly other uses of the Cana motif along lines similar to Rupert's (which derives from Augustine). None of them, including Rupert's, associates the jars specifically with the time after Christ. See Schmidt, "Aetates mundi," pp. 314-15.

miracle at Cana? More problematic are the considerable differences between Anselm and Eberwin. Anselm speaks of four attacks, not six; the Cana motif plays no role in his history, and he sees himself as living in the fourth state—well before the coming of the Antichrist— whereas we find Eberwin ready to drink from the sixth jug.

There is another individual more likely to have influenced Anselm, namely the recipient of Eberwin's letter, Bernard himself, whose thirty-third sermon on the Song of Songs comes closer to Anselm's periodization. There Bernard speaks of four temptations "in Christ's Own Body, which is the church." Eberwin does not mention the church in his divisions, but it is the major point with Anselm. Bernard's temptations proceed the one after the other in the same sequence Anselm uses: The saints were persecuted; the church then suffered from false teachings; in the present, it is afflicted with the hypocrisy of its own members; and finally the Antichrist will come.[86] While this sequence was rather commonplace by the twelfth century, when one compares Anselm's and Bernard's discussions of these persecutions, one finds fairly close similarities and one which is so close as to suggest strongly that Anselm read Bernard's sermon. For both writers, the church not only grows in these states but grows in the same ways, in endurance and then in wisdom, which is not, as far as I can tell, commonplace at all. Bernard says, "This pestilence [heresy] was repulsed in the wisdom of the saints just as the first [i.e. persecution] [was] in the patience of the martyrs" ("Sed haec quoque pestis [heresy] depulsa est in sapientia sanctorum, sicut et prima in patientia martyrum"), and Anselm, "In this state the church grew in marvelous wisdom against the heretics, just as in the earlier state it grew through persecution in the victorious patience of the martyrs" ("In hoc statu Ecclesia crevit mirabili contra haereticos sapientia, sicut in priori statu in persecutione martyrum victoriosa crevit patientia").[87] Both also begin their discussion of the present time of hypocrisy with descriptions of hypocrites hiding behind good deeds, though

---

[86] *Sermones super Cantica Canticorum* 33.7.14-16, *S. Bernardi opera* 1, ed. Jean Leclercq, *et al* (Rome, 1957), pp. 243-45. Eberwin, it may be pointed out, says how much he rejoiced in Bernard's writings on the Song of Songs (PL 182:676). Is it not then more likely that he derives his divisions from Bernard than from Rupert (n. 85 above)? This would also explain the similarity between Anselm and Eberwin, Bernard being their common source.

[87] *Sermones super Cantica Canticorum*, p. 243; *Antik.* 1.9, 1152B. The similarity is pointed to by Salet, *Anselme de Havelberg*, p. 83, n. 2.

Bernard limits his criticisms to the clergy, whereas Anselm casts a wider net.[88]

Bernard's view of the present is fraught with pessimism as he portrays the problem of hypocrisy as insurmountable. The church has sunk so low that all that remains is for "the noon-day demon" to appear. "[Christians] have scorned and dishonored [God] by a shameless life, shameless complaining, shameless dealing, and finally by the deeds of the thing that walks in darkness [i.e. hypocrisy]."[89] The dismal condition of the present church leads naturally into the reign of that noon-day demon, the Antichrist. Whereas Rupert of Deutz and Hugh of St. Victor subordinated history to theological concerns, Bernard made of it a pessimistic tool of prophecy.

d. *The general structure of* De una forma credendi
Anselm used his schemes of periodization to present ideas different than those of Rupert, Hugh, Eberwin, and Bernard. In doing this he ran up against the traditions which these writers represent. On the one hand, there was the Christocentric-theological view which held Christ's conquest of death to be the decisive historical event after the Fall, an event mirrored by the *historia* of Scripture but not allowing for much of an idea of development after Christ. On the other hand was the sense that what development there had been was downhill, ending in a world deserving of Antichrist. Anselm, as we will see, tried to show a line of historical development that went from Abel to the Second Coming in which Christ's centrality was the key, not the barrier, to further progress after the Assumption. Here, Anselm displayed a consciousness of history going well beyond his contemporaries in that he was explicitly concerned with understanding the present by comparing it with past periods. Moreover and in spite of seeing the same problems Bernard saw, Anselm maintained an optimistic view of the present and immediate future.

The overriding structure Anselm gives his work and into which he places his schemes of periodization is tripartite: a section dealing with time before Christ; one dealing with time after Christ; and between these, a middle section dealing with the *transpositiones*.[90] In the first

---

[88] Cf. *Antic.* 1.10, 1152C-53A to Bernard, *Sermones* 33.7.15, pp. 243-44.

[89] *Sermones* 33.7.16, pp. 244-45. Cf. Psalms 90:6.

[90] On Anselm's penchant for using a three part scheme in his writings, see Morrison, "Anselm of Havelberg," p. 242.

section, he defines time as generating and shaping the members of the church from Abel to the last of the elect. In the final section, he describes a state where, after a third and final earthquake, this process of educating the faithful will be complete. The end will be found in the silence of divine contemplation when "the truth of all symbols and sacraments which existed in different periods from the beginning of time will be revealed." This revelation will mark the end of the spiritual education of the just, an education in which "the signs of spiritual graces grow with the advance of time...[and] more and more declare the truth itself."[91] A temporal line could thus be drawn from Abel, moved by faith alone to sacrifice the first of his flock, to the end of time when truth will be revealed, a line on which stand all the faithful who make up the body of Christ which is the church. The criticisms of the those who would disparage change thus become criticisms of the church itself and derive from a lack of knowledge of the church's very nature.

Anselm's middle section on the *transpositiones* addresses the great obstacle to his concept of a church which has continued to make progress into the present, namely the Christocentric view of history which held the incarnate Christ to be the culmination of God's revelation to man.[92] Anselm's is a very different attitude toward the time after Christ, and it is with his chapters on the great *transpositiones* of history that he explains why change has continued.

3. *Old Testament images of faith*

In the early chapters of *De una forma credendi* dealing with the Old Testament, Anselm presents some complicated images that provide the foundation for his later explanation of change after Christ. For these images to make understandable a diversity of religious life as an expression of the one faith, they need to communicate both a sense of the sameness of the faithful as viewed over time and a sense of the changes in circumstances or knowledge which effect the way faith is expressed. Just as important, there must be a resonance between the images presented here and those presented for the time after Christ that will also communicate both continuity and change.

---

[91] *Antik.* 1.13, 1159C-60A.
[92] Bischoff, "Early Premonstratensian Eschatology," pp. 53-56.

Anselm first considers four Old Testament figures and then evokes the eleventh chapter of Paul's Letter to the Hebrews in which the apostle includes these four in a litany of faithful men who lived before Christ.[93] Anselm adopts Paul's famous "By faith...." (*Fidei....*) to introduce each of the faithful. In doing this, he asks his audience to compare his presentation of the Old Testament faithful with Paul's.

Paul presents these people as a panorama of the power of faith in demonstrations of righteousness, obedience, courage and prophetic powers: "By faith Abel offered God a more acceptable sacrifice.... By faith Enoch was taken up.... By faith Noah...constructed an ark..." etc. Only at the end of this litany does Paul ask his readers to compare their own faith with that of these Old Testament figures and understand that, coming after Christ, their faith should be all the stronger. Anselm, on the other hand, sharply contrasts the faith of his Old Testament figures with their lack of knowledge of how they should express that faith, and this negative aspect—completely lacking in Paul—must have rung clear to an audience well versed in the Scriptures. Abel, says Anselm, offered the first of his flock, "by faith," but "by no divine command was he commanded nor taught by any written law" and "no rite of sacrifice is read to have yet been established at that time." "By faith" Noah built the ark and after the flood made sacrifice on an altar, though "here, too, no rite of sacrifice had yet been established." "By faith" Abraham made sacrifice "still taught by no written law." "By faith" Jacob erected a monument to the Lord yet "was taught by no law but acted on the sole devotion of his faith."[94]

Anselm emphasizes that neither this lack of knowledge nor the different rites of worship demonstrates any difference in faith but that each rite was both unique to the individual practicing it and yet similar in being acceptable to God: Abel pleased God because of his righteousness (*iustitia*); Noah demonstrated the same faith as Abel

[93] Salet, *Anselme de Havelberg*, p. 46 n. 3.
[94] *Antik.* 1.3, 1144C-45A; Ber. 1, fol. 210r; Mun., fol. 3v; Wolf. 1, fol. 8v: "[Abel] hoc fecit primus in fide, nullo divino mandato specialiter jussus nec lege adhuc scripta doctus.... nullus ritus sacrificandi adhuc dispositus ibidem legatur.... Fide Noe...aptavit arcam...aedificavit altare...sed necdum hic quoque aliquis ordo sacrificandi dispositus erat. Fide Abraham obtulit sacrificium Domino, nulla lege adhuc scripta doctus..... Fide Jacob...erexit lapidem...nulla lege doctus, sed sola fidei devotione hoc faciens."

"but not the observance of the same ritual;"[95] Abraham was instructed on how to sacrifice in a vision (*visio*) directed to him alone and not to his posterity as a written law. Anselm creates similarities by using the same words to describe more than one figure. Abel and Abraham demonstrate *iustitia*; Abraham and Jacob have a *visio*. That this is a conscious effort on Anselm's part is seen in the fact that neither word is used to describe these figures by Paul. Anselm attributes *iustitia* to Abel and adopts Romans 4:9 for Abraham; he calls Jacob's dream (Gen. 28:12-16) a *visio* to draw the comparison with Abraham's vision (Gen. 15:1). From the Scriptures, Anselm shapes his images, forming them so that the deeds they communicate express to the reader both continuity and change.

This introduction to the faithful of the Old Testament touches on an idea of historical development only in that Anselm moves chronologically from one figure to the next.[96] For the moment, these Old Testament figures are presented as images of men of faith who yet expressed that same faith in different ways. Anselm asks his reader:

> These and many others proven by their witness to the faith, are they not judged to be part of the unity of the church, who, although one in faith, nevertheless worshiped the one God in diverse ways of living and with a diverse rite of sacrifice?[97]

He has intoned what his critics holds dear, the faith, one by its very nature and complete unto itself; but he has also drawn a firm distinction between the one faith and individual expressions of faith, and just as important he has moved his audience to a consideration of historical evidence as the basis for investigating variety in the church. The variety the critics fear is abundantly found in the past and in the Scriptures, and the question as to why this is so must be taken seriously.[98]

---

[95] *Antik.* 1.3, 1144D-45A; Ber. 1, fol 210r; Mun., fol. 3v; Wolf. 1, fol. 8v. Most of this quotation is not in Migne, and the mss. give many variants. It would follow "obtulit holocaustum super altare" in Migne (first line 1145A) and my reading is: "Odoratusque est dominus odorem suavitatis [Gen. 8:12]. Quidem et ipse ferit in eadem fide sed non eiusdem ritus observatione quia hic altare [Migne resumes] ibi vero non nominatur altare: hic de volucribus mundis, ibi de primogenitis gregis oblatio facta legitur, sed necdum hic quoque ordo sacrificandi dispositus erat."

[96] Cf. Rauh, *Bild des Antichrist*, pp. 274-75.

[97] *Antik.* 1.3, 1145BC.

[98] For another interpretation which views Anselm's early discussion of Abel, Abraham and Jacob as part of the history which follows rather than apart from it, see Edyvean, *Anselm of Havelberg*, pp. 15-16.

Anselm has already suggested his answer. His four Old Testament figures were "untaught" or given no written law by which they could know what was expected of them. That later, faithful people were given a law, Anselm soon makes clear, a law from God the teacher. History becomes the story of the faithful's education in what faith means, a story in which the image of the faithful progressively changes in accordance with what has been learned.

Anselm now begins another interpretation of the Old Testament, this time showing historical development from Adam through five ages of Old Testament history. He emphasizes not only that changing expressions of faith may indicate a growing understanding of God, but also that during the very first two ages, the faithful learned a great deal about living successfully with their neighbors. From Adam to Noah, he points to the faithful exercising a love of neighbor through love of self by doing "those things to a neighbor which they wished done to themselves."[99] From Noah to Abraham, love of neighbor was practiced through love of God as the faithful served "God the Creator and not the creation."[100] The message that the first principle the faithful needed to know is how to get along with their neighbors was certainly an important one for his audience of brothers and critics to grasp, and Anselm calls to their minds the simplicity of the golden rule. Perhaps, there is also here some self-criticism of the man who had written the uncharitable *Epistola apologetica*.

In the following two ages, from Abraham to Moses and from Moses to David, God the teacher begins to guide the faithful by instituting a law of obedience and then a written law. In the earlier period, the church grows and many "are counted and are in the unity of the church."[101] Anselm gives most of his attention to the customs and rites practiced during this time, including polygamy, circumcision and rites of sacrifice. These serve to remind Anselm's readers of the passage of time marked by changes in ritual and way of life.

---

[99] *Antik.* 1.3, 1145C; Mun., fol. 4r; Ber. 1 fol. 210v; Wolf. 1, fols. 9r-9v: "Ab Adam equidem usque ad Noe quam multi fideles fuere, qui hic non numerantur, qui naturalem legem secuti sunt, et Deum omnium creatorem cognoscentes coluerunt [cf. Wisdom 13:5], et proximo ea quae sibi fieri vellent naturaliter exhibuerunt ea vero quae sibi fieri nollent, nulli proximorum ad offensionem intulerunt."

[100] *Antik.* 1.3, 1145C.

[101] *Antik.* 1.3, 1145D.

In the fourth age, the faithful are gathered into one church by Moses under God's written law which institutes "a new rite and new rules of sacrifice." These he enumerates:

> The law of burnt offering, the law of sacrifice, the law of sin offering, the law of peace offering, the law of votive offering were fashioned in manifold variety. A new way of living, new commandments, new precepts, new prohibitions were written for that church.[102]

This passage does more than drive home the point that there are changes in the expression of faith. With it Anselm creates an image of the church moving from a time of natural law to one of law. He will later point to this change as the first of the great *transpositiones* associated with earthquakes. The second *transpositiones* is that from law to the Gospel; and when Anselm comes to describe the church after this second change, he gives it the same image as the one we have just seen:

> There arise new sacraments, new rituals, new commandments, new institutions. The gospels are written. The apostolic and canonical letters are written. By its doctrines and written decrees, the Christian law is instituted. The faith which is called catholic is announced throughout the world.[103]

Here, then, are the states of the church after the *transpositiones* of the two great earthquakes, states in which new forms mold the lives of the faithful.

With his fifth age, Anselm further prepares his readers for his description of the church after Christ as one full of a variety of expressions of faith. Likewise, the time from David to Christ exhibits a veritable explosion of new developments: Kings are chosen and anointed, the temple is built for the ark of the covenant, prophets and venerable men arise prophesying and writing of times to come, and to the written law new traditions, ceremonies, and observances are added. "Thus among the ancient fathers devotion was rendered in

---

[102] *Antik.* 1.3, 1146A; Mun., fol 4v; Ber. 1, fol. 210v; Wolf. 1, fol. 10r: "Lex holocausti, lex sacrificii, lex hostiae pro peccato, lex hostiae pacificae, lex hostie pro consecratione, lex hostiae pro voto multiplici varietate informatur. Novus ordo vivendi nova mandata, novae praeceptiones, novae prohibitiones illi Ecclesiae scribuntur." Cf. Lev. 1-8.

[103] *Antik.* 1.6, 1149A; Ber., fol. 212r ; Mun., fol. 6r; Wolf., fol. 14v: "Surgunt sacramenta nova, ritus novi, mandata nova, institutiones novae. Scribuntur evangelia. Scribuntur epistolae apostolicae et canonicae. Lex Christiana doctrinis et scriptis instauratur, fides quae vocatur catholica in universo mundo annuntiatur."

manifold and many ways with one faith in the one God."[104] The image Anselm paints of variety in the church before Christ is in color and outline the image of the church that comes after. It is a masterful construction, showing that the church has both changed and yet remained the same.

Anselm uses the traditional Christocentric view to make clear the vast difference between these two ages: Those before Jesus did not fully comprehend the sacraments of Christ and the church, for they could not see "the mystery of the incarnation, the nativity, the passion, the resurrection, the ascension with an uncovered face [*revelata facie*]." Those who come after recognize God made manifest through His Name which is His Word which is His Son.[105] It remains for Anselm to present his image of Christ and the effect that image has on developments since Christ.

There is one passage in these chapters on the Old Testament that stands apart from Anselm's periodization. In his treatment of the fourth age, from Moses to David, Anselm gives considerable attention—more than to any other Old Testament figure—to Job. Here is a man who stands completely outside of the organized church, a gentile of whom God Himself said that there was none like him on earth, a man "most strong in his faith."[106] Job's devotion was acceptable to God in spite of the fact that he did not use the same ritual as the Hebrews, and Anselm forthrightly confesses that he has no idea what rite Job used to worship God, for "the authentic Scriptures do not relate this to us."[107] In a work that Anselm says will answer questions, we find here an admission of ignorance. This willingness to admit that there are limits to what has been revealed will become an important issue in the debates with Nicetas; and, in fact, Job the gentile, whose rite Anselm does not understand but who was nevertheless acceptable to God, bears comparison with the Greek arch-

---

[104] *Antik.* 1.4, 1146CD; Ber. 1, fol.211r; Mun., fol. 4v; Wolf. 1, fol. 11r: "Nazaraei secundum tempora suscitantur; multa honesta ad decorem domus Dei devotissime disponuntur; et ita apud antiquos patres multifaria [Ber.: multivariis] multisque modis una fide uni Deo fideliter serviebatur."

[105] *Antik.* 1.4, 1146D-47B.

[106] *Antik.* 1.3, 1146B; Mun., fol. 4v; Wolf. 1, fol. 10v: "Job gentilis inventus fuisse putatur virtute patientiae praecipuus, fide futurae resurrectionis apertissimus, in sustinenda probrosa propriae uxoris tentatione fortissimus, in onerosa amicorum consolatione prudentissimus, in omnium temptationum mole gravissima fide robustissimus."

[107] *Antik.* 1.3, 1146B.

bishop of whose rites Anselm will at times portray himself as being woefully ignorant.[108] It may be suggested that with Job, Anselm is preparing the way for his audience to keep an open mind when they meet Nicetas.

4. *The transpositiones*

Before describing the states of the church from Christ to the end of time, Anselm address the Christocentric view that historical development culminated with Christ's incarnation and resurrection. Anselm introduces the idea of two massive breaks in the history of the faithful that create new standards by which faith is to be expressed.

The idea for these changes or *transpositiones* is not original with Anselm. Indeed, the two chapters in which he discusses them are in great part taken—without attribution—from the Fifth Theological Oration (oration 31) of the Greek church father Gregory of Nazianzus (d. 390). Nevertheless, Anselm has changed Gregory's ideas to fit his purpose.[109] He brings his history of religious development in

---

[108] See pp. 278-79 below.

[109] Salet, *Anselme de Havelberg*, p. 58 n. 1; Edyvean, *Anselm of Havelberg*, pp. 18-19; Amos Funkenstein, "Periodization and Self-Understanding in the Middle Ages and Early Modern Times," *Medievalia et Humanistica: Studies in Medieval and Renaissance Culture*, new ser. 5 (1974), 21 n. 36; idem, *Heilsplan und natürliche Entwicklung*, pp. 65-66, 184-86. Anselm's reliance on Gregory was first pointed out by Milo van Lee in a note on his doctoral dissertation in *Annuaire de l'université de Louvain* (1936-39), 750-53. Where Anselm got his translation of Gregory remains a mystery. As far as is known, there was no translation of the *Fifth Theological Oration* in general use in the West at this time, the first being that of Petrus Balbus in the fifteenth century. See Sister Agnes Clare Way, "Gregorius Nazianzus," *Catalogus translationum et commentariorum: Medieval and Renaissance Latin Translations and Commentaries, Annotated Lists and Guides* 2, ed. Paul Oskar Kristeller (Washington, 1972), pp. 43-192, esp. pp. 138-40, 192. Possibly the translation was made for Anselm by one of the three men who acted as interpreters for his debates in Constantinople. This is especially likely in that the oration deals with the relation of the Holy Spirit to the Father and Son, which, in the form of the *Filioque*, is the subject of the first debate. Indeed, Anselm also borrows from the oration in his rendering of that debate (see pp. 239 n. 233, 243 n. 242 below; also cf. *Antik.* 2.19, 1192CD with *On the Holy Spirit* 11, PG 36:143-45). As translator, Funkenstein (*Heilsplan*, p. 183 n. 67a) has suggested Burgundio of Pisa, as had been done before him by Joseph de Ghellinck, *Le mouvement theologique du XIIe siècle*, p. 376. However, no such claim is made by Peter Classen in his biography *Burgundio von Pisa*. Antoine Dondaine has pointed out the curious fact that Anselm does not mention Gregory by name—a name which would have carried some weight in the West and added authority to his argument "si Anselme avait connu la nature des textes qu'il utilisa." "'Contra Graecos': Premiers écrits polemiques des Dominicains d'orient," *Archivum Fratrum Praedicatorum* 21 (1951), 397 n. 31. It is, however,

the Old Testament to a jolting halt by beginning chapter five with "It must be noted, however...." and then proceeds to borrow from Gregory, "...that there are two renowned changes in life...," to which he adds, "...and religious devotion."[110] It is, of course, those changes in religious devotion that have disturbed the critics and on which Anselm will focus.

Borrowing from Gregory, Anselm calls these changes "two testaments" or "earthquakes," the one from idolatry to the law, the other from the law to the Gospel. Gregory uses the terms interchangeably, and he undermines the sense of drama as well as of an identifiable moment of change inherent in the earthquake image: "There was nothing sudden involved in the first movement to take their transformation in hand."[111] Anselm, on the other hand, uses the image of the earthquake to full advantage by presenting it as a geological event, an actual shaking of the earth. The change from idolatry to law takes place when Moses receives the commandments accompanied by "thunder and lightening and a dark cloud and the sound of a trumpet and terrible shaking."[112] While Anselm does not specifically mention the crucifixion, it is obvious that this is where he places the second change: "A great earthquake occurred, the sun was darkened, rocks were split, graves opened, and the barriers of hell were broken down."[113] No such descriptions are given by Gregory. The issue for

---

difficult to believe that Anselm stumbled on a now lost translation of Gregory which did not name the author. He could not have expected his audience to recognize his source; and by not mentioning Gregory, Anselm indicates either that he desired his own authority to carry more weight than the Greek's, or, and this I think more likely, that he has changed Gregory's ideas in such a way that a look at the original would have undermined his argument. It is, of course, speculation that Anselm got the translation from one of his Latin translators in Constantinople, but if he did, his use of it for Book One of the *Antikeimenon* would suggest that he was thinking about his experiences in Constantinople when he wrote the history, that is that he conceived of the *Antikeimenon* as a unified whole from the beginning.

[110] *Antik.* 1.5, 1147B; Gregory of Nazianzus, *On the Holy Spirit* 25, Migne, Patrologia Graeca 36:160D, English translation: Frederick Norris (intro. and commentary), Lionel Wickham, Frederick Williams, *Faith Gives Fullness to Reasoning: the Five Theological Orations of Gregory of Nazianzen*, Supplements to Vigiliae Christianae 13 (Leiden, 1991), p. 292.

[111] *On the Holy Spirit* 25, PG 36:160D-61A; Norris, *Faith Gives Fullness to Reasoning*, p. 292. Indeed, Gregory's point is that the transformations work on us by way of persuasion rather than force.

[112] *Antik.* 1.5, 1147B; cf. Ex. 19:16.

[113] *Antik.* 1.5, 1147BC; cf. Matt. 27:45, 51-52, 54. In the Middle Ages, the earthquake was often a sign of the Antichrist, a fact that Horst Dieter Rauh mentions in

Anselm's audience concerned the changes in the faithful, and Anselm brings these into focus by emphasizing points of change signaled by dramatic, historical events that set up new guideposts for further development.[114]

Anselm points first to the change from idolatry to law, which latter "certainly did not lead to perfection." Law then changes "to the perfection of the Gospel." This "perfection of the Gospel" was at the heart of the Christocentric view of the Scriptures and history, and Anselm is careful not to oppose it. However, the critics in his audience viewed that perfection as a conclusion, and Anselm's concern to explain changes in the time since Christ, including all those new orders the critics decried, meant that this "perfection of the Gospel" had to be presented in terms of a beginning rather than an end.

Anselm starts to push the reader in this direction by drawing attention to the teaching and healing nature of the Holy Spirit who has "pedagogically and medicinally" led the faithful from idolatry to the law and then to the Gospel until he could teach "the complete perfection of the Christian law." The perfection or completion thus comes with the Gospel, but that end is also a beginning in that the perfection of the Gospel can now be taught. In this Anselm finds the thread for his story of the church after Christ, that of the faithful learning and living the Gospel and moving toward "a third earthquake, namely from this earth to that which cannot be shaken or moved"[115] in the silence at the completion of time.

In chapter six, Anselm asks what the teaching of the Holy Spirit is and again relies heavily on Gregory. He drops the association of the two great changes with specific, dramatic events and turns to their other definition as the two Testaments. Almost quoting Gregory, he says that the Trinity has been revealed slowly to the faithful:

> The Old Testament preached God the Father openly, the Son, however, not so much openly as obscurely. The New Testament revealed

---

relation to this passage (*Das Bild des Antichrist*, p. 275). He does not develop this point, saying it is "nur hier angemerkt." However, it appears to me difficult to suggest that Anselm is trying to evoke thoughts of Antichrist here. The earthquake was also a common symbol of great change. See Spörl, "Das Alte und das Neue im Mittelalter," p. 516.

[114] This point is touched on by Funkenstein, *Heilsplan*, pp. 65-66. Gregory makes no mention of the ages and states of the church which Anselm uses for a narrower periodization of history before and after Christ.

[115] *Antik.* 1.5, 1147CD, from Gregory of Nazianzus, *On the Holy Spirit* 25, PG 36:160D-61B; Norris, *Faith Gives Fullness to Reasoning*, p. 293.

God the Son but suggested and hinted at the deity of the Holy Spirit. Afterwards the Spirit was proclaimed, giving us a more open manifestation of his divinity.[116]

The Spirit, Anselm goes on, acts as a teacher and doctor to bring the faithful slowly to an understanding of the Trinity. Relying yet again on Gregory, Anselm now begins to move into the time after Christ. The Spirit was with Christ, he says, during the Savior's life; but "the Son ascends into heaven; the Holy Spirit comes after Him to teach and complete all truth."[117] Anselm is not explicit about what the Spirit continuing to teach after Christ means or whether "all truth" is something more than an understanding of the Trinity; however, in the conclusion to *De una forma credendi*, he reveals the direction in which he wants his reader to move by saying that at the end of time: "The truth of all signs and sacraments which were to be found from the beginning of the world in diverse periods of time will be revealed."[118] In other words, even after Christ, man's understanding comes through signs and sacraments whose truth is not yet fully grasped. In effect, Anselm asks his reader to accept the notion that the historical centrality of Christ opened a new phase in the development of the church which would explain change after Christ and make both understandable and acceptable the profusion of new orders. He does not do this by attacking a contrary position as he had with Egbert in the *Epistola*, but by appealing to his readers' faith.

Anselm proceeds carefully to play on words that create an image of both the Son and the Spirit and of their relationship to the faithful. Borrowing a final time from Gregory, he says that "the Son performs miracles [*virtutes facit*]; the Holy Spirit follows everywhere and brings Himself to believers [*credentibus*]."[119] The image of the Son performing miracles could have been presented as readily and, perhaps, more clearly with the phrase *miracula facit*. *Virtutes* is a multifaceted word, resonating with ideas not only of miracles but of the elements that create a good image—strength, power, virtue. Indeed, elsewhere An-

---

[116] *Antik.* 1.6, 1147D-48A; cf. *On the Holy Spirit* 26, PG 36:161C; Norris, *Faith Gives Fullness to Reasoning*, p.293.

[117] *Antik.* 1.6, 1148AB; cf. *On the Holy Spirit* 29, col. 165B; Norris, *Faith Gives Fullness to Reasoning*, p. 293. Anselm describes the events of Christ's life much more concretely than Gregory, who says simply that the Spirit follows Christ.

[118] *Antik.* 1.13, 1159C.

[119] *Antik.* 1.6, 1148B; *On the Holy Spirit* 29, PG 36:165, Norris, *Faith Gives Fullness to Reasoning*, p. 295.

selm uses *miracula* to refer to miracles and makes a distinction between *virtus* and *miracula* by using the former to describe the latter:
virtus miraculorum, the strength of miracles.[120] Here, however, the vari-
able meaning of *virtutes* allows him to draw the Son together with the
faithful, much as he had earlier used words like *iustitia* and *visio* to pull
together images of Old Testament figures.[121] If we translate *virtutes
facit* to mean that the Son fashions an image for the world of
strengths and virtues, then Anselm is saying that the Holy Spirit
follows the Son by fashioning the faithful with those same virtues.
And it is on this sense of *virtutes* that Anselm plays as he links Son,
Spirit and faithful together: "Thus certainly the faith in the Holy
Trinity was slowly measured out and, as it were, distributed partially
according to the strength of the believers [*secundum virtutem credentium*],
and growing to completion was finally perfected. Therefore
[*Proinde*]," Anselm continues,

> from the coming of Christ until the day of judgment which is character-
> ized as the sixth age, the Son of God being now present whereby the
> one, same church is renewed, there is by no means one uniform state
> but rather many and multiformed states are discovered.[122]

Anselm has cautiously constructed his bridge into the present with
what he and his readers hold in common: Faith in the Trinity is
completed with Christ; Christ fashions *virtutes* through which the
Spirit strengthens the faithful; the Spirit remains as a teacher and
doctor; the Spirit gives his gifts to each according to the strength
(*virtus*) of the recipient. Nor would the reader disagree with the idea of
a sixth age after Christ, which Anselm here (and here alone) identifies
as such. This calls to mind the traditional division of time into a
world week with the present as the sixth day, and it links the time
after Christ to the five Old Testament ages Anselm had discussed in
the first part of his book. However, Anselm is drawing his readers
into something new. His chapters on the *transpositiones* and the break
which they create between the fifth and six ages serve notice that he
considers this sixth age to be fundamentally different from the first

---

[120] *Antik.* 1.7, 1149D; 1.10, 1156A. In Book Two of the *Antikeimenon*, Anselm shows
how the word *virtus* can also mean the Holy Spirit (2.17, 1188BC); and earlier, he
says that the Spirit has *omnis virtus* (1.2, 1144A).

[121] See pp. 192-93 above.

[122] *Antik.* 1.6, 1148BC. Shortly before this, Anselm has said that the Holy Spirit
does not burden the faithful "with food beyond their strength [*super virtutem*]." 1148A.

five. Unlike the others, this age is itself divided into periods called states, and this precisely because (*proinde*) the faith in the Trinity has been perfected.

To explain these divisions, Anselm moves the discussion to Jesus and the model His life presents to the faithful; and he uses the idea of the imitation of Jesus as the means of tracing development in the church since Christ. Jesus has shown the ideal (a beginning) toward which the body of faithful, the church, could progress (an end). Historical development could thus be traced through the efforts of the faithful to imitate the model which Jesus had presented them.

In an important passage, Anselm says:

> Truly there was *una facies* of the Christian life in the primitive church when Jesus, having returned from the Jordan and been led by the Spirit into the desert and, after the temptations, having been left by the tempter, crossed Judea and Galilee and chose the twelve apostles whom he ordained with the special doctrine of the Christian faith, taught them that they should be poor in spirit and the other things written in the Sermon on the Mount which was directed to them, instructed them that they should tread on this evil world, [and] shaped them with the wholesome and innumerable precepts of evangelic doctrine.[123]

The phrase "*una facies* of Christian life [*religionis*] in the primitive church [*ecclesia primitiva*]" is a particularly crucial one for understanding Anselm. Shortly after this passage, he refers to the description of the first Christian community found in Acts—a community having "one heart and one soul" and holding all possessions in common (4:32). If one starts with that community and looks back to Anselm's *una facies*, the latter can be interpreted as meaning that Christ's life was "one part" or "one aspect" of the primitive church whose other parts or aspects embraced the apostolic community of Acts.[124] This is

---

[123] *Antik.* 1.6, 1148C: "Fuit nempe una facies Christianae religionis in primitiva Ecclesia, quando Jesus regressus a Jordane, et ductus a Spiritu in desertum, et post tentationes relictus a tentatore, pertransiens Judaeam et Galilaeam duodecim apostolos elegit, quos speciali doctrina Christianae fidei instituit, quos ut essent pauperes spiritu, et caetera quae in sermone in monte ad eos habito scripta sunt, edocuit, quos, ut saeculum hoc nequam calcarent, instruxit, quos salubribus et innumeris evangelicae doctrinae praeceptis informavit."

[124] Edyvean, *Anselm of Havelberg*, pp. 56-57. In his translation of *De una forma credendi*, Salet also suggests this interpretation by translating *una facies* as "un aspect" (*Anselme de Havelberg*, p. 65). Cf. his translation of *una ecclesia* as "une seule Église" (p. 50).

surely wrong. For Anselm, the primitive church begins with Christ,[125] and this passage should be seen as a reference to his earlier statement that the mystery of Christ is not revealed "with an unveiled face [*revelata facie*]" to those who came before the Incarnation.[126] This phrase derives from Paul's Second Letter to the Corinthians 3:18: "We all, beholding the glory of the Lord with an unveiled face [*revelata facie*], are being transformed into his very image from glory to glory."[127] It was a favorite verse of monastic writers who interpreted it in terms of the goal of monastic contemplation. Bernard of Clairvaux, for example, contrasted those busy with the affairs of the world with Martha and the contemplatives with Mary. The latter have achieved the state in which "they look with unveiled face at the glory of the Bridegroom" and "are changed into his likeness from one degree of glory to another."[128] Here "beholding the glory of the Lord" is *the result* of contemplation. While it is impossible to say whether Anselm felt that his *una facies* would bring 2 Corinthians 3.18 to the minds of his readers, there can be little doubt that he himself had it in mind when he used the phrase. However, in contrast to the typical monastic interpretation, Anselm's is one of the Lord presenting himself in all clarity to the faithful in the historical sense of the incarnation *after which* they move from one degree of glory to another

---

[125] On the *ecclesia primitiva* see Giovanni Miccoli, *Chiesa Gregoriana: Ricerche sulla Riforma del secolo XI* (Florence, 1966), pp. 225-99, esp. 230-31; Glenn Olsen, "The Idea of the *Ecclesia Primitiva* in the Writings of the Twelfth-Century Canonists," *Traditio* 25 (1969), 61-86, esp. pp. 63-66. Miccoli says of Anselm's use of the term *ecclesia primitiva*: "In questo caso è la chiesa formatasi ancora presente Cristo." *Chiesa Gregoriana*, p. 294 n. 177.

[126] See p. 196 above; also *Epist. apol.*, 1131C: "...manifeste docens ea quae illis in figura contingebant, istos revelata jam facie videre" (p. 154 above); *Epist. apol.* 1133B: "Ecce Dei Filius forma summae contemplationis, forma perfectae actionis, utriusque vitae *in una sua persona exemplum* gessit" (my emphahsis).

[127] See also 2 Cor. 4:6. There is some comparison to Gregory of Naziansus who speaks of men advancing "from glory to glory" but not of the uncovered face. *On the Holy Spirit* 26, PG 36: 161-163; Norris, *Faith Gives Fullness to Reasoning*, p. 293. It may also be pointed out that Anselm gives the opposite of *una facies* by mentioning the critics complaint about *tot professionum facies* in the church. *Antik.*, proem, 1159D.

[128] *Sermones super Cantica Canticorum* 57.11, *Sancti Bernardi Opera* 2, ed. Jean Leclerq, et al (Rome, 1958), p. 126. In his Sermons on the Song of Songs, Bernard makes frequent use of 2 Cor. 3:18 in the monastic/contemplative sense: 12.11, *SBO* 1 (Rome, 1957), p. 67; 17.8, pp. 102-3; 24.5, p. 157; 25.5, p. 165; 31.2, p. 220; 36.6, *SBO* 2, p. 8; 62.5, p. 158; 62.7, p. 160; 67.8, pp. 193-94; 69.7, p. 206. See also Michael Casey, *Athirst for God: Spiritual Desire in Bernard of Clairvaux's Sermons on the Song of Songs*, Cistercian Studies Series 77 (Kalamazoo, 1988), pp. 231-34.

into His image. This is precisely what Anselm had in mind in tracing the church through a series of states after Christ.

In the *Epistola apologetica*, Anselm had used Jesus as the model of the combination of action and contemplation but had then discussed the relative merits of the two lives in an attempt to undermine the monk's claim to "the best part." In *De una forma credendi*, Anselm avoids the pitfalls of dispute into which such a close association of one group of religious with Jesus' life was sure to lead. There is no sense that any division can or should be made in the model presented by Jesus which might lead to arguments between Marys and Marthas. Rather than dividing the events of Christ's life into those one would call contemplative and those one would call active,[129] elements of contemplation and action are mixed together and the terms *vita contemplativa* and *vita activa*, around which so much of the argument of the *Epistola apologetica* revolves, are not mentioned. It is the unity of the faithful that Anselm emphasizes above all, and Jesus' life becomes the image not of the canonical life but of the church itself. Anselm responds to the implicit desire of the critics for *una facies* of religious devotion by showing them that what they seek is in Jesus, the one form or image of the church.

The historical centrality of Christ's mission as Savior is not ignored by Anselm. It is the great break in time to which he had earlier referred as one of the earthquakes. But as such, it creates a new time different from that which had gone before, and it is into this time which Anselm enters when he says:

> After Christ's passion, resurrection and ascension and after the Holy Spirit had been sent, many, seeing the signs and wonders done through the hands of the apostles, gathered themselves together in their own society.[130]

These form the apostolic community whose "one heart and one mind" echo the *una facies* of Jesus. In describing that community, Anselm says, "A new church of the faithful was gathered together through the grace of the Holy Spirit, renewed first from the Jews, then from the gentiles." This opens the time after Christ, the time of the church whose history he will trace through seven states.

As an appeal to faith, Anselm's chapters on the *transpositiones* are a

---

129 As Anselm had done in the *Epistola*; see pp. 157-58 above.
130 *Antik.* 1.6, 1148CD.

masterpiece of quiet persuasion. He has shown the critics that what he wants them to grasp is not contrary to anything they already believe. It is, quite simply, that being a Christian means imitating Jesus and that the success and completeness of that imitation can be traced through time from good to better to best as the faithful build a temple to the Lord on the foundation of faith in the Trinity.[131]

5. *The states of the church*

With Jesus, Anselm has shown his audience the unchanging ideal they seek and pointed to a relationship between that model and the faithful. It is the latter who change rather than the model. Anselm's church after Christ is both "new" and "renewed." It is new in comparison to the church of the Old Testament which saw only the veiled image of Jesus; and in its attempt to imitate that image, this new church renews the image of Christ. That renewal is repeated as the membership of this new church changes over time (Anselm gives the example of the change from the Jews to the gentiles).[132] An important aspect of this presentation for Anselm's audience is that it shifts responsibility for the faith from the Spirit, Who carefully taught the Old Testament faithful, onto the faithful of the new church. Having the *una facies* of Jesus clearly before them, they are responsible for its protection and imitation. It remains for Anselm to demonstrate the progressive development that is linked to protecting and imitating Jesus' image.

As the basic framework for time after Christ, Anselm uses the seven seals of the Apocalypse to symbolize the six states (*status*) through which the church passes on its journey to the seventh state of silence. In the Apocalypse, the first four of these seals are opened to present different colored horses: white, red, black and pale; and perhaps no aspect of Anselm's writings has received more attention than the four states he associates with these horses.[133] In looking at these states anew, the intent here is to understand them in the context of Anselm's audience and to see how he uses them to make clear what it means to renew the *una facies* of Jesus.

---

[131] *Antik.* 1.6, 1149AB.

[132] *Antik.* 1.6, 1148D-1149A.

[133] "Modern scholars have spilled rivers of ink on Anselm's theory." Smalley, "Ecclesiastical Attitudes to Novelty," p. 124.

a. *From Christ to Christ: the first state*

Anselm's view of history is an integration of the faithful's changing attempts to imitate Jesus with the changeless image itself. With his interpretation of the first seal, that of the white horse, Anselm demonstrates that the changes and variety which worry the critics are found within and contained by the unchanging image of Jesus. This first state of the church is uniquely complex as Anselm presents both the changeless Christ, unbound by time, and the temporal first state of the church. He says that there will be seven states of the church "from the coming of Christ until everything is consumed in the end [*novissimo*]." Then he interprets the white horse to symbolize the church in the first state "shining in the dazzling lustre of its miracles and most beautiful, which, in its newness [*novitate*], all marvel at and magnify."[134] Again, we find Anselm playing on the meaning of words: he gives his reader first *novissimus* meaning the end of time and then *novitas* meaning the beginning of the new church. The end is the beginning and the beginning is the end. He underscores this point by next saying that while the horse is the church, the rider is Christ, who governs the church, humbles the proud with the bow of apostolic doctrine, and lets the faithful know that in Him their confidence is well placed.[135] The image is of the rider of the white horse moving his conquest forward not to the end of the first state but to the end of time when all will be perfected in Him. Christ is beginning and end, not limited to one state but defining them all. The first state as a temporal entity is a time in which the church grows in size and strength of miracles (*virtus miraculorum*), which latter evokes the image of Christ who "performed miracles" (*virtutes facit*).[136] The church changes in that it grows; and yet that growth is contained within the unchanging Christ who is beginning and end. Thus the end of the church is also its beginning as it moves from Christ to Christ.

---

[134] *Antik.* 1.7, 1149BC, using Apoc. 6:2, cf. I Cor. 15:28.

[135] *Antik.* 1.7, 1149BC.

[136] *Antik.* 1.7, 1149CD: "Ecce in isto primo statu nascentis Ecclesiae magis ac 'magis augebatur credentium in Domino multitudo virorum ac mulierum' [Acts 5:14]; et quotidie clarescabat Ecclesia Dei virtute miraculorum et numero credentium." Anselm's final phrase is a play on Acts 5:12 ("Per manus autem Apostolorum fiebant signa et prodigia multa in plebe" (note his preceding citation of Acts 5:14) with the "signs and prodigies" changed to "strength of miracles" to evoke the earlier use of *virtus* (see pp. 200-1 above).

b. *The pattern for the present: the second and third states*

While the first state allows Anselm to give his readers a sense of change and variety contained within completion and immutability, their concerns were specifically with what they saw around them in their own time. With his second and third states, Anselm gives them an explanation for change which he will then trace into the present. Moreover, since these two periods are in the past, he can show the dynamic of change moving from a beginning to an end for each of these states, an end yet to be arrived at in the present state. If there is any real attempt to prophesy the future in Anselm's history, it is found in the pattern he finds in these second and third states and projects into his own time.

That pattern is one of the church mounting a successful defense against attack. Whereas the white horse symbolizes the church itself, the remaining three horses symbolize both a threat to the church and a period of time in which that threat is countered. The red horse indicates a period of persecution; the black, a period of heresy; and the pale, one of hypocrisy. While the symbolism associated with these horses is not unique to Anselm,[137] his interpretation is original. It both links the horses to periods of historical time and avoids any sense of resignation created by seeing temporal change in terms of decline toward a present on the verge of Antichrist. Anselm creates a pattern which offers hope rather than despair.

In the second and third states is a church which moves both forward and in a circle: forward by learning from its encounters with persecutors and heretics, in a circle by going from peace through disruption and back to peace. This latter is, of course, the same pattern for the general movement of the seven states—from Christ to Christ. With the red horse of persecution "peace was destroyed;" and the heretics of the black horse, says Anselm with startling imagery, "cruelly plucked and mangled the dove of God."[138] In both cases, the church successfully defends itself. Stephen and the martyrs are triumphant in their deaths, and the laws passed to persecute the Christians are rescinded and replaced by "another law for the peace of the church," bringing it full circle back to peace. In the third state, church councils also achieved peace by formulating a more explicit definition of the faith. Because of this, Anselm concludes that the

---

[137] See pp. 187-90 above.
[138] *Antik.* 1.8, 1149D; 1.9, 1151D.

heretics "were destroyed, pulverized, extinguished and utterly wiped out, so that from then on in no corner of the catholic church did they dare to sprout up again or boil up."[139] Anselm's point is clear: the church wins.

The sense is also of a church moving toward Christ through an ever changing variety of expressions of faith. In the second state, the "triumph" of the martyred Stephen was, says Anselm, enlarged upon by all of the apostles. Not only is martyrdom another expression of faith, but this persecution forced the Christian community to be "dispersed throughout the world." This is not the image of a primitive church that had been lost and was in need of recreation, but of a community grown larger through the efforts of those who carried the Gospel through the world. "The church of God blossomed like the palm in victory; and like the cedar of Lebanon, the more it endured, the more it multiplied." And so, the church returns to peace where law replaces persecution. The second state also ends in triumph, for through the missionary zeal of the apostles and their followers "the whole world now humbly venerates the Christian name, which before it persecuted."[140] The reaction to heresy in the third state also moves the church forward. The councils victoriously define the faith, and, says Anselm, just as the church grew in endurance through persecution, so in this state it "grew in marvelous wisdom against the heretics." Satan, however, does not rest but like "a roaring lion still wanders about seeking whom he may devour."[141]

With his statement that the church grows in wisdom as it had in endurance, Anselm makes clear that he is, indeed, giving us a pattern; and by ending his chapter on the third state with Satan ready to spring on the church again, he brings the fourth and present state of the church into that same pattern of defense and victory.[142]

c. *The present: the fourth state*
The enemy of the present church is revealed as the pale horse, "and he who sat on him, his name is Death; and Hell was following him"

---

[139] *Antik.* 1.8, 1149-1150; 1.9, 1151D-52A. See also Anselm's discussion of the importance of the councils in his debates with the Greeks, *Antik.* 2.22, 1197-1200.
[140] *Antik.* 1.8, 1150AB (cf. Psalm 91 (92):13); *Antik.* 1.8, 1150CD.
[141] *Antik.* 1.9, 1152B. Cf. I Pet. 5:8.
[142] One may note that at the end of his chapter on the second state Anselm also presents the "draco serpens ille antiquus" as being ready to spring on the church anew. *Antik.* 1.8, 1150BC.

(Apoc. 6:6-8). "This," says Anselm, "is undoubtedly the fourth state of the church, in which the most serious and mortal danger is from false brothers."[143] There are within the present church false men, he says, who deceive the faithful while professing holiness. The specific duty of the faithful is to strengthen their brothers so that they may weather attacks from sources so cleverly hidden that overt action against them is almost impossible.

These hypocrites hide under an almost perfect disguise of Christian actions. They publicly confess Christ, attend church, revere prelates, honor their neighbors, build churches, distribute alms, go on pilgrimages, and more, all in the name of the Lord. "Among them and with them, the status of the church seems to be peaceful; neither is it clearly assailed by the sword of persecution nor harassed by the crafty importunity of heretics."[144] In the *Epistola apologetica* Anselm had said that an individual's vocation—monk, cleric, layman—does not determine whether he is good or bad. In his discussion of the hypocrite he takes this idea a step further. Not even a man's actions are a strict sign of inner worth: "If, perchance, [these hypocrites] meet holy and truly religious men, they greet them with a bowed head but hiding a haughty heart."[145] As Anselm says repeatedly, faith is what commits the individual to God and gives unity to the church. Without it, an appearance of goodness remains only a facade: "For the intention—whether good or evil—establishes the nature of the deed and whether it deserves favor or the punishment of just retribution."[146] There has been a curious tendency on the part of historians to attempt to identify these hypocrites with a religious or social group: the black monks who had been attacked in the *Epistola apologetica* or, more recently, wealthy laymen.[147] This approach would surely surprise Anselm, the whole point of whose presentation is that the hypocrites cannot be identified. The problem for the church is precisely that its enemy is hidden.

---

[143] *Antik.* 1.10, 1152C.

[144] *Antik.* 1.10, 1153A.

[145] *Antik.* 1.10, 1152D.

[146] *Antik.* 1.10, 1154C. This idea is similar to Peter Abelard's emphasis on intention as the determinant of good and evil. See Winfried Eberhard, "Ansätze zur Bewältigung ideologischer Pluralität im 12. Jahrhundert: Pierre Abélard und Anselm von Havelberg," *Historisches Jahrbuch* 105 (1985), 353-87, esp. 375, 385-87; Berges, "Anselm von Havelberg," pp. 56-57.

[147] For further discussion of this interpretation see Lees, "Charity and Enmity," pp. 58-61.

Having presented the hypocrites, Anselm creates a marvelous juxtaposition by addressing his audience directly, something he has not done since his invitation to the critics at the beginning of *De una forma credendi* to ask their questions with him rather than against him. Now he speaks to his "dearest brothers," exhorting them to see the seriousness of the menace of hypocrisy: "Behold, dearest brothers, the terrible threats of the hypocrites which we have heard. Let us be weary of the pale death of our souls and the hell which follows with its chasm." Anselm also warns his readers that they must turn their gaze inward lest hypocrisy grow within them. They should not only flee "this detestable hypocrisy," but "cleanse and purify with a sincere confession that which is within and wash it with a repeated effusion of tears." His "dearest brothers" are members of all religious orders, not just his own, for he tells them: "We must in no way diverge from the standards of ecclesiastical discipline, everyone of us in the order to which he has been called, if we do not wish to cause or to suffer scandal."[148] While this may seem to hint at the problem Peter of Hamersleben had created by changing orders and the vituperative response of the *Epistola apologetica*, Anselm makes his point in the general terms of a call for ecclesiastical discipline and without attacking anyone. He had earlier called the critics of the new orders "false accusers" (*calumniatores*), a term he will soon use on the hypocrites;[149] but now the false accusers of the book's beginning have become "dearest brothers" on the common ground of the faith which Anselm has established. He has moved from the hypocrites to his audience and made of the latter the new tool of a church renewed in its imitation of Jesus and in its defense against evil. He then delivers a long invective against the hypocrites which stands both as a warning to the faithful and a condemnation of those who obdurately continue in their hypocrisy: "Woe unto you, miserable hypocrite, the most miserable of all the miserable, simulator of good, lover of evil, enemy of God, hostile to yourself...." He continues by calling the hypocrite, among many other things, a fox, a worm, a serpent, a cancer, a whitewashed wall, and the most foolish of the fools.[150]

---

[148] *Antik.* 1.10, 11153D-54.

[149] Of the critics: *Antik.* 1.1, 1143A, also 1141C: "Calumniosi inquisitores;" of the hypocrites: see n. 150 below.

[150] *Antik.* 1.10, 1154AC; Mun., fol. 9r; Ber. 1, fol 214r: "Vae tibi, miser hypocrita, omnium miserorum miserrime, simulator boni, amator mali, inimice Dei, hostis tui, seductor tui, deceptor tui, insidiator tui, fraudator tui, adulator tui, derisor tui, delusor tui, calumniator tui, damnator tui, traditor tui, judex tui, homicida tui,..." etc.

With this literary structure which goes from hypocrites to brothers and back to hypocrites, Anselm has moved his audience of critics "inside with us" surrounded by the threat of the hypocrites who clearly stand on the outside. Anselm has already shown martyrs ending persecution and councils defeating heresy in earlier states. In similar fashion, his former critics and the "certain brothers" upset by the criticisms—now all "dearest brothers"—help form the weapon of victory over hypocrisy.

The religious orders of Anselm's brothers present a united front. Although Anselm places them into those same categories of canonical and monastic orders that were faced off against each other in the *Epistola apologetica*, he displays an admirable desire to dispel completely the uncharitable spirit of his earlier work. He cautiously avoids any issues of contention between the orders and portrays them as working toward the same goal. The canons began with St. Augustine, whose rule "invited and assembled many men.to an imitation of the apostles...in a sacred society of the common life to this very day," and Anselm speaks of the founder of St. Ruf and his own Norbert of Magdeburg as men who continued this tradition by being part of "this same canonical profession" or by whom "this religious way of life was renewed." While he does say that canons live the apostolic life, nowhere does he use this as a criticism of the monks. The monastic way of life began in Egypt, was "renewed" in the West by St. Benedict, and expanded "with a new fervor" by Romuald of Camaldoli and "the new religious congregation of monks" at Vallombrosa. He prefaces his presentation of the religious orders, canonical and monastic, by saying, "In this state of the church religious men appear, lovers of truth, restorers of the religious life."[151]

His longest description of a monastic order, the Cistercians, is full of praise for their endurance, poverty and devotion. This, says Anselm, has won them "innumerable imitators of their way of life."[152] The monks for whom Anselm could find no ecclesiastical role in the *Epistola* are here portrayed as an integral part of the fight against hypocrisy. He cites not only the example of Bernard of Clairvaux, that "most religious man distinguished by the power of miracles," but that of Pope Eugenius III, himself a former Cistercian.[153] Here An-

---

[151] *Antik.* 1.10, 1154C-56A.
[152] *Antik.* 1.10, 1156A.
[153] *Antik.* 1.10, 1156AB.

selm does not use the fact that a monk has become a pope to elevate the clerical above the monastic order as he had done in the *Epistola*. If anything, Eugenius' former profession redounds here to the honor of monks. Moreover, in his description of the Cistercians, Anselm uses the same phrases he had applied to the church as a whole. These monks show "strength of endurance" (*virtus patientiae*) as did the church in the second state (as well as Job) and Bernard demonstrates "strength of miracles" (*virtus miraculorum*) which marks the first state of the church.[154]

Anselm's song of praise for the variety of religious orders expands to include the lay order of the Knights Templar who, he says, "are not inferior in merit to either the monks or the canons who live the communal life."[155] In this presentation of the religious orders, Anselm shows their variety to be a chief factor in their success. As the martyrs fought persecution by their steadfastness and the councils fought heresy with their wisdom, so does the variety of the new orders combat hypocrisy by rekindling spiritual commitment and enthusiasm.

Anselm has created here an image of variety unified in its goal to inspire all Christians. In the debates with Nicetas, he will address the issues that separate Christians into eastern and western camps. It is important, therefore, to note that in his description of the present state of the church, Anselm extends his image of the inspiring variety of religious orders to include the Greeks. He says that while the forms of worship may be different in the East, those who practice them are part of the one faith. There are religious orders among not only the Greeks but the Armenians and Syrians, as well, "which are no less

---

[154] In a footnote to his translation of *De una forma credendi*, Salet points out that Anselm deals first with the canons and then with the monks. From this he concludes, "Les chanoines revendiquaient en effet une priorité temporelle sur le monachisme, comme institution remontant á l'Église primitive" (*Anselme de Havelberg*, p. 92 n. 1). This is an example of how, and in spite of showing more interest in *De una forma credendi* than in the *Epistola*, historians have tended to read the former as an addenda to the latter rather than to see the *Antikeimenon* as a reaction against the very kind of argumentation Anselm had used in the earlier work. See Lees, "Enmity and Charity," pp. 58-62.

[155] *Antik.* 1.10, 1156BC; Mun., fol. 10r, Wolf. 1, fol. 25v: "Nempe congregati sunt ibi [Jerusalem] laici, viri religiosi...qui, relictis proprietatibus, communi vita vivunt, sub obedientia unius magistri militant, superfluitatem et pretiositatem vestium sibi absciderunt, parati ad defendendum gloriosum Domini sepulcrum contra incursus Saracenorum....in ea [vita] fideliter perseverent, remissionem omnium haberent peccatorum, affirmans eos non esse inferioris meriti, quam vel monachos, vel communis vitae canonicos."

united in the one catholic faith" in spite of differences in their ways of life. Anselm mentions his own trip to Constantinople as *apocrisiarius* for Lothar III, and as he has moved his audience to accept differences in the expression of faith in the West, so now he turns their gaze to the East and asks nothing less. He gives his audience their first look at Constantinople through his eyes. What they see is not a city of heterodoxy but of religious devotion; and in what is perhaps a gesture to the monks he had scorned in the *Epistola apologetica*, the devotion he shows them is monastic:

> While I was in the royal city of Constantinople...and was an avid explorer and diligent seeker of different forms of the religious life, I saw there many orders of the Christian religion. In the monastery which is called Pantocrator, that is Of the All Powerful, I saw about seven hundred monks serving under the rule of St. Anthony. In the monastery which is called Philanthropon, that is Of the Love of Man, I saw no less than five hundred monks serving under the rule of the blessed Pachomius. And I saw many congregations serving under the rule of the blessed Basil the Great, truly an extremely learned man.[156]

The Greeks share both the common ground of the one faith and a variety of religious life with the West. If his "dearest brothers" can grasp this, then many of the differences between East and West could not only be accepted but praised. As Anselm has worked to erase the line of divisive argument between his critics and himself that their questions may be asked with him rather than against him, so with his introduction of the Greeks, he moves his audience toward the debates which, if they are to have any chance of success, must be conducted in this same spirit of common faith.

Anselm ends his paean to the orders of the church, West and East,

---

[156] *Antik.* 1.10, 1156CD; Ber. 1, fol. 215r; Wolf. 1, fol. 25v; Mun. fol. 10v: "Ego cum essem in urbe regia Constantinopoli...et essem avidus explorator et diligens inquisitor diversarum religionum, vidi ibi multos ordines Christianae religionis. In monasterio quod dicitur Pantocratoros, id est, Omnipotentis, vidi septingentos ferme monachos sub regula beati Antonii militantes. In monasterio quod dicitur Philanthropon, id est amantis hominem, vidi non minus quingentos monachos sub regula beati Pachomii militantes. Vidi et quamplures congregationes sub regula beati Basilii Magni et doctissimi viri devote militantes." See Schreiber, "Anselm von Havelberg und die Ostkirche," p. 373. R. Janin (cited by Salet, *Anselme de Havelberg*, p. 102 n. 2) has pointed out that the numbers in Anselm's description of Greek monasteries are exaggerations. Pantocrator contained no more than eighty monks; Philanthropon, forty at the outside. It may be noted, however, that Anselm's contemporary John Kinnamos says that Pantocrator was famous for its size, though he gives no numbers. *Deeds of John and Manuel Comnenus* 1.4, p. 17.

by returning to the Holy Spirit. To those who despair over new forms of devotion, Anselm says, with more than a little insight into human nature, that it is through this very newness that the Spirit rekindles enthusiasm:.

> Indeed, the Holy Spirit...recognized the sluggish souls of men, long satiated with customary devotion, and knew how to renew the faithful in some way by the introduction of a new form of devotion, so that, when they saw others ascend higher and higher to a loftier summit of the religious life, they would be powerfully moved by these new examples; and having left behind indolence and the love of worldly things by which they had been held, they could rapidly and without fear grasp and imitate that which is perfect. For men are accustomed to marvel more at the extraordinary and unusual than at the ordinary and usual.[157]

Here is not just the individual's psychological need for change but an image of that change as moving upward "to a loftier summit." Nor is it just the individual but the Christian community that is reshaped and brought closer to its model of the *una facies* of Jesus.

In an often cited passage, Anselm sums up the effect of the Spirit's guidance by comparing the church to an eagle:

> And it happens by the marvelous dispensation of God that the youth of the church is renewed like the youth of an eagle with a new religious life always growing up from generation to generation, whereby it is able to fly more sublimely in contemplation and look more keenly on the rays of the true sun with, as it were, unbedazzled eyes.[158]

The idea of the eagle renewing its youth comes from Psalm 102 (103):5: "So that your youth is renewed like the eagle's." Anselm's interpretation of this verse is unique. Most medieval authors relied on Augustine's interpretation of this passage, namely that the beak of an old eagle grows so that he cannot eat; he then rubs it against a rock until it is serviceable once more. The eagle is the individual; the beak is the individual's sins; the rock is Christ who grants salvation

---

[157] *Antik.* 1.10, 1157A; Mun., fol. 10v; Ber. 1, fol 215v; Wolf. 1, fol 26r: "Novit quippe Spiritus sanctus, qui totum corpus Ecclesiae ab initio et nunc et semper regit, animos hominum torpentes, et diu usitata religione satiatos et fideles aliquo novae religionis exordio renovare, ut, cum viderint alios magis ac magis in altiorem religionis arcem conscendere, novis exemplis fortius excitentur, et relicta pigritia et amore saeculi, quo tenebantur, alacriter et sine formidine, quod perfectum est apprehendant et imitentur. Nam insolita et inusitata magis solent mirari homines, quam solita et usitata." See also Anselm's comments on the Holy Spirit, *Antik.* 1.6, 1148A.

[158] *Antik.* 1.10, 1157AB. For the eagle, see, along with Ps. 102:5, Is. 40:31.

through the resurrection.[159] But in Anselm's interpretation, the eagle is not the individual Christian but the whole community of the faithful, and the emphasis is not on individual salvation after death but on ecclesiastical action within history.[160]

The danger for Anselm here was that his clarion call for action could be seen as an affront to the monastic ideal and its emphasis on withdrawal from the world. To avoid this, he has carefully (and again, in sharp contrast to the *Epistola*) portrayed the new orders as causing men to leave "indolence and the love of worldly things" behind, something that did apply to the monks. Anselm turns more than Psalm 102:5 to his account, for he also borrows the belief that the eagle can look into the sun with unbedazzled eyes, and this was an image frequently used to support ideals of withdrawal and contemplation.[161] For example, with no reference to any sort of institutional renewal, Rupert of Deutz expresses the hope for those

> who are eager for venerable learning in the school of Christ [the monastery?] that in some ways they may be strong enough to imitate the eagle, who unbedazzled is able to contemplate the clarity of the eternal sun with the mind's eye.[162]

While Anselm's association of Psalm 102:5 with an idea of ecclesiastical renewal finds an echo in some of his contemporaries,[163] he appears unique in viewing rejuvenation as an historically traceable phenomenon.[164]

---

[159] *Enarrationes in Psalmos*, PL 36:1323-1324. A close reliance on Augustine can be traced through Cassiodorus, PL 70:720; Haimo of Auxerre, PL 116:539; Remigius of Auxerre, PL 131:668-669; the *Glossa ordinaria*, PL 113:114; Bruno the Carthusian, PL 152:1171; Peter the Lombard, PL 191:920. The ultimate source for Augustine's interpretation is the *Physiologus*. See Ladner, *The Idea of Reform*, pp. 314-15; Carol Neel, "Philip of Harvengt and Anselm of Havelberg: The Premonstratensian Vision of Time," *Church History* 62 (1993), 483-93.

[160] Ladner, *The Idea of Reform*, p. 423 and n. 93.

[161] This idea is found in the *Praefatio incerti auctoris* to Augustine's *Tractatus in Iohannis Euangelium*, which makes no reference to Psalm 102 but deals with the eagle as the symbol of the Apostle John. CCSL 36:xiv: "Unde merito in figura quatuor animalium aquilae uolanti comparatur: quae uolat altius ceteris auibus, et solis radios irreuerberatis aspicit luminibus."

[162] *In Euangelium Iohannis*, praefatio, CCCM 9:6-7.

[163] E.g. Peter Abelard, *Hymnarius Paraclitensis* 64, *Peter Abelard's Hymnarius Paraclitensis: An Annotated Edition with Introduction*, ed. Joseph Szövérffy, 2, *The Hymnarius Paraclitensis Text and Notes* (Albany, 1975), p. 138.

[164] Anselm's ideas of ecclesiastical renewal bear comparison with a passage at the end of the *Commentarium in Psalmos* of Honorius Augustodunensis. There Honorius says, "Deus est Pater Christi, corpus Christi est Ecclesia; nutritor Ecclesiae Spiritus

Anselm makes his call to ecclesiastical reform a joyful battle cry meant to unite all the faithful, monks, canons, laymen, Greeks, and Latins, in a common effort at spiritual renewal. It is also a call to Anselm's brothers to present a pacifistic model of commitment and endurance to the hypocrites: "Let us endure them in charity; and let us wait, praying that, laying aside their hypocrisy, they may become true [brothers]."[165] This unity of a multifaceted Christian community is precisely what Anselm had himself failed to demonstrate in the *Epistola apologetica*; but in *De una forma credendi*, there is not a single phrase which is critical of any form of religious devotion. Anselm had called on the Norbertines of Jerichow to set an example for the heathen.[166] In this work he gives himself as an example to those brothers of what a Christian model should be by offering the hypocrites of the fourth state the same invitation that he had offered the critics at the beginning of the book: to come inside the church with the faithful.

d. *The future: the end of the fourth state and the fifth, sixth, and seventh states*
Anselm's account of the future is brief; and it is punctuated by descriptions of huge changes in the church, some of them very bad. Because of this, it has become somewhat problematic for the interpretation of Anselm's entire history. At issue is the difficulty of bring-

---

Sanctus, cujus nutrimentum est sacra Scriptura, per quam in suis membris crescit in virum perfectum" (*Selectorum psalmorum expositio*, PL 172:308AB). As with Anselm, it is the Holy Spirit who helps the church grow. Honorius proceeds to divide the Psalms into fifteen *decades* taking the church from the *infantia* to the *decrepita aetas*. His interpretation of the eleventh decade or second *senior decas* shows an intriguing similarity to Anselm's exegesis of Psalm 102:5: "In undecima decade, eadem aetas Ecclesiae ad orationem instigatur, ut semen ejus in saeculum dirigatur, ut juventus ejus sicut aquila renovetur, et per emissum Spiritum Dei, recreetur, faciem Domini semper quaerat, judicium et justitiam in omni tempore faciat, misericordias Domini intelligat, paratum cor ad praecepta ejus habeat, et laudere eum in medio multorum; qui est principium a Patre genitus, in splendoribus sanctorum missus, redemptio populorum per Novum Testamentum" (PL 172:310B; in his exegesis of Ps. 102, PL 194:610, Honorius gives the traditional Augustinian interpretation). Here we find the eagle as the church rejuvenating itself and seeking "the face of the Lord." This would strongly suggest that Anselm read this work and borrowed from it for his idea of the *una facies* of Jesus. Honorius does not, however, tie his fifteen *decades* to any sort of historical periodization beyond the states of infancy to decrepitute nor does he specifically tie rejuvenation to new and different forms of religious life.

[165] *Antik.* 1.10, 1157C. See Eberhard, "Ansätze zur Bewältigung ideologischer Pluralität," 368-385, esp. 378ff.

[166] See p. 71 above.

ing his depiction of ecclesiastical progress together with his presentation of a church locked in a losing battle with Antichrist in the sixth
state. While this has caused some scholars to look for Antichrist
throughout Anselm's history[167] or to find a pessimistic tone coloring
his picture of progress,[168] one must be wary of reading too much of
Anselm's view of the future into his presentation of past and present.
Moreover, while the condition of the church in Anselm's fifth state is
tinged with foreboding and that in sixth is sad to behold, his treatment of the future includes the end of the fourth state and the seventh state as well, and they need also to be considered before the
work is labeled pessimistic.

Anselm says he is "afraid and by no means tranquil" about hypocrisy. It would, however, stand in contradiction to everything he has
presented to this point to interpret this as indicating that the church
might lose this battle or that the possibility of defeat is the message he
sends his brothers. He speaks of a time when the good will be separated from the bad, which has been taken to refer to the Augustinian
notion of an *ecclesia permixta* that would last until the end of time when
the wheat will be separated from the tares.[169] In fact, Anselm is quite
clear that at the end of the fourth state one will find the happy
completion of the pattern of defense and victory:

> Truly, [the hypocrites] will run together with us and we with them
> although in diverse ways and with a diverse intention until this fourth
> state of the church shall come to an end [*donec finiatur iste quartus status
> Ecclesiae*].

This is Anselm's only real attempt to prophesy the future, and it is a
most optimistic one reaffirming the pattern of victory set by his earlier states. The fourth state is a time of preparation for a division of
the false from the faithful at that state's, not the world's, end when
the faithful "shall follow the Lamb" and the false will "be buried in
hell."[170] At the same time, Anselm's shows little concern to explain
what this victory will entail, an indication that his interest in prophesying the future is limited, indeed.[171]

---

[167] Rauh, *Das Bild des Antichrist*, pp. 268-302.
[168] Morrison, "Anselm of Havelberg," pp. 242-43.
[169] Rauh, *Antichrist*, p. 289.
[170] *Antik.* 1.10, 1157BC.
[171] See Spörl, *Grundformen hochmittelalterlicher Geschichtsanschauungen*, p. 26, Kamlah,
Apokalypse und Geschichtstheologie, pp. 73, 86; Edyvean, *Anselm of Havelberg*, p. 33.

In his introduction to the fifth state, Anselm again gives a sense of the completion of the fourth state by affirming the idea that in its encounter with adversity the church grows as it had in the second and third states: "The church suffered persecution and grew in patience; it suffered from the subtle deceit of heretics and grew in wisdom; it suffered from the false brothers and hypocrites and grew in endurance." But of the fifth state, he gives only a laconic comment to the Apocalypse's description (6:9-11):

> Now, however, the spirits of the saints who, by having spilled their blood, truly deserved to rest under the altar which is Christ, seeing such endless miseries of the afflicted church, cry out for her with one great voice of compassion: 'How long, O Lord, will you not avenge our blood? [Apoc. 6:10]' And the rest which follows there pertaining to the fifth state of the church.[172]

Anselm's description is so brief as to open itself to any number of interpretations which have then been turned onto the entire work so that we look at past and present through the lens of this dismal future.[173] From this perspective, the fifth state becomes a time of despair for a church moving inexorably down an eschatological path straight to the Antichrist's own state; and Antichrist himself becomes the key to interpreting Anselm's history as one of the combat between good and evil.[174]

A major problem for this interpretation is presented by Anselm's history of the Old Testament church and his central chapters dealing with earthquakes and the two testaments. Nowhere in these sections

---

[172] *Antik.* 1.11, 1158A.

[173] Interpreting the fifth state as running concurrently with the fourth: Lauerer, *Anschauungen*, p. 78; Grundmann, *Studien über Joachim von Floris*, p. 94. Interpreting it as a period between persecutions which saves Anselm from describing the Antichrist in more detail: Rauh, *Das Bild des Antichrist*, pp. 290-91. Interpreting it as not referring to the church on earth at all but to those who have died and watch the church's battles from on high: Richard K. Emmerson, *Antichrist in the Middle Ages* (Seattle, 1981), p. 19; Rauh, *Antichrist*, p. 291 in addition to his above interpretation.

[174] Rauh, *Antichrist*, pp. 280-82; Emmerson, *Antichrist in the Middle Ages*, p. 19. On the various interpretations of Antichrist see in addition to Rauh, Bernard McGinn, *Antichrist: Two Thousand Years of the Human Fascination with Evil* (New York, 1994), Emmerson, *Antichrist*, esp. pp. 11-73; Jeffrey Burton Russell, *Lucifer: The Devil in the Middle Ages* (Ithaca, 1984), p. 103 n. 27; Classen, *Gerhoch of Reichersberg*, pp. 217-18; and the fine selection of translated texts in Bernard McGinn, *Apocalyptic Spirituality: Treatises and Letters of Lactantius, Adso of Montier-en-Der, Joachim of Fiore, the Franciscan Spirituals, Savonarola* (New York, 1979) and McGinn, *Visions of the End: Apocalyptic Traditions in the Middle Ages* (New York, 1979).

does he even mention a power of evil, little less the Antichrist. If his work were meant to trace a dualistic combat between the cities of Christ and Antichrist or to demonstrate the defense against evil to be the mechanism that has propelled the church forward from the beginning, then his story of Abel to the last of the elect would surely have established its counterpoint by mentioning Cain. It does not.[175]

Even if one ignores the first part of Anselm's book and considers only the seven states of the church, there are problems with reading Antichrist into more than the sixth state. A dualistic view of church history is not established by Anselm in his first state of the church. Christ is presented as the conqueror riding the white horse of the church in that state, but he faces no enemy. While Anselm does go on to present a church attacked by evil, he shows little concern with the ultimate source of the attacks. In the second state, he identifies not a single persecutor of the church. "Laws were written against the Christian name," is as far as he goes.[176] Only at the end of his description does he write of a force of evil, "the dragon, that old serpent who aroused such brutality against the church of God." Then, after saying that in defeat this dragon resolved to continue the fight,[177] Anselm moves on to describing the glories of the church after the persecution ended. The heresy of the third state is stirred up by the same "great dragon," and the heretics are identified by "the mark of

---

[175] Congar, "Ecclesia ab Abel," pp. 84-86; Edyvean, *Anselm of Havelberg*, p. 36 n. 104. Rauh (*Antichrist*, p. 291) says that Anselm held the fifth state to be a reflection of "die gesamte Zeit der Verfolgung...der die Kirche von Cain bis zum Antichrist ausgesetzt ist." I would suggest that this interpretation reads too much into *De una forma credendi*. Anselm does not mention Cain anywhere in his story of the faithful, either before or after Christ, nor, for that matter, in any of his extant writings.

[176] *Antik.* 1.8, 1150B.

[177] *Antik.* 1.8, 1150BC; Ber. 1, fol. 212v; Mun., fol. 7r; Wolf. 1, fol. 16v: "Draco serpens ille antiquus, qui tantam saevitiam adversus Ecclesiam Dei excitaverat ... iratus est in mulierem, et iterum statuit facere praelium cum reliquis de semine ejus, qui custodiunt mandata dei, et habent testimonium Jesu." Anselm draws here on Apoc. 12 by saying that the dragon attacks a woman clothed in the sun with the moon at her feet and a crown with twelve stars on her head (vs. 1). Furious that the flood he sends against her does not defeat her, the dragon resolves to fight on (vss. 15, 17). Anselm paraphrases only these verses. Apoc. 12 as a whole could lend itself to an interpretation in which the woman is identified as the Virgin Mary, and Rauh says that this is what Anselm means by the woman (*Bild des Antichrist*, p. 280). This reading risks making Anselm's book too arcane. In the context of his chapter, the woman is the church that has defeated persecution. See Kamlah, *Apokalypse und Geschichtstheologie*, pp. 130-31.

the beast."[178] But Anselm expresses so little concern for this beast[179] that he relies on First Peter rather than the Apocalypse to end this state, replacing dragons and beasts with a stalking lion still looking for someone to devour.[180] Finally, in the fourth state, Anselm makes no allusion to a leader of the power of evil until his invective against the hypocrites. There, it is a vague one only as he calls them "mar-tyr[s] of the devil," and "full of demons."[181] Moreover, in his list of epithets, there is no reference to the dragon, the beast, the lion, or to Antichrist, not even to the hypocrites as being forerunners of Anti-christ. Here Anselm's silence rings loudly for he seems to call the hypocrites every name he can think of.[182] Along with a final allusion to the hypocrites as being, like Judas, members of the devil" (*membra diaboli*),[183] this is the sum total of Anselm's references to a power of evil before the sixth state. *De una forma credendi* is concerned with the wonder of the unity of the faithful and the variety of ways in which they have expressed their faith. Antichrist, marks of the beast, drag-ons and demons are not what this work is about.

  Anselm's defense of variety ends precisely at the point at which he begins to consider the future.[184] What follows after the rich descrip-tion of the orders of the church in the fourth state is cursory and derivative. While he has given great care to preparing the pattern for the present fourth state, this fifth state and the sixth as well are described in ways that do not link them to anything Anselm has said about the second, third, and fourth states. What Anselm has not yet shown is the completion of the circle of time from Christ to Christ; and the Antichrist should be seen in the context of the closing of that

---

[178] *Antik.* 1.9, 1150D.

[179] One of the beasts in the Apocalypse marks his followers on the right hand or the forehead and was often identified with Antichrist. Apoc. 13:16-17, also 19:20; Emmerson, *Antichrist*, pp. 39-40, 94-95. But even here, Anselm is not clear, for his heretics carry a mark in their hearts.

[180] See p. 208 above.

[181] *Antik.* 1.10, 1154AB.

[182] This point is worth emphasizing. Rauh says that Anselm's invective against the hypocrite "ist ein Katalog von Antichrist-Symbolen" (*Antichrist*, p. 286). Still, in a list of epithets that fills two thirds of a column in Migne (*Antik.* 1.10, 1154AC), Anselm never once mentions Antichrist. For part of Anselm's invective see p. 210 n. 150 above.

[183] *Antik.* 1.10, 1157BC.

[184] Spörl, *Grundformen hochmittelalterlicher Geschichts-anschauungen*, p. 27. See also the apt comments of Walter Edyvean on Anselm's lack of interest in the future, *Anselm of Havelberg*, pp. 32-33.

circle of conquest in a battle where Christ Himself, rather than the faithful, must prevail. However, for Anselm to have presented the horrific time of the Antichrist as coming on the heels of the victory over hypocrisy could only have turned the enthusiasm he has tried to create into despair for the future. Anselm's fifth state creates something of a buffer between the victory over hypocrisy toward which the present is moving and the Antichrist,[185] and it gives the sense that the faithful will accomplish their task and then it will remain only for Christ to accomplish His.

The sixth state is one "in which there will undoubtedly be a great earthquake [Apoc. 6:12], namely the most powerful persecution that will take place in the times of the Antichrist."[186] Anselm shows so little regard for the future that he never says whether this is the third earthquake, the last of the *transpositiones*, he had mentioned in chapter five, though since he refers to no other, one may assume that it is. He had said that the third earthquake marks a time "when these things having been finished and perfected, the change will be to those things which will no longer be moved or shaken."[187] It may be suggested that what he felt would be "finished and perfected" before this earthquake is the earthly church, which reaches the culmination of its historical development in the clash between the new orders and hypocrisy. That accomplished, the earthquake of Antichrist makes the final *transpositio*, which is to say that we have entered into a time very different from what has gone before. This is precisely what Anselm describes as the fulfillment of the Lord's prophecy: "Then there will be such a tribulation as there had never been since the advent of man" (Mark 13:19).

Anselm is quite clear that this attack on the church is different not only in intensity but in kind from earlier ones:

> Although in other times of persecution many kinds of torment were contrived against the Christian name, nevertheless the right and undoubted faith was maintained [*tenebatur*]. Now in truth [in the sixth state] torments are revealed and a false faith under the name of Christ is convincing [*persuadetur*].

---

[185] Rauh, *Antichrist*, pp. 290-291; Kamlah, *Apokalypse und Geschichtstheologie*, p. 68; Edyvean, *Anselm of Havelberg*, p. 32.

[186] *Antik.* 1.12, 1158B.

[187] *Antik.* 1.5, 1147C. Note that while Anselm is using Gregory of Nazianzus for this passage, the phrase *istis finitis et consumatis* does not appear in Gregory.

This time of tribulation is not one of the persecution of pagans or the word play of heretics or the cancer of hypocrisy but of a full blown anti-church. In this fight, it is the impotence rather than the power of the faithful that comes clear, for they stand no chance "on account of the subversion of the faith, with men being ignorant of what they should believe and hold to."[188] None will be spared for the persecution "will seize even the elect."[189] Anselm concludes his description by interpreting Apocalypse 6:14, "And the heaven receded like a rolled up scroll":

> Heaven is the church in which are hidden the enveloped and enclosed ecclesiastical sacraments; these will recede from the use of Christians and will be concealed from public and solemn ritual.[190]

Anselm's description of a future state of confusion over what to believe in a time when the sacraments will be withdrawn and men will have "'dried up for fear' of the Antichrist" creates an image of a power greater than the faithful can combat. The church to which Anselm has attributed the basic properties of a diversity of expression of faith, a progressive development toward perfection, and the capability of defeating attacks crumbles in his description of the sixth state as he asks rhetorically: "Who will be able to stand?"[191] Anselm does not place the sixth state within the developmental process of the first four. The sixth is not a state in which the church faces all of its earlier afflictions to prove itself a final time.[192] Instead, the church, meaning the organization of the faithful on earth, is crushed.

---

[188] *Antik.* 1.12, 1158BC.

[189] *Antik.* 1.12, 1158C-1159A. Cf. Matt. 24:24. Here and for much of his description of the Antichrist, Anselm quotes Haimo of Auxerre (d. ca. 855), *Expositio in Apocalypsin* 2.6, PL 117:1132.

[190] *Antik.* 1.12, 1159A.

[191] *Antik.* 1.12, 1159A, quoting Luke 21:26 and Apoc. 6:17.

[192] Funkenstein, *Heilsplan und natürliche Entwicklung*, p. 66; Rauh, *Antichrist*, p. 290. While Anselm says the sixth state is a time of persecution, that persecution is not associated with the persecution of the second state; nor does he say anything about heresy or hypocrisy in the sixth state. There is no contest between church and Antichrist in which the faithful prove themselves again through a new form of devotion, and Rauh is mistaken when he says of Anselm's church: "Was die Kirche auf ihrem Weg zur Vollendung an Substanz gewonnen hat, muss sie im 6. Status aufs Spiel setzen, am Widerpart erproben." *Antichrist*, p. 294. While this is not a position taken by Anselm, it was common in his time. See for example, Honorius Augustodunensis, *Commentarium in Psalmos*, PL 194:507-10, 566; Otto of Freising, *Chronica sive historia de duabus civitatibus* 8.2, MGH SrG 45:394-95.

If read within the context of the church's earlier states, the sixth would appear to reveal a very pessimistic view. However, Anselm has pointed his own fourth state toward victory, and he has used the third earthquake to mark a decisive change from what has gone before, a change that includes the seventh as well as the sixth state. Antichrist is, for Anselm, the means of closing the circle which moves from Christ the conqueror to Christ the conqueror. The image Anselm sets against all of the terrors of Antichrist is that of "the moment, the twinkling of an eye" in which all is perfected by Christ in the silence of divine contemplation.[193] The removal of the church and the rise of the Antichrist become the means of revealing the power of the Savior, and the sixth state forms a unit with the seventh of ultimate victory.

Anselm's seventh state not only closes the historical circle of Christ to Christ, but the larger circle of the entire *De una forma credendi*. He began his work with the contention of the critics of the new orders that the faith is immutable, and Anselm shows that the silence they seek in quiet meditation is, indeed, the final resting place of the faithful. Anselm's position and theirs are, in the end, one and the same. He has demonstrated that the changes bothering his audience are the result of the growth of spiritual understanding and because man, moving through time from good to better to best, is mutable, not God:

> This variety does not come about on account of the mutability of the unvarying God, who is always the same and whose years never end [cf. Ps. 101 (102):28], but on account of the variable infirmity of the human species and temporal change from generation to generation.[194]

With this, Anselm could hardly have meshed his position with the critics more completely: Change is a sign of weakness, just as they have contended; but it is also a sign of the process of growing strong.

De una forma credendi takes its readers from the beginning to the end of history, showing them that, through His revelations, God fashions them in His own image but that they are responsible for fashioning themselves in that image as well. Above all, this is an image of a love of each other that does not merely tolerate diversity but glories in it, for the diversity of religious life itself unifies the faithful and converts

---

[193] *Antik.* 1.13, 1159B.
[194] *Antik.* 1.13, 1160AB.

the hypocrite. Anselm concludes by telling his readers what they should have learned from his book: "Therefore, now and in the future, no loyal believer will suspect there to be some scandal in this, if in his church the same faith is always believed, the same form not always lived."[195] In his letter to Pope Eugenius, Anselm said he was asked to show Latins what they could say to Greeks. This might be taken to mean that he will demonstrate why the Greeks are wrong. Anselm's message to his brothers indicates that he has something else in mind.

C. *The Debates*

1. *The Proem*

In attempts to determine the connection between *De una forma credendi* and Anselm's portrayal of his debates with Nicetas, it is curious that the *proemium* Anselm sets between his first and second books has been all but ignored. If commentators make reference to it, it is generally to associate it only with Anselm's account of the debates.[196] This is not what he intended, for the proem is clearly addressed to the readers of Book One and acts not only as an introduction to what follows but also as a bridge connecting *De una forma credendi* to the debates.

In his proem, Anselm says that the same brothers for whom he had written *De una forma credendi* have come to him once again with new questions. The readers of the first book have been transformed and "now changed, inquire with a more pious and humble spirit."[197] Anselm has drawn a picture of the faithful changing through history as the result of increased knowledge, and here he creates an image of his readers as having been transformed by the knowledge of what is expected of them in the fourth state: endurance in the face of hypocrisy. Clearly, the audience for the debates is the "now changed" reader of *De una forma credendi* who has dispelled the arrogance that

---

[195] *Antik.* 1.13, 1160C.

[196] Theodore N. Russell mentions the proem but misinterprets it as a letter to Eugenius III. He also considers the questions it contains to be questions Anselm asks of the Greeks rather than questions asked of Anselm by his brothers ("Anselm of Havelberg and the Union of the Churches," p. 95). This seriously oversimplifies the way Anselm defines his audience. See also Morrison, "Anselm of Havelberg," p. 241.

[197] *Antik.* 2. proemium, 1159D-60D. See p. 170 above.

had turned questions into weapons. In the debates that follow, Nicetas' major criticism of the Latins will be that they are arrogant; but through *De una forma credendi*, Anselm has shaped the Latin audience he will bring to a reading of those debates into a humble one that now stands with him rather than against him. Anselm has pointed to numerous examples of the variety of spiritual leaders in the fourth state. By avoiding criticism of any specific form of religious life, he has also, if obliquely, offered himself as an example of how Christians should charitably deal with fellow Christians. In the debates, we will find Anselm reshaping an event from his own past to give his brothers a model of how to deal with others as he had dealt with them.

The spirit of the change in his audience is shown in the way Anselm phrases the new question of his brothers: "Why is it that in the church some are seen to disagree about the faith in the Holy Trinity and in the rite of the sacraments, as the Greeks do with the Latins?"[198] The question, as posed, assumes that the Greeks are in the one church now accepted by Anselm's audience to be full of variety. It is neither rhetorical like those of the critics of the new orders nor even antagonistic toward the Greeks. It is followed by more specific inquiries dealing with three problems. The first concerns ritual practice: Why is it that sacramental ritual, which should be the same for all, is different for the Greeks? Second is the question of the *Filioque*: Why do "the wise Greeks, very erudite in the knowledge of the Scriptures" not believe that the Spirit proceeds from the Son as well as from the Father? And here Anselm accompanies the most serious doctrinal issue dividing East from West with praise of the Greeks, speaking of the thousands of Greek saints who suffered in the name of the Lamb and whose feasts are solemnly celebrated.[199] Finally, the *Filioque* is connected to the issue of the papacy: How is it that there have been Greek saints and popes "if they have been so mistaken in the faith in the Holy Trinity that they say and believe the Holy Spirit proceeds from the Father only and not from the Son?"[200] These

---

[198] *Antik.* 2. proemium, 1161A; Wolf., fol. 31r: "Verum quid est, inquirunt, quod aliqui in Ecclesia, in fide sanctae Trinitatis et in sacramentorum ritu videntur discrepare, quemadmodum Graeci a Latinis?"

[199] *Antik.* 2. proemium, 1161BC.

[200] *Antik.* 2. proemium, 1161C-62B; Mun. 13r-13v; Wolf. 1, 33r: "Et mirum in modum, quomodo Graeci in numero sanctorum computentur, et ex ipsis Romani pontifices electi inveniantur, si in fide sanctae Trinitatis adeo erraverunt, ut dicerent et crederent Spiritum sanctum a Patre tantum, et nequaquam a Filio procedere; nisi forte quis audeat dicere, quod nihil obsit fidei Christianae, et credentium saluti, sive

questions put the purpose for writing about the debates on a different footing than that suggested by the request of Pope Eugenius for Anselm to show what could rationally be used to oppose Greek positions. Indeed, the way he poses his brothers' questions comes close to putting a Greek argument against the *Filioque* in their mouths—namely that some of the popes had not believed in it. As Anselm portrays his audience, the brothers are not asking questions in order to defend one position or attack another but because they want to understand their faith.

2. *From action to image*

The man whom Anselm uses to explain the Greek positions is Archbishop Nicetas of Nicomedia, and it is important to see how Anselm manipulates both the image of Nicetas and that of the debates as a whole to create a sense of confrontation and to show how real commitment to understanding can bring opposing sides together.

That Anselm was quite conscious of the distinction between an event and the reshaping of that event with words into an image suited to a specific purpose comes clear from a consideration of the opening of his earlier *Epistola apologetica* to Abbot Egbert of Huysburg.[201] There Anselm writes of the need to teach with love a man who "has been tempted to struggle against love" and has created confusion among Christians by

> asserting light to be darkness, darkness light, sweetness to be bitter and bitter sweet, saying bad is good and good bad; he stumbles from good to bad, deserts light to grasp darkness, spits out the sweet to choose the bitter by not tasting with a healthy palette.[202]

Here is the image of one who sows confusion. He then proceeds to reveal that the one who is guilty of fitting this description is Abbot

---

hoc, sive illud dicat, sive hoc non dicat vel credat; quasi ille articulus fidei, quo Spiritus sanctus creditur a Filio procedere, vel non procedere, nulli Christiano sit necessarius. Proinde quomodo, inquiunt, potuit esse quod aliquis, natione Graecus, pontifex Romanus, secundum Graecos Spiritum sanctum a Filio non procedere crederet, et secundum Latinos eumdem Spiritum Sanctum a Filio procedere in Romana Ecclesia praedicaret? Nam quod aliter crederent, et aliter praedicarent, nefas est dicere. Si autem quod credebant, id etiam praedicabant, quomodo Romana Ecclesia eos patienter audivit, quorum doctrinam de processione Spiritus sancti a Patre tantum, et non a Filio, nec tunc approbavit, nec hodie approbat?"

[201] See p. 54 above.
[202] *Epist. apol.*, 1119A.

Egbert who had defended a change in religious profession from canon to monk. Anselm is calculating about making this revelation. He gives what might be taken as a simple account of what he was doing when Egbert's tract defending the monks was brought to his attention: sitting and reading "as was my custom." And the tome in his hand happens to be the letters of St. Jerome. Now, this must strike one as a remarkable coincidence: A tract arrives from a monk who has thrown himself into stirring up confusion, and it is given into the hands of a quiet canon who is calmly reading the letters of St. Jerome, the great defender of the monastic life! There can be little doubt that Anselm is not interested here in historical reportage but in shaping an image of himself that contrasts with Egbert. That image has little to do with Anselm the active diplomat and adviser to kings, rather it is, remarkably enough, that of the contemplative. If his custom is quietly to study the Fathers, what then is Egbert's custom? Anselm expresses his surprise, even shock, to discover that Abbot Egbert has been spending his time authoring this "onerous" work, and then attacks the abbot for being petty, appealing to rumor, and twisting authorities to support his position. In doing this, Anselm has quite smoothly fashioned an image of the person who undermines Christian love, and then vilified Egbert by showing that he fits this image. At the same time he presents himself as a man of love who would prefer quiet study but whose sense of duty requires him to respond to the abbot.[203] And, of course, this is precisely the image of the canon, namely the active clergyman who is also the contemplative, that Anselm goes on to portray as the summit of Christian spirituality. No doubt, Egbert's tract did arrive for him to read, but from that incident Anselm has formed images designed to impress his reader.

In his prologue to the *Antikeimenon*, we find Anselm again shaping images out of events. He tells us that Pope Eugenius' request for the *Antikeimenon* was made on account of "a certain bishop." Eugenius has told Anselm about this bishop who recently had come to the pope with "a delegation from the emperor of Constantinople and a letter written in Greek." Anselm learns that

> this same bishop, well schooled in Greek scholarship and endowed with a distinguished eloquence of speech and self-assured in its use, proposed

---

[203] This same topos of the man who only writes out of duty is repeated by Anselm both in the prologue and the proem of *Antikeimenon*, 1141A-42B; 1162BC.

much from the doctrine and the ecclesiastical ritual of the Greeks that
but little accords with the doctrine of the Roman church and differs
greatly from its ritual.

It is very difficult to find a specific individual in this description; and
yet, ultimately, this "certain bishop" is Anselm's opposition: the Egbert, so to speak, of the *Antikeimenon*. However, Anselm does not give
this bishop a name, nor does he have any personal contact with him.
In fact, he does not even directly identify this bishop as a Greek, clear
though that may be. Nor does the man defend the Greek position
because it is Greek. He defends it only because "it was his, not
because it was true, and to disprove completely that which was ours
because it was ours and not his."[204] In the *Epistola*, Anselm had contrasted an image of the monk who withdraws and perverts Scripture
for his own purpose with that of the clergyman who is useful to the
church. It is, therefore, important to note that the closest Anselm
comes to revealing this man's identity is with the word "bishop."
Here is the image of a clergyman gone wrong.

The proof that this is Anselm's intent comes as he moves immediately to his own mission to Constantinople in 1136, for there his
presentation of the "certain bishop" is both echoed by and contrasted
to Anselm's description of himself. In position and circumstance, the
two men are almost identical. Both are bishops, both deal with religious differences between Greeks and Latins. Most telling is the fact
that Anselm has said that the "certain bishop" served on a *legatio* for
the Greek emperor, and then Anselm describes himself as a *legatus* for
the western emperor. Toward the end of the first book of the *Antikeimenon*, he again refers to his position on the delegation, only this
time he calls himself an *apocrisiarius*, a term which, had he used it in
his earlier description of himself, would not have created the *legatio-
legatus* parallel between the two bishops.[205] Here, however, the similarities end. Where the "certain bishop" flaunts his learning and tries
to prove "that which is his own," Anselm describes himself as spending time discussing and conferring about doctrine and ritual with
both Latins and Greeks. He says he will report not just what he said
about these things but what he heard as well, and this because Latins
have frequently misunderstood spoken Greek, having been "mislead

---

[204] *Antik.*, prol., 1139BC.
[205] *Legatio-legatus*: *Antik.*, prol., 1139B, 1140B; *apocrisiarius*: *Antik.* 1.10, 1156CD.

by the sayings of the Greeks because they hear them only as flights of words...judging them to affirm what they do not affirm and to deny what they by no means deny."[206] Here we have a subtle yet important aspect of the image of the good clergyman: whereas Eugenius asked for what a Latin could say in opposition to the positions of the Greeks, Anselm nicely holds out the possibility not only that misunderstandings rather than differences may be at the heart of the divisions in Christendom, but that it is the Latins—supposedly the side he will defend—who have misunderstood. The door to compromise is open as Anselm's image of himself begins to reflect that of the mediating Norbert.

The comparisons go a step further, as Anselm proceeds to present Archbishop Nicetas in the prologue, as well; and the archbishop is described in terms which contrast him with the "certain bishop" while demonstrating similarities with Anselm. The "certain bishop" twists Scripture to attack the Latins, but Nicetas is the first of the twelve *didascalos*, the most learned men of Greece to whom difficult theological questions are brought and whose decisions "are held to be irretractable and definitive and are written down."[207] Anselm is acting much like Nicetas in responding to the questions of his brothers with the written *Antikeimenon*. In the structure of the prologue Anselm places himself between the "certain bishop" and Nicetas. On the one side is a man with whom he can have a shouting match in which winning is everything, and he can thus play much the same game he had played with Abbot Egbert. On the other is Nicetas, a man who is preeminent among those whose job it is to listen and consider carefully before responding. Anselm appears to be able to choose his opponent, and the contentious "certain bishop" is never mentioned again. It is the thoughtful Nicetas with whom Anselm will debate.

The careful and complex structure of the prologue shows that the hand at work on the debates is that of an artist rather than of a reporter, and Anselm's manipulation of the images of himself and Nicetas will continue in those debates. When Anselm admits in the prologue that he has added "certain things no less necessary to the faith than adaptable to this work" to his account of the debates, it is a tacit admission that the characters of Nicetas and Anselm the de-

---

[206] *Antik.*, prol., 1141A.
[207] *Antik.*, prologus, 1141AB.

bater are literary constructs of the work's author over whom he has assumed complete control.[208]

Moving to Anselm's proem, we find a very different presentation of Nicetas from that in the prologue. Instead of being reintroduced in terms which would draw Anselm and the archbishop together, the Greek appears as an adversary. Anselm presents the reader with a situation rife with the possibility of attack and counterattack. He heightens the drama by making it appear that a David is going to meet a Goliath and stones will be hurled:

> Since among the [Greeks], Archbishop [Nicetas] was noble in his devout bearing, sharpest in his ability, most learned in the study of Greek letters, most eloquent in speech, and most cautious in giving and receiving answers, he neglected none of these things whether in a disputation [*disputatione*] or in a quiet deliberation which seemed capable of being turned to the advantage of his opinion and the destruction [*destructionem*] of ours; and this was especially the case since among the twelve elect *didascalos*, who by custom preside over the schools of the Greeks, he was, at the time, their leader. And from them all, in our disputation [*disputationis*] he was elected for the task of serving against [*adversum*] me.[209]

Here Anselm uses the words *disputatio, destructio,* and *adversum* to convey a sense of opposition, words that do not appear in the prologue to the *Antikeimenon* at all. On the other hand, at the beginning of *De una forma credendi,* he says that those who criticize the new orders are "against [*adversus*] every kind of religious life," "they dispute [*disputant*] about religious devotion," and they find the spiritual life sunk "in scandal and ruin [*destructionem*]."[210] Those critics have been changed by *De una forma credendi*; and with his description of Nicetas, Anselm draws two distinct and opposing sides, placing his former critics with him facing Nicetas. In effect, he has put them in the same position he had held when he faced their criticisms. If they have learned the lesson of the first book, they should not expect David to use his sling.

---

[208] *Antik.*, prologus, 1141A: "...addens quaedam non minus fidei necessaria, quam huic operi congrua." This is an understatement. See pp. 232-33 below; also Morrison, "Anselm of Havelberg," pp. 244-45, on Anselm's presentation of himself and Nicetas.

[209] *Antik.* 2. proemium, 1162.

[210] *Antik.* 1.1, 1143BC.

3. *The first debate*

a. *Catching words in flight: the dialogue format and the connection with* De una forma credendi

In presenting the Latin and Greek views of doctrine, ritual practice, and the papacy, Anselm does not simply give the Latin positions and show how they rebut those of the Greeks. Instead, he chooses to write his account in the form of a dialogue between himself and Nicetas.

As Peter von Moos has admirably demonstrated, the dialogue format was endemic to the writers of the Middle Ages. This was not, argues von Moos, the dialogue as Catechism in which responses were to be memorized and based on unquestioned authority, but a quest for truth.[211] As an example of the dialogue format, von Moos focuses on the *Dialogus Ratii* of Everard of Ypres, written at the end of the twelfth century and in defense of Gilbert of Poitiers. Von Moos points out that Everard begins with a letter to the pope (Urban III), presents a dialogue with himself as one of the participants, and finally a letter from an unnamed brother commenting on the letter to the pope and on the dialogue. Moos traces this tripartite division back to Sulpicius Severus and his use of an epistolary, dialogic and historical defense of the memory of Martin of Tours,[212] though the order of Sulpicius' defense is epistolary, historical and dialogic. A parallel organization is found in Anselm's work with its letters to Pope Eugenius and the brothers, its *De una forma credendi*, and finally its dialogue between Anselm and Nicetas. Just as important, von Moos argues that the three parts of Everard work form a united whole in "a literary fiction, perhaps written in a single burst."[213] This statement can as easily be applied to Anselm's work if we understand that the entire *Antikeimenon* stands within a literary tradition that uses several different approaches to address a single issue rather than accepting the notion that Anselm has stuck disparate elements tenuously together.

---

[211] Peter I. von Moos, "Literatur- und bildungsgeschichtliche Aspekte der Dialogform im lateinischen Mittelalter: Der *Dialogus Ratii* des Eberhard von Ypern zwischen theologischer *disputatio* und Scholaren-Komödie," in Günter Bern, et al, eds., *Tradition und Wertung*, FS Franz Brunhölzl (Sigmaringen, 1989), pp. 165-209; idem, "Le dialogue Latin au Moyen Age: L'exemple d'Evrard d'Ypres," *Annales: Économies, Sociétés, Civilisations* 44 (1989), 993-1028.

[212] Von Moos, "Le dialogue Latin," p. 1001.

[213] Von Moos, "Le dialogue Latin," p. 1001: "une fiction littéraire, peut-être écrite d'un seul jet."

The use of a dialogue by medieval writers took several forms with their roots in the classical world. One often finds the pedagogic device of using the characters of a student or friend and a teacher such as in Augustine's *De libero arbitrio* and *De magistro* and (in Anselm's time) Anselm of Canterbury's *Cur Deus Homo* and Honorius Augustodunensis' *Elucidarium*; or the tradition of a dialogue taking place within the context of a dream as in Boethius' *De Consolatione Philosophiae* and Abelard's *Dialogus inter philosophorum, Judaeum, et Christianum*.

Anselm of Havelberg departs from these standard forms of dialogue in an important way that has frequently caused a misinterpretation of his debates: He portrays his dialogue with a realism that draws the reader into accepting it as having actually taken place. Abelard and Boethius' use of the dream setting is an obvious literary device used to get archetypes (e.g. the Christian) or personifications (e.g. Philosophy) onto the stage. Everard makes no attempt to present his counterpart Ratius as a real person,[214] and even where Anselm of Canterbury names an actual student as the one with whom he debates (Boso in *Cur Deus homo*), he makes it clear to the reader that he is doing this as an honor to the student and not recounting an actual debate.[215] Augustine explains that he based *De Magistro* on an actual discussion with his son, but like Anselm of Canterbury, he does this by way of creating a memorial rather than because the historicity of the account is important for understanding it.[216] In other words, the dialogue was a literary form used as a pedagogical tool and viewed as such rather than as some sort of stenographic record of a past event.

When we turn to Anselm of Havelberg, we find that he gives us not only the names of his debaters, but he places them in what comes across to the reader as a historical construct: a debate which the reader has been told actually took place in Constantinople during the reign of Lothar III; and he starts his account by mentioning the date of the first debate and its exact location in Constantinople. Indeed, Anselm is so careful about giving his debates a historical setting that he, in effect, creates a historical event by making the reader believe that he is witnessing the actual, historical performance of Anselm and Nicetas in front of a crowd of onlookers in Constantinople in 1136.

---

[214] Von Moos, "Literatur- und bildungsgeschichtliche Aspekte der Dialogform," pp. 175-182; "Le dialogue Latin," p. 1002.

[215] *Cur Deus Homo* 1.1.

[216] Indeed, had Augustine not told us this in his *Confessions* 9.6, we would not know of the actual discussion between father and son.

He has done this so well, that while recognizing some reworking of his material, scholars have accepted Anselm's version of the debates as a fairly accurate recounting of what happened in 1136, even suggesting that Anselm relied on some stenographic record.[217] Two points should be made here. First, there can no longer be any doubt that Anselm does not even attempt to give an accurate account of the debates of 1136. Hermann-Joseph Sieben has decisively and with overwhelming evidence demonstrated the debates to be full of citations from many western theological works placed in the speeches of both debaters in such a way as to preclude the notion of historical accuracy;[218] moreover, Anselm even goes so far as to place a passage from the *Epistola apologetica* in the mouth of Nicetas.[219] In summing up his assessment of the historicity of Anselm's account, Sieben concludes that it is more sensible to see the written debates in terms of an "overall non-historicity" in that they do not report the course of the actual debates but rather form "a literary construct with a fabricated dialogue."[220] Second, I would suggest that it is largely because Anselm's account has, to one extent or another, been taken as a piece of historical reportage that its connection with *De una forma credendi* has been held to be tenuous. The work is not one of reportage, and the question becomes: Why does Anselm want us to think it is?

Generally, scholars have seen a concern with charity or Christian unity as the connective factor between *De una forma credendi* and the debates. Certainly, they do have these themes in common, but it is also possible to find a much closer connection between the two since the same argument is being made both with the narrative and the dialogue. Most important is that we understand that Anselm's argument is not made through reason and logic. Instead, Anselm argues through creating a charismatic model, the *una facies*. *De una forma credendi* offers historical examples of the unity of the faith, a unity that

---

[217] See Beumer, "Ein Religionsgespräch," p. 466; Russell calls Anselm's account "a report, based on a verbatim record." "Anselm of Havelberg and the Union of the Churches," p. 85 n. 1. Recently, Karl Morrison has described Anselm's account as being "composed by revising transcripts of public debates held in 1136." "Anselm of Havelberg: Play and the Dilemma of Historical Progress," p. 226.

[218] *Die Konzilsidee*, pp. 157-67. Sieben points to examples where Anselm places part of another author's argument in the mouth of one debater and then continues it in that of the other.

[219] See pp. 244-45 below.

[220] *Die Konzilsidee*, p. 167: "globale Nichthistorizität"; "ein literarisches Produkt, mit einem fingierten Dialog."

shines through differences in expressing that faith. In the section on the church after Christ, the work communicates a sense of Christians fighting against forces that threaten the faithful. The debates create, quite literally, a full-fledged historical example from the not-too-distant past of two men expressing their faith differently but working together to overcome issues conducive to disunity. In *De una forma credendi*, the reader is made aware of the *una facies* of Christ as the example to be followed in combating threats to Christian unity and shown that the imitators of Christ have defended the church. In the debates, the reader is taken by the hand and seated before the stage of contention to see how men of faith should act with each other. Anselm's readers are made into an audience in the true sense of the term. They not only consider the theological positions of Latins and Greeks, but they also observe two men presenting those positions. By using a dialogue format, Anselm draws attention to how the opposing positions are presented as much as or even more than to their content.

Paul Zumthor has said that the power of the medieval dialogue derived from its theatricality, its ability to render a teacher present to a reader.[221] For Anselm this was particularly important. He was of the old school, so to speak, having studied at the feet of men who taught not by argumentation but by projecting a model to their students of proper and useful behavior. In the *una facies* of Jesus we find the ultimate teacher of this kind; but that image must be emulated by all Christians, and this, I would suggest, is why it was vital to Anselm that his debates come across as "real". Their power to persuade has little to do with the rules of logical argumentation or the weight of authority but everything to do with the projection of personality in a way that will win the love of one's audience. The abstraction of a nameless Latin and a nameless Greek debating in an obviously fictional setting would never have worked as well as showing a real Latin named Anselm and a real Greek named Nicetas having an "actual" debate in which they get along quite well together. Indeed, much of Anselm's fame in the modern world has rested on the notion that he actually furthered the cause of unity with the Greeks in 1136; and that notion, of course, rests entirely on our (mis)reading of Anselm's account.

---

[221] Paul Zumthor, *La lettre et la voix: De la "littérature" médiévale* (Paris, 1987), p. 92.

Anselm the author actually has his counterpart in the debate explain his use of the dialogue format. In the middle of the first debate, the debaters discuss how words are understood. Anselm the debater supports the *Filioque* by saying that when Christ breathed on the apostles and told them, "Receive the Holy Spirit" (John 20:22), procession from the Son is demonstrated. He supports this inference with analogies to the blind who have eyes and are then given sight or the deaf with ears who are made to hear. Nicetas warns him that it is dangerous to make comparisons between corporeal and spiritual things because of their different natures. In the response we find the author's explanation of the dialogue format. Anselm the debater says that comparison by its very nature cannot mean that two things are the same,

> but we give or receive similitudes in the fashion of theatrical representation [*similitudines scenicas*], not because they capture the pure truth of things but because they conduct the spirit of the listener to a better understanding of things; and it often happens that, by such a method of instruction, that which is not understood because of its highly elevated nature can be understood.[222]

Within the context of the specific analogies toward which Nicetas' warning is directed, Anselm's use of the phrase *similitudines scenicae* is a curious one; *similitudines* would have served his purpose just as well. However, the debates themselves are very much a theatrical presentation of the unity of the faithful, an image of performed action in which Anselm invites his readers to participate as members of the audience.

There is yet more evidence that Anselm is referring here to his act of creating through writing rather than to the analogies used by Anselm the debater. "Very often," he writes, "through the recognition of visible things, words are invisibly formed in the invisible spirit; one forms equally visibly the visible characters of letters on visible parchment,"[223] which is exactly what Anselm the author is doing in writing but not what Anselm the debater is doing in speaking. In his prologue to the *Antikeimenon*, he had stated that Latins often misjudged what Greeks said because they heard the spoken phrases as flights of words passing by too quickly to be examined;[224] and the

---

[222] *Antik.* 2.16, 1187BC.
[223] *Antik.* 2.16, 1187D.
[224] See pp. 228-29 above.

image he creates here is not of spoken words connecting with the mind of a listener, but of written words connecting with the mind of a reader where, in a beautiful turn of phrase, "in silence [the words] speak, and in speaking they fall silent." He describes the effect of written words on the reader: "And it follows that through the same visible characters an invisible understanding is engendered in the soul of the reader."[225] With the debates, Anselm attempts to engender an understanding of the unity of the faith in the souls of readers concerned with differences between Greeks and Latins. He goes beyond an analysis of those differences, for by using the dialogue format he moves the reader beyond reading words to hearing them spoken and seeing the speakers. He creates a moving picture, a picture of a Latin and a Greek discussing their differences on the assumption that their faith is one. By using a dialogue which gives the impression of recreating an actual event, Anselm, rather brilliantly, has it both ways. The image conjured up in the mind of the reader is that of a Greek and a Latin speaking to each other, and Anselm's words are thus both written and, in *similitudines scenicae*, spoken as well.[226] In his description of the literary dialogue, von Moos has captured exactly what Anselm consciously accomplishes: "The literary dialogue is necessarily paradoxical: it is a text that tends to forget that it is a text."[227]

To draw the reader into the debate, the first thing Anselm does is to place him at the center of the action by invoking the drama and tension of the occasion. The place is the Pisan quarter of Constantinople near the church of Hagia Eirene. Anselm scans the assembly of court officials, judges, and Latin translators. There are also notaries there to write down what is said, giving the reader the sense that the

---

[225] *Antik.* 2.13, 1187D-1188A; Mun., fol. 28r; Wolf 1, fol. 73r: "Et rursus per eosdem apices visibiles formatur invisibilis intellectus in anima legentis: et fit quoque, ut si quando primi intellectus, ad quorum formam idem apices primo facti sunt, oblivione superveniente deleantur, per eosdem apices inspectos renascantur. Ac ita vicissim ad similitudinem invisibilium intellectuum fiunt verborum sermones et visibiles apices: et iterum ad similitudinem sermonum , seu apicum visibilium, vel [Wolf. adds: non visibilium] novi intellectus invisibiles generantur; vel antiqui invisibiles regenerantur quamvis tamen visibilia et invisibilia non ejusdem, sed prorsus diversae naturae inveniantur."

[226] For a somewhat different interpretation of this passage see Morrison, "Anselm of Havelberg: Play and the Dilemma of Historical Progress," p. 221, who sees it as a presentation of the hermeneutic problem inherent in moving between things, words, and thoughts.

[227] Von Moos, "Le dialogue Latin," p. 994: "Le dialogue littéraire est nécessairement paradoxal: c'est un texte que tend à faire oublier qu'il est texte."

spoken words, moving from one language to the other, have been caught in flight and that he is vicariously present. A crowd of onlookers, eagerly awaiting the beginning of the debate, is moved to silence.[228]

That crowd is also an audience, only this time of Greeks, and thus Anselm posits a Greek counterpart for his brothers, who also witness the debates by reading the dialogue in silence, letting the words speak. Thus, even in the way he sets his stage, Anselm is obscuring the line between Greeks and Latins. The dual audience comprises the faithful facing a division amongst them represented by the debaters Anselm and Nicetas. At issue is not only what is believed but those who believe, Latins and Greeks. Anselm's readers are, as well, partisans standing with Anselm on one side of a line of divergent beliefs and practices. From this vantage point, they can expect him to present the Latin positions in such a way as to make apparent their strengths against the weaknesses of those of the Greeks. But on the other hand, they stand with Anselm precisely because, with *De una forma credendi*, he has eliminated a similar dividing line by showing them the common ground of faith they share with him. From this perspective, they must expect Anselm to do the same with the line dividing them from the Greeks. In this sense, they are not the partisan audience of one side in a contest but rather an audience of students whom Anselm is teaching about the ways of making peace and of maintaining the unity of the faith. It is Anselm's readers who must learn from the debates, for Nicetas is a literary construct howsoever much he may be based on a real man. The brothers are the only ones Anselm can actually win over to anything.

Nicetas is a complicated figure. In both the *Epistola apologetica* and *De una forma credendi*, Anselm addressed his remarks to an opposition that never had a chance to state its own case. In using Nicetas, it is apparent that he wants his opponent's views stated as well as his own. More than that, by saying that he has relied on his memory of an actual debate and by basing Nicetas on his actual opponent in that debate, Anselm is able to state the Greek position much more forcefully, even passionately, than would otherwise be possible. By portraying Nicetas neither as a straw man nor a buffoon but as a sympathetic man of faith to whom the reader owes the same consideration as to the debater named Anselm, Anselm the writer has found a safe

---

[228] *Antik.* 2.1, 1163C.

mouthpiece for his own criticisms of western Christendom.[229] At the same time, Nicetas serves yet another function. He also becomes the mouthpiece of Anselm's audience of brothers who watch the debate to see how Anselm the debater will maintain the unity of the faith. Here Nicetas acts as a judge evaluating not only what Anselm the debater says but, more importantly, how he says it.

b. *Setting the tenor of the debates*

In Anselm's portrayal of the first debate, he is not introduced to the crowd nor are the issues to be debated formally presented by one of the judges or by the contestants themselves. Instead Anselm speaks first. This may, in fact, reflect the actual debate of 1136;[230] but be that as it may, in the written account it allows the Latin side to set the tenor of what follows. If Anselm had wanted to have his readers see a Greek opponent crushed, here was the place to draw a line between opposing positions and move to the attack. But this is not what happens. Instead, Anselm the writer creates tension and then presents Anselm the debater as a man attempting to relax it:

> "When all was ready, the seats [for the debaters] arranged facing each other, silence imposed, everyone eager and waiting, Bishop Anselm of Havelberg said: 'Reverend fathers, I did not come seeking a quarrel....
> I came to inquire about and understand the faith, yours and mine, and above all because it pleases you.'[231]

It is, therefore, the Greeks who have come to Anselm, and here he draws them together with his anxious readers who had come to him twice with their questions. To those readers he had responded in a similar vein that if the questions are to be answered, they must be treated as inquiries posed by the faithful to the faithful.[232] The tension

---

[229] See Walter H. Principe, "Monastic, Episcopal and Apologetic Theology of the Papacy, 1150-1250," in Christopher Ryan, ed., *The Religious Roles of the Papacy: Ideals and Realities 1150-1300*, Papers in Mediaeval Studies 8 (Toronto, 1989), pp. 132-33; cf. another article in this same work: Jannis Spiteris, "Attitudes fondamentales de la théologie byzantine, en face du rôle religieux de la papauté au XIIème siècle," pp. 174-79.

[230] Anselm may be reflecting Greek practice. In 1149 Wibald wrote: "Ariopagitae, castigatissimi Greciae et Athenarum iudices, neque proemiis nec epilogis quemquam uti permittebant, set simplici et minime colorata narratione" (Ep. 167, p. 285). Indeed, Anselm's debaters give neither a general introduction to what is to be debated nor an epilogue summing up their conclusions.

[231] *Antik.* 2.1, 1163C.

[232] *Antik.* 1.2, 1143D.

is further relaxed by Nicetas' response that he appreciates Anselm's humility because in a humble discussion truth will be arrived at much sooner than "if, in our eagerness to conquer, we dispute arrogantly." To this Anselm responds that they should accompany each other on the path of truth by avoiding arrogant argument.

All this good will establishes more than the ground rules for a debate. Anselm draws the same circle of faith around the debaters he had previously drawn around himself and his brothers; and in discussing the faith, it is vital that the circle not be broken. It can be assumed that, manipulating both debaters as he does, Anselm the writer will not allow Nicetas to break it. To do so would end in blaming the Greeks for divisiveness, and Anselm's brothers would learn nothing. At center stage is Anselm the debater. The issue is whether he can maintain the circle he has drawn and eliminate the divisive line by the debates' end.

The subject of the first debate is the *Filioque*. Of the issues raised in the debates, it is the one most fraught with problems over the meanings of words. That two languages are involved adds to the complications. What does "to proceed" mean? Is it different from "to be given" or "to be sent"? And what are the dangers of using words to describe the mystery of the Trinity? A debate on the *Filioque* would inevitably revolve around making such linguistic determinations. It is, therefore, somewhat surprising that Anselm the debater prefaces the discussion by resisting Nicetas' desire to improve mutual understanding by having the translators translate everything word for word. It would be better, says Anselm, to avoid disputes over words by allowing the translators to give the sense of what is being said.[233] Beyond this, Anselm humbly tells Nicetas that he feels unprepared for the debate and asks indulgence if he should happen to say something which might offend; then he introduces the issue of the *Filioque*.[234]

Anselm's comments seem curious on two counts. First, to introduce the *Filioque* after saying that sense rather than words should be translated appears an incredible *non sequitur*. Avoiding precise translations was going to be, quite simply, impossible. Second, Anselm the

---

[233] Possibly influenced by Gregory of Nazianzus, *On the Holy Spirit* 24, PG 36:159; Norris, *Faith Gives Fullness to Reasoning*, p. 292 or by Pope Gregory I who expressed a similar sentiment; *Registrum epistularum*, ed. Dag Norberg (Turnholt, 1982), CCSL 140, 7.27, p. 485 and CCSL 140 A, 10.21, p. 855.

[234] *Antik.* 2.1, 1164AB.

writer is under none of the constraints of a spoken debate. He can be as exact in his use of words and spend as much time preparing himself to write as he wants.[235] However, in his prologue, Anselm suggested that Latins had problems when they listened to Greeks because hearing the Greek words left no time to examine their meaning.[236] With his request for translations according to the sense of what is said and his protestations of a lack of preparedness, he leaves the impression that his audience is listening to, rather than reading about, a debate and that they will hear words in flight but with time to ponder them in their written form.

Anselm also addresses here a problem created by the format of using a Greek adversary, namely that Anselm the debater cannot win the debate in the sense of actually resolving divisive issues. At the end of the debate, Nicetas and Anselm may embrace, a sense of the integrity of the faith may be maintained; but outside of Anselm's literary invention, the divisive issues will still confront his readers. It is only their view of the issues, not the issues themselves, that can change at the end of Anselm's work; and it is their new view of the issues that is all important for a unity of the faith.

c. *Logical traps*

The debaters discuss the *Filioque* from three perspectives: reason, scriptural authority, and the decrees of church councils. With the first, Anselm the writer presents Nicetas stating the Greek position, then he gives a discussion in which Anselm the debater responds to the queries of the Greek, and finally, he allows Nicetas to react to what the Latin has said.

The Greek expresses concern that the belief in the Father as the unique principle and the highest perfection sufficient unto itself is threatened by the *Filioque*: If the Spirit proceeds both from the Father and the Son, then the principle which is the Father must not be sufficient. If it is sufficient, then the principle which is the Son is superfluous for the procession of the Spirit.[237] In his response, Anselm

---

[235] Here, by the way, is further evidence that Anselm's audience is not first and foremost Pope Eugenius III. If Anselm were responding specifically to Eugenius' request for what a Latin could say to a Greek, the suggestion that one could claim to be unprepared has not only a hollow ring of special pleading but sounds rather comical as well.

[236] *Antik.* prologus, 1141A.

[237] *Antik.* 2.1, 1165AD.

the debater begins by doing exactly what we have seen Anselm the writer do with the critics in *De una forma credendi*: He emphasizes how much common ground there is between Greeks and Latins. Their faith is one in their agreement that "in God there are not many principles nor is there no principle, but He is one principle unto Himself, through Himself, in Himself, holding exclusively the most free principle of monarchy."[238] But after this, we find each debater striving to create logical traps in which to ensnare his opponent and force him to say something contrary to what he believes. More important for Anselm's readers is the fact that these traps do not work, and this precisely because the debaters are not dealing only with the *Filioque* but with each other.

First Anselm lays a trap for Nicetas. He takes up the word "principle" and shows that it can have a variety of meanings. If one speaks of the Trinity according to persons, then the Father is a principle unto Himself and the Son is a different principle engendered by the principle which is the Father. Thus, there are, as Nicetas suggests, two principles. If, however, principle is taken to mean substance, then the Son is of one principle with the Father. On this basis, the Spirit can proceed from Father and Son without the conclusion that Father and Son must be two principles. While Nicetas may accuse Anselm of positing two principles for the procession of the Spirit when one is sufficient, it is really the Greek who is guilty of dividing Father from Son by suggesting too complete a distinction between them. And so the debater springs his trap:

> Since you have first denied the one thing, that is the procession from the Son, and affirmed the other, that is procession from the Father, now you must either dare to acknowledge neither or you must admit both with me according to the catholic faith as well as these rational propositions.

Nicetas should be caught no matter which way he turns. But after showing the debater very carefully laying this trap, Anselm the writer allows Nicetas to step around it ("The things presented in your discussion concerning 'principle' seem to be enough."[239]) and immediately set about baiting his own. If Anselm is right, he points out, then the Spirit is also one principle with the Father and the Son, and thus

---

[238] *Antik.* 2.2, 1165D-1166C.
[239] *Antik.* 2.3, 1170C.

must proceed from Himself. When Anselm responds by falling back on a distinction between the members of the Trinity which would be obscured if one said the Father engenders Himself or that the Son is engendered from Himself or that the Spirit proceeds from Himself, Nicetas puts his question to Anselm:

> What or of what nature in your opinion is this procession of the Holy Spirit about which we speak? Does it seem to you that the Holy Spirit should be said to proceed according to a common substance or according to the distinct and proper person?[240]

If Anselm says the former, then the Spirit must proceed from Himself; if he says the latter, then the procession from Father and Son would mean procession from two principles.

While historians have frequently pointed to an imbalance which favors the Latin in the amount each debater has to say, it should be emphasized that Nicetas' trap is a response to Anselm's. This is to say that Anselm the writer shows his namesake and supposed champion of the Latins to have taken up a mistaken line of argument which has no impact on the opposition. The real trap here is sprung on the reader who, following Anselm the debater's reasoning toward victory, finds the tables turned. The message is that logical traps produce logical traps, not agreement.[241]

Indeed, in his response to Nicetas' trap, Anselm the debater points to the very limitations of the kind of argumentation in which the two are engaged. "You tell me," he says to Nicetas,

> what or of what nature is the unbegottenness of the Father, and what or of what nature is the begottenness of the Son, and I will explain to you what or of what nature is the procession of the Holy Spirit, and we will both go mad together investigating divine mysteries.

Anselm the debater's conclusion is to abandon logical argument entirely and fall back on his faith: "It should be sufficient for you to hear what it suffices me to believe: Of a certainty, it is enough for me to believe that the Father is unbegotten, the Son begotten, and that the Holy Spirit proceeds." This mystery deserves to be honored in reverent silence, "because certainly it exceeds the foggy cloud of our

---

[240] *Antik.* 2.4, 1171C.

[241] See von Moos, "Le dialogue Latin," p. 996 who says that the true dialogue was to be conducted "sans avoir recours ni à la force ni à la ruse ni à l'argument d'autoritié." Anselm's debaters will try all three and fail to accomplish anything.

insignificant condition where vanity sometimes passes for truth."[242]
Here, in their mutual faith in the mystery of the Trinity, the two sides
do come together without the need of compromise.

When a second series of exchanges over similar ground again fails
to produce agreement, Anselm the writer pursues the discussion
through the voice of an exasperated Latin debater intent on forcing
Nicetas to admit he is in error; and it is this exasperation that would
have been lost had Anselm the writer chosen not to use the format of
a debate and the character of Nicetas. For brothers seeking the unity
of the faith, these moments of exasperation are critical ones and must
be gotten around. Otherwise, the object of debate will no longer be
to understand the faith, one's fellow debater will become the opposition, and arguments will begin to be directed *ad hominem*.

These consequences begin to threaten as Anselm the debater accuses Nicetas of slyly reintroducing what has already been dealt with
and then asks him to listen patiently as he explains his position again.
However, it is Anselm the debater who reveals impatience by coming
very close to calling Nicetas a heretic:

> What, indeed, is a greater blasphemy against the Holy Spirit than to
> believe and teach that the Holy Spirit does not proceed from the Son?...
> Clearly he who commits this sin of blasphemy or faithlessness, or impa-
> tience, unless he reconsiders, will neither be forgiven in this age nor in
> the future.[243]

This *ad hominem* argumentation could only serve to undermine whatever sense of unity had already been created by the Latin and the
Greek, and significantly, Anselm the writer puts it in the mouth of his
namesake. While Anselm the debater's humility becomes suspect at
this point, Anselm the writer's comes clear, for he quite humbly
portrays himself as the one who turns a discussion into an attack and
risks a violent reaction from Nicetas. The debater's arrogance is high-
lighted by Nicetas, who does not respond in kind but says that he will

---

[242] *Antik.* 2.5, 1171D-1172B. Anselm's statement about going insane together with
Nicetas by attempting to explain the mystery of the Godhead is borrowed from
Gregory of Nazianzus, *On the Holy Spirit* 9, PG 36:141; Norris, *Faith Gives Fullness to
Reasoning*, p. 283.

[243] *Antik.* 2.11-12, 1180C-81C. Anselm has just quoted Matt. 12:32, "Qui peccaverit in Patrem, seu in Filium, remittetur ei; qui autem peccaverit in Spiritum sanctum, non remittetur ei, neque in hoc saeculo, neque in futuro," which, he says
applies, equally to the Macedonian heresy of calling the Holy Spirit a creation of
God rather than God and to Nicetas' position on the *Filioque*.

patiently endure Anselm's insults (a nice play on Anselm the debater's accusation of impatience) and then affirms his belief in the Trinity and the Holy Spirit in terms with which no Christian, Greek or Latin, could find fault.[244]

Whatever the merits of Anselm's argument supporting the *Filioque*, in the context of the act of discussion, the message to the reader is that Anselm the debater has trapped himself. If Nicetas counterattacks, the debate will disintegrate into a series of insults and must be lost by both sides, for no unity of the faith could be affirmed. But Nicetas does not respond in kind, and this puts Anselm the debater in an even worse light as Nicetas takes on the image of Jesus enduring persecution and even of the brothers Anselm described as patiently enduring the hypocrites of the fourth state in *De una forma credendi*. This is a replay of the end of the first round of the debate where Anselm had affirmed his faith, only now with Nicetas standing steadfastly by his. We are left with the principle that unifies the two men, Greek and Latin.

d. *Scripture's own sense: Latin arrogance and Greek neutrality*
The next part of the debate deals with the use of Scriptural authority to determine the validity of the *Filioque*. At this point, the two debaters appear estranged. Anselm expresses the feeling that it is impossible to teach Nicetas anything. The Greek is like a wolf trying to learn his A-B-C's. What is in his heart takes precedence, and he merely repeats over and over, "Lamb, lamb, lamb." He then expresses fear that Nicetas will bend Scripture to conform to his beliefs.[245] Nicetas' response bears careful consideration.

In the *Epistola apologetica*, Anselm had warned Abbot Egbert about misusing Scripture and had suggested that it has a clear meaning which needs only to be found and adopted. "Truly," he told Egbert,

> no one accustomed to devoting time to Scriptural exegesis ought to be ignorant of how great an evil it would be to leave the sense of divine Scripture behind rather than to adopt divine Scripture's own sense.

Now in the *Antikeimenon*, Anselm takes this statement and puts it in the mouth of Nicetas responding to Anselm the debater:

---

[244] *Antik.* 2.12, 1181. Nicetas gives a long series of names of the Holy Spirit, a list which distinctly echoes Anselm's fondness for giving lists of names and qualities.
[245] *Antik.* 2.14, 1183CD.

No one accustomed to devoting time to Scriptural exegesis ought to be ignorant of what an evil it would be to distort the understanding of Scripture that deserves to be called divine from its proper sense by violent exposition rather than humbly to release and apply completely the proper meaning of divine Scripture; and therefore your advice is well taken.[246]

Well taken, indeed! The Anselm who seemed so sure of the clear meaning of Scripture in the *Epistola* now quite consciously posits a Greek telling him to be careful of his exegesis. There is here, as well, more than an echo of Pope Eugenius III's complaint given in the prologue to the *Antikeimenon* of the "certain bishop" who defended the Greek position by using Scripture "violently twisted to fit his sense." According to Anselm, Eugenius accused the "certain bishop" of

using every means to prove that which was his own because, of course, it was his, not because it was true, and to disprove completely that which was ours because it was ours and not his.

That Anselm means to call this to mind comes clear as he has Nicetas tell Anselm the debater:

Do as you have advised me, and if you want to bring forth sacred authorities, explain them in such a way that you do not seem to wish to prove your meaning by distorted exposition because it is yours and not because it is true.[247]

Had Anselm the debater told Nicetas these things, Anselm's Latin readers could have maintained the feeling that the other side was always the one guilty of distorting Scripture. But by having Nicetas address this advice to the Latin, Anselm the writer draws a different

---

[246] *Epist. apol.*, 1119BC: "Quantum vero malum sit, quamvis sacram Scripturam suo sensui emancipare, et non potius divinae Scripturae suum sensum adaptare, nulli incognitum esse debet qui sacris lectionibus vacare consuevit." *Antik.* 2.14, 1183D-84A: "Quantum malum sit, intellectum Scripturae, quae divina meruit appellari, ad proprium sensum quasi violenta expositione distorquere, ac non potius proprium sensum omnino divinae Scripturae humiliter mancipare et accommodare, nulli debet esse incognitum qui sacris lectionibus vacare consuevit, et ideo bene monuisti."

[247] *Antik.* prologus, 1139C: "Et ipse quidem nonnullis auctoritatibus sanctarum Scripturarum ad suum sensum violenter retortis, universa in quibus Graeci a Latinis discordant tamquam recta visus est affirmare; ea vero, in quibus Latini a Graecis discrepant, tamquam non recta visus est infirmare: illud nimirum quod suum erat, non quia verum erat, per omnem modum probando; hoc autem quod nostrum, quia nostrum et non suum erat, omnino improbando." *Antik.* 2.14, 1184A: "Fac ergo et tu quod tu in me monuisti; et si vis proponere sacras auctoritates, ita eas exponas, ne videaris tuam sententiam, quia tua est, non quia vera est, extorta expositione, velle probare."

kind of attention to it, one that requires a bit of soul searching from his readers by tacitly asking them to turn their criticism of others around to see if it fits themselves. It is Nicetas who reminds the Latin, "He who presses the udder hard to get milk brings forth butter, and he who violently blows his nose, brings forth blood."[248] And it is Nicetas who makes the valuable point that the two should recognize that Scripture often lends itself to more than one interpretation, and thus dissent among the debaters does not necessarily mean one of them is in error.[249]

A further element of the debate at this point should be mentioned: its humor. As the debaters dig in their heels and the line between them appears etched all the deeper, Anselm the writer diffuses an explosive situation with humorous sayings and proverbs—the wolf learning his ABC's and the person milking a cow or blowing his nose—which take the edge off the exasperation while nevertheless allowing it to be expressed. Thus, when Nicetas suggests that Scriptures which apparently have little to do with the subject at hand may nevertheless be useful, Anselm warns him not to search for "a knot on a bulrush."[250] But while this may have raised a smile from Latin readers, what follows should have given them pause.

In this debate over scriptural authority, the Latin proceeds to support his position by giving numerous scriptural citations, but not a single one clearly makes his point about procession from the Son. Nevertheless, he concludes by telling Nicetas that their meaning should be obvious:

> It is clear, therefore, that the Holy Spirit proceeds from the Son, unless perchance, willing your eyes to remain closed, you do not wish to see what is more clear than light, and willing your ears to remain deaf, you do not wish to hear the Scriptures crying out and pouring upon you.[251]

This is an uncharitable reference to Anselm's use of the blind receiving sight and the deaf being made to hear as analogous to Jesus

---

[248] *Antik.* 2.14, 1184A, quoting Prov. 30:33. Perhaps Anselm hoped this would bring the end of this verse to mind: "Et qui provocat iras producit discordias."

[249] *Antik.* 2.14, 1184BC.

[250] *Antik.* 2.14, 1184C, an old Roman proverb. On the use of humor in dialogues and specifically in Everard's *Dialogus Ratii,* see von Moos, "Literatur- und bildungs-geschichtliche Aspekte der Dialogform," pp. 170-180; "Le dialogue Latin," p. 1008.

[251] *Antik.* 2.17, 1188C. Anselm cites John 20:22 (2.15, 1185A) and Luke 8:46, 1:35, 24:49 (curiously omitting the beginning of this verse: "Et ego mitto promissum Patris mei in vos"), Acts 1:8, Luke 6:19 (2.17, 1188BC).

saying "Receive the Holy Spirit." Again, it is Anselm the debater who is turning the argument *ad hominem*;[252] again, Nicetas does not respond in kind but simply cites the verse of Scripture most clearly relevant to the question of the *Filioque*, asking why it is that Jesus said, "[The Spirit] proceeds from the Father" (John 15:26), but said nothing about procession from the Son.[253]

When he wrote the *Epistola apologetica*, Anselm used "Scripture's own sense" to defend his position at the expense of the monks. Now, in the first debate, we find him allowing the Greek to turn this strategy against the Latin debater: what the Scriptures say stands on the side of Nicetas. The thrust of the next portion of the debate is to demonstrate a lack of clarity in the Scriptures that makes the Greek position understandable, if not acceptable, to a Latin audience. Here, one may suggest, is an indication that Anselm recognized the arrogance he had expressed in the *Epistola* and that it was threatening to the unity of the faithful.

Anselm the debater defends himself by asking Nicetas why, if Scripture provides clear answers, the Son did not say, "[The Spirit] does not proceed from Me"?[254] Together the two men then use Scripture to affirm their common belief in the unity of the Trinity, and Nicetas admits the Holy Spirit "to be of the Father and the Son." But he goes on to show that the sticking point is still the word "proceed": "Yet we do not dare to admit that [the Holy Spirit] proceeds from both because perhaps it is one thing for Him to be from the Father and to be from the Son and another for Him to proceed."[255] The two sides appear to be drawing together; but once again, Anselm the debater shows some anger with Nicetas. He demands to be shown how the Spirit can be from the Father in one way and from the Son in another, yet again from Them both, and yet in some other way can proceed. Show that, he says, "and you have differentiated [the

---

[252] See p. 243 above and Russell, "Anselm of Havelberg and the Union of the Churches," p. 105.

[253] *Antik.* 2.17, 1188CD.

[254] *Antik.* 2.17, 1188D.

[255] *Antik.* 2. 17, 1189BC; Mun. fol. 29r; Wolf. 1, fol. 80r: "Propter haec itaque et multa alia testimonia quibus instruimur, bene, sicut dixi, confitemur Spiritum sanctum qui in Trinitate tertia persona est, Patris esse et Filii: nec tamen ab utroque eum procedere fateri audemus, quia fortasse aliud est eum a Patre esse [Wolf. adds: et a filio esse], et aliud est eum procedere."

Spirit] from Himself, and thus you have quite shamelessly made
empty the sound Faith which is from the Holy Spirit."[256]

What is coming clear for Anselm's Latin reader is that the Greek
position is remarkably close to that of the Latin, in fact, may even be
the same, but that the semantic argument over the meaning of "to
proceed" is threatening reconciliation. Far from following the hope
expressed at the debate's beginning to concentrate on what is believed, the debaters have fallen to quibbling over the meaning of
words. Finally Anselm the debater demands,

> What now? Will we dispute about words signifying now one thing, now
> another? Is it proper for us to follow letters or syllables or sayings,
> leaving the truth of things behind? We should rather leave this to boys
> playing with grammar and dialectic, for truly it would suit us better to
> investigate the proposition rather than to cling to words."[257]

Anselm, in fact, reduces the argument from one over the troublesome
word *Filioque* to one over the little word *non* in his assertion that the
Scriptures do not say the Spirit does not (*non*) proceed from the Son.
"At least do this," he tells Nicetas,

> namely, remain silent concerning what I acknowledge and do not deny
> with the impudent, monosyllabic, little, negative word *non* that of which
> you are doubtful and uncertain, and which I am certain and secure in
> affirming.[258]

In very sympathetic terms, Nicetas matches Anselm's claim of humbly asserting his faith with one of humbly doubting what is ambiguous in matters of the faith. He tells Anselm that mortals are easily
deceived, and since the Greeks have been taught to avoid "offending
Scripture," he cannot affirm that the Spirit does or does not proceed
from the Son.[259]

---

[256] *Antik.* 2.18, 1190A; Mun. 29v; Wolf. 77v: "Proinde ostende, si potes, Spiritum
sanctum habere aliud esse a patre et aliud esse a Filio; et iterum ostende, si potes
aliud esse eum esse a Patre et Filio, et aliud esse eum procedere: et sic eum a seipso
diversificasti, et ita sanam fidem quae de Spiritu sancto est, [Wolf. adds: doctrinam]
satis impudenter evacuasti."

[257] *Antik.* 2.20, 1195B.

[258] *Antik.* 2.21, 1196B.

[259] *Antik.* 2.21, 1197AB: "Homines enim sumus, unde aliter aliquid sapere, quam
se res habet, humana tentatio est; nimis autem amando sententiam suam, vel invidendo melioribus usque ad praecidendae communionis, vel condendi schismatis, vel
haeresis sacrilegium praevenire, diabolica praesumptio est. In nullo autem sapere
aliter quam se res habet, angelica perfectio est. Ergo quia homines sumus, et plerum-
que fallimur et dubitamus, interim caveamus diabolicam praesumptionem, donec

The Greek position here is neutral. The concern is not to affirm some positive belief but to avoid commitment one way or the other. This, of course, stands at odds with virtually all Nicetas has had to say about the *Filioque* to this point, and the Greek certainly had himself earlier maintained the negative "[The Spirit] does not proceed from the Son."[260] However, to Anselm's Latin audience the writer is communicating a sense that the *Filioque* is not an indication of a serious division in the faith. As Anselm the writer presents it, the neutral Greek position stems from honest, understandable caution. In a telling passage, Anselm the writer has Nicetas explain why the *Filioque* has become such a problem. The Greeks have not taken a stand on the *Filioque*, he says,

> unless perhaps [they were] irritated and aroused by the impudence of certain Latins heedlessly asserting [their position], coming to us in censorious arrogance, strutting about with lofty speech, and beating the air in noisy disputes. They wanted to show off their puny knowledge and strove in disdainful haughtiness to obscure the great wisdom of the Greeks in clouds of sophistries, or even to smother it if they could. We did not yield to them for even an hour, but always sent them away full of confusion, just as they deserved.[261]

Nicetas' description focuses on the behavior of the Latins and the way they presented their arguments rather than on the contents of those arguments. The sense is that a proper presentation will go a long way toward resolving conflicts.[262] Nicetas' description also turns

---

perveniamus ad angelicae sententiae perfectionem; siquidem majores nostri hujus processionis verbum affirmativum, *procedit a Filio*, humiliter hactenus vitaverunt, ignorantes quidem rei veritatem, et caventes vocis temeritatem; verbum vero negativum, *non procedit a Filio*, etiam nunquam dixerunt, metuentes errorem, et fugientes offensionem Scripturae neutrum manifeste dicentis." A persuasive indication of the literary nature of the debates is the fact that Anselm the writer is borrowing from Augustine's *De baptismo contra Donatistas* for Nicetas' speech. *De baptismo* 2.5.6, PL 43:130: "Homines enim sumus. Unde aliquid aliter sapere quam res se habet, humana tentatio est. Nimis autem amando sententiam suam, vel invidendo melioribus, usque ad praecidendae communionis et condendi schismatis vel haeresis sacrilegium pervenire, diabolica praesumptio est. In nullo autem aliter sapere quam res se habet, angelica perfectio est. Quia itaque homines sumus, sed spe angeli sumus, quibus aequales in resurrectione futuri sumus, quamdiu perfectionem angeli non habemus, praesumptionem diaboli non habeamus."

[260] *Antik.* 2.1, 1165C.

[261] *Antik.* 2.21, 1197B; see Nicetas' similar comments at *Antik.* 3.14, 1231B.

[262] For the same criticism of the way an argument is presented in Everard's *Dialogus*, see von Moos, "Literatur- und bildungsgeschichtliche Aspekte der Dialogform," p. 183-85.

Pope Eugenius' meeting with an arrogant Greek on its head. Rather than showing how to deal with the arrogance of the Greeks, Anselm the writer sends the message to his Latin readers that they may be the ones guilty of arrogance and bear some responsibility for the division between Greeks and Latins. Nicetas follows his criticisms of the Latins with praise for Anselm the debater, his humility, gentle manner, and avoidance of contention. And when he indicates that had Anselm displayed the arrogance of other Latins, a public debate would not have been allowed, the message to Anselm's readers is clear: Without a humble willingness to avoid contentious dispute, the line between Latins and Greeks will remain sharply drawn with no means of erasing it.[263]

e. *The hope for a church council*
A true discussion among humble Greek and Latin Christians is Anselm's answer to the *Filioque*; but for that discussion to occur, he has to provide a means of moving outside of the confines of his written work and into the real world. The final section of the debate addresses this problem. When Nicetas asks how Anselm can accept the *Filioque* when the profession of the faith agreed on at the Council of Nicaea does not mention it, he opens the subject of church councils; and it becomes apparent that Anselm the writer is not so concerned with what councils have said about the *Filioque* as about the possibility of a future council and the spirit in which it should be held.

That spirit is conveyed by the care Anselm the debater displays to convince Nicetas that in his response he is not laying another trap, "but [asking] in order that I may learn something from you, or, if perchance it is possible, you may learn something from me, and we may mutually recognize and be recognized by the faith, yours and mine."[264] When Nicetas answers positively a series of questions about the tenets of the Nicene Creed, Anselm points out that the faith is not

---

[263] *Antik.* 2.21, 1197BC. Russell says that at this point in the debate, "Once again Anselm and Nicetas have reached an impasse" ("Anselm of Havelberg and the Union of the Churches," p. 107.). This, I feel, does not do justice to Anselm the writer's careful attempt to render the *Filioque* less volatile in the minds of his readers as a threat to the unity of the faithful. Of course, Russell has approached the debate as if Anselm had given an accurate transcription of what was actually said in 1136 (p. 45 n. 25 above).

[264] *Antik.* 2.22, 1198D; Mun., fol. 34v; Wolf. 1, fol. 92r: "Sed ut aliquid discam a te; vel si forte fieri potest, ut tu discas aliquid ex me, et invicem cognoscamus et cognoscamur de fide tua atque mea."

stated so explicitly in the Scriptures and therefore Nicetas must believe that the faith has been made more explicit by the councils. Nicetas is willing to agree that the Holy Spirit is the author of both the Scriptures and the councils and even says that "we and many of our wise men do not disagree with you about the sense of this procession [from the Son]."[265] This is what Anselm had requested at the debate's beginning: that the two concentrate on the sense of what is said rather than on defining words.

The debate begins to come full circle to its amicable beginning, much as the states of the church in Anselm's history had moved from peace to disruption and then back to peace. Nicetas explains that the Greek doctors had "suggested to us the same sense of this procession clearly enough" but that they did not use the word procession.[266] Here, it may be suggested, Anselm the writer shows his hand as he creates an opportunity for the Latin debater to respond with citations from an assortment of Greek theologians: Athanasius, Didymus, Origen, Cyril, and John Chrysostom. While these citations, along with many from the Latin Fathers as well, serve to buttress Anselm's case for the *Filioque*, it is not this to which Nicetas reacts but rather to the fact that Anselm the debater cites Greek authors at all: "The fact that you wish to introduce our doctors pleases me; but since you are a Latin, I would like to know if you accept the authority of those you have named as well as that of our other doctors." This allows Anselm the writer to show his readers that the world of learning is not divided into Greeks and Latins:

> As for myself, I do not separate the gift of the Holy Spirit from any Christian, Greek or Latin, or from a faithful Christian of any people; I condemn no one, I reject no one, nor do I believe such should be rejected; but I welcome and embrace with an open mind every person who speaks justly and writes those things which are not contrary to apostolic doctrine.[267]

Here is the message of *De una forma credendi*, and to it Nicetas responds with an effusion of praise for Anselm the debater and, just as important, a desire that all Latins would behave the same way. Anselm the writer has shown Nicetas growing in his trust of Anselm as he realizes that no attack on the Greeks is intended, and it is significant that, this

---

[265] *Antik.* 2.22-23, 1198C-1202CD.
[266] *Antik.* 2.23, 1202C.
[267] *Antik.* 2.24, 1202D-1204B.

established, it is Nicetas who points the way to a compromise on the *Filioque* by asking, "What do you say to this, namely that certain wise men among the Greeks say that the Holy Spirit proceeds from the Father *through* the Son?"[268] Anselm the writer has nicely turned around a debate which for the most part presents the Latin position on the *Filioque*, so that it is now the Latin who is asked whether he can agree with a Greek formulation. The debater responds positively if cautiously, saying that more study of both Latin and Greek writers is necessary.[269]

The debate moves to a happy conclusion with Nicetas saying that the Latin should not think the Greeks have been defeated and that the charity and concord necessary to address the *Filioque* will depend on Latin humility. It is Nicetas who draws the new line on one side of which he stands together with Anselm, on the other side of which stand all those who squabble with each other, Latins and Greeks alike. "It is of no importance to us," Nicetas says, "what either foolish Greeks or arrogant Latins say and argue about among themselves."[270]

In the final speeches of the debaters, Anselm the writer, perhaps carried away by the spirit of reconciliation he has created, holds out great hopes for a unified church. Anselm the debater makes no mention of any compromise formula on the *Filioque*, but tells Nicetas that all that remains is for the Greeks to accept the *Filioque* and the leadership of the Roman church.[271] Nicetas accepts all of this with the single qualm that before the formula "the Holy Spirit proceeds from the Son" is made public in the East, a general council of the church should be called to make a determination lest the debaters "run in a vacuum." This council, he says, should be held under the authority of the of Roman pope, and afterwards the *Filioque* will be freely accepted by the Greeks.[272] Anselm the debater agrees with all of this, emphasizing the role of the pope at such a council. To this sugges-

---

[268] *Antik.* 2.25, 1206D.
[269] *Antik.* 2.26, 1208B.
[270] *Antik.* 2.26, 1208D.
[271] *Antik.* 2.27, 1209A; Mun., fol. 39v; Wolf. 1, fol. 104v: "Nihil ergo jam aliud restat, nisi quod Spiritum sanctum a Patre et Filio procedere, sine aliqua haesitatione, sicut credis, ita dicas, ita doceas, ita scribas, et cum sancta Romana Ecclesia quae mater est omnium Ecclesiarum, et quae hoc docet et scribit, ejusdem fidei concordiam habeas."
[272] *Antik.* 2.27, 1209B-10A.

tion, the crowd shouts, "Let the things that have been said and gathered by the notaries be diligently preserved," and everyone responds with a rousing, "It is good! It is good! It is good! Thus let it be done! Let it be done! Let it be done!"[273] This enthusiasm is surely Anselm the writer's wishful thinking. On the other hand, it is also a call to action in the real world. This open-ended and hopeful conclusion, along with the whole debate, is, in fact, preserved in the *Antikeimenon*; and Anselm's debaters will, indeed, "run in a vacuum" inside of a closed book if their words are not read and heeded.

A Greek reading this debate would surely have been surprised at Nicetas' acceptance of the *Filioque* and desire for a council headed by the pope;[274] but to Anselm's Latin reader, it sends a message of hope and encouragement. The *Filioque* appears to be a great, complicated misunderstanding, rather than a rent in the fabric of the faith. Anselm's brothers could come away from the debate with a sense that there truly was a unity of the faith, East and West; it only needed patience and understanding to be made clear. The brothers have witnessed the debate through words and seen what Anselm wants them to be: promoters of unity and peace. They are Anselm's audience and therefore the ones who should shout: "It is good! Thus let it be done!"

Anselm the writer's presentation of the debates has recently been interpreted as the intentional formulation of a dilemma from which there is no escape, and the debaters' suggestion of a church council interpreted as "a gracious escape from the impasse of debate."[275] To the contrary, Anselm the writer has engineered his debaters out of a dilemma as they come back around to the debate's beginning and the desire to investigate sense rather than words. What they have discovered is that words have gotten in the way of their common faith. The idea of a church council is not an escape from an impasse. It is the means of moving from an optimistic literary construct into the real world. The idea for that church council comes from Nicetas, as if the writer thought that giving it a Greek origin would help clear away the problems of bringing it into being. Anselm the diplomat

---

[273] *Antik.* 2.27, 1210B; Mun., fols. 40r-40v; Wolf. 1, fol. 106r: "Item alii clamantes dixerunt: 'Ea quae dicta sunt, et a notariis excerpta diligenter conserventur.' Omnes dixerunt: 'Bonum est, bonum est, bonum est. Ita fiat, fiat, fiat.'"

[274] Cf. Russell, "Anselm of Havelberg and the Union of the Churches," pp. 108-10.

[275] Morrison, "Anselm of Havelberg," pp. 234-45, citing p. 240.

and man of affairs knew that this was not enough, and it is to the
problem of holding such a council that he returns in the second
debate.

4. *The second debate*

a. *Custom versus papal primacy*
The second debate is ostensibly about differences in sacramental
practice: Should one follow the Latin custom of using unleavened
bread in the mass or the Greek custom of using leavened bread?
Should water be mixed with the wine before consecration according
to Latin practice or after as the Greeks would have it? And did the
Greeks practice a form of rebaptism? But Anselm the writer does not
begin the debate with the first of these nor are they treated as isolated
issues. They are used to explore the deeper problem touched on at
the end of the first debate concerning the authority by which disputes
over such differences could be decided. The second debate's discussion of ecclesiastical authority has been taken to indicate Anselm's
thoroughgoing commitment to papal primacy, and certainly Anselm
the debater presses for obedience to the Roman pope at almost every
turn. But if one distinguishes between Anselm the debater and Anselm the writer, then the words of Nicetas must be taken into consideration in determining the views of the latter.

Anselm the writer begins with a clear affirmation by both debaters
of the mutual charity established in the first debate, and it is important to note that while the procession of the Holy Spirit is mentioned,
neither debater uses the word *Filioque*. It is the spirit in which the
debate was conducted that Anselm the writer chooses to emphasize.
The Latin says: "[The Holy Spirit] informed us sufficiently in mutual
deliberation, and after the many turns of a not contentious but fraternal dispute, brought us humbly together at last in the law of love and
in the concord of the same opinion."[276] And the Greek responds in
kind: "Thanks be to God that we completed the earlier question with
the wholesome love of peace-making words, so that indeed it is pleasant for us to confer with you, not in a debate over words, but in an

---

[276] *Antik.* 3.1, 1209; Mun. fol. 41r; Wolf. 1, fol. 108r: "Ipse nos mutua collatione
sufficienter edocuit, et post multos non contentiosae sed fraternae disputationis an-
fractus, tandem in legem charitatis, et in ejusdem sententiae concordiam nos humiliter composuit."

inquiry concerning meaning." He goes on to say that the Greeks do not intend to attack Anselm but want to listen to what he has to say about Greek customs, for "they want to learn something new which is good."[277] In the *Epistola apologetica*, Anselm discussed whether a man or the office he holds is good. Now in the debates, it is this sense of unity and fraternal inquiry created by a "wholesome love of peace-making words" that is good. For all the praise of Anselm the debater that issues from Nicetas in the two debates, the Greek never calls him "good." What is good is the situation in which both parties try to understand each other.

In the previous debate, the question of whether the Roman pope's authority extended to the eastern church was not discussed, nor did Anselm express the idea that the voice of the Roman pope should be decisive in determining dogma.[278] In the second debate, the writer steers the debaters toward the issue of papal leadership as he has Anselm the debater begin the discussion by pointing to the Roman church as the voice of authority on sacramental practices.[279]

---

[277] *Antik.* 3.1, 1210D-11A: "Gratia Dei nos ita priorem quaestionem salva charitate pacificis verbis consummavimus, ut jam sit jucundum nobis tecum conferre, non in disceptatione verborum, sed in inquistitione sententiarum; ideoque non sit tibi meticulosa praesentia tantorum virorum, quia non idcirco huc convenereunt, ut tibi aliquam calumniam quacunque occasione inferrent, sed ut te loquentem consueta Graecorum mansuetudine audirent...cupiunt aliquid novi quod bonum sit, apprehendere." This follows on Anselm the debater's protestation of apprehension in facing so august a body of learned men. Since in the first debate Anselm has done what appears to be a fine job of moving the Greeks toward the Latin position on the *Filioque*, an expression of stage fright at this point seems forced and rhetorical. Nicetas' response, which amounts to a paternal pat on the back, sounds particularly out of place given Anselm's earlier performance. Perhaps, we have here a glimpse of the actual debate of 1136 where a kind Nicetas, capable of embarrassing the young Latin bishop, tells him instead not to be afraid and to do his best.

[278] Cf. Beumer, "Ein Religionsgespräch," pp. 468-69.

[279] Sieben says that the issue of papal primacy is subsumed under that of the use of unleavened bread in the mass, that it is not treated on the same plane as the *Filioque* or sacramental practice: "Will [Anselm] durch diese Disposition andeuten, dass die Primatsfrage nicht zu den Dingen gehört, in denen unbedingt Konsens bestehen muss? Wenn schon logische Unterordnung der Primatsfrage, warum dann, kann man sich weiter fragen, Subsumption nicht unter die Frage der *fides*, sondern des *ritus sacramentorum?*" (*Die Konzilsidee,* p. 167) As will be shown, Anselm is particularly concerned to mitigate the Greeks' fear that a church led by the pope will run roughshod over Greek learning and wisdom; and in the proem, Anselm's brothers asked him specifically to address the issue of the papacy. For all of the talk about sacramental ritual, papal primacy is the issue of the second debate. That Anselm nicely avoids making it an article of faith and thereby allows room for discussing the role of the Greeks in a council is more a sign of diplomacy than that consensus on

In dealing with the type of bread to be used in the mass, Anselm the debater says that while there is such a thing as local custom governing individual congregations, "the whole church is bound together by authority; no less is the whole also under obligation to the universal tradition of the ancients." The Roman church, which uses unleavened bread, is the authority for other churches because it teaches the tradition of the ancients which is the custom of Christ. The Greeks have broken from Rome and thus from universal usage by using leaven. While on the one hand, this serves to establish a foundation for Anselm the debater's defense of papal primacy, on the other, it turns the debate in a direction which allows Anselm the writer to present the fears of the Greeks. Anselm the debater has first said that local custom is important in the church, but then tacitly changed this to the custom of Christ and said that this is what the Roman church teaches.[280] Following this line of reasoning, the Greeks could well wonder whether there was any room left for local custom at all. What was to prevent Rome from saying that whatever customs it followed were Christ's and therefore binding on all churches? And more important, if one wanted a unified church of East and West, where was the common ground between Roman authority and Greek custom on which such unity could be established?

As with the first debate, we find the direction of the second moving rapidly from peace and mutual understanding to disruptive antagonism; and again it is Anselm the debater whose lack of tact precipitates this. Anselm the writer has written about the unity of the faith in the first book and argued against those who condemn new forms of religious devotion. Yet on the issue of papal primacy, Anselm the debater condemns the eastern church for creating a schism because it "prefers to build up something new and unique" as if the term *novum* were one of censure.[281] The students of *De una forma*

---

papal primacy is not important. Again, one must look at the debates from the perspective of Anselm's audience of brothers. To them he is showing the care that must be taken to find middle ground while remaining true to one's own beliefs. On the issue of papal primacy, Anselm the debater does both.

[280] *Antik.* 3.2-3, 1211B-12A.

[281] *Antik.* 3.3, 1211D: "Orientalis Ecclesia...mavult aliquid novum et singulare moliri, quam tenere universalem consuetudinem." This may draw on Augustine, *De baptismo* 2.9.14, PL 43:133: "[Consuetudo] sola opponebatur inducere volentibus novitatem, quia non poterant apprehendere veritatem."

credendi could hardly help but be puzzled at such a charge which mouths their own earlier criticisms of the new orders. Moreover, Anselm the debater gives his Greek opposite no room in which to build unity. This comes very clear from the responses of Nicetas which may be summarized as saying that if the Latins demand absolute obedience to the pope, there will be no reconciliation with the East. Indeed, this comes so clear as to suggest that Anselm the writer uses Anselm the debater to highlight this point and create sympathy for Nicetas rather than to make a strong case for papal primacy.

Nicetas supports the rule of local custom: Erudite and devoted men have served in the patriarchate of Constantinople, governed the eastern church, and established the venerated and inviolate customs of the East. He does not criticize Rome, saying that if the Roman church leads the churches of the West in different customs, it does so because it exercises its own local authority. There is nothing wrong with this, but the Greeks will follow and defend their own customs. "We want to hold on to what was acquired of our predecessors by defending custom," says Nicetas, "and now weary, to lie down in the small bed of authority more than to reject customary things by still making inquires and working to introduce new things." Here is Anselm the writer's own earlier description of those who question the new orders in the church and seek a place to lay their weary heads in expectation of eternal salvation,[282] the very people who now stand on Anselm's side in the debates. That their own former image is projected here onto Nicetas is aimed, one suspects, at capturing some sympathy for the archbishop.

Anselm the debater's long response has nothing to do with unleavened bread but rather addresses the place of custom in the church. That Anselm the writer is manipulating the discussion in this direction is clear from the fact that Nicetas' sigh of weariness has been lifted from St. Augustine's *De baptismo*,[283] as has much of Anselm

---

[282] Cf. *Antik.* 3.3, 1212D "Magis autem volumus praedecessorum nostrorum inventum et institutionem defendendo tenere, et in lectulo tantae auctoritatis jam fessi accumbere, quam inquirendo amplius etiam usitata reprobare, et ad inducenda nova laborare" to *Antik.* 1.1, 1143A: "Utinam alicubi aliquid certi inveniamus, ubi caput nostrum fiducialiter in exspectationem salutis aeternae reclinemus."

[283] *De baptismo* 2.8.13, PL 43:134: "[Cyprianus] maluit praedecessorum suorum tanquam inventum defendere, quam inquirendo amplius laborare. Nam in fine epistolae ad Quintum ita ostendit, in quo tanquam lectulo auctoritatis quasi fessus acquieverit."

the debater's response.[284] At the end of this debate, Anselm will bring up the Latin suspicion that the Greeks practice rebaptism, and rebaptism is precisely the issue addressed by Augustine in *De baptismo*. Thus, this work was probably at Anselm's side as a reference for writing the last part of the debate. But *De baptismo* deals with rebaptism within the context of Christian unity and conciliar authority. Paraphrases and quotations of it at this point in the debate are indications that the issue Anselm the writer has in mind is not the kind of bread to be used for the Eucharist but who has the authority to make decisions for the entire church.

b. Fermentum: *the Latin attack*

Anselm the debater first attacks the idea that custom should rule in the church. Stringing together passages from *De baptismo*, he says, that "no one should doubt that custom gives way to manifest truth because reason and truth always exclude custom." Custom, he goes on, should not be followed if it is in error; and if something new is found which is better and "more useful, let him embrace it."[285] Here is the Anselm of the *Epistola*, arguing for the utility of a thing and using that utility to attack someone else; for as far as Anselm the debater is concerned, what is "better and more useful" is the Roman church. He draws a sharp line between himself and Nicetas, calling himself "the special son of the Roman church," saying he is "not embarrassed to be its servant," and expressing his displeasure with the archbishop for saying things about Rome which he cannot let pass, especially since leaders of the eastern church have on occasion erred in matters of the faith.[286]

Standing on its own, Anselm the debater's speech appears a courageous defense of his beliefs in the face of attack. In context, how-

---

[284] Sieben, *Die Konzilsidee*, pp. 158, 161. Anselm also borrowed from *De baptismo* in Book Two, see pp. 248-49 n. 259 above.

[285] *Antik.* 3.4, 1212D-13A. Cf. *De baptismo* 3.6.9, 3.8.11, 2.8.13, PL 43:143-44, 134. Anselm's attitude toward custom here reflects that of the reform papacy of the late eleventh and early twelfth centuries. Either Gregory VII or Urban II used the formula, "Nam Dominus in evangelio: Ego sum, inquit, veritas. Non dixit: Ego sum consuetudo," and may have found it in Augustine's *De baptismo* 3.6.9 and 6.37.71, PL 43:143, 220. See Gerhart B. Ladner, "Two Gregorian Letters: On the Sources and Nature of Gregory VII' Reform Ideology," *Studi Gregoriani* 5 (1958), 221-42. It is interesting to note, however, that even though Anselm relies on 3.6.9, he does not cite "Nam Dominus...."

[286] *Antik.* 3.4, 1213BC.

ever, this is not the case. Anselm the writer could have given Nicetas
a speech worthy of a spirited response, but at no point does the
archbishop attack either Rome or Anselm the debater; he only insists
that the eastern and western churches be allowed to follow their own
customs. Given that Anselm the writer has concocted both the archbishop's tolerant acceptance of custom and Anselm the debater's
aggressive response, one must conclude that it is the negative effect of
a contentious insistence that the Greeks capitulate to Rome that
Anselm the writer wants to impress on the minds of his readers. In
the strongest terms, Anselm the debater lays out the case for Rome as
the leader of the church, West and East, and the arbiter of custom.
The speech is neither an answer to any question asked by Nicetas nor
an attempt to understand the Greeks, nor is it punctuated with Nicetas agreeing, disagreeing or asking for more information. It is a statement of why Westerners accept the authority of the Roman pope,
not an effort to educate the Greeks or win their acceptance of the
Latin position. Indeed, it appears a conscious effort to offend the
Greeks.

Anselm begins his attack by turning to the Council of Nicaea
because of its supposed affirmation of Rome's primacy in the church.
He cites the council as saying that Christ Himself had given primacy
to the Roman church which he founded on Peter, that Rome was
consecrated with the blood of both Peter and Paul, and that in the
hierarchy of bishoprics Rome holds first place over Alexandria and
Antioch.[287] Anselm does not so much as mention Constantinople but
only repeats the ranking of Rome, Alexandria and Antioch and that
"Peter the prince of the apostles honored the first seat, which is in the
most eminent and triumphant city of Rome, with his body." The
Roman church is the preeminent church of God and has remained
firm while others wavered in heresy.[288]

When Anselm the debater moves on to speak of the church of
Constantinople, it is to associate it again and again with heresy and
schism. With no subtlety at all, he constantly identifies the evil caused

---

[287] *Antik.* 3.5, 1213D-14C: "Sciendum sane est...exortum est." Anselm relies here
on the *Praefatio Nicaeni concilii* of the first half of the fifth century rather than on the
Council of Nicaea itself. *Decretales Pseudo-Isidorianae et capitula Angilramni*, ed. Paul
Hinsch (1863, reprint: Aalen, 1963), p. 255; see Sieben, *Die Konzilsidee*, pp. 158-59.
The *Praefatio* was not recognized in the East, and one can only wonder what the real
Nicetas would have made of it in an actual debate.
[288] *Antik.* 3.5, 1214C-15A.

by Constantinople and the churches of the East with the words *fermentum* or *fermentare*. Thus Constantinople was often exited (*fermentata*) by innumerable heresies and was polluted "by the very poisonous ferment" (*venenoso fermento*) of Arianism. His first example of an Arian is Eusebius of Nicomedia—the very place where Nicetas is archbishop—who infected Constantinople "by the same ferment" (*eodem fermento*). Of course, *fermentum* in the sense of the leaven used in bread is the issue at hand, and Anselm's use of the word is no coincidence. In his presentation of the East as a hot bed of heresy and without ever mentioning the kind of bread to be used for the Eucharist, he nevertheless uses various forms of the word *fermentum* fully twelve times.[289] "Who," he asks, "is able to enumerate all of the heretics and all of their errors which have been in this city and fermented the holy and immaculate church of God with false teachings and attempted to tear the tunic of Christ with impious schism?" Heresies have collected in Constantinople "like bilge water," and sat there "like dirty frogs." "Indeed, from this pool of heresy the multitude of the simple became drunk as if on wormwood wine." He compares Constantinople to Babylon giving drink to the world from a poisoned cup of heresy; and here he calls Babylon "the first and great Babylon," allowing the reader to draw the conclusion that Constantinople is a second (not so great) Babylon rather than a second Rome.[290]

Anselm refers again to Rome, calling it the little boat (*navicula*) of Peter.[291] Other members of the ecclesiastical navy have suffered shipwreck—and lest there be any doubt which vessels Anselm numbers among them, he lists Constantinople, Alexandria, and Antioch by name. Only the boat of Peter has weathered the storm of heresy, and "in order to expunge the ferment of malice and wickedness by which the heretics were corrupting the church of God, [the Roman church]

---

[289] *Antik.* 3.6, 1215-17. In *De una forma credendi*, Anselm not only associated heresy with *fermentum* but truth with *azymum*: "Expurgatum est fermentum malitiae et nequitiae, et solidata est mater Ecclesia in azymis sinceritatis et veritatis" (1.9, 1151D).

[290] *Antik.* 3.6, 1216.

[291] *Antik.* 3.6, 1216D-17A, also 3.10, 1222BC. On the *navicula Petri*, see Hugo Rahner, *Symbole der Kirche: Die Ekklesiologie der Väter* (Salzburg, 1964), pp. 473-90. Rahner traces the idea of the little boat of Peter as the church back to Tertullian and Pseudo-Clement, but he points to no one before Anselm who explicitly associated the *navicula* with the Roman church. While he says that Anselm sees Peter as the good "Steuermann" (p. 490), he does not mention Anselm's references to the *navicula* nor take into account that this association of the *navicula* with the Roman church is precisely the one Anselm—who may very well be the first—makes.

always labored by itself and through its legates and still labors today."
Those who wish to call themselves sons of God and of Rome, the
mother of all churches, should imitate Rome in sacramental ritual.[292]

This blatant attack stands in stark contrast to the tolerant, mediating image created by Anselm in the first book. The humility that
Nicetas has attributed to him is not to be found in a single word of
this speech which threatens the common ground between Greeks
and Latins that had carefully been claimed in the first debate. Suggesting that Constantinople collected heresy like bilge water, that
Rome not only had labored but still labors against heresy and does
this through its legates, among whom Anselm, "the special son of the
Roman church" debating with a Greek, would be numbered, was
hardly a way of charitably steering the debates toward a happy resolution. Anselm the writer has gone out of his way to make a reasoned
defense of Rome into an insult to the Greeks. He has presented the
Roman position in such stark, uncompromising and pugnacious
terms as to make clear not why the pope should have primacy but
why the Greeks are so resistant to the idea. The result is that Nicetas
can now express the Greek fear of papal primacy in a way that
should be understandable even to a Latin.[293]

It is Nicetas who drily points out that the charitable nature of the
debate is at risk by telling Anselm:

> You have said enough great and sublime things about the dignity and
> sublimity of the Roman church, but the things that you have added
> concerning that church, your restraint was able to have expressed more
> cautiously.

As he has listened to Anselm, now, he says, Anselm should listen to
him. "This, surely, the charity in which we have convened demands." Anselm the debater responds with a final uncharitable play

---

[292] *Antik.* 3.6, 1217A.

[293] Peter Classen, assuming the historicity of Anselm's account, says that for the
most part the debaters avoided calling each other heretics. "Der Häresie-Begriff,"
pp. 40-41; see also Morrison, "Anselm of Havelberg," p. 253 n. 123. I would suggest
that in Anselm the debater's play on the word *fermentum* and in his insulting remarks
about Constantinople as a sink of heresy, the element of a past time is not stressed at
all. The attempt is to create an association between the words Constantinople and
heresy; and the image left in the mind of the reader is one of a heretical Constantinople. It remains for Nicetas to insist that a distinction be made between the city in
the past and the city in the present. Through Nicetas, Anselm the writer draws
attention to and makes the reader conscious of the artifice of Anselm the debater's
speech.

262 PART TWO – CHAPTER TWO

on the word *fermentum* that only serves to underscore his arrogance rather than his love:

> In pure charity, I have sincerely spoken the pure truth without any ferment of falsity. Respond whatever you wish in this same charity, and may it be with the ferment set aside.[294]

Setting the ferment aside is, of course, exactly what Anselm the debater wants the Greeks to do in their sacramental practice. Heresy and leaven have been implicitly tied together, and the debater is asking for unconditional surrender.

c. *Nicetas' fears: the Greek response*

Given Anselm the debater's insults, it is noteworthy that Nicetas does not follow suite. He begins his speech with many concessions to Rome: He neither denies nor rejects Rome's primacy; says that while Rome, Alexandria, and Antioch were sister sees, Rome was preeminent; declares that for guidance in problematic ecclesiastical concerns all churches looked to Rome; and affirms that Rome adjudicated matters which could not be dealt with locally.[295] Here is the stuff of compromise. Nicetas is even willing to concede the primacy of the Roman pope if it means the primacy of the first among equals rather than monarchical rule. In a superbly diplomatic use of historical evidence, Nicetas points to the seventh-century Greek Emperor Phocas and his affirmation to Pope Boniface III that "the apostolic see of the blessed Apostle Peter was the head of all churches" in the face of Constantinople's claim of primacy.[296] Rome's primacy is affirmed— and by a Greek emperor, at that— but it is a *primus inter pares* kind of primacy. Nicetas opens the door for a council, saying that Rome, Alexandria, and Antioch were like sisters maintaining "the concord of sound doctrine" and, when necessary, holding a general council. Because of Constantine's *translatio imperii*, Constantinople became the second Rome and part of this sister-like relationship in which Rome is the first church and holds the place of honor at a general council.[297]

---

[294] *Antik.* 3.6, 1217C: "Ego in mera charitate meram veritatem sincere, et sine omni fermento falsitatis locutus sum, tu quoque in eadem charitate, utinam fermento dimisso, responde quidquid vis." In Migne, these lines come at the end of Anselm's long speech in support of the papacy. Mun. fol. 45r and Wolf. 1, fol. 118v place them after Nicetas' plea to be heard.

[295] *Antik.* 3.7, 1217D-18A.

[296] *Antik.* 3.7, 1218A. For Nicetas' discussion of Phocas and Boniface III, Anselm the writer has relied on the *Liber pontificalis* 1. 68, p. 316.

[297] *Antik.* 3.7, 1218A-19A.

Only after these concessions, does Nicetas present the very human fears of the Greeks concerning the implications of a church governed by the Roman bishop alone. In what must be counted one of the most important passages of the debates, Anselm the writer allows Nicetas to give full voice to Greek concerns about a church ruled by the pope. The Roman church, he says, has made of her position a monarchical one at odds with the nature of her primacy, and this has divided the eastern bishops from the western. How, he asks, can the Greeks be expected to acquiesce to the decisions of councils called by western popes that include only western bishops?

> Indeed, if the Roman pontiff, sitting on the lofty throne of his glory, wishes to thunder at us and to hurl his mandates as if from on high, and wishes to pass judgments on—yea, rule over—us and our churches without our counsel but on his own authority alone and for his own good pleasure, what fraternity or even paternity is there in this? Who would ever be able to resign himself to supporting this? Truly, we would then be called—would be!—slaves of the church, not sons.[298]

Surely, he says, Rome could use assistance with her labors in the vineyard of the Lord and would do better not to condemn her brothers, since "it is not ascertained by any creed that we are especially commanded to acknowledge the Roman church; we are rather everywhere taught to confess one holy, catholic and apostolic church." Nicetas will honor the Roman church along with Anselm, "but I will not follow all things along with you, nor do I think it necessary that all things be followed in common."[299] This is where Anselm the debater's defense of papal primacy has led.

Nicetas began his speech by saying that as he had listened to Anselm, so charity required Anselm to listen to him. However, Anselm the debater is now portrayed as interrupting Nicetas with the hope that this will not offend the archbishop's charity.[300] An interruption is necessary, says the Latin, in order to spare the Greek from adding to his numerous "inept ironies against the Roman church." It is difficult to construe Nicetas' temperate and conciliatory speech as

---

[298] *Antik.* 3.8, 1219C.

[299] *Antik.* 3.8, 1220AB.

[300] Nicetas' last comment could easily stand as the end of his speech. Anselm the writer is thus under no constraint to have Anselm the debater "interrupt" the Greek. This points to a conscious desire of the writer to have his debater appear to demonstrate a lack of the charity Nicetas has requested.

inept.[301] If this were Anselm the writer's purpose, surely he would have placed an insult or two in the mouth of Nicetas to justify Anselm the debater's interruption. On the contrary, Nicetas appears at pains constantly to reaffirm his belief in Rome's primacy. As it stands, it is the interrupting Anselm who comes across as not only uncompromising but willing to take advantage of Nicetas for conceding to Rome any sort of primacy at all. If Nicetas is willing to recognize Roman spirituality, sincerity, equanimity, etc., then, Anselm tells him, he should be running to accept Rome's ways.[302] This obtuse lack of understanding for Nicetas' fears serves only to highlight them. In Nicetas' speech, Anselm the writer has presented those fears eloquently and pointed to common ground on which to fashion a compromise. That he does not have Anselm the debater join Nicetas on that middle ground indicates a more far reaching purpose to the debates than to construct arguments which would prove the Greeks wrong. Anselm the writer is moving down a more subtle path. Neither of his debaters is a caricature of meek submission or fanatic commitment; both are honestly devout. On the subject of papal authority, Anselm the debater is aggressive, uncompromising, and insulting, and he maintains what for Anselm's readers would be the correct position. Nicetas is moderate, polite, and willing to stake out common ground. Anselm the writer presents these men to those readers of De una forma credendi who have learned to accept a variety of forms of worship and the importance of diversity for the unity of the faithful. His brilliant portrayal of Nicetas as a man of conviction standing above the sly word games of his Latin counterpart serves to draw a distinction between the man and his cause and opens up the possibility that the former might be embraced even if the latter cannot be completely accepted. This is to say that Anselm the writer is humbly attempting to move his audience to see in Nicetas a man who is good because he is good.

Unlike his behavior in the debate on the *Filioque*, Nicetas does not deliver brief comments or ask questions that simply allow the Latin to clarify his position and lead the Greek into making concessions. In speeches of like length to Anselm's, the archbishop makes the impli-

---

[301] Russell says Nicetas presents his case "in courteous and moderate terms," "Anselm of Havelberg and the Union of the Churches," p. 112.

[302] *Antik.* 3.9, 1220CD.

cations of the Latin position clear.[303] Thus when Anselm the debater tries to demonstrate papal power by giving an example of a pope taking precedence over a council,[304] Nicetas says the Latin appears to be suggesting that Christ gave the power to bind and loose to Peter alone and that the Holy Spirit descended only to Peter at Pentecost; and then he cites Scripture to prove otherwise.[305] This shifts the discussion from Peter's successors to Peter himself, and Anselm the debater's response is for the most part a thorough-going defense of this apostle as having been specially favored by Jesus and holding a unique position among the twelve in guiding the new church. He constructs a line of authority in which the Roman pontiff alone holds the place of Christ by taking the place of Peter; the rest of the bishops take the place of the apostles under Christ and thus under Peter. Since the pope stands in Peter's place, the other bishops are subordinated to the pope.[306]

While this may appear to show a commitment to a monarchical kind of papal primacy, Anselm the writer has placed this argument between introductory and concluding remarks that mitigate its force. The debater begins by conceding that Nicetas is right: The Holy Spirit did descend on all of the apostles, and Christ did give power over sin to them all. And he concludes by telling Nicetas: "Nor in this is there anything at all derogatory to any of the apostles if each one is humbly assigned his proper office."[307] These comments are far removed from Anselm's earlier attack on the Greeks. Anselm the writer has created an ambiguity about Peter's authority through Nicetas' scriptural citations concerning the authority of all of the apostles and the Latin's admission that the Greek is correct. And when the Greek ends this part of the discussion by saying, "It may well be as you say," he leaves the issue open-ended, allowing room for future discussion that earlier appeared impossible to find.[308]

---

[303] See the comments of Steven Runciman, *The Eastern Schism: A Study of the Papacy and the Eastern Churches during the XIth and XIIth Centuries* (Oxford, 1955), p. 115.

[304] *Antik.* 3.9, 1221A. The example is Leo I and the Council of Chalcedon.

[305] *Antik.* 3.9, 1221BD.

[306] *Antik.* 3.10, 1223A.

[307] *Antik.* 3.10, 1222A, 1223A.

[308] *Antik.* 3.11, 1223B. On the ambiguity in Anselm the debater's comments see the trenchant remarks of Richard Kay, *Dante's Swift and Strong: Essays on Inferno XV* (Lawrence, Ks., 1978), pp. 130-31.

d. *Church councils and popes*

The debate now moves to the pivotal issue involved in a possible future church council: the role of the pope at such a gathering. Nicetas first establishes that councils have functioned without the participation of a pope. Conceding that the East was at one time full of heresies, he points out that these were destroyed because of the work of church councils. Anselm the writer has already written about these councils in his first book, describing them as the third state of the church. That earlier description is linked to Nicetas' speech both by the use of similar words and phrases[309] and by having Nicetas say that the councils were held "for strengthening the faith and the unity of all churches," a phrase that captures the thrust not only of the third state but of *De una forma credendi* as a whole. And if this were not enough to bring the description of the third state to the mind of the reader, Nicetas evokes the idea of the church growing through its combat with heresy "more and more in the knowledge [*scientia*] of Scripture," a distinct echo of the church of the third state growing in wisdom (*sapientia*).[310] Nicetas wryly concludes by suggesting why heresy was not the great problem in the West that it was in the East: "Perhaps in Rome...there just were not the subtle, wise men and investigators of Scripture that there are among us."[311] It is his single uncharitable comment about the Latins, and even it appears more amusing than mean-spirited. Moreover, it echoes Anselm's own concern that men of learning lead the western church.[312]

There is one more very important similarity between Nicetas' words and Anselm's description of the third state of the church: In neither is there a reference to papal participation in the great church councils. However committed to papal primacy Anselm the debater appears to be, Anselm the writer has evoked his own earlier descrip-

---

[309] Cf. *Antik*. 1.9, 1152AB with 3.11, 1223B-24B. In the former there were "celebrata multa concilia congruis in locis et temporibus," in the latter, "per diversa loca diversis temporibus...multa concilia celebravit;" in the former "fides orthodoxa post tot impulsiones adeo est roborata," in the latter, "Majus robur fidei post exstinctas haereses acceperit;" in the former "a sanctis Patribus convenienter inhibitum est ut de caetero nemo disputet publice de fide," in the latter "a sanctis Patribus inhibitum sit, quod nemo amplius de fide publice disputare audeat."

[310] *Antik*. 3.11, 1224A: "Ecclesia Dei occasione haeresum magis ac magis in scientia Scripturarum creverit." Cf. 1.9, 1152B: "Ecclesia crevit mirabili contra haereticos sapientia."

[311] *Antik*. 3.19, 1224C.

[312] See pp. 82-83 above.

tion of the state of the councils that makes not a single reference to the papacy or to Rome. This, it may be suggested, must inevitably mitigate the force of his namesake's reply.

The ensuing discussion brings in the use of historical evidence to determine the role of the pope. After arguing that there can logically be but one head of the church,[313] Anselm the debater attempts to demonstrate that Roman bishops had, in fact, guided earlier councils. Using the *Liber pontificalis*, he gives historical evidence to that effect.[314] This argument from historical example is one we have seen Anselm use often. It is therefore striking that the writer has Nicetas immediately cut the ground out from under the debater's evidence by pointing out that there are documents in the archive of the Hagia Sophia relating the deeds of the Roman bishops and the acts of the councils. He can find nothing among them suggesting that Roman pontiffs or their legates had any authority in a church council except in so far as they acted in concert with the other bishops. If Anselm the debater has the evidence, then,

> You tell me, I beseech you, which of the Roman pontiffs decreed that it is necessary to use unleavened bread in the sacrifice of the altar in such a way that necessity should demand that we be compelled to accept it, and should we not accept it, that we would be subject to just damnation.[315]

Also relying on the *Liber pontificalis*, Nicetas proceeds to give the specific examples of popes Miltiades (311-314) and Siricius (384-399) as men who did decree the use of leaven for the Host,[316] saying, "If the

---

[313] *Antik.* 3.12, 1226A.

[314] *Antik.* 3.12, 1226-28 dealing with various popes and deriving from the *Liber pontificalis*: 1.34, pp. 170-71 with the *Epistola vel praefatio Niceni concilii*, *Decretales Pseudo-Isidorianae*, pp. 254-55 (Silvester I); 1.42, p. 220 (Innocent I); 1.47, p. 238 with the *Synodus Chalcedonensis*, *Decretales Pseudo-Isidorianae*, pp. 287-88 (Leo I); 1.50, p. 252 (Felix III); 1.51, p. 255 (Gelesius I); 1.59, p. 287 (Agapitus); 1.75, pp. 331-32 (Theodore); 1.76, pp. 336-37 (Martin I); 1.80, p. 348 (Donus); 1.81, pp. 350-54 (Agathos). See also Sieben, *Die Konzilsidee*, p. 158.

[315] *Antik.* 3.12, 1228D.

[316] *Antik.* 3.13, 1229; cf. the *Liber pontificalis* 1.33, p. 168; 1.40, p. 216. It should be noted that before Nicetas presents this evidence, Anselm the debater is designated in the Migne edition (1228D-29A) as saying of the contention that popes held sway over councils, "Fateor ego in ecclesiasticis libris qui apud nos sunt, nusquam scriptum inveni." The manuscripts do not support this, giving Nicetas as the speaker (Mun. fol. 51v; Wolf. 1, fol. 136v; as well as the manuscript(s) used for Migne, see col. 1228 n. 36). It is possible to read "fateor" with a sense of irony and thus leave the words in Nicetas' mouth. On the other hand, the next clear statement of Anselm (3.15, 1232A) does not mention Nicetas' discussion of church councils at all, suggesting that

authority of the Roman pontiffs seems to you to be sufficient for opposing me, it should also be sufficient for me in opposing you."[317]

Nicetas does not argue that Greek practice should be followed everywhere, but that the issue is one of custom. He expresses disbelief that the Greek popes of earlier times spent their days arguing with their Latin subjects about different kinds of bread, and he points to Greek congregations of monks in or near Rome who still use leavened bread with no scandal to Latins or to the pope—evidence Anselm the writer would have known firsthand from his trips to Italy.[318] Nicetas gives his own history of the church, using the issue of the bread of the Host to draw a temporal line between a unified church and one rent into eastern and western parts. From the time of the apostles to Charlemagne, he says, East and West were united. The apostles made no issue of the bread of the altar but used whatever came to hand as they traveled from province to province. From this the custom of using unleavened bread developed in the West, that of using leavened in the East. Even if Christians were not uniform in their choice of Host, "nevertheless in mutual peace and fraternal charity, they faithfully loved and supported one another in Christ, and if mutual agreement should fail, they celebrated a council together whenever it was opportune." Only with the Frankish invasion of the Roman Empire and Charlemagne did religious and political divisions appear between East and West.[319]

Nicetas ends his speech by reminding Anselm of the continued presence of Greek ideas in the Latin church in such words as patriarch and metropolitan. This is not hurled pretentiously at the Latin debater but given as an indication that the church is, indeed, one. Here again the view of Anselm the writer comes clear, for in his litany written at the behest of the archbishop of Magdeburg around the same time as the *Antikeimenon*, he stresses the use of the Greek *Kyrie Eleison* as a means of demonstrating the unity of the church.[320]

"Fateor..." is meant to be Anselm the debater's response. But whether Nicetas or Anselm the debater is supposed to say these words, they come from Anselm the writer who gives no evidence from either side to refute them.

[317] *Antik.* 3.13, 1229A.

[318] *Antik.* 3.13, 1229B-30B. The monasteries referred to are St. Caesarius in Rome and Grottaferrata outside of Rome.

[319] *Antik.* 3.14, 1230D. For Nicetas' discussion of Charlemagne and the division of the empire, see pp. 271-73 below.

[320] See p. 91 above.

It is in light of Nicetas' expression of the writer's ideas, that Anselm the debater's response needs to be read. There, the Latin is reduced to pursuing a contorted path around Nicetas' evidence which is less than satisfying given his uncompromising commitment to papal primacy. He says that Miltiades and Siricius were only two early popes out of many, that the church has developed since then, and that the authority of the majority rules. The debater buttresses this argument by asking Nicetas to consider the fact that at times a church synod may "loosen" (*solvit*) the pronouncements of another synod for the sake of better reasoning, necessity, utility, or temporal conditions, and this on account of the "keys [*claves*] of discretion and power" which God has committed to those who make up the synod.[321] The use of the words *claves* and *solvit* cannot but conjure up the apostolic power of loosening and binding claimed by the pope. Anselm the debater has drawn a parallel between papal and synodal power: A pope can change what was affirmed by an earlier pope as a synod can change the affirmation of an earlier synod, which leaves the door open to the possibility that a church council can function in the same way.

Most noteworthy in assessing Anselm the writer's presentation of papal authority is that by having the debater say that the decisions of a majority of the popes outweigh that of the two Nicetas has shown to have sided with the Greeks, the reader cannot but expect the Latin debater to produce clear, pro-Latin pronouncements on the bread of the Host by at least three popes since Miltiades and Siricius. However, Anselm does not (cannot!) produce a single one. Rather Anselm the debater suggests (*puto*) that Miltiades and Siricius may have been talking not about the Eucharist but about bread that had been blessed but not consecrated (*eulogia*). This technical if important point can only be suggested, perhaps as the grist for further discussion. As Anselm must have known full well, his source for the papal decrees, the *Liber pontificalis*, is at best not clear and would, in fact, appear to support the Greek position.[322] The significant point to be made here is that Anselm the writer has chosen to place his entire discussion of papal primacy within the framework of an issue on which the only papal statements to be found support the Greeks.[323] The Latin de-

---

[321] *Antik.* 3.15, 1232AC.

[322] *Antik.* 3.15, 1232; *Liber pontificalis*, 1.33, 40, pp. 74-75, 216-217.

[323] Nicetas later reiterates this point, *Antik.* 3.16, 1234C.

bater, who starts out uncharitably condemning Constantinople and touting the monarchical authority of the pope, ends up trying to argue his way around papal pronouncements.

Not only is Anselm the writer showing that further clarification is necessary for establishing what bread to use in the mass, but he has his Latin debater admit that Nicetas may be right. Perhaps, the kind of bread does not matter:

> What you have said about the concord of ancient wise men, Latins and Greeks, to whom, as you assert, there was no scandal in offering either unleavened or leavened bread, certainly this thing which you say does not displease me.

Nevertheless, he says—and this almost in response to the contention that Latins or Greeks were defending what was their own rather than what was true, it is not for him to make such decisions but for his betters, adding, "especially the Roman pontiffs." This amounts to a call for further discussion between the pope and others.[324]

The end of Anselm the debater's speech is another attempt to defend Rome's right to lead the church, but it is as if he has run out of substantive things to say about the popes. Nicetas expresses just this with a curt response: "Enough has been said on both sides about the authority of the Roman church." The Greek then moves the discussion back to the bread of the Host.[325]

The debate now proceeds in much the same direction as the earlier one on the *Filioque*, which is to say toward Nicetas' qualified acceptance of the Latin position. Anselm the debater quotes passages which play on his earlier association of heresy with leaven by condemning *fermentum*, such as: "Beware of the leaven of the Pharisees, which is hypocrisy" (Luke 12:1).[326] That the cautious Nicetas begins to show some willingness to concede the strength of the Latin position and the weakness of his own must, however, be placed in the context of the entire debate to this point rather than seen to depend solely on Anselm the debater's use of Scripture critical of *fermentum*. Anselm the writer has carefully brought Nicetas to this point by edging the two debaters away from making the Greek's concessions hinge on an acceptance of papal leadership of the eastern church. Moreover, Anselm the debater has shown himself open to Nicetas'

---

[324] *Antik.* 3.15, 1232D.

[325] *Antik.* 3.16, 1234B.

[326] *Antik.* 3.17-18, 1237-38. Anselm also cites Matt. 16:6; Mark 8:15; I Cor. 5:7.

feeling that conformity in the matter of the bread of the Host may not be particularly important.

The first debate ended with the desire for a church council, and in the second debate Anselm the writer could have had his Greek and Latin immediately pursue the idea of a conciliar statement on differences of ritual practice. But it is only after both sides have made some concessions and after the presentation of conflicting views reveals mutual uncertainty, that Nicetas again suggests that a general council might decide the issue of the bread of the Host.[327] Nicetas prefaces this suggestion with an image of the dichotomy between discord and harmony, an image that captures the message of the entire *Antikeimenon*. He says that while God is offended by sinful discord, so he is "appeased by the truly wholesome Host made perfect by devotion." Discord "sharply blames that people may be condemned." This disharmony is what Anselm's critics had been guilty of, and like the hypocrites of the fourth and present state, those guilty of discord are on a path that, as Nicetas says, "leads to hell." "[Discord] provokes God the judge by offending Him; [the Host] appeals to the kind God by appeasing Him.... Through the former we are alienated from God, through the latter we are made one with God." While Nicetas focuses on the bread of the Host, his message is that variety cannot be allowed to undermine "a unity of love": "For clearly, when that love is absent, all other good things are possessed in vain, and when present, things that are good are not lightly held."[328] Were there to be a council, Nicetas says that this would be his message even to the pope. One can safely say that this is also Anselm the writer's message to his readers.

e. *The two emperors*

Nicetas goes on to speak of the possibility of a council, and he says it should be one called by "the pious emperors," which can only mean

---

[327] *Antik.* 3.19, 1239CD.

[328] *Antik.* 3.19, 1240CD: "Discordia autem tanquam peccato plena Deus offenditur; hostia vero salutari tanquam devotione perfecta Deus placatur. Illa damnandos acriter accusat, ista salvandos salubriter excusat. Illa Deum judicem offendendo provocat, ista Deum pium propitiando placat. Illa in tartara, ista mittit ad supera. Per illam a Deo alienamur, per istam Deo incorporamur. Per illam terreni, per istam coelestes efficimur." This passage has the ring of Anselm's letter to Wibald probably written around the same time and in which Anselm compares life in Havelberg to life at court: "Christus in presepio, Christus in pretorio; aliter ibi, aliter ibi," etc. See p. 89 above.

the two emperors, East and West.[329] What was Anselm's reader to make of this? Earlier, Nicetas had criticized Charlemagne for splitting the empire, yet now the archbishop is portrayed as seeing a chance for unity in a council called by the two emperors, both of whom he appears willing to recognize. To understand this apparent turnabout, we must look back to his discussion of Charlemagne and digress somewhat from the theme of East-West unity. For in Nicetas' words, Anselm confronts his reader not only with the historical division of the empire but with the contemporary possibility of a renewed outbreak of the struggle between the pope and the German ruler in the West.

What is startling about Nicetas' earlier speech is that he does not use Charlemagne's imperial coronation as the cause of the division of the empire. The division was created, he says, by Charlemagne's invasion of Rome and claim to the title "protector of the city of Rome" (*patricius Romanae urbis*). This is curious, indeed. Charlemagne as western emperor would have indicated a clear-cut division between East and West;[330] Charlemagne as *patricius Romanae urbis* does not make the division clear at all. Nicetas even has this title strangely wrong. Long before Charlemagne's imperial coronation, he bore the title "protector of the Romans" (*patricius Romanorum*). Neither this nor the title really significant to Nicetas' apparent point, namely *imperator*, is mentioned.[331] What Nicetas' speech accomplishes is to focus Anselm's audience squarely on the city of Rome rather than on either the empire or on the vague notion of "the Romans." And at the time Anselm the writer penned these words, a "protector of the city of Rome" was an immediate and dangerous possibility.

Nicetas refers to Charlemagne as *rex Francorum*. When Anselm was exiled to Havelberg, Conrad III, king not emperor, had entered into negotiations with the Roman commune concerning the possibility that he would defend Rome against the pope. While both pope and commune offered to crown Conrad emperor, only the pope had a clear right to do so. Conrad's choice was either to aid the pope and become emperor in the usual way or to become Rome's protector. Nicetas points to Charlemagne as the cause of "scandal and schism"

---

[329] *Antik.* 3.19, 1240D.

[330] So much so that scholars assume that this is what Anselm is saying; e.g. Spiteris, "Attitudes fondamentales," pp. 177-78.

[331] *Antik.* 3.14, 1231A.

between Greeks and Latins. It is a charge to which Anselm the debater does not respond, a sign that the writer wants to leave his
readers with a sense of Latin complicity in the problems between
East and West. Beyond this, however, "scandal and schism" is undoubtedly what Anselm thought would ensue in the West should
Conrad accept Rome's bribe. Nicetas' speech thus both attacks Latins as responsible for the East-West schism and warns against a Latin
schism as well.

When Nicetas later makes his suggestion that a church council
should be called by the two emperors, it would have been apparent
to Anselm's Latin reader that Latin Christendom could not act on
Nicetas' offer. There was no emperor in the West, Conrad III not
having been crowned by the pope. The possibility of unity with the
East depended on establishing good relations between the German
ruler and the pope without which there would be no western emperor. It is clear why Anselm the writer has Nicetas criticize Charlemagne for taking the title *patricius* rather than *imperator*: Conrad as
patricius, i.e. allying with the Roman commune, threatened Christian
unity, whereas Conrad as *imperator* furthered it. For a king to become
an emperor is not criticized; for him to become Rome's protector
leads to disaster. Anselm's was a message of more than academic
value, for his brothers had a far better chance of influencing their
king than they did of playing a role in negotiations with the East.

f. *The perfect pope*
While the emperors' part in a future council is briefly touched on by
Nicetas, that of the pope remains central; and when he returns to the
issue of the papacy, Nicetas rather than Anselm the debater tries to
define the role of a pope at a council. But behind Nicetas is Anselm
the writer expressing what he thinks it will require for a pope to win
over those not yet willing to follow Rome's unqualified leadership of
a united Christendom. The relationship of the pope to the council
should be that of Peter to Paul. The pope, says Nicetas, should listen
to him, that is to the Greeks, as Peter was willing to listen to and take
advice from Paul. Nicetas admits to being very much the inferior of
Paul, but the Roman pope "ought not to be inferior to Peter." Anselm the writer then has his Greek portray the ideal man needed on
the chair of St. Peter:

> Certainly it could happen that the Roman pontiff, having become all
> things to all people, a Latin to the Latins, a Greek to the Greeks, could

enlighten them all, and by the humble authority of the Apostolic See, bring together the things over which we dispute, either by completely abolishing one interpretation and instituting the other as universal custom, or abolishing the scandal of both by establishing without bias that both of them be allowed.

This is a tremendous concession to the Latins, but Anselm the debater's response is as curt as Nicetas' was on the authority of Rome: "It appears that enough has been said concerning this question." He moves the discussion to an entirely new subject.[332]

Is this because Anselm the writer is pessimistic about a pope's ability to fit Nicetas' description? Or does he feel that having described his perfect pope he can do no more? Whatever it may be, Anselm the writer's view of the papacy is certainly not that the vicar of St. Peter can or should rule by fiat but that he must act as a Peter among Pauls, a bishop among bishops, whose ability to settle divisive issues depends on the combination of authority and personal charisma that moves the disputants to look to him for non-partisan judgments.

Nicetas' ideal is one Anselm would apply to more than the pope. It is the image of the man who holds the middle ground and has an office which gives him the power to act. Because he is good, opposing sides come together in him. It is the image of Norbert of Magdeburg in his dealings with secular and ecclesiastical leaders; it is the image of what Anselm wanted his brothers to reflect, and it is the image of what Anselm himself wanted to present: all things to all people, the perfect diplomat, the perfect negotiator, the perfect peacemaker, the man who is good because he is good. It is a description of Paul, not the Paul whom Anselm divided into contrary apostolic and monastic lives in the *Epistola*, but a complete Paul. For Nicetas' description of the perfect pope is a reworking of a passage of Paul's First Letter to the Corinthians (9:20-23):

> To the Jews I became as a Jew, in order to win Jews; to those under the law I became as one under the law...that I might win those under the law...I have become all things to all men, that I might at all costs save some [9:20-23].

This is what Anselm the writer has tried to do in the debates, become all things to all men: a Latin to the Latins and a Greek to the Greeks,

---

[332] *Antik.* 3.19, 1241B.

and he has played both parts as fairly as he is able. This is his imitation of Christ, the Christ who moves things toward perfection with God who, in the end of time, as Anselm said in the first book of the *Antikeimenon*, "will be all things to all men."[333]

g. *Eucharistic wine and the unity of the church*

In the final portion of this second debate, Anselm the writer addresses two more issues: the Greek custom of consecrating the wine of the altar before mixing it with water versus the Latin custom of consecrating a mixture of wine and water, and the Latin suspicion that the Greeks practice a form of rebaptism. These issues should not be seen as two relatively unimportant items which Anselm has relegated to quick dismissal as he brings the debate to a close. For Anselm ends the *Antikeimenon* with the end of the debate, and the chapters dealing with these issues constitute his conclusion to his entire work.

In moving from the Host to the wine of the altar, the debaters again face the problem that Scripture gives no clear indication of whether wine alone or wine and water were used by Christ at the Last Supper. Each debater begins by defending his position with rather academic arguments, Nicetas insisting that the Gospels say Christ used wine and Anselm countering by referring to the Jewish custom of using wine mixed with water.[334] However, Anselm's defense of consecrating the mixture of wine and water quickly draws in ideas from *De una forma credendi* and becomes an expression of his overriding concern for a unified church.

From the scriptural description of water flowing with the blood from Christ's side at the crucifixion (John 19:34), Anselm fashions an image of the church of the faithful. The water is "the people who are saved in the communion of the same blood of the new and eternal Testament." It is "the one body of the church with its head who is Christ" that is offered in the mixture of wine and water.[335] *De una forma credendi* has presented the idea of an imitation of Jesus who presents the *una facies* of the church, the image toward which and within which the community of Christians develops by continually renewing that image. By consecrating a mixture of wine and water,

---

[333] *Antik.* 1.7, 1149BC; see also *Antik.* 1. 13, 1160C.
[334] *Antik.* 3.20, 1241CD.
[335] *Antik.* 3.20, 1242B.

Christ and the faithful are unified. To do otherwise, is to risk separating the head from the members and thus "to remove Christ and church from our midst and to confound everything."[336] The debater had shown himself open to the possibility that the bread of the Host may be treated as a matter of custom. In contrast, the wine and water of the mass embrace for him the mystery of the unity of Christ and the faithful in the church. The mixture of wine and water is a "liquid of purification and renovation" which brings grace to the sinner, who "is renewed again from day to day."[337] For Anselm this mystery of unity, the mystery that stands at the heart of his entire work, is captured by using diluted wine, lost by using wine alone.

When Nicetas responds that he has no intention of dividing head from body and can present many rational arguments to defend Greek practice, Anselm the debater cuts him off with some impatience by pointing to the danger inherent in this constant recourse to reason, namely that it can have no end. "Always to respond by always rebutting leads on infinitely," the debater tells Nicetas. On this issue, Anselm will not compromise at all: "I know and do not doubt that I have spoken the truth." However, what is striking about the Latin debater's attempt to stop the discussion at this point is how much of it both contradicts what he has already said and would fit better in the mouth of Nicetas. In his prologue, Anselm said that Latins do not fully understand Greek beliefs; and in the beginning of the first debate, he requested that he and Nicetas concentrate on the sense of what is said rather than on the definitions of words. Now, however, he criticizes Nicetas' subtle eloquence in concocting new defenses of the Greek position. To the Greek he says:

> But in something like this, modest and sober wisdom, for which the terms [*termini*] written by the Holy Fathers suffice, is more to be recommended than cunning sagacity [*prudentia*] excessively searching beyond its limits [*supra modum*] and trying to extend itself beyond itself and beyond the terms [*supra terminos*] of the Holy Fathers.[338]

In this passage, with its play between *termini* and *modum* and swipe at Nicetas whose *prudentia* has so often cautioned him to stay precisely within the limits of what Scripture and councils say, Anselm is being slyly eloquent about telling Nicetas to beware of eloquence. More-

---

[336] *Antik.* 3.20, 1242BC, 1243AB.
[337] *Antik.* 3.20, 1243CD.
[338] *Antik.* 3.20, 1244CD.

over, he is suggesting that the written words of the Fathers are in
need of no emendation, exactly what Nicetas has been arguing. It is
Anselm the debater who had earlier ventured the view that what
Scripture and councils do not make clear may be further probed. Yet
here, the debater not only takes his stand on the side of the clarity of
truth but does so in such a way as to evoke the critics addressed in *De
una forma credendi* and their aversion to change: The Scriptures speak
of water and blood coming from Christ's side and "we know and
believe without doubt in the witness of the Gospel." For this reason,
the wine and water are mixed before consecration, "and for us it is
sufficient that the form of the passion of Christ be imitated, because
we do not wish to be ensnared [*impediri*] by some new inventions."
Here is the voice of the critics of change to whom *De una forma credendi*
was addressed, the ones to whom Anselm said they ought not "to
turn their foot [*pedem*] from some [new] religious society."[339] Yet here,
Anselm is using those critics' position to defend Latin practice.

There is a magic quality to this short speech. A critic of change
and novelty can read it as a commitment to a faith long since revealed and as being adverse to change; a Greek can take heart in its
reliance on the plain sense of Scripture; a Latin can see it as a defense
of Latin practice. And Anselm of Havelberg ties what he writes directly to the cherished imitation of Jesus that he has championed in
the *Epistola apologetica* and *De una forma credendi*:

> Moreover, whatever we do in this [i.e. the consecration of wine and
> water] as in other ecclesiastical sacraments, either we do according to
> the figure which preceded or according to the truth which appears in
> Christ, and we deem nothing to come from us but all from God, who
> sacramentally and truly sanctifies all things.[340]

Within the frame of his literary construct, Anselm the writer is not
only Anselm the Latin debater but he has become his critics and
Nicetas the Greek, as well. And in doing this, he is himself the man
devoted to imitating Jesus Who is all things to all people. All this in
a passage which begins with a caveat about manipulating words.

Nicetas responds positively by praising Anselm and comparing
(very eloquently, one may say) the unified church of Greeks and
Latins to the grains of wheat in the Host, whether leavened or un-

---

[339] *Antik.* 1.13, 1160C.
[340] *Antik.* 3.20, 1244D-45A.

leavened, or the bunches of grapes pressed for the wine; and he again calls for a church council to continue the discussion. He balances Anselm the debater's commitment to Latin ritual by saying that whatever differences the two groups of people may have, "a dangerous contention ought to be feared both by us and by you more than a different custom of the same sacramental offering."[341] Nicetas expresses here the overriding concern of Anselm the writer that the debaters avoid contention while yet discussing the issues that divide them, and it should be noted that it is again the Greek who most clearly sends this message, thus drawing Latin readers toward him rather than repelling them.

h. *Rebaptism: the end of the* Antikeimenon

It has been Anselm's goal to bring the two men together. With every issue they have debated, the line dividing them has perforce remained. It is in this context that the last of the issues they address should be seen. That issue is the Latin concern that the Greeks practice a form of rebaptism.

Anselm the debater asks whether the Greek custom of pouring sanctified oil over a Latin woman before she marries a Greek is a form of rebaptism. He does not, however, give Nicetas a chance to answer but launches into a fairly lengthy attack on rebaptism, showing it to be heretical and giving examples of popes who have opposed it.[342] Nicetas' response is to the point:

> If the Latins would acquaint themselves anew with Greek rites, they would not malign them as being so superficial, nor be so easily offended by them.

It is Latin ignorance that has caused the problem, he says, precisely the point Anselm the writer made in the prologue to his work.[343] Nicetas goes on to show as much abhorrence of rebaptism as Anselm,

---

[341] *Antik.* 3.20, 1245BC; Mun., fol. 60v; Wolf. 1, fol. 162r: "Et sicut ex multis purissimi frumenti granis tam azyma quam fermentata hostia conficitur, et sicut ex multis uvis in unum collectis vinum expressum colligitur; ita ex multis tam Graecorum quam Latinorum turbis una et concors, et id ipsum sentiens constituatur Ecclesia, ne vel nobis vestrum azyma, vel vobis nostrum fermentum in die Domini fiat damnationis judicium, dum altrinsecus inde surgimus in contentionem quod utrisque institutum est ad salutem. Magis enim tam nobis quam vobis timenda est periculosa contentio, quam ejusdem oblationis [Migne: obligationis] diversa consuetudo."
[342] *Antik.* 3.21, 1245C-46D.
[343] *Antik.* 3.21, 1246D-47A. Cf. *Antik.* prologue, 1141A.

saying that neither is sanctification with oil to be equated with baptism, nor is this rite or baptism itself ever repeated where it is known to have already been performed.[344]

In this exchange, Anselm the writer has Anselm the debater ask the question about rebaptism but then turn it into an accusation by not allowing Nicetas a chance to refute the charge. Anselm the writer has nicely, and at the cost of his namesake and the Latins he represents, portrayed that assault as very learned only to have Nicetas show that its foundation is one of ignorance. Ignorance dispelled, there is no line between Greek and Latin.

Anselm the writer's choice of rebaptism as the last issue to be discussed is, thus, a conscious one, allowing him to bring his debate to a close with an affirmation of the unity of the church; and it is, perhaps, significant that by expressing his wish that Latins would acquaint themselves "with Greek rites" rather than "with the Greek rites of sanctification and baptism," Nicetas tacitly gives the sense that Latins have still more to learn. "Thanks be to God," Anselm the debater exclaims,

> who has cleared this dissension away from me and spared me from dealing the Christian name a reproach which until now I have suspected of the very wise Greek people.[345]

While obviously Anselm cannot solve the problems of the *Filioque*, the place of the papacy in the church, or the Eucharist, within the parameters of his literary construct, he has left his readers with a sense of the possibility of finding solutions. The issue of rebaptism allows him to end where he began by making this optimism abundantly clear and minimizing the differences that remain. Nicetas declares his happiness that the faith and rites of the Greeks might please Anselm the debater and says: "Truly, we seem to differ not in the great things but in the smallest." The problem caused by these differences is not that Latins or Greeks risk their salvation by not adopting the other's beliefs or customs, but that the differences "do not build charity."[346] It is Nicetas who gives expression to this sentiment rather than Anselm the debater, who makes no such remarkable concession about Latin beliefs and ritual. This makes an offer out of Nicetas' call for a

---

[344] *Antik.* 3.21, 1247AB. Though not named by Nicetas, he is referring to the Greek rite of "chrismation," the Eastern equivalent of the Western confirmation.

[345] *Antik.* 3.22, 1247B.

[346] *Antik.* 3.22, 1247B-48A.

church council to form from Greeks and Latins "one people under
one Lord Jesus Christ, in one faith, in one baptism, in one ritual of
sacraments." Here, at the end of the debate we have come full circle
once again from peace to dissension and back to peace. We are also
back at the beginning of *De una forma credendi* and the critics' cry for
the unity of the faithful. That unity is offered in the council Nicetas
proposes. It is Anselm the writer's Latin readers who must accept or
reject it.

Anselm—and here it is safe to drop the writer/debater distinction—shows great hopes for such a council. He draws a final line. On
the one side stand those who follow the path of heretics and "seek out
corners and hiding places"—perhaps an echo of the critics at the
beginning of *De una forma credendi* who sigh for a place to rest their
heads and of the earlier Nicetas looking for tranquility on the bed of
authority. On the other side of this line are those who, along with the
debaters, desire a universal council.

Anselm says that to speak at such a council will be to speak "before
the face of the whole church." Here he brings in the word *facies*
which was so important in his first book. Jesus is the *una facies* of the
church; the council is the *facies totius Ecclesiae*. While Anselm does not
explicitly draw the two together (though Nicetas has called for "one
people under one Lord Jesus Christ"), the latter can only be possible
if those attending the council imitate Jesus, which is to say the body
must be coordinated with the head—the point of the discussion over
the wine and water of the Eucharist. Anselm's closing remarks can be
read superficially as the Latin debater's polite hope that Nicetas will
be able to attend and speak at such a council. However, it is not the
two men to whom Anselm refers but rather to certain qualities they
posses, the qualities which can project such a council into reality and
the qualities necessary for its success. The hope expressed is not that
Nicetas will attend the council but that his wisdom, eloquence, sanctity, maturity, discretion, consideration, moderation, spirituality, con-
stancy, piety, and perfection will be there. These qualities will make
the council a success. And it is not Anselm who hopes for this but his
humility, insignificance, smallness, devotion, good will, and longing.
The debaters are the models of the qualities necessary to move the
council into being.[347] When the crowd of onlookers declares its ap-

---

[347] *Antik.* 3.22, 1248AB.

proval, it comes together with Anselm's readers from whom he undoubtedly wished the same response.

It is, in fact, the crowd that ends both the debate and the *Antikeimenon* by shouting, *"Calos dialogos"*—"Beautiful dialogue." This would denote two sides speaking well with each other. But Anselm is writing for Latins, and he gives a Latin translation of the Greek which captures far better the intent of the *Antikeimenon*. In Latin, the crowd shouts, *"Bonus dualis sermo"*—"A good dual discourse." The sense is of two men giving a single speech which captures the good. The dividing line between them has disappeared.

Beyond this, Anselm has the crowd end the debate with a repeated shout of "Let it all be written down!"[348] And Anselm's *Antikeimenon* gives the impression that that is precisely what he has done for them —crowd and reader alike. One recalls Anselm the debater's earlier statement: "And it follows that through the same visible characters an invisible understanding is engendered in the soul of the reader."

---

[348] *Antik.* 3.22, 1248B

CONCLUSION

The quest for fresh forms of the spiritual life which swept western Europe in the eleventh and twelfth centuries produced new schools of thought concerning what kind of life was lived closest to God. While Anselm of Havelberg provides us with an example of a "court bishop" whose career can be reconstructed in some detail, the idea of such service was itself touched by the new spirituality. Anselm was a product of what, in the face of a rising interest in scholastic inquiry, was rapidly becoming a conservative program of education. This entailed training a student to assume a place in the clerical hierarchy as an adviser at royal and ecclesiastical courts. Its teachers wrote little but taught by presenting living models of how their students should behave in order to render such courtly service.

Anselm moved along the traditional court bishop's career path by taking an episcopal position and finding a place at the court of the German ruler. He also attached himself closely to Norbert, observing the archbishop serve as an advocate of peaceful understanding between popes and rulers in times of crisis. In doing this, Norbert brought his own brand of charismatic spirituality and the notion of the active court bishop nicely together.

Anselm himself was not so successful. With the death of Lothar III, fortune's wheel spun rapidly for him. The scope for his activities shrank to the virtually non-existent diocese of Havelberg and to trotting around in an auxiliary capacity for an archbishop other than his own. His attempts to ingratiate himself with Conrad III were lackluster, halting, and fairly ineffectual. With no secure position at Conrad's court, Anselm's activities focused on his diocese. There he worked cautiously to define his power as bishop in legal terms. While this allowed for an active clerical life, Anselm found himself ousted from court with little opportunity even to attempt taking on the peace-making role of a Norbert. His acceptance of the chance to reengage himself with court life at the accession of Frederick Barbarossa is a good indication that he aspired to more than a humble episcopal position. We should, however, be careful about ascribing this to crass personal ambition. Frederick reopened the possibility for Anselm to play precisely the role for which his education and apprenticeship under Norbert had prepared him. Moreover, in his writings, Anselm has given us a good idea of how he defined that role.

The misfortunes Anselm met in his attempts to attain the life to which he aspired are our gain. The *Epistola apologetica* and the *Antikeimenon* were produced in times of relative inactivity in Anselm's life, lacking which they may not have been written at all. These writings are, in essence, a twelfth-century attempt by someone who had chosen the active life to define what it meant for him and what he thought this active service should mean for those around him.

For Anselm, the church had been fashioned by God through the deeds of men, and Anselm relied on a biblical exegesis that emphasized Scripture as the history of action proceeding from faith. Anselm's writings are tied together by their author's concern with forming the deeds of the past into a model of the active clerical life. By showing how the differences in the expression of faith define periods of time, he could use the uniqueness of past times to make the present understandable. This consciousness of history is, however, anything but objective. For the model Anselm built out of the deeds of Old and New Testament figures and Christ Himself is the model Anselm saw in the present. He read back into the past the ideal court bishop as embodied by Norbert.

Anselm also demonstrates a complex consciousness of himself as model. The active life of the court bishop and of Norbert of Magdeburg required dealing with conflicting factions, either as a partisan or a peacemaker. In the *Epistola apologetica* and in both parts of the *Antikeimenon*, Anselm engages in debates with a variety of opponents: a Benedictine abbot, the critics of new religious orders, and a Greek archbishop. In all three cases, he attains a kind of victory. Thus in his writings, he grants himself the success that more often than not escaped him in his real life of clerical service. With his pen, Anselm could script the outcome.

In the *Epistola*, Anselm tried to make his case for the superiority of the canonical life with reasoned arguments rather than with himself as a model of that life. The paradox of the work is that in it he called for charity while demonstrating none. In the *Antikeimenon*'s *De una forma credendi*, on the other hand, he made every effort to show the critics that they stand with him on the common ground of faith and that he is not trying to argue them into a corner. And in the debates, he gave the Greek side a voice in order to show that the kind of argument he had tried in the *Epistola* does not work and to demonstrate that both he and his opponent can agree that their faith is one. Thus, if we compare the *Epistola* with the *Antikeimenon*, we find that Anselm has become self-conscious in the latter about the model he was projecting of himself, and it is that model which is the heart of the work.

Most intriguing is Anselm's presentation of the debates. In biblical history he found models of faith leading to the *una facies* of Christ; and in the history after Christ, models of wisdom and patience leading to the endurance demanded by the present age of hypocrisy. These latter qualities are seen in the debaters Anselm and Nicetas, who express their faith as people had done in the past and move toward understanding that their faith is one, even if their expression of it differs. Here the paradox is, of course, that Anselm has invented a moment of history. This entails a wonderful playfulness which should bring him much more attention from scholars of medieval literature. He has invented the harmony not to be found in his world and then validated his creation by encasing it in a historical setting. The setting is not only Constantinople, the Pisan quarter, on April 10, but also that of *De una forma credendi* and its impressive presentation of historical models of faith. The success of Anselm's creation goes well into modern times. Scholars dealing with Greek-Latin relations in the Middle Ages have repeatedly used Anselm's debates as evidence that a Greek and a Latin honestly and cordially tried to open the door to compromise.

There is little indication that Anselm's written work influenced contemporary writers. It may be suggested that the *Epistola apologetica* was too uncharitable to have found a permanent place among the readings of those dedicated to charity. The intricacy and integrity of the *Antikeimenon* was apparently missed. The account of the debates perhaps favored the Greeks too much to be used as a reference point for further discussions. Finally, Anselm's history was narrowly focused on the new religious orders which would rapidly become the old as engagement with the world became more clearly defined and defended by the Dominicans and the Franciscans. The work also demonstrated almost no concern with prophesying. By looking into the future, Joachim of Fiore's use of history would be far more fascinating and appealing than Anselm's could ever be.

For modern scholars, Anselm represents the generation of royal advisers that had witnessed the chaos of the Investiture Controversy from the sidelines. Their challenge was to put the pieces of Christendom back together. Anselm learned that the duty of a peacemaker was to control passionate fervor lest it tear the tunic of Christ; and the charisma he sought in his perfect pope was that of the man who could become all things to all people. He and men like Wibald of Stablo and Arnold of Wied cautiously tried to steer conflicting forces away from a renewed outbreak of divisive argumentation. When men like Anselm passed from the scene, it was Christendom's loss; divisions, not unity, were embraced.

Anselm is also an important as a representative of the intellectual developments of his time. Believing as he did in the constant renewal of the church, he would have been pleased by the idea of a "twelfth-century renaissance." He is one of that generation caught up in the excitement of intellectual discovery and taking delight in the ambiguity and flexibility of words. He stretched their meanings and molded them into a model of what it meant to be one of the faithful.

BIBLIOGRAPHY

1. *Writings of Anselm of Havelberg*

a. *Manuscripts consulted*

Antikeimenon
Berlin, Staatsbibliothek der Stiftung Preussischer Kulturbesitz, Theol. fol. 80, saec. XV, fols. 208r-52r.
Munich, Bayerische Staatsbibliothek, Lat. 6488 (anno 1437) aus Freising, fols. 1r-62r.
Wolfenbüttel, Herzog-August-Bibliothek, 2135 (August. 11.14), saec. XVI, fols. 1r-164v.

Epistola apologetica
Berlin, Staatsbibliothek der Stiftung Preussischer Kulturbesitz, Theol. fol. 80, saec. XV, fols. 252v-61r.
Wolfenbüttel, Herzog-August-Bibliothek, Helmst. 494, saec. XII, fols. 9r-10v (frag.).

b. *Printed works*

Antikeimenon
J.L. D'Achery, ed. *Spicilegium sive collectio veterum aliquot scriptorum* 13:88-252. Paris, 1677.
St. Baluze, E. Martène, F. J. de la Barre, ed. *Spicilegium sive collectio veterum aliquot scriptorum* 1:161-207. Paris, 1723.
PL 188:1139-1148.

Epistola apologetica
E. Amort, ed. *Vetus disciplina canonicorum regularium et saecularium* Pp. 1048-65. Venice, 1747.
PL 188:1117-1140.

Letter to Peter the Venerable.
Recueil des chartes de l'Abbay de Cluny 5:4176, pp. 526-27. Ed. Auguste Bernard and Alexandre Bruel. Paris, 1894.

Letters to Wibald of Stablo.
Wibald of Stablo, *Epistolae* 158, pp. 263; 221, pp. 339-41. Ed. Philip Jaffé. Bibliotheca rerum Germanicarum 1. Monumenta corbiensia. Berlin, 1864.

Tractatus de ordine pronuntiandae letaniae
Ed. Franz Winter. "Zur Geschichte des Bischofs Anselm von Havelberg." *ZKG* 5 (1882), 144-55.

c. *Works in translation*

Antikeimenon, book one, *De una forma credendi*
Gaston Salet. *Anselme de Havelberg: Dialogues, Livre I, "Renouveau dans l'"Église": Texte Latin, note préliminaire, traduction, notes et appendice.* Source Chrétiennes 118. Paris, 1966.

Antikeimenon, book two, the first debate
Paul Harang. "Dialogue entre Anselme de Havelberg et Néchitès de Nicomédie
sur la procession du Saint Esprit." *Istina* 17 (1972), 375-424.
Letter 221 to Wibald of Stablo
Karl Pfändtner. "Ein Brief des Praemonstratenserbischofs Anselm von Havel-
berg." *AP* 7 (1931), 100-103.

                              2. *Primary Sources*

Abelard, Peter. *Peter Abelard's Hymnarius Paraclitensis: An Annotated Edition with Introduc-
tion 2: The Hymnarius Paraclitensis Text and Notes.* Ed. Joseph Szövérffy. Albany,
1975.
Acta et scripta quae de controversiis ecclesiae graecae et latinae saeculo undecimo composita extant.
Ed. Cornelius Will. Leipzig-Marburg, 1861.
Ailred of Rievaulx. *Aelredi Rievallensis opera ominia* 1. *Opera ascetica.* Ed. C. H. Talbot.
CCCM 1. Turnhout, 1971.
Albinus-Cencius. *Liber Censuum.* In *Pontificum Romanorum vitae* 2. Ed. J. M. Watterich.
Leipzig, 1862.
Annales Colonienses Maximi. Ed. Karl A. F. Pertz. MGH SS 17:723-847. Hanover,
1861.
Annales Erphesfurdenses. Ed. G. H. Pertz. MGH SS 6:536-41. Hanover, 1844.
Annales Magdeburgenses. Ed. Georg Heinrich Pertz. MGH SS 16:105-96. Hanover,
1859.
Annales Palidenses. Ed. Georg Heinrich Pertz. MGH SS 16: 48-98. Hanover, 1859.
*Annales Patherbrunnenses. Eine Quellenschrift des 12. Jahrhunderts, aus Bruchstücken wieder-
hergestellt.* Ed. Paul Scheffer-Boichorst. Innsbruck, 1870.
Annalista Saxo. Ed. Georg Waitz. MGH SS 6:542-777. Hanover, 1844.
Augustine. *De civitate Dei* XI-XXII. CCSL 48. Turnhout, 1955.
—. *Sermones ad populum.* PL 39:1493-1638.
—. *Enarrationes in Psalmos.* CCSL 39. Turnhout, 1956.
—. *Tractatus in Iohannis Euangelium.* CCSL 36. Turnhout, 1954.
Basilius of Achrida. *Das Basilius aus Achrida, Erzbischofs von Thessalonich, bisher unedierte
Dialoge: Ein Beitrag zur Geschichte des griechischen Schismas.* Ed. Joseph Schmidt.
Munich, 1901.
Bernard of Clairvaux. *Sermones super Cantica Canticorum. S. Bernardi opera* 1-2. Ed. Jean
Leclercq, *et al.* Rome, 1957, 1958.
Boso. *Adrien IV. Liber Pontificalis* 2:379-446. Ed. L. Duchesne. 1882, reprint: Paris,
1955.
Burchard of Worms. *Decretum.* PL 140:537-1066.
Byzantium: Church, Society, and Civilization Seen through Contemporary Eyes. Ed. and trans.
Deno John Geanakoplos. Chicago,1984.
Carmina medii aevi posterioris Latina 2.3, *Proverbia sententiaeque Latinitatis medii aevi, Latei-
nische Sprichwörter und Sentenzen des Mittelalters in alphabetischer Anordnung.* Ed. Hans
Walther. Göttingen, 1965.
Chronicon Montis Sereni, ed Ernst Ehrenfeuchter. MGH SS 23:138-226. Hanover,
1874.
Chronographus Corbeiensis. Ed. Philipp Jaffé. *Bibliotheca rerum Germanicarum* 1. *Monumenta
Corbeiensia.* Berlin, 1864.
Codex diplomaticus Anhaltinus 1. Ed. Otto von Heinemann. Essau, 1867.
Continuatio Praemonstratensis. Ed. D. L. C. Bethmann. MGH SS 6:447-56. Hanover,
1844.

Decretales Pseudo-Isidorianae et capitula Angilramni. Ed. Paul Hinsch. 1863, reprint: Aalen, 1963.

Ebo of Michaelsberg. *Vita Ottonis Episcopi Babenbergensis.* Ed. R. Köpke. MGH SS 12:822-83. Hanover, 1856.

Encyclica de Anacleto antipapa damnato. Ed. Ludwig Weiland. MGH Const. 1:114. Hanover, 1893.

Eugenius III. *Epistolae et privilegia.* PL 180:1013-1642.

Ex vita Ludovici VI. Francorum Regis auctore Sugerio. Ed. A. Molinier. MGH SS 26:46-59. Hanover, 1882.

Fundatio monasterii Gratiae Dei. Ed. Hermann Pabst. MGH SS 20:683-91. Hanover, 1868.

Gesta archiepiscoporum Magdeburgensium. Ed. Wilhelm Schum. MGH SS 14:361-486. Hanover, 1883.

Gregory I. *Dialogi: Libri IV.* Ed. Umberto Moricca. Fonti per la Storia d'Italia. Rome, 1924.

—. *Homiliae in Hiezechihelem prophetam* Ed. Marc Adriaen. CCSL 142. Turnhout, 1972.

—. *Homiliarum in Evangelia.* PL 76:1075-1310.

—. *Moralia in Iob.* Ed. Marc Adriaen. CCSL 143, 143B. Turnhout, 1979-1985.

Gregory of Nazianzus. *Theologica* 5. Migne, Patrologia Graeca 36:133-71. English translation: Frederick Norris (intro. and commentary), Lionel Wickham, Frederick Williams, *Faith Gives Fullness to Reasoning: the Five Theological Orations of Gregory of Nazianzen,* Supplements to Vigiliae Christianae 13. Leiden, 1991.

Haimo of Auxerre. *Expositio in Apocalypsim.* PL 117:937-1220.

Hamburgisches Urkundenbuch 1. Ed. Johann Martin Lappenberg. Hamburg, 1907.

Helmold of Bosau. *Cronica Slavorum.* Ed. Bernard Schmeidler. MGH SS r. G. Hanover, 1909.

Hermann of Laon. *De miraculis S. Mariae Laudunensis.* Ed. R. Wilmans. MGH SS 12:653-60. Hanover, 1856.

Honorius Augustodunensis. *Commentarium in Psalmos.* PL 172:269-312. PL 194:485-730.

—. *Expositio in Cantica Canticorum.* PL 172:347-496.

Hugh of St. Victor. *Allegoriae in Vetus Testamentum.* PL 175:635-750.

—. *De arca Noe morali.* PL 176:617-80.

—. *De sacramentis.* PL 176:173-618.

—. *De vanitate mundi,* PL 176:703-40.

—. *Didascalicon.* PL 176:739-812. Trans. Jerome Taylor. *The Didascalicon of Hugh of St. Victor: A Medieval Guide to the Arts.* New York, 1961.

Idung of Prüfening. *Le moine Idung et ses deux ouvrages: "Argumentum super quatuor questionibus" et "Dialogus duorum monachorum".* Ed. R. B. C. Huygens. Biblioteca degli "Studia Medievali" 11. Spoleto, 1980.

Innocent II. *Epistolae et privilegia.* PL 179:53-674.

Ivo of Chartres. *Decretum.* PL 161:9-1036.

John Kinnamos. *Deeds of John and Manuel Comnenus.* Ed. and trans. Charles M. Brand. New York, 1976.

John of Salisbury. *Historia Pontificalis.* Ed. and trans. Marjorie Chibnall. London, 1956.

Leo of Ochrida. *Epistola missa ad quemdam episcopum Romanum.* Migne, Patrologia Graeco-Latina 120:836-844.

Liber Pontificalis. 2 vols. Ed. L. Duchesne. Paris, 1886-1892.

The Life of Pachomius (Vita Prima Gaeca). Trans. Apostolos N. Athanassakis. Society of Biblical Literature: Texts and Translations 7, Early Christian Literature Series 2. Missoula, Montana, 1975.

Magdeburger Schöppenchronik. Ed. Karl Janicke. Die Chroniken der deutschen Städte 7. 1869, reprint: Gottingen, 1962.

Mainzer Urkundenbuch. 1: *Die Urkunden bis zum Tode Erzbischof Adalerts I. (1137).* Ed. Manfred Stimmins. Darmstadt, 1932. 2: *Die Urkunden seit dem Tode Erzbischof Adalberts I. (1137) bis zum Tode Erzbischof Konrads (1200)*, pt. 1: *1137-1175.* Ed. Peter Acht. Darmstadt, 1968.

Notae dedicationum Montis S. Petri Erfordensis, ed. O. Holder-Egger, MGH SS 30.1:481-88.

Orderic Vitalis. *Ecclesiastical History* 4. Ed. and trans. Marjorie Chibnell. Oxford, 1973.

Otto of Freising and Rahewin. *Gesta Friderici I. imperatoris.* 3rd ed. Ed. Georg Waitz and Bernard von Simson. MGH SS r. G.1 Hanover, 1912.

Otto of Freising, *Cronica sive Historia de duabus civitatibus*, ed. Adolf Hofmeister, MGH SS r. G.. Hanover, 1912.

Peter the Deacon. *Chronica Monasterii Casinensis.* Ed. Hartmut Hoffmann. MGH SS 34. Hanover, 1980.

Peter the Venerable. *The Letters of Peter the Venerable.* 2 vols. Ed. Giles Constable. Cambridge, Mass., 1967.

—. *De miraculis libri duo.* Ed. Dyonisia Bouthillier. CCCM 83. Turnhout, 1988.

Regesta archiepiscopatus Magdeburgensis 1. Ed. George Adalbert von Mülverstedt. Magdeburg, 1876.

Regesta Pontificum Romanorum 2. Ed. Philip Jaffé. 1888, reprint: Graz, 1956.

Regesta Pontificum Romanorum Italia Pontificia 5: *Aemilia sive provincia Ravennas.* Ed. Paul Kehr. 1911, reprint: Berlin, 1961.

Regesten der Markgrafen von Brandenburg aus Askanischem Hause. Ed. Hermannn Krabbo and Georg Winter. Berlin, 1955.

Regesten zur Geschichte der Mainzer Erzbischöfe von Bonifatius bis Uriel von Gemmingen 742-1514 1: *Von Bonifatius bis Arnold von Selehofen 742?-1160.* Ed. Johann Friedrich Böhmer and Cornelius Will. Innsbruck, 1877.

Regesto della chiesa di Ravenna: Le carte dell'archivio Estense 1. *Regesta chartarum Italiae.* Ed. V. Federici and G. Buzzi. Rome, 1911.

Regesto della chiesa cattedrale di Modena 1. *Regesta chartarum Italiae* 16. Ed. Emilio Paolo Vicini. Rome, 1931.

Regesto di S. Apollinare Nuovo. Regesta chartarum Italiae. Ed. V. Federici. Rome, 1907.

Registrum, oder merkwürdige Urkunden für die deutsche Geschichte 2. Ed. H. Sudendorf. Berlin, 1851.

Reinhardsbrunner Briefsammlung. Ed. Friedel Peeck. MGH Epp. sel. 5. Weimar, 1952.

Romoald of Salerno. *Annales.* Ed. Wilhelm Arndt. MGH SS 19:387-461. Hanover, 1866.

Rubeus. *Historiarum Ravennatum* 6. Venice, 1572.

Rupert of Deutz. *De victoria verbi Dei.* Ed. Hrabanus Haacke. MGH Quellen zur Geistesgeschichte des Mittelalters 5. Weimar, 1970.

—. *Altercatio monachi et clerici quod liceat monacho praedicare.* PL 170:537-542.

—. *Super quaedam capitula Regulae Divi Benedicti Abbatis.* PL 170:477-538.

—. *Commentaria in Euangelium Sancti Iohannis.* Ed. Hrabanus Haacke. CCCM 9. Turnhout, 1969.

—. *In Apocalypsim.* PL 169:825-1214.

—. *De Sancta Trinitate et operibus eius.* Ed. Hrabanus Haacke. CCCM 21-24. Turnhout, 1971-1972.

—. *Epistola ad Everardum.* PL 170:541-544.

S. Petri Erphesfurtensis Auctarium et Continuatio Chronici Ekkehardi. Monumenta Erphesfurtensia saec. XII, XIII, XIV. Ed. Oswald Holder-Egger. MGH SS r. G. Hanover, 1899.

Stephen of Muret. *Regula venerabilis uiri Stephani Muretensis.* Ed. Johannes Becquet. CCCM 8. Turnhout, 1968.
Theodore of Engelhusen. *Chronicon continens re Ecclesiae et Reipublicae ab o.c. usque ad a.d. 1421.* Ed. G. W. Leibniz. Scriptores rerum Brusvicensium 2. 1710.
Thietmar of Merseburg. *Chronicon.* Ed. Robert Holtzmann. MGH SS rer. Germ. NS 9. Berlin, 1935.
Translatio Godehardi episcopi Hildesheimensis. Ed. Philipp Jaffé. MGH SS 12:639-52. Hanover, 1856.
Urkunden Friedrichs I. Ed. Heinrich Appelt, *et al.* MGH DD 10.1-2. Hanover, 1975, 1979.
Urkunden Konrads III. und seines Sohnes Heinrich. Ed. Friedrich Hausmann. MGH DD 9. Vienna, 1969.
Urkunden Lothars III. und der Kaiserin Richenza. Ed. Emil von Ottenthal and Hans Hirsch. MGH DD 8. Berlin, 1927.
Urkundenbuch der Stadt Halle, ihrer Stifter und Kloster 1: *806-1300.* Ed. Arthur Bierbach. *GQPS NR* 10. Magdeburg, 1926.
Urkundenbuch des Erzstifts Magdeburg 1: *(937-1192).* Ed. Friedrich Israël and Walter Möllenberg. GQPS NR 18. Magdeburg, 1937.
Urkundenbuch des Hochstifts Halberstadt und seiner Bischöfe 1. Ed. Gustav Schmidt. Publicationen aus den K. preussischen Staatsarchiven 17. 1883. Reprint: Osnabrück, 1965.
Urkundenbuch des Hochstifts Hildesheim und seiner Bischöfe. Ed. K. Janicke. 1896, reprint: Osnabrück, 1965.
Urkundenbuch des Hochstifts Naumberg (967-1207). Ed. Felix Rosenfeld. GQPS NR 1. Magdeburg, 1925.
Urkundenbuch des Klosters Unser Lieben Frauen zu Magdeburg. Ed. Gustav Hertel, GQPS 10. Halle, 1878.
Vincent of Prague. *Annales.* Ed. Wilhelm Wattenbach. MGH SS 17:658-83. Hanover, 1861.
Vita Norberti archiepiscopi Magdeburgensis [Vita Norberti A]. Ed. R. Wilmans. MGH SS 12:663-720. Hanover, 1856.
Vita Norberti archiepiscopi Magdeburgensis [Vita Norberti B]. Acta Sanctorum, Juni 1:807-45. Antwerp, 1695.
Vita prima Bernhardi. PL 185:225-466.
Wazelinus. *Epistola ad Liezelinum.* Ed. R. Vander Plaetse. In "Notities betreffende Wazelinus abt van Saint-Laurent." *Sacris erudiri* 24 (1980), 243-64.
Wibald of Stablo. *Epistolae.* Ed. Philip Jaffé. Bibliotheca rerum Germanicarum 1. Monumenta Corbeiensia. Berlin, 1864.

3. *Secondary sources*

Acht, Peter. "Die Gesandtschaft König Konrads III. an Papst Eugen III. in Dijon." *HJ* 74 (1955), 668-73.
Baker, Derek. "Reform as Protest: the Evidence of Western Eremitical Movements." In *The Church in a Changing Society: Conflict--Reconciliation or Adjustment?*, *Proceedings of the CIHEC Conference in Uppsala August 17-21, 1977*, Publications of the Swedish Society of Church History, New Series 30, pp. 55-62. Uppsala, 1978.
Barmann, Lawrence F. "Reform Ideology in the *Dialogi* of Anselm of Havelberg." *Church History* 30 (1961), 379-95.
Barni, Gian Luigi Barni. "La lotta contro il Barbarossa." *Storia di Milano* 4. Pp. 3-112. Milan, 1954.

Bauermann, Johannes. "Die Frage der Bischofswahlen auf dem Würzburger Reichstag von 1133." In *Kritische Beiträge zur Geschichte des Mittelalters: Festschrift für Robert Holtzmann*. Historische Studien 238. Ed. Emil Ebering. Pp. 103-34. Berlin, 1933.

Bayol, A. "Anselme." *Dictionnaire d'histoire et de géographie ecclésiastiques* 3:458-59. Paris, 1924.

Beck, Hans-Georg. *Kirche und Theologische Literatur im Byzantinischen Reich. Handbuch der Altertumswissenschaft* 12, 2.1: *Byzantinisches Handbuch* 2.1. Munich, 1959.

Beinert, Wolfgang. *Die Kirche--Gottes Heil in der Welt: Die Lehre von der Kirche nach den Schriften des Rupert von Deutz, Honorius Augustodunensis und Gerhoch von Reichersberg.* Beiträge zur Geschichte der Philosophie und Theologie des Mittelalters, Neue Folge 13. Münster, 1973.

Benson, Robert L. *The Bishop-Elect: A Study in Medieval Ecclesiastical Office.* Princeton, 1968.

Berges, Wilhelm. "Anselm von Havelberg in der Geistesgeschichte des 12. Jahrhunderts." *JGMOD* 5 (1956), 39-57.

—. "Reform und Ostmission im 12. Jahrhundert." In Beumann, *Heidenmission*, 317-36

Berlière, U. "Anselme d'Havelberg." *Dictionnaire de théologie Catholique* 1.2, 1360-61. Paris, 1909.

Bernhardi, Wilhelm. *Konrad III.* Jahrbücher der Deutschen Geschichte. 1883; repr., Berlin, 1975.

—. *Lothar von Supplinburg.* Jahrbücher der Deutschen Geschichte. 1879; repr., Berlin, 1975.

Berry, Virginia G. "The Second Crusade." In *A History of the Crusades* 1, ed. Kenneth Setton. *The First Hundred Years*, ed. Marshall Baldwin. 2nd ed. Pp. 463-512. Madison, 1969.

Berschin, Walter. "Anselm von Havelberg und die Anfänge einer Geschichtstheologie des hohen Mittelalters." *Literaturwissenschaftliches Jahrbuch im Auftrage der Görres-Gesellschaft*, NF 29 (1988), 225-32.

—. *Griechisch-lateinisches Mittelalter: Von Hieronymus zu Nikolaus von Kues.* Bern-Munich, 1980.

Beumann, Helmut, ed. *Heidenmission und Kreuzzugsgedanke in der deutschen Ostpolitik des Mittelalters.* Wege der Forschung 7. Darmstadt, 1973.

—. "Kreuzzugsgedanke und Ostpolitik im hohen Mittelalter." *HJ* 72 (1953), 112-32. Also in Beumann, *Heidenmission*, 121-45.

Beumer, Johannes. "Ein Religionsgespräch aus dem zwölften Jahrhundert." *Zeitschrift für katholische Theologie* 78 (1951), 465-82.

Bischoff, Guntram. "Early Premonstratensian Eschatology: The Apocalyptic Myth." In *The Spirituality of Western Christianity*, ed. Rozanne Elder. Pp. 41-71. Kalamazoo, 1976.

Bloomfield, Morton. "Joachim of Flora: A Critical Survey of His Canon, Teachings, Sources, Biography, and Influences." *Traditio* 13 (1957), 249-311.

Bogumil, Karlotto. *Das Bistum Halberstadt im 12. Jahrhundert: Studien zur Reichs- und Reformpolitik des Bischofs Reinhard und zum Wirken der Augustiner Chorherren.* Cologne, 1972.

Bosl, Karl. *Regularkanoniker (Augustinerchorherren) und Seelsorge in Kirche und Gesellschaft des europäischen 12. Jahrhunderts.* Bayerische Akademie der Wissenschaften, philosophisch-historische Klasse, Abhandlungen-NF. Heft 86. Munich, 1979.

—. "Anselm von Havelberg." *Biographisches Wörterbuch zu deutschen Geschichte* 1:113-14. Munich, 1973.

Braun, Johann W. "A[nselm] von Havelberg," *Lexikon des Mittelalters* 1:678-79. Munich, 1980.

Braun, Johann W. "Anselm von Havelberg." *Die deutsche Literatur des Mittelalters, Verfasserlexikon* 2nd ed., 1:384-91. New York, 1978.

—. "Studien zur Überlieferung der Werke Anselms von Havelberg I: Die Überlieferung des Anticimenon." *DA* 28 (1972), 133-209.

Brüske, Wolfgang Brüske. *Untersuchungen zur Geschichte des Lutizenbundes: Deutsch-wendische Beziehungen des 10.-12. Jahrhunderts.* Mitteldeutsche Forschungen 3. Münster, 1955.

Buchholz, Torsten. "Die Havelberger Bischöfe von Dudo bis Gumpert und ihre Zeit (946/48-1125). *Havelberger Regionalgeschichtliche Beiträge* 4 (1995), 4-23.

Bünding-Naujoks, Margret. *Das Imperium Christianum und die deutschen Ostkriege vom Zehnten bis zum zwölften Jahrhundert.* Historische Studien 366. Berlin, 1940. Also in Beumann, *Heidenmission,* pp. 65-120.

Büttner, Heinrich. "Erzbischof Heinrich von Mainz und die Staufer (1142-1153)." *ZKG* 69 (1958), 247-67.

Bynum, Caroline Walker. "The Spirituality of Regular Canons in the Twelfth Century," in *Jesus as Mother: Studies in the Spirituality of the High Middle Ages.* Berkeley, 1982. Pp. 22-58.

—. *Docere verbo et exemplo: An Aspect of Twelfth-Century Spirituality.* Harvard Theological Studies 31. Missoula, 1979.

Carr. David R. "Frederick Barbarossa and the Lombard League: Imperial Regalia, Prescriptive Rights, and the Northern Italian Cities," *Journal of the Rocky Mountain Medieval and Renaissance Association* 10 (1989), 29-49.

Casey, Michael. *Athirst for God: Spiritual Desire in Bernard of Clairvaux's Sermons on the Song of Songs.* Cistercian Studies Series 77. Kalamazoo, 1988.

Caspar, Erich. *Roger II. und die Gründung der normannisch-sicilischen Monarchie.* Innsbruck, 1904.

Chalandon, Ferdinand. *Les Comnène: Etudes sur l'empire byzantin au XIe et au XIIe siècles* 2.1: *Jean II Comnène (1118-1143) et Manuel I Comnene (1143-1180).* Paris, 1912.

—. *Histoire de la domination Normande en Italie et en Sicile.* 2 vols. Paris, 1907.

Chenu, M.-D. *La theologie au douzième siècle.* Etudes de philosophie médiévale 45. Paris, 1957.

Chodorow, Stanley. *Christian Political Theory and Church Politics in the Mid-Twelfth Century: The Ecclesiology of Gratian's Decretum.* Berkeley, 1972.

Christiansen, Eric. *The Northern Crusades: The Baltic and Catholic Frontier 1110-1525.* Minneapolis, 1980.

Classen, Peter. "Der Häresie-Begriff bei Gerhoch von Reichersberg und seinem Umkreis." In *The Concept of Heresy in the Middle Ages (11th-13th C.),* ed. W. Lourdaux and D. Verhelst. Medievalia Lovaniensia, series 1, studia 4. Proceedings of the International Conference Louvain May 13-16, 1973. Pp. 27-41. Louvain, 1976.

—. *Burgundio von Pisa: Richter, Gesandter, Übersetzer.* Heidelberg, 1974.

—. "Das Wormser Konkordat in der deutschen Verfassungsgeschichte." *Vorträge und Forschungen* 17: *Investiturstreit und Reichsverfassung,* ed. Josef Fleckenstein. Pp. 411-60. Sigmaringen, 1973.

—. "La politica di Manuele Comneno tra Frederico Barbarossa e le città italiane." *Popolo e stato in Italia nell'età di Federico Barbarossa: Alessandria e la Lega Lombarda.* Relazioni e communicazioni al XXXIII congresso storico subalpino per la celebrazione del'VIII contenario della fondazione di Alessandria. Pp. 263-89. Turin, 1970.

—. *Gerhoch von Reichersberg: Eine Biographie.* Weisbaden, 1960.

Claude, Dietrich. *Geschichte des Erzbistums Magdeburg bis in das 12. Jahrhundert.* Mitteldeutsche Forschungen 67/1-2. Cologne, 1972, 1975.

Cohn, Willy. *Die Geschichte der Normannisch-sicilischen Flotte unter der Regierung von Rogers I. und Rogers II. (1060-1154)* Breslau, 1910.

Colvin, H. M. *The White Canons in England.* Oxford, 1951.

Congar, Yves. *L'Église de Saint Augustin à l'époque moderne.* Histoire des Dogmes 3. Christologie-Sotériologie-Mariologie, fascicule 3. Paris. 1970.

—. "Ecclesia ab Abel." In *Abhandlungen über Theologie und Kirche: Festschrift für Karl Adam,* ed. Marcel Reding. Pp. 79-108. Düsseldorf, 1952.

Constable, Giles. *Three Studies in Medieval Religious and Social Thought: The Interpretation of Mary and Martha; The Ideal of the Imitation of Christ; The Orders of Society.* New York, 1995.

—. "Baume and Cluny in the Twelfth Century," in *Tradition and Change: Essays in honour of Marjorie Chibnall.* Ed by Diana Greenway, Christopher Holdsworth, and Jane Sayers. New York, 1985. Pp. 35-61.

—. "Renewal and Reform in Religious Life: Concepts and Realities," in *Renaissance and Renewal in the Twelfth Century.* Ed. Robert L. Benson and Giles Constable. Cambridge, Mass., 1982. Pp. 37-67.

—. "The Second Crusade as Seen by Contemporaries." *Traditio* 9 (1953), 213-79.

Cremaschi, G. *Mosè del Brolo e la cultura a Bergamo nei secoli XI-XII.* Bergamo, 1945.

Crone, Marie-Luise. *Untersuchungen zur Reichskirchenpolitik Lothars III. (1125-1137) zwischen reichskirchlicher Tradition und Reformkurie.* Europäische Hochschulschriften: Reihe 3, Geschichte u. ihre Hilfswiss. 170. Frankfurt am Main, 1982.

Curschmann, Fritz. *Die Diozese Brandenburg: Untersuchungen zur historischen Geographie und Verfassungsgeschichte eines ostdeutschen Kolonialbistums.* Leipzig, 1906.

De Ghellinck, Joseph. *Le mouvement théologique du XIIe siècle.* 2nd ed. Bruges, 1948.

De Lubac, Henri. *Exégèse mèdièvale: Les quatre sens de l'écriture.* 2 vols., vol. 2 in 3 pts. Aubier, 1959-1964.

Demm, Eberhard. *Reformmönchtum und Slawenmission im 12. Jahrhundert: Wertsoziologisch-geistesgeschichtliche Untersuchungen zu den Viten Bischof Ottos von Bamberg.* Historische Studien 419. Lübeck, 1970.

Derbes, Anne. "The Frescoes of Schwarzrheindorf, Arnold of Wied and the Second Crusade." In *The Second Crusade and the Cistercians.* Ed. Michael Gervers. Pp. 141-47. New York: 1992.

Dereine, H. "La réforme canoniale en Rhénanie (1070-1150)." *Memorial d'un voyage d'études de la Société Nationale des Antiquaires de France en Rhénanie.* Pp. 235-40. Paris, 1953.

Dereine, Charles. *Les Chanoines réguliers au diocèse de Liège avant saint Norbert.* Bruxelles, 1952.

—. *Les Chanoines réguliers au diocèse de Liège avant Saint Norbert.* Memoires de l'Academie royale de Belgique, Classe des Lettres et des Science morales et politiques, Mémoires 47. Brussels, 1952.

—. "Clercs et moines au diocèse de Liège du Xe au XIIe siècles." *Annales de la Société archéologique de Namur* 45 (1949-1950), 183-203.

Deutz, Helmut. "Norbert von Xanten bei Propst Richer im Regularkanonikerstift Klosterrath." *AP* 68 (1992), 5-16

Dickinson, J. C. *The Origin of the Austin Canons and Their Introduction into England.* London, 1950.

Dombrowski, Eugen. *Anselm von Havelberg.* Inaugural-Dissertation. Königsberg, 1880.

Dondaine, Antoine. "'Contra Graecos': Premiers écrits polemiques des Dominicains d'orient." *Archivum Fratrum Praedicatorum* 21 (1951), 320-446.

Dräseke, Johannes. "Bischof Anselm von Havelberg und seine Gesantschaftsreisen nach Byzanz." *ZKG* 21 (1901), 160-85.

Dunken, Gerhard. *Die politische Wirksamkeit der päpstlichen Legaten in der Zeit des Kampfes zwischen Kaisertum und Papstum in Oberitalien unter Friedrich I.* Historische Studien 209. Berlin, 1931.

Duranti, Angelo. "Il collegio dei cardinali di Ravenna." *Ravennatensia* 4 (1974), 529-618.

Eberhard, Winfried. "Ansätze zur Bewältigung ideologischer Pluralität im 12. Jahrhundert: Pierre Abélard und Anselm von Havelberg." *Historisches Jahrbuch* 105 (1985), 353-87.

Edyvean, Walter. *Anselm of Havelberg and the Theology of History.* Rome, 1972.

Ehlers, Joachim. "Deutsche Scholaren in Frankreich während des 12. Jahrhunderts." *Schulen und Studium im sozialen Wandel des hohen und späten Mittelalters.* Ed. Johannes Fried. *Vorträge und Forschungen* 30. Sigmaringen, 1986. 97-120.

—. *Hugo von St. Viktor: Studien zum Geschichtsdenken und zur Geschichtsschreibung des 12. Jahrhunderts.* Wiesbaden, 1973.

Eichmann, Eduard. *Die Kaiserkrönung im Abendland: Ein Beitrag zur Geistesgeschichte des Mittelalters mit besonderer Berücksichtigung des Geistesgeschichte des Mittelalters mit besonderer Berücksichtigung des kirchlichen Rechts, der Liturgie und der Kirchenpolitik.* 2 vols. Würzburg, 1942.

Elm, Kaspar, ed. *Norbert von Xanten Adliger-Ordensstifter-Kirchenfürst.* Cologne, 1984.

—. "Norbert von Xanten: Bedeutung-Persönlichkeit-Nachleben." In Elm, *Norbert von Xanten Adliger-Ordensstifter-Kirchenfürst*, pp. 267-318.

Emmerson, Richard K. *Antichrist in the Middle Ages.* Seattle, 1981.

Engels, Odilo. "Zum Konstanzer Vertrag von 1153." *Deus qui mutat tempora. Festschrift für A. Becker zu seinem 65. Geburtstag.* Eds. E.-D. Hehl, H. Seibert and F. Staab. Pp. 235-258. Sigmaringen, 1987.

Evans, Gillian R. "Unity and diversity: Anselm of Havelberg as ecumenist." *AP* 67 (1991), 42-52.

—. *The Language and Logic of the Bible: The Earlier Middle Ages.* Cambridge, 1984.

—. "Anselm of Canterbury and Anselm of Havelberg: The Controversy with the Greeks." *AP* 53 (1977), 158-75.

Fantuzzi, Marco. *Monumenti Ravennati.* Venice, 1802.

Felton, Franz J. "Norbert von Xanten: Vom Wanderprediger zum Kirchenfürsten." In Elm, *Norbert von Xanten Adliger-Ordensstifter-Kirchenfürst*, pp. 69-157.

Ficker, Julius. *Beiträge zur Urkundenlehre* 2. 1878; repr., Aalen, 1966.

Fina, Kurt. "Anselm von Havelberg: Untersuchungen zur Kirchen- und Geistesgeschichte des 12. Jahrhunderts." *AP* 32 (1956), 69-101, 193-227; 33 (1957), 5-39, 268-301; 34 (1958), 13-41.

—. "'Ovem suam requirere': Eine Studie zur Geschichte des Ordenswechsels im 12. Jahrhundert." *Augustiniana* 7 (1957), 33-56.

Fincke, Hanns-Joachim. "Wie alt ist der Havelberger Dom?" *Havelberger Regionalgeschichtliche Beiträge* 4 (1995), 55-83.

Fitzthum, Martin. "Anselm von Havelberg als Verteidiger der Einheit mit der Ostkirche." *AP* 36 (1961), 137-41.

Freund, Walter. *Modernus und andere Zeitbegriffe des Mittelalters.* Neue Münstersche Beiträge zur Geschichtsforschung 4. Graz, 1957.

Fuhrmann, Horst. *Germany in the High Middle Ages: c. 1050-1200.* Trans. Timothy Reuter. Oxford, 1986.

Funkenstein, Amos. "Periodization and Self-Understanding in the Middle Ages and Early Modern Times." *Medievalia et Humanistica: Studies in Medieval and Renaissance Culture.* New ser. 5 (1974), 3-23.

—. *Heilsplan und näturliche Entwicklung: Formen der Gegenwartsbestimmung im Geschichtsdenken des hohen Mittelalter.* Munich, 1965.

Gehrt, Wolf. *Die Verbände der Regularkanonikerstifte S. Frediano in Lucca, S. Maria in Reno bei Bologna, S. Maria in Porto bei Ravenna und die cura animarum im 12. Jahrhundert.* Europäische Hochschulschriften series 3, 224. New York, 1984.

Georgi, Wolfgang. *Friedrich Barbarossa und die auswärtigen Mächte: Studien zur Aussenpolitik 1159-1180.* Europäische Hochschulschriften, Reihe 3, 442. New York, 1990.

Giunta, Francesco. *Bizantini e bizantinismo nella Sicilia normanna* 2nd ed. Palermo, 1974.

Glaeske, Günter. *Die Erzbischöfe von Hamburg-Bremen als Reichsfürsten (937-1258).* Quellen und Darstellungen zur Geschichte Niedersachsens 60. Hildesheim, 1962.

Gleber, H. *Papst Eugenius III. (1145-53).* Jena, 1936.

Goetting, Hans. *Das Bistum Hildesheim.* 3 vols. Die Bistümer der kirchenprovinz Mainz, Germania Sacra, Neue Folge 7, 8, 20. New York, 1973-1984.

—. "Die Reichenberger Fälschungen und das zweite Königssiegel Lothars III." *Mitteilungen des Instituts für österreichische Geschichtsforschung* 78 (1970), 132-66.

Goetz, Hans-Werner. "Die Gegenwart der Vergangenheit im früh- und hochmittelalterlichen Geschichtsbewußtsein." *Historische Zeitschrift* 255 (1992), 61-97.

Gössmann, Elizabeth. *Antiqui und Moderni im Mittelalter: Eine geschichtliche Standortsbestimmung.* Veröffentlichungen des Grabmann-Institutes. NF 23. Munich, 1974.

Grabmann, Martin. "Anselm." *Neue Deutsche Biographie* 1:309-10. Berlin, 1953.

Grauwen, Wilfried Marcel. "Norberts reis naar Laon, Kamerijk en Nijvel en de inbezitneming van Prémontré, 1120." *AP* 69 (1993), 41-50.

—. "De crisissituatie van Norbert begin november 1119 en zijn belangstelling voor psalm 119 (118)." *AP* 64 (1988), 5-18.

—. *Norbertus Aartsbisschop van Maagdenburg (1126-1134).* Verhandelingen van de Koninklijke Academie voor Wetenschappen, Letteren en Schone Kunsten van België: Klasse der Letteren, Jaargang XL nr. 86. Brussels, 1978.

Greenaway, George William. *Arnold of Brescia.* Cambridge, 1931.

Grumel, V. "Notes d'histoire et de littérature Byzantines." *Echos d'Orient* 29 (1930), 334-338.

Grundmann, Herbert. *Neue Forschungen über Joachim von Fiore.* Münstersche Forschungen 1. Marburg, 1950.

—. *Studien über Joachim von Floris.* Beiträge zur Kulturgeschichte des Mittelalters und der Renaissance 32. Leipzig, 1927.

Guth, Klaus. "The Pomeranian Missionary Journeys of Otto I of Bamberg and the Crusade Movement of the the Eleventh and Twelfth Centuries." In *The Second Crusade and the Cistercians.* Ed. Michael Gervers. Pp. 13-23. New York, 1992.

Hampe, Karl. *Deutsche Kaisergeschichte in der Zeit der Salier und Staufer.* 1969; repr.: Darmstadt, 1981.

Haskins, Charles Homer. *Studies in the History of Mediaeval Science.* Cambridge, Mass., 1924.

Hauck, Albert. *Kirchengeschichte Deutschlands.* 5 vols. Berlin, 1954.

Hausmann, Friedrich. "Die Anfänge des staufischen Zeitalters unter Konrad III." *Vorträge und Forschungen* 12: *Probleme des 12. Jahrhunderts,* ed. Theodor Mayer. Pp. 53-78. Constance, 1968.

—. *Reichskanzlei und Hofkapelle unter Heinrich V. und Konrad III.* MGH Sch 14. Stuttgart, 1956.

Haverkamp, Alfred. *Herrschaftsformen der frühstaufer in Reichsitalien.* 2 vols. Monographien zur Geschichte des Mittelalters 1. Stuttgart, 1970.

Heineman, Wolfgang. *Das Bistum Hildesheim im Kräftesspiel der Reichs- und Territorialpolitik vornehmlich des 12. Jahrhunderts,* Quellen und Darstellungen zur Geschichte Niedersachsens 72. Hildesheim, 1968.

Herkenrath, Rainer Maria. "Regnum und Imperium in den Diplomen der ersten Regierungsjahre Friedrichs I." In Wolf, *Friedrich Barbarossa,* pp. 323-59. Reprint of chapt. 3 of *Regnum und Imperium. Das "Reich" in der frühstaufischen Kanzlei (1138-1155)*. Sitzungsberichte der Österreichische Akademie der Wissenschaften. Phil.-hist. Klasse 264, pt. 5. Vienna, 1969.

Higounet, Charles. *Die deutsche Ostsiedlung im Mittelalter*. Trans. from the French by Manfred Vasold. Berlin, 1986.

Hoffmann, Hartmut. "Die älteren Abtslisten von Montecassino." *Quellen uund Forschungen aus italienischen Archiven und Bibliotheken* 47 (1967), 224-354.

Hofmeister, Adolf. "Puer, Iuvenis, Senex. Zum Verständnis der mittelalterlichen Altersbezeichnungen." In *Papstum und Kaisertum: Forschungen zur politischen Geschichte und Geisteskultur des Mittelalters. Paul Kehr zum 65. Geburtstag dargebracht*. Ed. Albert Brackmann. Pp. 287-316. Munchen, 1926.

—. "Kaiser Lothar und die grosse Kolonizationsbewegungen des 12. Jahrhunderts." *Zeitschrift der Gesellschaft für schleswig-holsteinische Geschichte* 43 (1913), 353-60.

Hofmeister, Philipp. "Der Übertritt in eine andere religiöse Genossenschaft." *Archiv für katholisches Kirchenrecht* 108 (1928), 419-481.

Holtzmann, Robert. "Zum Strator- und Marschalldienst." *HZ* 145 (1932), 301-50.

—. *Der Kaiser als Marschall des Papstes: Eine Untersuchung zur Geschichte der Bezeihungen zwischen Kaiser und Papst im Mittelalter*. Schriften der Strassburger Wissenschaftlichen Gesellschaft in Heidelberg. Neue Folge 8. Berlin, 1928.

Hoppe, Willy. *Die Mark Brandenburg Wettin und Magdeburg: Ausgewählte Aufsätze*. Ed. Herbert Ludat. Cologne, 1965.

Hucke, Richard G. *Die Grafen von Stade, 900-1144. Genealogie, politische Stellung, Comitat und Allodialbesitz der sächsischen Udonen*. Einzelschriften des Stader Geschichts- und Heimatvereins 8. Stade, 1956.

Jaeger, C. Stephen. *The Origins of Courtliness: Civilizing Trends and the Formation of Courtly Ideals, 939-1210* Philadelphia, 1985.

—. "Cathedral Schools and Humanist Learning, 950-1150," *Deutsche Vierteljahrsschrift für Literaturwissenschaft und Geistesgeschichte* 61 (1987), 569-616.

Jakobi, Franz-Josef. *Wibald von Stablo und Corvey (1098-1158): Benediktinischer Abt in der frühen Stauferzeit*. Veröffentlichungen der Historischen Kommission für Westfalen X; Abhandlungen zur Corveyer Geschichtsschreibung 5. Münster, 1979.

—. *Henry the Lion: A Biography* Trans. P. S. Falla. Oxford, 1986.

—. *Investiturstreit und frühe Stauferzeit (1056-1197)*. Gebhardt Handbuch der Deutschen Geschichte 4. Stuttgart, 1970.

Jordan, Karl. *Die Bistumsgrundungen Heinrichs des Löwen. Untersuchungen zur Geschichte des Ostdeutschen Kolonization*. MGH Sch 3. Leipzig, 1939.

Kahl, Hans-Dietrich. *Slawen und Deutsche in der Brandenburgischen Geschichte des Zwölften Jahrhunderts: Die letzten Jahrzehnte des Landes Stodor*. 2 vols. Cologne, 1964.

—. "Zum Ergebnis des Wendenkreuzzugs von 1147. Zugleich ein Beitrag zur Geschichte des sächsischen Frühchristentums." *Wichmann-Jahrbuch* 11/12 (1957/58), 99-120. Also in Beumann, *Heidenmission*, pp. 275-316.

Kamlah, Wilhelm. *Apokalypse und Geschichtstheologie. Die Mittelalterliche Auslegung der Apokalypse vor Joachim von Fiore*. 1935; repr., Vaduz, 1965.

Kay, Richard. *Dante's Swift and Strong: Essays on Inferno XV*. Lawrence, Ks., 1978.

Klebel, F. W. "Norbert von Magdeburg und Gerhoch von Reichersberg." *AP* 38 (1962), 323-34.

Krabbo, H. "Ein Verzeichnis von Urkunden des Prämonstratenserstifts Jerichow." *Geschichts Blätter für Stift und Land Magdeburg* 56-60 (1924), 96-110.

Kunisch, Johannes. *Konrad III., Arnold von Wied und der Kapellenbau von Schwarzrheindorf*. Düsseldorf, 1966.

Kupper, Jean-Louis. *Liége et l'église impériale, XIe-XIIe siècles*. Bibliothèque de la Faculté de Philosophie et Lettres de l'Université de Liège 28. Paris, 1981.

La Piana, George. "Joachim of Flora: A Critical Survey." *Speculum* 7 (1932), 257-82.

Ladner, Gerhart B. *The Idea of Reform: Its Impact on Christian Thought and Action in the Age of the Fathers.* Rev. ed. New York, 1967.

—. "Two Gregorian Letters: On the Sources and Nature of Gregory VII' Reform Ideology." *Studi Gregoriani* 5 (1958), 221-42.

—. "The Concepts of "Ecclesia" and Christianitas" and Their Relation ot the Idea of Papal "Plenitudo Potestatis" from Gregory VII to Boniface VIII." *Miscellanea Historiae Pontificiae* 18 (1954), 49-77.

Lambert, Malcolm D. *Medieval Heresy: Popular Movements from Bogomil to Hus.* New York, 1976.

Lamma, Paolo. *Comneni e Staufer: Ricerche sui rapporti fra Bisanzio e l'occidente nel secolo XII.* 2 vols. Rome, 1955-1957.

Larner, John. *The Lords of Romagna: Romagnol Society and the Origins of the Signorie.* Ithaca, 1965.

Laudage, Johannes. *Gregorianische Reform und Investiturstreit.* Darmstadt, 1993.

Lauerer, Hans. *Die theologischen Anschauungen des Bischofs Anselm von Havelberg (+1158) auf Grund der kritischgesichteten Schriften dargestellt.* Erlangen, 1911.

Lawrence, C. H. *Medieval Monasticism: Forms of Religious Life in Western Europe in the Middle Ages* 2nd ed. New York, 1989.

Leclercq, Jean, François Vandenbroucke, Louis Bouyer. *A History of Christian Spirituality* 1: *The Spirituality of the Middle Ages.* New York, 1968.

Leclercq, Jean. "La crise du monachisme aux XIe et XIIe siècles." *Bullettino dell' Istituto Storico Italiano per il Medio Evo* 70 (1958), 19-41.

Lees, Jay T. "Charity and Enmity in the Writings of Anselm of Havelberg," *Viator: Medieval and Renaissance Studies* 25 (1994), 53-62.

—. "La lettera di Anselmo di Havelberg a Pietro il Venerabile: Federico Barbarossa e Baume-Les-Messieurs," *Benedictina* 40 (1993), 49-56.

—. "Confronting the Otherness of the Greeks: Anselm of Havelberg and the Division between Greeks and Latins," *AP* 68 (1992), 224-240.

—. "Anselm of Havelberg's 'Banishment' to Havelberg." *AP* (1986), 5-18.

Lefèvre, Pl. "Prémontré, ses origines, sa première Liturgie, les relations de son Code législatif avec Citeaux, et les Chanoines du Saint-Sépulcre de Jérusalem." *AP* 25 (1949), 96-103.

Leyser, Henrietta. *Hermits and the New Monasticism: A Study of Religious Communities in Western Europe 1000-1150.* London, 1984.

Little, Lester K. *Religious Poverty and the Profit Economy in Medieval Europe.* Ithaca, 1978.

—. "Intellectual Training and Attitudes toward Reform, 1075-1150." In *Pierre Abélard-Pierre le Vénérable: Les courants philosophiques, littéraires et artistipues en occident au milieu du XIIe siècle.* Colloques internationaux du Centre National de la Recherche Scientifique 546. Pp. 235-49. Paris, 1975.

Lotter, Friedrich. *Die Konzeption des Wendenkreuzzugs. Ideengeschichtliche, kirchenrechtliche und historisch-politische Voraussetzungen der Missionierung von Elb- und Ostseeslawen um die Mitte des 12. Jahrhunderts. Vorträge und Forschungen:* Sonderband 23. Sigmaringen, 1977.

—. "Bemerkungen zur Christianisierung der Abodriten." In *Festschrift für Walter Schlesinger* 2, ed. Helmut Beumann. Mitteldeutsche Forschungen 74/2, 395-442. Cologne, 1974.

Maccarrone, Michele. *Papato e impero: Dalla elezione di Federico I alla morto di Adriano IV (1152-1159).* Rome, 1959.

Maleczek, W. "Das Kardinalskollegium unter Innozenz II. und Anaklet II." *Archivum historiae Pontificiae* 19 (1981), 27-78.

Manteuffel, Tadeusz. *The Formation of the Polish State: The Period of Ducal Rule, 963-1194.* Trans. Andrew Gorski. Detroit, 1982.

McGinn, Bernard. *The Calabrian Abbot: Joachim of Fiore in the History of Western Thought.* New York, 1985.

—. *Antichrist: Two Thousand Years of the Human Fascination with Evil.* New York, 1994.

—. *Apocalyptic Spirituality: Treatises and Letters of Lactantius, Adso of Montier-enDer, Joachim of Fiore, the Franciscan Spirituals, Savonarola.* New York, 1979.

—. *Visions of the End: Apocalyptic Traditions in the Middle Ages.* New York, 1979.

Melville, Gert. "Zur Abgrenzung zwischen Vita canonica und Vita monastica: Das Übertrittsproblem in kanonistischer Behandlung von Gratian bis Hostiensis." In *Secundum regulam vivere: Festschrift für P. Norbert Backmund O. Praem.*, ed. Gert Melville. Pp. 205-43. Windberg, 1978.

Miccoli, Giovanni. *Chiesa Gregoriana: Ricerche sulla Riforma del secolo XI.* Florence, 1966.

Minio-Paluello, L. "Jacobus Veneticus Grecus Canonist and Translator of Aristotle." *Traditio* 8 (1952), 265-304.

Moore, R. I. *The Origins of European Dissent.* 2nd edition. Oxford, 1985.

Morrison, Karl F. "Anselm of Havelberg: Play and the Dilemma of Historical Progress." In *Religion, Culture and Society in the Early Middle Ages: Studies in Honor of Richard E. Sullivan*, ed. Thomas F. X. Noble and John J. Contreni. Studies in Medieval Culture 23. Pp. 219-56. Kalamazoo, 1987.

Munz, Peter. *Frederick Barbarossa: A Study in Medieval Politics.* Ithaca, 1969.

Neel Carol. "Philip of Harvengt and Anselm of Havelberg: The Premonstratensian Vision of Time." *Church History* 62 (1993), 483-93.

Neuss, Wilhelm. *Das Buch Ezechiel in Theologie und Kunst bis zum Ende des XII Jahrhunderts.* Beiträge zur Geschichte des alten Mönchtums und des Benediktinerordens. Münster, 1912.

Oediger, Friedrich Wilhelm. *Vom Leben am Niederrhein: Aufsätze aus dem Bereich des alten Erzbistums Köln.* Düsseldorf, 1973.

—. *Das Bistum Köln von den Anfängen bis zum Ende des 12. Jahrhunderts* (2nd edition). *Geschichte des Erzbistums Köln* 1. Cologne, 1972.

Ohnsorge, Werner. "Zu den aussenpolitischen Anfängen Friedrich Barbarossas." *Quellen und Forschungen aus Italienischen Archiven und Bibliotheken* 32 (1942), 13-32.

Olsen, Glenn. "The Idea of the *Ecclesia Primitiva* in the Writings of the Twelfth-Century Canonists." *Traditio* 25 (1969), 61-86.

Opll, Ferdinand. *Friedrich Barbarossa.* Darmstadt, 1990.

—. "Amator ecclesiarum: Studien zur religiösen Haltung Friedrich Barbarossas." *Mitteilungen des Instituts für Österreichische Geschichtsforschung* 88 (1980), 70-93.

—. *Das Itinerar Kaiser Friedrich Barbarossas (1152-1190).* Cologne, 1978.

—. *Stadt und Reich im 12. Jahrhundert (1125-1190).* Forschungen zur Kaiser- und Papstgeschichte des Mittelalters. Beihefte zu J.F. Böhmer, Regesta imperii 6. Vienna, 1966.

Orioli, Giorgio. "Cronotassi dei vescovi di Ravenna." *Felix Ravenna* 127-130 (1984-1985), 323-332.

Pacaut, Marcel. *L'Ordre de Cluny (909-1789).* Paris, 1986.

Partner, Peter. *The Lands of St Peter: The Papal State in the Middle Ages and the Early Renaissance.* Berkeley, 1972.

Patze, Hans. "Friedrich Barbarossa und die deutschen Fürsten." In *Die Zeit der Staufer* 5. Ed. Reiner Haussherr und Christian Väterlein. Pp. 35-75. Stuttgart, 1979.

Petersohn, Jürgen. *Der südliche Ostseeraum im kirchlich-politischen Kräftespiel des Reichs, Polens und Dänemarks vom 10. bis 13. Jahrhundert: Mission-Kirchenorganisation-Kultpolitik.* Vergangenheit und Gegenwart 17. Cologne, 1979.

Petit, François. "L'Ordre de Prémontré de Saint Norbert à Anselme de Havelberg." In *La vita comune del clero nei secoli XI e XII.* Atti del settimana di studio: Mendola, settembre 1959, 1. Relazioni e questionario. Pp. 456-79. Milan, 1962.

—. *La spiritualité des Prémontrés aux XIIe et XIIIe siècles*. Études de théologie et d'histoire de al spiritualité 10. Paris, 1947.

Petke, Wolfgang. *Kanzlei, Kapelle und Königliche Kurie unter Lothar III. (1125-1137)*. Forschungen zur Kaiser- und Papstgeschichte des Mittelalters: Beihefte zu J. F. Böhmer, Regesta Imperii 5. Cologne, 1985.

—. *Die Grafen von Wöltingerode-Wohldenberg. Adelsherrschaft, Königtum und Landesherrschaft am Nordwestharz im 12. und 13 Jahrhundert*. Veröffentlichungen des Instituts für historische Landesforschungen der Universität Göttingen 4. Hildesheim, 1971.

Principe, Walter H. "Monastic, Episcopal and Apologetic Theology of the Papacy, 1150-1250," In Christopher Ryan, ed., *The Religious Roles of the Papacy: Ideals and Realities 1150-1300*. Papers in Mediavel Studies 8. Toronto, 1989. Pp. 117-170.

Puhle, Matthias, ed. *Erzbischof Wichmann (1152-1192) und Magdeburg im hohen Mittelalter: Stadt-Erzbistum-Reich*. Magdeburg, 1992.

Rahner, Hugo. *Symbole der Kirche: Die Ekklesiologie der Väter*. Salzburg, 1964.

Rassow, Peter. *Honor Imperii: Die neue Politik Friedrich Barbarossas 1152-1159*. Darmstadt, 1974.

Rauh, Horst Dieter. *Das Bild des Antichrist im Mittelalter: Von Tyconius zum deutschen Symbolismus*. 2nd ed. Beiträge zur Geschichte der Philosophie und Theologie des Mittelalters, Neue Folge 9. Münster, 1979.

Reeves, Marjorie. "The Originality and Influence of Joachim of Fiore. *Traditio* 36 (1980), 269-316.

—. *Joachim of Fiore and the Prophetic Future*. New York, 1976.

—. "History and Prophecy in Medieval Thought." *Medievalia et Humanistica: Studies in Medieval and Renaissance Culture*. New Series 5 (1974), 51-76.

Renardy, Christine. "Les écoles Liégeoises du IXe au XIIe siècle: Grandes lignes de leur évolution." *Revue belge de Philologie et d'Histoire* 57 (1979), 309-28.

—. *Le monde des maîtres universitaires du diocèse de Liège 1140-1350: Recherches sur sa composition et ses activités*. Bibliothèque de la Faculté de Philosophie et Lettres de l'Université de Liège 227. Paris, 1979.

Reuter, Timothy. "Zur Anerkennung Papst Innocenz II.: Eine neue Quelle." *DA* 39 (1983), 395-416.

Richards, Jeffrey. *Consul of God: The Life and Times of Gregory the Great*. Boston, 1980.

Riedel, Adolph Friedrich. "Nachrichten über den Bischof Anselm von Havelberg, Gesandten der Deutschen Kaiser Lothar und Friedrich I. am kaiserl. Hofe zu Constantinopel, nachmaligen Erzbischof und Exarchen von Ravenna." *Leopold von Ledeburs Allgemeines Archiv für die Geschichtskunde des preussischen Staates* 8 (1832), 97-136, 225-67.

Rubeus, Hieronymous. *Historiarum Ravennatum* 6. Venice, 1572.

Runciman, Steven. *The Eastern Schism: A Study of the Papacy and the Eastern Churches during the XIth and XIIth Centuries*. Oxford, 1955.

Russell, Jeffrey Burton. *Lucifer: The Devil in the Middle Ages*. Ithaca, 1984.

Russell, Theodore N. "Anselm of Havelberg and the Union of the Churches." *Kleronomia* 10 (1978), 85-120.

Scheffczyk, Leo. "Die heilsökonomische Trinitätslehre des Ruperts von Deutz und ihre dogmatische Bedeutung." In *Kirche und Überlieferung*, ed. Johannes Betz and Heinrich Fries. Pp. 90-118. Freiburg, 1960.

Schlesinger, Walter. *Kirchengeschichte Sachsens im Mittelalter*. 2 vols. Cologne, 1962.

—. "Bemerkungen zu der sogenannten Stiftungsurkunde des Bistums Havelberg von 946 Mai 9." *Jahrbuch für die Geschichte Mittel- und Ostdeutschlands* 5 (1956), 1-38.

Schmale, Franz-Josef. *Studium zum Schisma des Jahres 1130*. Forschungen zur kirchlichen Rechtsgeschichte und zum Kirchenrecht 3. Cologne, 1961.

—. "Die Bemühungen Innocenz II. um seine Anerkennung in Deutschland." *ZKG* 65 (1953/54), 240-96.

Schmidt, Roderich. "Aetates mundi: Die Weltalter als Gliederungsprinzip der Ge-
schichte." *ZKG* 57 (1955-1956), 288-317.
Schreiber, Georg. "Anselm von Havelberg und die Ostkirche: Begegnung mit der
byzantinischen Welt. Morgenländisches und abendländisches Zönobium."
ZKG 60 (1941), 354-411.
—. "Studien ueber Anselm von Havelberg. Zur Geistesgeschichte des Hochmittel-
alters." *AP* 18 (1942), 5-90.
—. "Praemonstratenserkultur des 12. Jahrhunderts." *AP* 16 (1940), 41-107; 17
(1941), 5-33.
Schirge, Alfred. *Dom zu Havelberg*. Berlin, 1970.
Schultze, Johannes. "Der Wendenkreuzzug 1147 und die Adelherrschaften in Prig-
nitz und Rhingebiet." *JGMOD* 2 (1953), 95-124.
Schulze, Eduard Otto. *Die Kolonisierung und Germanisierung der Gebiete zwischen Saale und
Elbe*. 1896; repr., Wiesbaden, 1969.
Schütz, Christian. *Deus Absconditus, Deus Manifestus: Die Lehre Hugos von St. Viktor über die
Offenbarung Gottes*. Studia Anselmiano 56. Rome, 1967.
Schwineköper, Berent. "Norbert von Xanten als Erzbischof von Magdeburg." In
Elm, *Norbert von Xanten Adliger-Ordensstifter-Kirchenfürst*, pp. 189-209.
Semmler, J. *Die Klosterreform von Siegburg. Ihre Ausbreitung und ihr Reformprogramm im 11.
und 12. Jahrhundert*. Rheinisches Archiv 53. Bonn, 1959.
Seppelt, F. X. *Geschichte der Päpste* 3. Munich, 1956.
Severino, Gabriella. "La discussione degli `Ordines' di Anselmo di Havelberg." *Bul-
lettino dell'Istituto Storico Italiano per il Medio Evo e Archivo Muratoriano* 78 (1967), 75-
122.
Sieben, Hermann-Josef. *Die Konzilsidee des lateinischen Mittelalters (847-1378)*. Konzi-
liengeschichte: Reihe B, Untersuchungen. Paderborn, 1984.
—. "Die eine Kirche, der Papst und die Konzilien in den Dialogen des Anselm von
Havelberg (+1158)." *Theologie und Philosophie* 2 (1979), 219-51.
Silvestre, Herbert, "Notes sur la controverse de Rupert de Saint-Laurent avec An-
selme de Laon et Guillaume de Champeaux." In *Saint-Laurent de Liège: Église,
Abbaye et Hopital militaire: Mille ans d'histoire*, pp. 63-80. Liège, 1968.
—, "La tradition manuscrite des oeuvres de Rupert de Deutz: A propos d'une étude
récente de Rhaban Haacke," *Scriptorium* 16 (1962), 336-45.
Simonsfeld, Henry. *Jahrbücher des Deutschen Reichs unter Friedrich I (1152-1158)* 1. 1908;
repr., Berlin, 1977.
Smalley, Beryl. "Ecclesiastical Attitudes to Novelty c. 1100-1250." In *Church and
Society*, Papers read at the Thirteenth Summer and the Fourteenth Winter
Meeting of the Ecclesiastical History Society. Ed. Derek Baker. Oxford, 1975.
Pp. 113-31.
—. *The Study of Bible in The Middle Ages*. Notre Dame, Indiana, 1964.
Sommerfeldt, J.R. "Anselm of Havelberg." *New Catholic Encyclopedia* 1, 583-84. New
York, 1967.
Southern, R. W. "Aspects of the European Tradition of Historical Writings. 2. Hugh
of St. Victor and the Idea of Historical Development." *Transactions of the Royal
Historical Socity* 5th ser. 21 (1971), 159-79.
Spicq, P. C. *Esquisse d'une histoire de l'exégèse latine au Moyen Âge*. Paris, 1944.
Spiteris, Jannis. "Attitudes fondamentales de la théologie byzantine, en face du rôle
religieux de la papauté au XIIème siècle." In Christopher Ryan, ed., *The
Religious Roles of the Papacy: Ideals and Realities 1150-1300*. Papers in Mediavel
Studies 8. Toronto, 1989. Pp. 171-192.
Spörl, Johannes. *Grundformen hochmittelalterlicher Geschichtsanschauungen. Studien Zum
Weltbild der Geschichtsschreiber des 12. Jahrhunderts*. Munich, 1935.

—. "Das Alte und das Neue im Mittelalter. Studien zum Problem des mittelalter-lichen Fortschrittsbewusstseins." *HJ* 50 (1930), 297-341, 498-524.

Staemmler, Georg. "Havelberg." In *Repertorio delle Cattedrali Gotiche,* ed. Ernesto Brivio, 781-90. Milan, 1986.

Stephan-Kühn, Freya. *Wibald als Abt von Stablo und Corvey und im Dienste Konrads III.* Cologne, 1973.

Stoob, Heinz. "Gedanken zur Ostseepolitik Lothars III." In *Festschrift Friedrich Hausmann* Ed. Herwig Ebner. Graz, 1977. Pp. 531-51.

Stroll, Mary. *The Jewish Pope: Ideology and Politics in the Papal Schism of 1130.* Brill, 1987.

—. Symbols of Power: The Papacy following the Investiture Contest. Leiden 1991.

Taylor, Jerome. *The Origin and Early Life of Hugh of St. Victor.* Texts and Studies in the History of Medieval Education 5. Notre Dame, 1975.

Tellenbach, Gerd. *The Church in Western Europe from the Tenth To The Early Twelfth Century.* Trans. Timothy Reuter. New York, 1993.

Töpfer, Bernard. "Kaiser Friedrich I. Barbarossa und der deutsche Episkopat." in Alfred Haverkamp, ed., *Friedrich Barbarossa. Handlungspielräume und Wirkungsweisen des staufischen Kaisers.* Vorträge und Forschungen 40. Sigmaringen, 1992. Pp. 389-433.

—, and Evamaria Engel, *Vom staufischen Imperium zum Hausmachtkönigtum: Deutsche Geschichte vom Wormser Konkordat 1122 bis zur Doppelwahl von 1314* (Weimar, 1976), pp. 41-43.

Torre, Augusto. "La Romagna e Federico Barbarossa." In *Popolo e stato in Italia nell'etá di Federico Barbarossa: Alessandria e la lega Lombarda.* Relazioni e comunicazioni al XXXIII congresso storico subalpino per la celebrazione del'VIII contenario della fondazione di Alessandria. Pp. 595-607. Turin, 1970.

Ughelli, Ferdinand. *Italia sacra sive de episcopis Italiae* 2. 1717; repr., Nendeln, 1970.

van Engen, John. *Rupert of Deutz.* Berkeley, 1983.

van Lee, Milo. Dissertation abstract. *Annuaire de l'université de Louvain* (1936-1939), 750-53.

—. "Les idées d'Anselme de Havelberg sur le developpement des dogmes." *AP* 14 (1938), 5-35.

Versteylen, A. "Anselme d'Havelberg." *Dictionnaire de spiritualité: ascetique et mystique: doctrine et histoire* 1:697-98. Paris, 1937.

von Guttenberg, Erich. "Albrecht der Bär." *Neue Deutsche Biographie* 1:160-61. Berlin, 1953.

von Heinemann, Otto. *Albrecht der Bär: Eine quellenmässige Darstellung seines Lebens.* Darmstadt, 1864.

von Moos, Peter I. "Literatur- und bildungsgeschichtliche Aspekte der Dialogform im lateinischen Mittelalter: Der *Dialogus Ratii* des Eberhard von Ypern zwischen theologischer *disputatio* und Scholaren-Komödie." In Günter Bern, et al, eds., *Tradition und Wertung,* FS Franz Brunhölzl (Sigmaringen, 1989), pp. 165-209.

—. "Le dialogue Latin au Moyen Age: L'exemple d'Evrard d'Ypres." *Annales: Économies, Sociétés, Civilisations* 44 (1989), 993-1028

von Ottenthal, Emil. "Die Urkundenfälschungen von Hillersleben." In *Papstum und Kaisertum: Forschungen zur politischen Geschichte und Geisteskultur des Mittelalters. Paul Kehr zum 65. Geburtstag dargebracht,* pp. 317-46. Munchen, 1926.

Ward, Benedicta. *Miracles and the Medieval Mind: Theory, Record and Event 1000-1215.* Philadelphia, 1987.

Way, Agnes Clare. "Gregorius Nazianzus." In *Catalogus translationum et commentariorum: Medieval and Renaissance Latin Translations and Commentaries, Annotated Lists and Guides* 2. Ed. Paul Oskar Kristeller. Pp. 43-119. Washington, 1972.

Weinfurter, Stefan. "Norbert von Xanten als Reformkanoniker und Stifter des Prämonstratenserordens." In Elm, *Norbert von Xanten*, pp. 159-87.
—. "Norbert von Xanten--Ordensstifter und 'Eigenkirchenherr.'" *Archiv für Kultur-
geschichte* 59 (1977), 66-98.
Weise, Erich. *Die Amtsgewalt von Papst und Kaiser und die Ostmission besonders in der 1.
Hälfte des 13. Jahrhunderts*. Marburger Ostforschungen 31. Marburg/Lahn,
1971.
Wentz, Gottfried, and Berent Schwineköper. *Das Erzbistum Magdeburg* 1.1, *Das Dom-
stift St. Moritz in Magdeburg*. Germania Sacra. Die Bistümer der Kirchenprovinz
Magdeburg. New York, 1972.
Wentz, Gottfried. *Das Bistum Havelberg*. Germania sacra 1.2. Berlin, 1933.
—. "Havelberg, Jerichow und Broda: Probleme der märkischen Kirchengeschichte
und Beiträge zu ihrer Lösung." In *Festschrift A. Brackmann*, ed. L. Santifaller. Pp.
324-46 Weimar, 1931.
—. "Die Staatsrechtliche Stellung des Stiftes Jerichow." *Sachsen und Anhalt: Jahrbuch
der Historischen Kommission für die Provinz Sachsen und Für Anhalt* 5 (1929), 266-99.
Werner, Ernst. *Pauperes Christi: Studien zu sozial-religiösen Bewegungen im Zeitalter des Re-
formpapstums*. Leipzig, 1956.
West, Delno C. and Sandra Zimdars-Swartz, *Joachim of Fiore: A Study in Spiritual
Perception and History*. Bloomington, 1983.
Winter, Franz. "Zur Geschichte des Bischofs Anselm von Havelberg," *ZKG* 5 (1882),
138-55.
—. *Die Prämonstratenser des zwölften Jahrhunderts und ihre Bedeutung für das nordöstliche
Deutschland. Ein Beitrag zur Geschichte der Christianisierung des Wendenlandes*. 1865;
repr., Aslen, 1965.
Wisplinghoff, Erich. *Die Benediktinerabtei Siegburg. Das Erzbistum Köln 2: Die Bistumer der
Kirchenprovinz Köln*, Germania Sacra NF 9. New York, 1975.
Wolf, Gunther, ed. *Friedrich Barbarossa*. Wege der Forschung 390. Darmstadt, 1975.
—. "Der 'Honor Imperii' als Spannungsfeld von Lex und Sacramentum im Hoch-
mittelalter." In Wolf, *Frederick Barbarossa*, pp. 297-322. Reprint from *Lex et Sac-
ramentum im Mittelalter*. Miscellenea Mediaevalia 6:189-207. Berlin, 1969.
Wolter, Heinz. *Arnold von Wied, Kanzler Konrads III. und Erzbischof von Köln*. Veröffent-
lichungen des Kölnischen Geschichtsvereins e.V. 32. Cologne, 1973.
Zatschek, Heinz. *Beiträge zur Geschichte des Konstanzer Vertrages vom Jahre 1153*. Vienna,
1930.
Zerfass, Rolf. *Der Streit um die Laienpredigt: Eine pastoralgeschichtliche Untersuchung zum
Verständnis des Predigtamtes und zu seiner Entwicklung im 12. und 13. Jahrhundert*.
Untersuchungen zur praktischen Theologie 2. Freibug, 1974.
Zöllner, Walter. *Die Urkunden und Besitzaufzeichnungen des Stifts Hamersleben (1108-1462)*.
Studien zur katholischen Bistums- und Klostergeschichte 17. Leipzig, 1979.
—. "Ekbert von Huysburg und die Ordensbewegung des 12. Jahrhunderts." *For-
schungen und Fortschritte* 38 (1964), 25-28.

INDEX OF PEOPLE

INDEX OF PLACES

INDEX OF SUBJECTS

Subjects dealt with by Anselm in his written works are indexed separately from those works.

active life: 2, 18, 23-27, 29, 55, 90, 126, 131-34, 138, 143, 147, 150, 152-58, 160-63, 165-66, 172, 190, 204, 284

advovatus of Jerichow: 64-65

allegory: 1-2, 126, 131, 135-37, 152-54, 156-57, 160, 184. *See also*: biblical figures; history

Antichrist: 6, 12, 178, 188-90, 198-99 n. 13, 207. *See also*: history—periodization—Anselm's states of the church—sixth

Antikeimenon: 4-8, 13, 19, 42-47, 50-52, 55, 70, 82, 85, 91, 121, 125, 163, 165, 268, 271, 275, 281, 284-85.
   Anselm as teacher and model in: 173, 216, 225, 227-29, 233-34, 237-39, 253, 274-75, 285
   circumstances of composition: 125, 164-66
   Dialogi as alternative title for: 8
   integrity of the whole: 163, 166-72, 175, 231
   manuscript tradition of: 7-8
   proem: 166-67, 169-71, 203 n.127, 224-26, 230, 255
   prologue: 165-71, 173, 175, 227-30, 235, 240, 245, 276, 278
   See also: De una forma credendi; Debates with Nicetas

Apocalypse, seven seals: 178, 182-83, 187-88, 205. *See also*: history—periodization—Anselm's states of the church

apocrisiarius: 43, 213, 228

apostolic life: 25-26, 55, 144, 158, 160, 211

Arianism: 260

Armenians: 212

Augustinian Rule: 24-25, 64, 132

Benedictine monks: 130, 209

Benedictine Rule: 145

bonus: 137-38, 140, 142, 146, 153, 159-60, 165, 209, 255

bread, leavened and unleavened in the Eucharist: 45, 255 n. 279, 256-58, 260, 267-71, 276. *See also: fermentum*

brothers, audience for the *Antikeimenon*: 82, 166-67, 169-72, 175, 177, 210-11, 213, 216-17, 224-26, 229, 231, 237-46, 248, 250, 253, 255-56 n. 279, 273-74. *See also*: critics

canon law: 143

canons regular, canonical life: 12, 16-18, 23-26, 54, 126, 130-32, 134, 136, 138-39, 141-43, 148-53, 156, 158-59, 162-63, 171-72, 204, 211-12, 216, 227. *See also*: active life; change of religious profession; Norbertines

care of souls: 17, 23-24, 150

cathedral schools: 18, 142-43, 283

celibacy: 129

change of religious profession: 16-17, 54-55, 126, 227.

chrismation: 279 n. 344

church, definition of: 129-30, 159-60, 176, 187, 191, 204

circumcision: 194

Cistercians: 12, 29, 211-12

clergy, clerical life: 2, 16-18, 55, 125, 129-32, 134, 136, 138, 143-44, 146-48, 151, 155-63, 190, 209, 212. *See also*: active life

commune of Rome: 75, 78, 85-88, 103, 272-73

Concordat of Worms: 11-12, 33, 34, 100 n. 14, 101-2 n. 18

contemplative life: 2, 18, 22, 23-26, 29, 55, 90, 126, 130-33, 140, 143, 152-58, 160, 162, 165, 172, 204. *See also*: monastic life; change of religious profession

Studies in the History
of Christian Thought

EDITED BY HEIKO A. OBERMAN

50. HOENEN, M. J. F. M. *Marsilius of Inghen*. Divine Knowledge in Late Medieval Thought. 1993
51. O'MALLEY, J. W., IZBICKI, T. M. and CHRISTIANSON, G. (eds.). *Humanity and Divinity in Renaissance and Reformation*. Essays in Honor of Charles Trinkaus. 1993
52. REEVE, A. (ed.) and SCREECH, M. A. (introd.). *Erasmus' Annotations on the New Testament*. Galatians to the Apocalypse. 1993
53. STUMP, Ph. H. *The Reforms of the Council of Constance (1414-1418)*. 1994
54. GIAKALIS, A. *Images of the Divine*. The Theology of Icons at the Seventh Ecumenical Council. With a Foreword by Henry Chadwick. 1994
55. NELLEN, H. J. M. and RABBIE, E. (eds.). *Hugo Grotius – Theologian*. Essays in Honour of G. H. M. Posthumus Meyjes. 1994
56. TRIGG, J. D. *Baptism in the Theology of Martin Luther*. 1994
57. JANSE, W. *Albert Hardenberg als Theologe*. Profil eines Bucer-Schülers. 1994
59. SCHOOR, R.J.M. VAN DE. *The Irenical Theology of Théophile Brachet de La Milletière (1588-1665)*. 1995
60. STREHLE, S. *The Catholic Roots of the Protestant Gospel*. Encounter between the Middle Ages and the Reformation. 1995
61. BROWN, M.L. *Donne and the Politics of Conscience in Early Modern England*. 1995
62. SCREECH, M.A. (ed.). *Richard Mocket, Warden of All Souls College, Oxford, Doctrina et Politia Ecclesiae Anglicanae*. An Anglican Summa. Facsimile with Variants of the Text of 1617. Edited with an Introduction. 1995
63. SNOEK, G.J.C. *Medieval Piety from Relics to the Eucharist*. A Process of Mutual Interaction. 1995
64. PIXTON, P.B. *The German Episcopacy and the Implementation of the Decrees of the Fourth Lateran Council, 1216-1245*. Watchmen on the Tower. 1995
65. DOLNIKOWSKI, E.W. *Thomas Bradwardine: A View of Time and a Vision of Eternity in Fourteenth-Century Thought*. 1995
66. RABBIE, E. (ed.). *Hugo Grotius, Ordinum Hollandiae ac Westfrisiae Pietas (1613)*. Critical Edition with Translation and Commentary. 1995
67. HIRSH, J.C. *The Boundaries of Faith*. The Development and Transmission of Medieval Spirituality. 1996
68. BURNETT, S.G. *From Christian Hebraism to Jewish Studies*. Johannes Buxtorf (1564-1629) and Hebrew Learning in the Seventeenth Century. 1996
69. BOLAND O.P., V. *Ideas in God according to Saint Thomas Aquinas*. Sources and Synthesis. 1996
70. LANGE, M.E. *Telling Tears in the English Renaissance*. 1996
71. CHRISTIANSON, G. and T.M. IZBICKI (eds.). *Nicholas of Cusa on Christ and the Church*. Essays in Memory of Chandler McCuskey Brooks for the American Cusanus Society. 1996
72. MALI, A. *Mystic in the New World*. Marie de l'Incarnation (1599-1672). 1996
73. VISSER, D. *Apocalypse as Utopian Expectation (800-1500)*. The Apocalypse Commentary of Berengaudus of Ferrières and the Relationship between Exegesis, Liturgy and Iconography. 1996
74. O'ROURKE BOYLE, M. *Divine Domesticity*. Augustine of Thagaste to Teresa of Avila. 1997
75. PFIZENMAIER, T.C. *The Trinitarian Theology of Dr. Samuel Clarke (1675-1729)*. Context, Sources, and Controversy. 1997
76. BERKVENS-STEVELINCK, C., J. ISRAEL and G.H.M. POSTHUMUS MEYJES (eds.). *The Emergence of Tolerance in the Dutch Republic*. 1997
77. HAYKIN, M.A.G. (ed.). *The Life and Thought of John Gill (1697-1771)*. A Tercentennial Appreciation. 1997
78. KAISER, C.B. *Creational Theology and the History of Physical Science*. The Creationist Tradition from Basil to Bohr. 1997
79. LEES, J.T. *Anselm of Havelberg*. Deeds into Words in the Twelfth Century. 1997

Prospectus available on request

KONINKLIJKE BRILL — P.O.B. 9000 — 2300 PA LEIDEN — THE NETHERLANDS

DATE DUE
